XVI

The Cognition of the
Literary Work of Art

Northwestern University
STUDIES IN *Phenomenology &*
Existential Philosophy

Roman Ingarden

Translated by

The Cognition
of the
Literary Work of Art

RUTH ANN CROWLEY

and KENNETH R. OLSON

NORTHWESTERN UNIVERSITY PRESS

EVANSTON   1973

Permission to quote from English translations of the following poems by Rainer Maria Rilke has been granted by the publishers:

For "Initial" and "Closing Piece," from *Translations from the Poetry of Rainer Maria Rilke*. Translation by M. D. Herter Norton. Copyright 1938 © 1966 by W. W. Norton & Company, Inc., New York. Permission also granted by The Hogarth Press, Ltd, London.

For "It began as a feast . . . ," from *The Lay of the Love and Death of Cornet Christopher Rilke*. Translation by M. D. Herter Norton. Copyright 1932 © 1959 by W. W. Norton & Company, Inc. Permission also granted by The Hogarth Press.

For "In the deep nights . . ." (from *The Book of Hours*), from *Rainer Maria Rilke: Poems*. Translation by Jessie Lemont. Copyright © 1943 by Columbia University Press, New York. Permission also granted by The Hogarth Press.

Permission to quote from *Lord Jim*, by Joseph Conrad, has been granted by J. M. Dent & Sons, Ltd, London, and by the Trustees for the Joseph Conrad Estate.

Contents

Translators' Introduction

ROMAN INGARDEN (1893–1970) was a Polish philosopher who studied philosophy and mathematics in Poland and Germany and whose works show a blending of speculative metaphysics, phenomenology, and the Polish analytical tradition. Born in Cracow, he studied philosophy under Twardowski at Lvov and under Husserl at Göttingen. When Husserl moved to Freiburg, Ingarden followed him and received his doctorate in 1918 with a dissertation on "Intuition und Intellekt bei Henri Bergson."[1] He returned to Poland and taught mathematics in secondary schools while completing his habilitation with his "Essentiale Fragen."[2] In 1924 he became a Privatdozent in philosophy at Lvov, and in 1933 he received a professorship there. It was during the time of his tenure at Lvov that he published his major works in aesthetics, *The Literary Work of Art*[3] and *The Cognition of the Literary Work of Art*.[4] From 1939 to 1944, Polish universities were closed, and Ingarden again taught mathematics in a secondary school in Lvov. During these five years he also finished his major work in general ontology, *Spór o istnienie*

1. *Jahrbuch für Philosophie und phänomenologische Forschung*, V (1921).

2. *Jahrbuch für Philosophie und phänomenologische Forschung*, VII (1925).

3. *Das literarische Kunstwerk* (Halle: Max Niemeyer, 1931; Tübingen: Max Niemeyer, 1960, 1965). Ingarden published this work in Polish under the title *O dziele literackim* (Warsaw, 1960). English translation by George Grabowicz (Evanston, Ill.: Northwestern University Press, 1973).

4. Original Polish title: *O poznawaniu dzieła literackiego* (Lvov: Ossolineum, 1937). Published in a revised and enlarged form in German as *Vom Erkennen des literarischen Kunstwerks* (Tübingen: Max Niemeyer, 1968). This translation is based on the German version.

świata (The Controversy over the Existence of the World).[5] In 1945, when eastern Poland was annexed by the USSR, Ingarden was expelled from Lvov and given a chair of philosophy at Jagellonian University in Cracow but from 1949 to 1956 was barred from teaching by the Polish government because of his supposed idealism. He was able, however, to carry on his own research in connection with the Polish Academy of Sciences in Cracow and also to translate Kant's *Critique of Pure Reason* into Polish. He was reinstated at the university in 1956 and remained there until he became professor emeritus in 1963. As early as 1957 he began publishing his complete works in Polish through the Polish Academy of Sciences; five volumes appeared in his lifetime, and several more are planned. He also spent the latter part of his life revising his works and rendering them into German; in addition to the two works on aesthetics and the work on ontology mentioned above, he published *The Ontology of the Work of Art*[6] as an extension of his considerations in *The Literary Work of Art,* and *Erlebnis, Kunstwerk und Wert,*[7] a collection of essays from thirty years which show his growing interest in the problems of value in art.

Like his teacher Husserl, Ingarden saw philosophy not as one intellectual discipline or one branch of knowledge among others but as a "rigorous science" which should furnish a foundation for all other sciences, should explain their concepts and procedures and give a basis for evaluating the certainty of their results. Both men were thus concerned with cognitive philosophy. Phenomenology for them was not a system of philosophy but a way of doing philosophy, a way of submitting objects of consciousness—whether internal or external, things or processes— to analysis in order to determine their essential and necessary features, how they are given to consciousness, and what kind of knowledge we can have about them. Phenomenology is descriptive in its concentration on objects, but it does not reach its conclusions about the invariant features of an object by generaliza-

5. 2 vols. (Cracow: Polska Akademia Nauk, 1947–48; 2d ed., Warsaw: Państwowe Wydawn. Naukowe, 1961–62). A German version of this work appeared as *Der Streit um die Existenz der Welt,* 3 vols. (Tübingen: Max Niemeyer, 1964–66). The third volume is not published in Polish. Volume I has been partially translated by Helen R. Michejda as *Time and Modes of Being* (Springfield, Ill.: Thomas, 1964).

6. *Untersuchungen zur Ontologie der Kunst: Musikwerk, Bild, Architektur, Film* (Tübingen: Max Niemeyer, 1962). English translation forthcoming from Northwestern University Press.

7. (Tübingen: Max Niemeyer, 1969). Also in Polish as *Przeżycie–dzieło–wartość* (Cracow: Wydawn Literackie, 1966).

tion from many particular cases of observation. Instead, it is nonempirical in that it brackets the real existence of its object in order to arrive at the type of which any really existing object is the token, in order, that is, to arrive by intuition at the essence of the object. The German for "intuition" is *Anschauung,* which can also mean simply "looking at"; in phenomenological terms, however, its implication is an immediate experience of the necessary conditions for recognizing the object as such an object. Phenomenology is also reflective; it concentrates on bringing to clear awareness those elements which are merely latent in our normal performance of mental acts. The knowledge gained by phenomenological analysis and reflection is to be self-evident and self-validating, its own criterion of adequacy. To conduct phenomenological analyses yielding self-evident knowledge, Husserl felt it was necessary to assume that our consciousness is transcendental. Husserl's transcendental idealism aroused Ingarden's opposition as early as 1918; Ingarden wished to establish the existence of the real world as independent of consciousness, and this desire guided his philosophical activity to a greater or lesser degree for the rest of his life.

Rather than concentrate on pure consciousness to establish the bases of our knowledge, Ingarden wanted to analyze the nature and the mode of being of the objects of our knowledge. Although still centrally concerned with cognitive philosophy, he came to consider ontology the basic philosophical discipline, because our cognition is adapted to the objects of cognition. The way we cognize a given object will depend on the object's mode of being and its formal structure. There are as many types of immediate experience as there are types of objects and relationships obtaining among objects; hence we need to consider the types of objects there are before discussing the kind of experience we have of them and evaluating the knowledge it is possible to gain of them. It was to the analysis of the basic structures of real and possible objects that Ingarden devoted his *Spór,* his work on general ontology. And although about half the volume of his works deals with aesthetics, in a very important sense these studies are also manifestations of his concern with ontology. Works of art seem to have a particularly problematic mode of being, and they provided Ingarden with excellent subject matter for his deliberations. In *The Literary Work of Art* and *The Ontology of the Work of Art* he established a regional ontology for existentially heteronomous, purely intentional objects, and his ontological studies of art furnish the basis for his investigation of our experience of art and the kinds of knowledge this experience can yield.

This is not to deny Ingarden's genuine interest in aesthetics, but it may help the reader understand the relationship of Ingarden's work to, say, literary scholarship. The charge has been raised against him from various sides that he is overly abstract; he never approaches literature on the level of actually existing works. To do so was not his aim; rather, he wanted to ascertain the formal structure common to all members of this class of objects, in order to show scholars in aesthetics exactly what their object of inquiry is and how it is constituted, so that the methods for dealing with it can be adapted to what is under investigation. In keeping with the phenomenological goal of providing a groundwork for the various areas of knowledge, Ingarden wanted to make literary scholarship a rigorous discipline by clarifying its object, how the object is given to consciousness, and what kinds of knowledge we can legitimately expect to gain of it in view of these considerations. His work is in the philosophy of literature, and he is both establishing a firm basis for literary scholarship and setting it investigative tasks. It is up to literary scholars to deal with actually existing works, to do empirical studies which will either bear out or disprove the statements Ingarden offers as hypotheses about, say, genre theory or about the relation of artistic values to aesthetic values, a problem he treats in Chapter 5 of the present work. The undertaking of literary scholarship can make greater progress if answers to the basic questions about the object of investigation have been provided. As in any science or rigorous discipline, once a community of scholars agrees on a view of its object, it is free to proceed in detailed empirical studies suggested by this view. Thus, while Ingarden comes to his consideration of aesthetic problems through his interest in ontology, the results of his deliberations are of primary importance to students of literature.

In deciding to examine the mode of being and formal structure of works of literary art, Ingarden was also launching a polemic against two views of the mode of being of the literary work which were current when he began writing on aesthetics and which he felt were the results of inadequate concern with the phenomenon itself and detrimental to any attempts to make a rigorous discipline of literary studies. One was the conception—Ingarden identifies it as neopositivist—that the work of art is identical with its physical foundation (with ink marks on paper, for instance). This reductionist view would make it impossible to distinguish literary works of art from any other kind of printed matter and would thus preclude the possibility of literary studies. The second view he repeatedly attacks is the psychologistic identification of the work of art with the mental experience of it. If this view were true, it would mean that the work of art is a unique, temporal, and nonrepeatable object. It would therefore be accessible only to the experiencing subject and could not be the object of scientific investigation because it would not be an intersubjective object. At best one could analyze the subject's report of his experience, but then we would be dealing in individual psychology and not in aesthetics. Ingarden's view of the literary work of art will solve the problems posed by both of these conceptions.

The Literary Work of Art and *The Cognition of the Literary Work of Art* are companion pieces in establishing certain fundamental principles for dealing with literature as an object of knowledge. Ingarden felt that two basic questions about literary works of art and the experience of them had to be answered before one could even begin to discuss the proper methodology of literary studies. The first question is: How is the object of cognition, the literary work of art, structured, and how does it exist? The second is: What process or processes lead to the cognition of the literary work of art, what are the possible ways of cognizing it, and what results can we expect of this cognition? Only after answering these two questions can we consider what methods of cognition should be employed in order to obtain satisfactory results. Ingarden addressed the first question in *The Literary Work of Art* and the second in the present work.

The Literary Work of Art presents Ingarden's conception of the literary work as a complex, stratified object depending for its existence on the intentional acts of author and receiver but not identical with these acts. It has its origin in the creative acts of consciousness on the part of the author, but it also has as its ontic basis a physical foundation (in the case of a literary work, printed letters on paper, as one possible means of transmission) which makes possible its continued existence after the conscious acts of the author have run their course. The literary work of art has four strata: the stratum of verbal sounds, or the phonetic stratum; the stratum of verbal and sentence meanings, or the semantic stratum; the stratum of objects projected by the states of affairs, the intentional correlates of the sentences; and the stratum of aspects under which these objects appear in the work. The artistic intention creates an interplay among these strata, so that they all work together to form a polyphonic harmony in the constitution or reconstitution of the work. The material substratum of the work is the guarantee that the artist's intentional form can be reconstituted by an aesthetic receiver who will decipher the physically perceivable signs of the substratum and fulfill the meaning intentions fixed by these signs. Primarily because of its stratum of semantic units, the work is an intersubjective object. But the work of art is not itself an aesthetic object. It contains, for example, many potential elements and places of indeterminacy, places, that is, in which a thing, an action, an event, or a stretch of time is not supplied with a full qualitative determination. In constituting the work, however, the aesthetic receiver tends to take an attitude toward the portrayed world which is related to the perception of physical objects; he tends to fill in the indeterminate areas in imagination just as if the portrayed objects really existed and were fully determined, as real objects are. Ingarden calls a constitution of the work which fills in undetermined areas and actualizes potential elements, such as the aspects under which objects appear, a "concretization" of the work. An adequate concretization of the work will contain the work of art as a skeleton, but it will flesh out the schematic structure of the work and reveal the aesthetic value that is present in the work in potential form. Concretizations may vary in details from reading to reading but are admissible as concretizations of a given work so long as they do contain the work as an identical core and so long as they fill in places of indeterminacy in a way that is in keeping with what is explicitly determined in the work. If a concretization is constituted in the aesthetic attitude, the result will be an aesthetic object. It may sound from the above as if any reading necessarily results in a concretization and as if "the work of art itself" is then a convenient hermeneutic fiction to solve the problem of the identity of a work or to account for the similarity of concretizations, to avoid both the reductionist view that the work exists in its physical foundation and the psychologistic view that it is identical with the mental experiences of its receiver. Ingarden was aware of this problem and discusses the work of art itself as an object of knowledge in the present book. In *The Literary Work of Art* Ingarden performs a reflective analysis on the mode of being and formal structure of a purely intentional object. He opens vistas on many problems which he addresses from a different perspective in *The Cognition of the Literary Work of Art*. Ingarden determined in the first work how the object of cognition is structured; in this work he analyzes the receiving intention of this object, discussing how the object is given to consciousness, how we gain knowledge of it, and, in consideration of its structure and mode of givenness, what kind of cognitive results we can hope to gain and how we can assess their validity.

Ingarden remains true to his phenomenological precepts in the present work, as he did in *The Literary Work of Art*. He does not examine the individual psychology involved in becoming acquainted with and gaining knowledge of a given work but rather the essential and necessary features which must be present in an experience in order for it to qualify as a cognitive experience of a literary work of art. He begins by defining "cognition" very broadly, to include even the acquaintance with the work in ordinary reading, which can serve as a basis for more specifically directed kinds of cognition. As he proceeds, he refines his analysis to distinguish the varieties of cognition which are relevant for literary studies and the kinds of objects—a literary work of art itself, a reconstruction of a literary work, a concretization of a literary work, an aesthetic object—to which each type of cognition is geared. For the remainder of this introduction we should like to sketch Ingarden's concerns and some of his arguments in this work, chapter by chapter.

Introduction. Ingarden here delineates his methodological presuppositions for dealing with the cognition of the literary work of art. There are many attitudes in which one can encounter a literary work of art, ranging from that of the literary consumer, who uses it simply as a springboard for his own fantasy or as a way of passing the time, to that of a literary scholar who assumes that its statements are either veiled references to the author's biography or a peculiarly encoded system of knowledge and uses it as a document in a context essentially alien to the literary work of art. But Ingarden will be primarily concerned with just three of the possible attitudes: the aesthetic, in which an aesthetic object is constituted, the preaesthetic, in which we gain reflective knowledge about the work of art itself as opposed to its concretizations, and the attitude of reflective cognition of the aesthetic concretization, which we could also call "postaesthetic." He will analyze each of these attitudes with a view to its object, the essential features of the experience in which the object comes to givenness, and the kind of cognitive results each attitude yields. Because cognition is adapted to its object, Ingarden supplies (§ 4) a summary of his ontological investigations of the structure of the literary work of art. The nine points which he lists here serve as a synopsis of *The Literary Work of Art* and as basic assumptions guiding his cognitive analysis. To these he adds several limiting conditions for his consideration of the first phase of cognizing the literary work of art: the work must be finished and available in a fixed form, it must be in a language the reader knows well, and it must be assumed to be read in a solitary situation at one sitting. Even though these conditions are idealizing abstractions, they enable Ingarden to discuss the most basic type of an extremely complex experience. Variations on this basic experience can be worked out in empirical research, but it is important to bring to awareness the features which are essential in any act of reading, and to do that Ingarden finds it helpful to consider a somewhat idealized process of consciousness. Finally, Ingarden feels that he can already make two basic assertions about the cognition of the literary work, based on his analysis of the basic structure of the work: the cognition will be composed of different but closely related processes, as the work itself is composed of heterogeneous but interconnected elements; and it will necessarily take place in a temporal process, since it is only in a temporal process that the work is given to us.

Chapter 1. Ingarden here treats those functions or operations which contribute to the constitution of the literary work of art as an object of knowledge. Both in the Introduction and in Chapter 1 Ingarden relies heavily on the argument and conclusions of *The Literary Work of Art* to guide his presentation in the present work. In §§ 7–12 he proceeds through the four strata of the work, from the simplest in terms of mental activity to the most complex, discussing the subjective operations which must be performed for each of the strata to be brought to givenness. Ingarden does not consider the printed signs a new stratum of the work; they are apprehended in their typical form and are automatically accompanied by an imaginary hearing of the verbal sound they designate, which is also apprehended as a type. The first stratum in the constitution of a literary work of art is the phonetic stratum. While it may be of great importance for the aesthetic value of the work, it is generally heard and registered in a fleeting way; the transition to the meaning intention connected with it is almost immediate. In asking what the reader must do to intend the meanings of words and how he can be sure he has intended them correctly, Ingarden confronts the problem of how to guarantee the intersubjective accessibility and the identity of the work of art. It is the stratum of meanings which makes it possible for the author to inform a literary work of art with his intentions and for readers to intend the meanings of a work again; it is by means of this stratum that we can talk about the existence of the literary work itself as something transcendent to our individual acts of consciousness. In *The Literary Work of Art* (§ 66), Ingarden called verbal meanings ideal entities, although he was manifestly uncomfortable at having to do so, since his entire argument about the mode of being of the literary work of art was that it was neither real nor ideal, and calling the verbal meanings ideal meant that this existentially heteronomous, purely intentional object had an ideal foundation. In § 8 of the present work, Ingarden no longer finds it necessary to speak of verbal meanings as "ideal." He characterizes them as the objective intentional correlates of mental acts which will have the same structure whenever the same meaning is intended. The meaning is transcendent to these acts; it will be the same in any number of acts which intend it. And it is not an ideal entity; at some point in time it was conferred on, or joined with, a verbal sound. This explanation of verbal meaning is structurally analogous to Ingarden's explanation of the mode of being of the work of art itself. Understanding a sentence means actualizing the meaning intentions in that sentence. Because of the intersubjective accessibility of the linguistic strata, one's understanding can always be checked against that of other members of the speech community. Problems of ambiguity are removed, in case a word is not intended to be ambiguous, largely by the context and by the expectations created by the sentence-generating operation set in motion by reading the first few words of the sentence. Previously intended meanings also influence what one reads later, as does one's expectation for the meanings not yet read.

Ingarden continues his analysis of the acts necessary to constitute a literary work of art with comments on active reading, that is, the ability to follow the cues in the semantic stratum for imaginatively projecting the world of the work, actually concretizing the portrayed objects, and gaining a sense of the whole. To do this, the reader must be cocreative with the aesthetic transmitter. Understanding the semantic stratum is a relatively simple matter compared to what is demanded of the reader by the two remaining strata. Each sentence meaning projects a state of affairs as its intentional correlate. The states of affairs project the objects which constitute the world of the work. But in order to pass from the disparate states of affairs to a synthetically constituted portrayed world, we must perform what Ingarden calls "objectifications" of the states of affairs; these can be of various kinds. How we summarize and store the information provided by the states of affairs about the portrayed world will influence the formal structure of the world in our concretization; it may turn it, for instance, from dynamic to static. The ways of objectification are one source of differences among individual concretizations of the same work. The process of objectification makes the stratum of portrayed objects somewhat independent of the stratum of semantic units; it gives it a different order than the one of presentation in the text. Without his synthetic activity in objectifying the states of affairs on the basis of understanding the meaning of the sentences, the reader would be unable to have direct aesthetic contact with the world of the work. Because the work is a schematic formation, the reader is also called upon to fill in places of indeterminacy in the objects portrayed and to imagine the objects clothed in the sense aspects under which they are presented; the aspects are present only potentially in the work of art itself. The aspects are what the reader actually experiences of the portrayed objects he concretizes, and they are often of great aesthetic importance. They are suggested by the work, but, of all the strata, they depend most on the reader for their actualization.

The apprehension of the work of art as a whole, however, requires more than just an acquaintance with all the strata of the work. It requires a considerable synthetic effort on the part of the reader as well as an insight on his part into the "idea" of the work of art. Ingarden defines the idea of the work as a "synthetic, essential complex of mutually modulated, aesthetically valent qualities which is brought to concrete appearance either in the work or by means of it" (p. 85). These qualities lead to the intuitive constitution of the aesthetic value which may emerge from the work of art and form a unity with it. The idea of the work of art is thus not a paraphrasable statement or series of statements contained in the work but becomes known only in the immediate experience of the actualized artistic intention of the work. The complex of mutually modified valuable qualities make evident the "organic" structure of the work: "organic" in that the various functions contributing to actualization of the work as it is apprehended in concretization are mutually adapted and are hierarchically subordinated to one main function, just as with a living organism. The main function of a living organism is to preserve life; the main function of the work of art, in

Ingarden's view, is to enable the receiver to constitute a possible aesthetic object and to bring to appearance the aesthetic value appropriate to the work of art. Any other functions which the work of art might perform—transmission of information about really existing entities, expression of moral or political standpoints, etc.—are not essential to its nature as a work of art. It should be judged as a work of art solely on the basis of how well it fulfills its main function. Ingarden feels that one of the most important areas of inquiry for literary scholarship is an examination of the relationship among the aesthetically valent qualities in the concretization and how they are founded in the artistic (potential) features of the work of art itself. He deals with this more extensively in Chapters 4 and 5. However, the basis for any knowledge about the aesthetic value of a work and its constitutive aesthetically relevant qualities is the concrete experience of the idea of the work through an adequate reading resulting in an aesthetic concretization.

Chapter 2. Because the work of art as given in concretization is a synthetic composite which demands a great number of difficult operations for its constitution, it is entirely possible that some strata or parts of them will not be fully realized, while others may be overemphasized. Either error will result in a foreshortening of certain aspects of the work in concretization. It is theoretically possible to correct this type of distortion in a concretization by a return to the text, once one has become aware of it. But in Chapter 2 Ingarden deals with a perspectival foreshortening which cannot be corrected because it is the result of an essential feature of the work as given in concretization: the effects of temporal perspective on the reader's experience of the work and the possible consequences of temporal perspective for cognition of the work. In one sense the work of art possesses all its parts at once, as a finished object; but we have access to the work only in a series of temporally extended acts, so that the parts of the work become, in our concretization, the phases of reading, and the phases read earlier will always be subject to some modification of temporal perspective as we progress in reading. As we constitute our concretization, only one phase of the work will be vividly present to us; it will fill and qualitatively determine our present moment, and when it is recalled in an act of memory, it will be remembered as a unit of time. The scope of the present moment varies with the reader and with the material, but usually it encompasses a sentence. Whatever fills our present moment in reading a literary work of art will be influenced to a certain extent by the double horizon surrounding any present moment, toward the past and toward the future. We are able to make a connection between our present moment of reading and the phases of the work preceding it as belonging to the same experience largely because of what Ingarden calls "active memory." This is a phenomenon which has received little attention. It is not what Husserl calls "retention," a sort of echo of the moment just passing, nor is it memory of past moments, which has to be activated voluntarily. Rather, it is a peripheral feeling that this present moment is connected with other moments as part of the same experience. Active memory seems to involve the process of objectification mentioned above and also a kind of summarizing operation of sentences or even of whole chapters of longer works. It is mainly the objective stratum which is retained in active memory. The way we view what is past, both in active memory and in voluntary and involuntary acts of recollection, will change as the reading progresses, being influenced by new knowledge about the portrayed world, so that there is retroactive influence by the new present moment. The work is never totally present to us in actuality; even when we have finished reading, we still do not have the whole work all at once before us. We have its phases from the perspective of the end, all in some kind of modification of temporal perspective. Therefore, in discussing the knowledge we can have of the work of art, we must bear in mind that some or all of the knowledge will be based on acts of memory, and we must take into account the role of memory in supplying information. In § 17, Ingarden discusses the various ways of remembering the past and brings these to bear on the reader's experience of the work.

But the reader's own succession of present moments in the experience of the work and the modifications they undergo as they become past are not the only phenomenon of temporal perspective with which we have to deal in a literary work of art. The portrayed world of the work is also presented to us under temporal aspects. Ingarden uses his typology of memory also to discuss the portrayal of time in the work. His typology could furnish a point of departure for the stylistic analysis of novels, for instance, starting with an examination of the function of the narrative past tense and considering such features as the relationship of portrayed time to time of portrayal. In a further suggestion for the practice of literary scholarship, Ingarden mentions the possibility of a genre theory based on the way in which lyric poetry, the novel, and the drama portray time and on the experience the reader has of the time portrayed in the world of each of these genres.

Chapter 3. Ingarden has discussed how we constitute the literary work of art. Before he turns to the varieties of cognition of the constituted object, he further delimits the object of cognition with which he is concerned by distinguishing between the literary work of art and the scientific work. Ingarden uses the term "literary work" to refer to written (or spoken) works of all kinds, reserving "literary work of art" for works of belles-lettres. The most important works which do not belong to the latter category Ingarden calls "scientific works"; it must be noted that "scientific" is used here in a much broader sense than usual, in connection not only with the natural sciences but also with any serious field of study, just as the German *wissenschaftlich* is used. The main difference between the two kinds of work is their function. Broadly speaking, the function of the scientific work is to transmit knowledge about an objectivity which exists independently of the work; the function of the literary work of art is to serve as the basis for an aesthetic experience. From this characterization of scientific works, Ingarden concludes that all declarative statements in such a work are genuine judgments. That is, they claim to determine an independently existing object exactly as that object is determined in reality. They may or may not be true, but they claim to be true and can be validated with reference to external evidence. Ingarden distinguished these judgments from what he calls quasi-judgments, which are peculiar to the literary work of art. (Ingarden discusses quasi-judgments at greater length in §§ 25 and 25a of *The Literary Work of Art.*) A judgment and a quasi-judgment are not differentiated by formal features; the same sentence can often serve as an example of either. But a genuine judgment posits its object as existing, whereas a quasi-judgment does not claim to be making a statement about anything existing independently of the world of the work which that quasi-judgment helps project and determine. The objects portrayed in the work of art exist solely because the intentional correlates of the sentences, the states of affairs, are able to combine in projecting them. The consequence for the reader of the scientific work is that he should direct his attention beyond the work to the objects under discussion, whereas the reader of the literary work of art should focus on the objects constituted in the work as having a quasi-reality of their own. The differences which follow from the basic distinction between genuine and quasi-judgments need little elucidation.

Aesthetic qualities are viewed as inessential to the scientific work and may even be detrimental to its main function. The stratum of portrayed objects should be transparent in the scientific work; the semantic stratum should lead the reader directly to external objects. The stratum of aspects may be entirely absent with no harm done. If we add to the above that the stratum of verbal sounds in a scientific work functions solely to mark distinctions of meaning and not, as in the literary work of art, as a possible repository of aesthetically relevant qualities, we can see that the proper apprehension of a scientific work is, if not simpler, at least more single-minded than the apprehension of a literary work of art. It is largely limited to a proper understanding of the semantic stratum, whereas with a literary work of art all strata must be taken into account, since all may harbor aesthetically relevant qualities, often as a result of specific relations obtaining between elements in one stratum and elements in another.

Chapter 4. In this chapter Ingarden continues his descriptive analysis of cognitive activity with the literary work of art as object. Having defined his object and detailed how it comes to be constituted, he now describes the various ways of cognizing it. Ingarden's aim here is to prepare the way for an epistemological theory of literary studies. He will distinguish the kinds of cognition of the literary work of art or of its concretizations according to the intention with which the cognitive activity is undertaken and the object with which it is concerned. Here, and in Chapter 5, Ingarden is presenting material which is not closely based on his investigations in *The Literary Work of Art,* so that much of what he says will be a tentative exploration of problems which have rarely even been recognized and will therefore be less accessible than the material in the first three chapters. On the other hand, the last two chapters are the central chapters in terms of Ingarden's contribution to the philosophy and epistemology of literary studies in this work, and deserve careful consideration.

Although our cognition will certainly be modified according to the basic type of literary work under consideration, Ingarden feels that our knowledge of basic types of literary art is inadequate, and he restricts himself to varieties of cognition determined by the reader's attitude. Ingarden will consider two attitudes: that of the scholar, who reads for purposes of research, and that of the reader who wishes to form an aesthetic concretization of the work. If the first attitude prevails, there are two kinds of cognition of the work possible, the preaesthetic investigative cognition having the work of art itself as its object, and the reflective cognition of an aesthetic concretization of the work. These two kinds of cognition may be brought into conjunction in a further phase of literary study in order to assess the relationship between the work itself and its concretizations; it is this phase that will give us knowledge about the foundation of the aesthetically valuable qualities of the concretization in the artistic features of the work itself and will allow us to evaluate individual concretizations as to their adequacy in respect to the work itself.

It will be remembered that the difference between the work itself and one of its concretizations is that in the latter at least one place of indeterminacy is filled in or one potential element is actualized. An especially important class of actualized elements are the aesthetically relevant qualities. These are founded in potential features of the work itself, which Ingarden calls "artistic values." Ingarden seems reluctant to furnish examples of aesthetically relevant qualities, probably because he wishes to describe them in the most general way possible in order to include any possible aesthetically relevant quality. It is clear, however, that they include qualities from various strata of the work. It is also clear that the aesthetic relevance of the elements will depend in large measure on the system of relations in which they stand to other qualities. The relationships of a set of qualities to one another can lead to the emergence of a new quality. Ingarden describes a relationship between two or more aesthetically relevant qualities, in the same stratum or from different strata, as a "qualitative harmony." The emergent quality is called the "quality of the harmony" and is said to be founded in the qualities from whose relation to one another it emerges. Ingarden notes that this is the same as what Ehrenfels called a Gestalt quality. The emergent quality can in turn enter into relations with other qualities (emergent or primary) and lead to the founding of emergent qualities of higher order. A concretization may thus be organized in terms of relations of ascending complexity, culminating in a dominant emergent quality, the value of the work. Ingarden defines the literary work of art in terms of its function, which is to lead to the concretization of an aesthetic object. A literary work has value in proportion as it performs this function. Accordingly, Ingarden distinguishes between the artistic value of the work itself and the aesthetic value of the aesthetic object.

It remains to consider the various attitudes which the reader can take toward the work. Ingarden deals first (in § 24) with the aesthetic attitude in which the aesthetic object is constituted. His treatment of the aesthetic experience was based on an earlier paper which was not concerned mainly with the literary work of art, and little attempt has been made to integrate it into the present book. He devotes § 25 to justifying his discussion of the general aesthetic experience by arguing that the literary aesthetic experience is simply a variation of this general experience. Some of the main features of the aesthetic experience are the following.

The experience begins with our being emotionally affected by some quality of the work. Our reaction to this quality Ingarden calls the original emotion. It initiates a change in our everyday attitude; we fasten on the quality as such, forgetting our practical concerns. We are not interested in the real existence of the object but solely in the fact that it manifests a quality which attracts us, something a merely portrayed object can also do. This is probably the source of the claim, mentioned above, that all the sentences in a literary work of art should be read as quasi-judgments. Influenced by the original emotion, we look for other qualities to harmonize with the one we have perceived. In the case of a literary work of art, we try to form a concretization which contains a maximal number of aesthetically relevant qualities arranged in a system of relations and dependencies. In case an ultimate value emerges from this system, then the aesthetic experience culminates in an emotionally colored acknowledgment of this value.

One could object to the above analysis on the grounds that it seems to be an exercise in introspective psychology and not a phenomenological analysis. The aesthetic experience is not even acknowledged to exist in all quarters; thus, to reach agreement on which of its features are essential and necessary, much research remains to be done. Still, there is a good deal in Ingarden's account which rings true from a subjective point of view and which may serve as a corrective to other views.

Passing to a consideration of the investigative attitude toward the literary work, Ingarden opens an important issue, the question of the possibility of objective knowledge of the literary work itself as opposed to its possible concretizations. The question of whether it is possible to know the work itself reduces to the question of whether it is possible to read the work and form a faithful reconstruction of it without actualizing potential elements or filling in places of indeterminacy. Ingarden decides this question affirmatively, leaving for Chapter 5 the consideration of what constitutes a faithful reconstruction of the work. Ingarden's name for this study of the literary work is the preaesthetic investigation, although it need not be temporally prior to an aesthetic concretization of the work. Such an investigation even requires partial concretizations of an aesthetic object in order to uncover the founding relationships between the literary work itself and the aesthetic object and thus to determine the artistic effectiveness and value of the work. In the main, however, this type of investigation suppresses the original emotion, should it arise during reading, and takes cognizance of the places of indeterminacy in the text without filling them in.

We have considered the aesthetic experience and the problem of knowledge of the literary work as a schematic structure. Problems of a different kind arise in connection with the reflective cognition of the aesthetic concretization of a literary work. Among these may be distinguished problems of obtaining such knowledge, on the one hand, and problems of communicating it, on the other. Ingarden's general strategy for overcoming objections concerning the objectivity and sharability of knowledge of the aesthetic object is to observe first of all that it is possible for a reader to concretize the same aesthetic object on a number of occasions. A concretization is not identical with the reader's experiences during reading but is rather an abstract object correlated with a subset of those experiences. All that Ingarden is saying is that the same abstract object can be correlated with different experiences. Second, it is possible for different readers to concretize the same aesthetic object, where a certain amount of "nonessential" variation is permitted. Thus with the development of the proper tools of research, knowledge about aesthetic concretizations could be made intersubjectively accessible. One of the problems of transmitting knowledge about the aesthetic object is the lack of refined vocabulary for dealing with it, since the distinction between the work itself and its concretizations has generally gone unrecognized. Concentration by literary scholars on the aesthetic object could result in the creation of a vocabulary adequate to deal with the properties of the object and to check the truth of judgments about it by reference to the object itself (say, in a renewed aesthetic experience).

Chapter 5. In the final chapter, Ingarden takes the results of Chapter 4 and poses questions concerning the epistemological value of the results of the various types of cognition of the literary work of art. He is concerned with determining the basic value of the knowledge which each type of cognition yields and with discovering the possible sources of errors in achieving this knowledge. This chapter, more than any of the preceding, is a set of tasks for practical scholarship, since most of the ways Ingarden suggests of checking his assertions about the results of cognition would involve a great deal of empirical research. As literary scholars, our aim is to gain a set of true judgments about the literary work or about its concretizations. How, Ingarden asks here, can we assess the truth of our judgments about literature?

The central cognitive problem connected with the preaesthetic investigation of the work itself is whether we can determine that our reconstruction of the work is faithful to the work and gives objective knowledge of it. How can we be sure that we are dealing with the work itself and not with our reconstruction of it? Ingarden catalogues the possible types of deviation from the work itself in reconstruction and concludes that careful attention to the phonetic and semantic strata will eliminate most serious errors in the reconstruction. We can constantly check our reconstruction against the work in successive readings, thus gaining an ever more exact reconstruction. Comparing our reconstruction with that of other scholars can also be helpful in pointing up possible inaccuracies. Because the work continues to exist after our conscious experience of it, it is possible to keep reintending it and refining our reconstruction of it until we are satisfied that—in the limiting case—our reconstruction exactly resembles and reflects the work itself. We can have no absolute guarantee of the fidelity of the reconstruction to the work, beyond our careful checking and comparing; but in dealing with an actually existing work, we are gaining empirical knowledge, and this is the case with all empirical knowledge.

The primary task of the aesthetic experience is not to furnish knowledge but to make possible the constitution of the aesthetic object. Still, the aesthetic experience can be interwoven with cognitive moments if we plan to use it as the basis for the aesthetic cognition of a value-bearing object. Ingarden considers the questions of how we judge the effectiveness of an aesthetic experience in actualizing the values potentially present in the work, how we determine the acceptable variations in actualizing potential elements, and how we choose the most desirable completion for places of indeterminacy in terms of constituting the most valuable aesthetic object permitted by the work. In a favorable case the aesthetic experience will culminate in the emergence of an ultimate value and the subject's response to this value. Ingarden cautions against confusing the response to value with judgments about the artistic or aesthetic values present in the work or its concretization. He feels that a confusion of these two entities is responsible for skepticism about the possibility of objective value judgments. In a protracted consideration of value response as opposed to value judgments, Ingarden tries to establish an objective foundation for determining what values are present in the work, to avoid begging the question by reference to the relativity of taste. Finally, he suggests ways of constituting a concretization which will be as close as possible to the work itself. Since a concretization necessarily goes beyond the work itself, we can only choose the most probable completions suggested by the work. The work is not completely inert; it contains factors which must be actualized and which limit the set of possible aesthetically relevant qualities in the concretization. We also begin to sense the "idea" of the work during the aesthetic experience and can try to form a concretization which embodies this idea. The more concerned we are that our concretization contain a true reconstruction of the work itself, the more adequately it will serve as an object of knowledge. And if we are aware during the course of the aesthetic experience that we want to gain knowledge about the object being constituted, and not merely to have direct contact with it, the experience can be punctuated with insights into the emerging object which can serve as the point of departure for later cognitive acts and which have the advantage of being formed in direct contact with the object, not on the basis of acts of memory, with their incumbent dangers for cognition.

Once the aesthetic object is constituted, our access to it is only through our acts of memory. The aesthetic object is a unique entity, and its unique temporal character cannot be shared. But if we bracket this temporal quale, we can find what is repeatable and intersubjectively accessible in aesthetic concretizations. This is a task for the reflective cognition of aesthetic concretizations. A further task, and indeed the main task of this type of cognition, is the determination of the necessary interconnections among the aesthetically valuable qualities and the relation between a given set of qualities and the value it determines. Only a determination of the ontic connection among aesthetic qualities and between them and the value they found in the aesthetic experience will give us an understanding of the structure of the aesthetic object. To accomplish this, we must be able to share information about our concretizations and to compare them and the values emerging in them. If we form aesthetic concretizations with careful attention to the work embodied in them, we have a good chance of developing a branch of inquiry with aesthetic concretizations as its object. Ingarden had previously believed that concretizations were the domain of literary criticism, that is, a field dealing strictly with the receiver's subjective experiences of the works; now he believes that concretizations can at least in part become the objects of literary scholarship, although we are standing at the very beginning of a science of aesthetic objects.

In this chapter Ingarden seems to pose as many questions as he answers, in keeping with his desire to make literary scholarship reflect on itself and its object. This is not meant as a definitive work but as a first exploration of problems which must be considered if we are to establish literary studies as the science of literary works and aesthetics as the science of the experience of such works.

THIS TRANSLATION grew out of a seminar given by Professor Kurt Mueller-Vollmer on the ontology of the literary work of art (Stanford University, 1969). We would like to thank him for his encouragement and support in this project. To Mrs. Virginia Seidman, of Northwestern University Press, we would also like to offer thanks for her excellent editorial work on the manuscript.

R. A. C., K. O.

Stanford University
August, 1973

The Cognition of the
Literary Work of Art

Introduction

§ 1. *The area of investigation*

THE STUDY OF THE VARIOUS WAYS in which we become
acquainted with and possibly gain effective knowledge of the
literary work, and of the literary work of art in particular, is
part of the broad field of epistemology and deals with a special
group of very important problems. On the one hand, the solution
of these problems is important for the epistemological foundation of literary studies and, in a different way, for the theory of
science in general. On the other hand, it forms the basis for at
least one area of aesthetics, specifically, for establishing the
possibility of an objective apprehension of artistic and aesthetic
values in literary art.

In the period between the two world wars there was animated activity in various countries in the field of the methodology of literary studies. At the same time, concrete examinations of individual works showed a great disunity in the
conception of the literary work of art; this led to noticeable
differences in critical tendencies and in the manner of treating
individual works of art. What with the tendencies to psychologism in aesthetics which were still active at the beginning of
the century (especially in Germany, for instance in the works
of Theodor Lipps and Johannes Volkelt) and the aftereffects of
the psychology and historicism of Dilthey, literary study was
constantly diverted into other fields of investigation, primarily
into a historically colored individual psychology of the poets. Husserl's antipsychologism and the attempts to reorient aesthetics

[3]

took effect very slowly in the field of literary study. The first investigations in stylistic analysis directed the attention of scholars to the literary works themselves and made them aware of specific artistic problems. These investigations also made scholars conscious of the fact that psychologism was no longer compatible with the general conception of the literary work of art. Still, scholars seemed to feel no need for a radical revision of the philosophical theory of the literary work of art. New theories about the literary work of art were ignored because it was feared that they could lead to sweeping changes in the established method of investigation, which was understandably not desired. Nonetheless, there were differences in both the tendencies and the methods of scholarship in the practical investigation of individual works, and these differences provoked various methodological debates. But on the whole these discussions were not very productive, because they were often limited to a defense of one's own method. Scholars discussed methods of investigation or of "criticism" without even having asked themselves two crucial questions: (1) How is the object of cognition —the literary work of art—structured? and (2) What is the procedure which will lead to knowledge of the literary work; that is, how does the cognition of the work of art come about and to what does or can it lead? Only after having answered these two questions can one meaningfully ask how the literary work of art *should* be cognized in order to achieve satisfactory results.

In my book *The Literary Work of Art* I tried to answer the first question. It is now time to take up the second question, before we can even begin to consider methodological problems. I proffered an answer to this question as early as 1936, in the Polish version of my book *The Cognition of the Literary Work of Art*. I do not doubt that much has changed since that time, in Germany as well as other western European countries. Nevertheless, it seems to me that there is still no satisfactory treatment of the problems concerning the cognition of the literary work of art, and thus my book, now in an expanded edition, can be useful even today. The only important work which is thematically related to part of the problems under discussion here, Emil Staiger's *Die Kunst der Interpretation*, gives too little consideration to the stratified structure of the literary work of art [1] and is too sketchy in its theoretical section to press forward

1. Traces of this view can be detected in the *Grundbegriffe der Poetik* (Zurich: Atlantis, 1946; 2d ed. 1951–52), although Staiger never

to the important basic problems in the cognition of the literary work of art.[2] The discussion which has developed about the "New Criticism" in recent years in France also bypasses the problems of how literary works are cognized and understood and deals more with possible different concretizations of the literary work of art (under the obvious influence of Russian Formalism). Thus it was certain conclusions which I drew from reading many Western publications which prompted me to make my old book, *The Cognition of the Literary Work of Art,* available in a foreign language.

The present edition of the book has been expanded with regard to various points; it maintains, however, all the positions of the first Polish version, and it has been expanded only to give more detailed treatment to problems which were already formulated in the first version. In these past thirty years I have added to my knowledge by continuing my own research [3] and not through the research of others. Wherever I do owe something to another scholar, I shall make specific note of it.

§ 2. *Preliminary sketch of the problem*

THE MAIN QUESTION which I am trying to answer is: How do we cognize the completed literary work set down in writing (or by other means, e.g., in a tape recording)? Cognition is, however, only one kind of intercourse a reader can have with the literary work. To be sure, we will not completely ignore the other ways of experiencing the work, but neither will we pay particular attention to them at the moment. Even "cognition"

refers to my book, which is only natural since the problems of his book are of a much more specialized nature and presuppose, so to speak, the stratified structure. At least this is clear in his chapter on the epic. Staiger, by the way, has acknowledged in a letter to me that he "recalls" having read my book once.

2. This book is nevertheless interesting for the analyses of interpretations of individual works, with which it deals at length. But what that involves is really "interpretation" and not becoming acquainted with and understanding the literary work of art—hence it involves problems which relate to different possible concretizations of one and the same work of art. I shall return to this question later.

3. This is contained in part in my *Studia z estetyki* (Studies in Aesthetics) which appeared in Polish in 2 volumes (Warsaw: Państwowe Wydawn. Naukowe, 1957–58). The *Studia* also contained the second edition of *The Cognition of the Literary Work of Art.*

itself can take place in many different ways, which can bring about various results. The type of work read also plays an essential role in determining how cognition takes place.

I use the word "cognition" here for want of a better.[4] It should be taken for the moment in a rather vague and broad sense, beginning with a primarily passive, receptive "experience," in which we, as literary consumers, "become acquainted with" a given work, "get to know" it somehow, and thereby possibly relate to it in a more or less emotional way, and continuing on to the kind of attitude toward the work which leads to the acquisition of effective knowledge about the work. All these extremely diverse attitudes lead to some kind of knowledge about a work, whether it be a novel (for instance, Thomas Mann's *Buddenbrooks*) or a lyric poem (like "Shall I compare thee to a summer's day") or a drama (for instance, Ibsen's *Rosmersholm*). We shall not exclude from consideration other written works, either, such as newspaper articles, essays, and scientific works. On the contrary, one of the matters we are extremely concerned with is becoming aware of how we "understand" scientific works and how we apprehend cognitively the works themselves as well as what is portrayed in them. "Cognition" should thus be taken to mean a kind of intercourse with literary works which includes a certain cognizance of the work and does not necessarily exclude emotional factors. Of course, we take into account from the outset that acquaintance with a work, as well as its cognition, can take place in different ways and lead to various results, according to the peculiar character of the work in question. However, I hope to be able to show in the following that despite this considerable diversity every "cognition" of a literary work has a stock of operations which are always the same for the experiencing subject and that the process of "cognition" follows a course which is characteristically the same in all these diverse cases, provided it is not disturbed or interrupted by external circumstances. And the concluding investigations will show that in certain specific cases one can achieve genuine knowledge of the literary work and even of the literary work of art. We can remove the dangers arising from uncritical use of an unexplicated and possibly much too narrow idea of "cognition" as a basis for our investiga-

4. In particular, it does not correspond to the word used in the Polish version, *poznawać*, which clearly indicates an activity, not necessarily completed, and which can be opposed to the Polish *poznać*, which designates a successful cognitive activity leading to effective knowledge.

tion only in this way of gradual progress, which does not lead to a delimitation of the ideas involved until its last stage. The exact notion of the cognition of a literary work, and in particular of a literary work of art, will thus be determined only as a result of our investigations. At the same time, we shall consider under what conditions this cognition can be accomplished. But on the way to such a result there are many difficulties to be overcome which are connected with the problem of "objective" knowledge and which can be solved only in a general epistemological investigation. We shall have to content ourselves here with preparing the way to this goal.

By "literary work" I mean primarily a work of belles-lettres, although in the following the term will also apply to other linguistic works, including scientific works. Works of belles-lettres lay claim, by virtue of their characteristic basic structure and particular attainments, to being "works of art" and enabling the reader to apprehend an aesthetic object of a particular kind. But not every work of art is "successful" and thus in a specific sense a "genuine," "valuable" work of art. And not every object of an aesthetic experience is the object of an experience culminating in pleasure or admiration or in a positive value judgment. This is especially true of works of belles-lettres. They can be "genuine" and "beautiful"; generally speaking, they can be of artistic or aesthetic value; but they can just as well be "bad," "not genuine," "ugly"—in short, of negative value. We can experience all these works aesthetically; we can also apprehend them in a preaesthetic cognition or in a cognition which is itself not aesthetic but which builds upon the aesthetic experience. Only the results of the latter cognitive apprehension of the work can give us valid information about the value of the work.[5] Our investigations must therefore encompass both groups of works, those of positive and those of negative value; but we will take into consideration from the outset that the cognition, especially the aesthetic cognition, of a work of positive value follows a different course and can have different properties than that of "bad" works, works of negative value.[6]

5. The word "value" and the word "work" are both used here with a certain double meaning, which will become clear later. We cannot say everything at once.

6. I assumed an analogous standpoint as to method in the investigation of the basic structure of the literary work of art in my book *The Literary Work of Art* [*Das literarische Kunstwerk* (Halle: Max Niemeyer, 1931; 2d ed., Tübingen: Max Niemeyer, 1960; 3d ed., 1965); English translation by George Grabowicz (Evanston, Ill.: Northwestern University

§ 3. *Adaptation of cognition to the basic structure of the object of cognition*

BEFORE WE PROCEED to the description of the "cognition," in our broad sense, of the literary work, we must first consider what is to constitute the object of this "cognition." The epistemological investigations which have been carried out by the phenomenologists since Husserl's *Logical Investigations* show that between the mode of cognition and the object of cognition there is a special correlation; there is perhaps even an adaptation of the cognition to its object. This correlation is especially evident in which attitudes or cognitive operations enter into the process of cognition, in the order of sequence or of simultaneity they follow, in how they reciprocally condition and possibly modify one another, and in the total result to which they all lead, the cognitive value of which depends on the course they take and on their cooperation. For all the basic types of objects of cognition, there are corresponding basic kinds and modes of cognition. For instance: one can gain knowledge of a physical object only by beginning the cognitive process with a sensory perception of the object. Sometimes, of course, we learn about an object through information from another person, but even then this information must be based on a perception. We must use different kinds of perception to gain knowledge of different kinds of attributes of the object. We cannot hear colors or see or touch tones. When we wish to gain knowledge of our own psychological states or processes, we must employ acts of inner perception which are differently structured and proceed differently from those of outer perception; we can neither smell nor taste these processes and states. The situation is analogous in other cases: one must understand and prove mathematical propositions through their meaning; sensory perception plays no part in understanding them. In every case there is a strong correlation between the structure and qualitative constitution of the object of cognition, on the one

---

Press, 1973)]. This method has been misunderstood from many sides. It does not mean at all that I exclude the artistic or aesthetic value of the literary work of art from consideration.

hand, and the kind of cognition, on the other.[7] In view of this correlation, analysis of a cognitive process is made easier if we examine the basic formation of the object of cognition. Thus it will be useful in our case to begin by calling to mind the basic attributes and structures of the literary work.

But before we do this, we must first consider a possible reproach against our procedure. Are we not becoming involved in a vicious circle when we refer to the basic attributes and structures of literary works in order to explain the way in which we learn about a literary work? Is such reference not tantamount to presupposing the validity and effectiveness of the cognition which informs us about those basic attributes? At the outset of our investigation we do not yet have any positive knowledge about the cognition of a literary work and cannot assume anything about the value and effectiveness of this cognition. Nor do we make such assumptions. It is merely a question of directing our attention to certain processes of consciousness which take place during the reading of an individual work, not in order to apprehend their individual course and individual function, but rather to apprehend what is essentially necessary in that course and function. We refer not to the individual peculiarities of a specific literary work but rather to the essentially necessary structure of the literary work of art as such. We merely use the individual cognition of a work performed during a reading as an example which allows us to look for the essentially necessary structural elements and interconnections among the cooperating functions. These *correspond* in an intelligible way to the essentially necessary structural properties of the literary work in general and can be correlated with individual factors in the work; in fact, they help us to discover and apprehend such factors.

Thus, when we describe the cognitive processes involved in reading a text in their unfolding and their specific character and judge whether they are positively effective—that is, whether they can lead to objectively valid knowledge of the literary work—we presuppose neither the validity of the results of an individual reading nor the effectiveness of the cognitive functions

---

7. Even when we use artificial apparatus (e.g., a microscope, electron microscope, radar, various electrical measuring devices, etc.) to observe objects (or processes), the structure of the apparatus is designed to function in a certain way which is adapted to the type of object or process which is to be "observed."

involved in it. We must distinguish here between two different procedures: first, the reading of a specific literary work, or the cognition of that work which takes place during such reading, and, second, that cognitive attitude which leads to an apprehension of the essential structure and peculiar character of the literary work of art as such. These are two different modes of cognition and yield two quite different kinds of knowledge. The first is accomplished in an individual reading of an individual work. It is a particular kind of experience in which we establish the actuality of this work and its details. The second is not accomplished in a reading at all and does not give us an experience of the actual qualitative constitution of a particular work, say of the *Magic Mountain,* by Thomas Mann. The second kind of cognition differs from an individual reading to such an extent that, even if we completely described the course and functions of an individual reading in our investigation, we would still be merely at the threshold of the difficult problem: What constitutes the general nature (to use the inappropriate but common term) of the literary work of art? Phenomenologists would say that in this case it is a question of an a priori analysis of the substance of the general idea "the literary work of art." This analysis, even if accomplished on the example of a particular literary work of art, or rather on various appropriately chosen examples, is not carried out in reading and understanding the successive sentences of these examples. It is rather a question of the essential differences among various basic elements of the literary work (and the literary work of art) as such: e.g., the difference between the phonetic patterns and phenomena and the sentence meanings (or, more generally, the different types of semantic units) or between the sentence meanings and the intentional sentence correlates projected by them (especially the states of affairs). It is a question of apprehending the constitutive formal and material factors of such elements and the essential differences among the elements which follow from those factors, as well as the various interrelations and connections among the elements. None of this can be discovered in the ordinary reading of a literary work, since the necessary possibilities which must be comprehended in the idea of "the literary work of art" far surpass the individual determinations of any particular work of art. On the other hand, the reading of a particular work can reveal far more about the individual work with respect to the details of the work than the a priori analysis, which is oriented toward the substance of the general idea of the literary work of art. The a priori analysis establishes only the "skeleton" of that which forms the full body of the individual work. It does not, for instance, apprehend the full meaning of the whole sequence of sentences in a work, which is indispensable for the reading of a work; but it attends to the general form of any possible sentence and to other things which cannot be specially heeded and analyzed in a specific reading. To be sure, it cannot be said that there is no relation at all between a general "eidetic" analysis (as Husserl calls it) of the idea of the literary work of art as such and the reading of a particular work. For example, an empirically oriented person might deny the existence or even the possibility of an a priori analysis of the substance of a general idea and yet still be inclined to recognize the possibility of general knowledge about literary works. He would then perhaps say that, on the basis of reading many individual works, one compares the results obtained and establishes the "common" characteristics of the individual works in an "act of generalization." This act of comparison and generalization goes beyond any individual reading; but it is presupposed in this empiricist view of "general" knowledge that the facts found in an individual reading really do exist and, thus, that the knowledge gained in such a reading has its validity. But an "eidetic" analysis of the "general nature" of the literary work of art (that is, of the substance of the general idea) in a phenomenological sense makes no such presupposition. The individual readings only give us a supply of phenomena which can be apprehended in their essential content; we need not presuppose the individual, real existence of the objects which come to givenness in these phenomena. Through these eidetically apprehended phenomena we can establish essential relations among the perceived phenomena and thus determine the essential, necessary structure of the literary work of art as such.

In other words, when in the following we adduce some characteristics of the general structure of the work, we presuppose neither the validity of the cognition of the works accomplished in the individual reading nor their real qualitative constitution. We use the data about the general structure of the literary work of art as such as a heuristic device which allows us to direct our attention to the process of consciousness wherein the cognition of the individual works is accomplished. At the same time it allows us to prepare ourselves for what we can find in the analysis of this process of consciousness, if we remember that the experiences making up this process should lead to, or help in, disclosure of the form and qualitative constitution of individual literary works. The confrontation of the analysis of the experiences in which the reading is accomplished with the essential, necessary structural elements of the literary work of art will, however, give us a better understanding of why those experiences are so complex in themselves and why they proceed in just this essential, typical way.

§ 4. *Basic assertions about the essential structure of the literary work of art*

THE FOLLOWING GENERAL ASSERTIONS about the essential structure of the literary work of art will be helpful in our further investigations.

1. The literary work is a many-layered formation. It contains (*a*) the stratum of verbal sounds and phonetic formations and phenomena of a higher order; (*b*) the stratum of semantic units: of sentence meanings and the meanings of whole groups of sentences; (*c*) the stratum of schematized aspects, in which objects of various kinds portrayed in the work come to appearance; and (*d*) the stratum of the objectivities portrayed in the intentional states of affairs projected by the sentences.

2. From the material and form of the individual strata results an essential inner connection of all the strata with one another and thus the formal unity of the whole work.

3. In addition to its stratified structure, the literary work is distinguished by an ordered sequence of its parts, which consist of sentences, groups of sentences, chapters, etc. Consequently, the work possesses a peculiar quasi-temporal "extension" from beginning to end, as well as certain properties of composition which arise from this "extension," such as various characteristics of dynamic development, etc.

The literary work actually has "two dimensions": the one in which the total stock of all the strata extends simultaneously and the second, in which the parts succeed one another.

4. In contrast to the preponderant majority of the sentences in a scientific work, which are genuine judgments, the declarative sentences in a literary work of art are not genuine judgments but only quasi-judgments, the function of which consists

in lending the objects portrayed a mere aspect of reality without stamping them as genuine realities. Even sentences of other types—for example, interrogative sentences—undergo a corresponding modification of their function in the literary work of art. Depending on the type of work—e.g., in a historical novel—still other varieties of these modifications are possible.[8]

The presence of quasi-judgments in literary works of art constitutes only one feature which distinguishes them from scientific works. Other characteristic features are attached to this one, namely:

5. If a literary work is a work of art having positive value, each of its strata contains special qualities. These are valuable qualities of two kinds: those of artistic and those of aesthetic value. The latter are present in the work of art itself in a peculiar potential state. In their whole multiplicity they lead to a peculiar polyphony of aesthetically valent qualities which determines the quality of the value constituted in the work.

Even in a scientific work, literary artistic qualities can appear which determine certain aesthetically valuable qualities. In a scientific work, however, this is only an ornamentation which has little or no connection with the essential function of the work and which cannot of itself make it a work of art.[9]

6. The literary work of art (like every literary work in general) must be distinguished from its concretizations, which arise from individual readings of the work (or, for instance, from the production of a work in the theater and its apprehension by the spectator).

7. In contrast to its concretizations, the literary work itself is a schematic formation. That is: several of its strata, especially the stratum of portrayed objectivities and the stratum of aspects, contain "places of indeterminacy." These are partially removed in the concretizations. The concretization of the literary work is thus still schematic, but less so than the work itself.

8. The places of indeterminacy are removed in the individual

8. It is a special problem whether the declarative sentences which are only quoted in the text, for example the sentences spoken by the persons portrayed, also undergo such a modification. This is of particular importance for the drama. The question as to which linguistic and perhaps also extralinguistic means produce the character of quasi-judgments constitutes another problem, which has been investigated by Käte Hamburger. I shall return to this problem in connection with the question of how the reader recognizes that he is dealing only with quasi-judgments and not with genuine judgments, for instance in a novel.

9. I shall later have occasion to speak of the further differences between scientific works and literary works of art.

concretizations in such a way that a more or less close determination takes their place and, so to speak, "fills them out." This "filling-out" is, however, not sufficiently determined by the determinate features of the object and can thus vary with different concretizations.

9. The literary work as such is a purely intentional formation which has the source of its being in the creative acts of consciousness of its author and its physical foundation in the text set down in writing or through other physical means of possible reproduction (for instance, the tape recorder). By virtue of the dual stratum of its language, the work is both intersubjectively accessible and reproducible, so that it becomes an intersubjective intentional object, related to a community of readers. As such it is not a psychological phenomenon and is transcendent to all experiences of consciousness, those of the author as well as those of the reader.

§ 5. *The literary work as fixed in writing*

THERE WAS A TIME when literary works of art endured without being fixed in writing. In those days they owed their continuance through many generations to the purely oral reproduction from memory by those who recited or sang them to others. This resulted in a number of variants in which, however, the basic text survived for centuries as the identical core. The first eight assertions, above, referred to such an orally transmitted work of art. The work was a purely phonetic formation. But once it was set down in manuscript form, and later in printing, and hence was predominantly read rather than heard, this purely phonetic character was changed. The print (the printed text) does not belong to the elements of the literary work of art itself (for instance as a new stratum, as Nicolai Hartmann, for one, proposed) but merely constitutes its physical foundation. But the printed format does play a modifying role in the reading, so that the verbal sound enters into a close connection with the printed word, although they do not blend to form a unity. The printed signs are not grasped in their individual physical form but rather—as is also the case with verbal sounds—as ideal types, and in this form they are connected with the verbal sound. This introduces a certain contamination into the whole of the literary work of art, but, on the other hand, it allows the identity of the work to be preserved much more faithfully than is possible with purely oral transmission.

§ 6.   *Delimitation of the topic and first basic theses*

THE CONDITIONS under which the actual processes of reading or hearing literary works of art take place are extremely complex and variable. Thus it is very difficult to take them all into account in the exact consideration of how we achieve cognition of the work and to evaluate correctly the role they play in gaining knowledge of it. Therefore it is advisable to simplify these conditions and make the investigation easier by narrowing its topic somewhat. I thus intend to treat the cognition of a completed literary work presented to the reader in a language completely mastered by him and present in his mind. The condition that the work be "complete" means not only that it should not be taken in the shifting form it has during the process of poetic creation but also that, once it has been finished by the author, it remain unchanged in the form given it by him, thus that it change in neither of its two linguistic strata, in neither the sound stratum nor the semantic stratum. Since living languages do in fact slowly change in many of their elements and functions according to circumstances, we impose the second limiting condition, that the work be composed in a language contemporary with the reading (where this "contemporaneity" is to be taken with a grain of salt), at least in a relatively stable epoch of language development. We do not wish to discuss here the possible or actual stability of language. Since this far surpasses our present subject, we are quite willing to let this requirement be viewed as an idealized abstraction. To a certain degree, an analogous idealized abstraction is contained in the third condition we impose, that the language of the work be completely familiar to the reader and mastered by him, thus be, ideally, his native language. But even this condition is imposed as an approximation, because there are various degrees even in the mastery of one's own native language. Each of us exhibits greater or lesser deficiencies in his ability to use his own native language correctly. But it is not so difficult, once we have really mastered our own language and can think and speak in it without hesitation, to deepen our knowledge of it so that we can read a literary work of art without hesitation, "fluently." With works in a foreign, even though "familiar" language, the limits of our mastery of the language are usually much narrower, so that we often have to expand our knowledge of the language significantly before reading the work. Our requirement is thus only that the reader be sufficiently prepared for reading the work.

One further delimitation of the subject of our investigations: I shall consider only those cases where the literary work is acquired in solitary reading, without consultation with other readers or hearers. I introduce this restriction because then the experiences of the readers are much simpler, are bound only by the text, and consequently develop more freely and fluently. The course of the reading is not interrupted by consultation with others; the artistic unity of the work is much better preserved. We thereby also exclude external influences on the understanding of the work which is cognized through reading, for the reason that the role they play in the effort for correct, adequate understanding of the work is very difficult to judge. On the other hand, we are concerned with avoiding any interruption in the process of becoming acquainted with the work. Thus we shall also abstract from the fact that there are many works too voluminous to be read through without interruption. We shall restrict our consideration to the reading of relatively short works, and only later shall we consider the role of the necessary breaks in reading. We exclude external influences on the process of gaining knowledge of a work, also, in order to avoid, for the present, the complication arising from the fact that every conversation with another reader is accomplished only by taking cognizance of a new (unwritten) literary work—that is, of another person's speech. Understanding this speech presents us with the same problems as understanding the work we have read, except that, in listening to the other person's speech, two basically different works, the work of art and the speech of the other person, are intermingled, modify each other, and must be apprehended by the reader in a superimposed unity, so that the work can no longer be known in its purity.

Along with these limiting conditions we believe that we can set up two basic assertions about the cognition of the literary work of art: first, that this cognition is composed of heterogeneous but closely connected processes (operations); second, that it is accomplished in a temporal process. These two essential facts are bound up with the basic character peculiar to the literary work. We shall now proceed to develop and substantiate these two assertions.

1 / The Processes Entering into the Cognition of the Literary Work of Art

§ 7. *Apprehension of the written signs and verbal sounds*

UNTIL RECENTLY, the usual way of becoming acquainted with a literary work of art was to read a printed text; it was rather seldom that we encountered orally presented works. What happens when we prepare to read? At the beginning of our reading, we find ourselves confronted with a book, a volume in the real world consisting of a collection of pages covered with written or printed signs. Thus the first thing we experience is the visual perception of these "signs." However, as soon as we "see" printed signs and not drawings, we perform something more than, or rather something different from, a mere visual perception. In the perception which takes place during reading, we do not attend to the unique and individual features but rather to the typical: the general physical form of the letters as determined by the rules of the written language or, in the case of "fluent" reading, the form of the verbal signs. The individual features do not, of course, vanish entirely from the reader's awareness; the apprehension of the typical form of the verbal signs is thus not the pure apprehension of a species. We do see, for instance, how one letter is repeated in successive verbal signs. But the individual features here are subsumed only under the aspect of their typical form, and in general the quality of individuality recedes unless for some reason it becomes especially important; but it never disappears completely from awareness.[1] In fluent, fast reading we do not perceive the individual letters themselves, although they do not disappear from our consciousness. We read "whole words" and thus easily overlook typographical errors. There are also other details about the printed paper of which one is not completely unaware but to which one does not attend for their own sake. And if we did attend to them, that would prove to be a distraction in reading, because our main attention in visual reading is directed at the apprehension of the typical verbal forms. The same thing happens in hearing a speech or a "recited" literary work, where we do not attend to the details of the concrete sound as such but rather to the verbal sounds as typical forms. If for some reason we do not succeed in apprehending the typical forms, even though the speaker's voice is loud enough, we often say we "didn't hear" the speaker and consequently didn't understand him.

The first basic process of reading a literary work is thus not a simple and purely sensory perception but goes beyond such a perception by concentrating attention on the typical features in the physical or phonetic form of the words.[2] There is still another way in which the basic process of reading goes beyond simple sensory seeing. First, it takes the writing (printing) to be "ex-

1. An attentive, purely sensory perception (or, better, a series of continual perceptions of the same thing, in sequence) gives us an object which is in every sense individual. In a fleeting perception we tend to see clearly only a general aspect of the object; we then say: "I see a mountain" or "a table." These words are general nouns and are applied to the object of perception, which is indeed before us in its individuality without every detail being strictly individualized. Only a further, more attentive perception leads to a more exact apprehension of the uniqueness of many details, so that we understand its difference from other "similar" objects. In reading a printed text, the individual letters and verbal signs do not have individual qualities for us; they simply do not matter to us. On the contrary, it would disturb us in our reading if we noted individual differences in letters too much. This becomes especially evident in reading manuscripts, where we purposely ignore individual deviations in the physical form of the letters and direct ourselves to the "character" of the person's handwriting—that is, to what is typical in his handwriting. If we are unsuccessful in apprehending the character of the writing, we will be unable to "decipher" the text at all.

2. I would not place such emphasis on this essentially trivial fact were it not for the neopositivists, who once tried to reduce sentences to mere writing and this writing, as a linguistic formation, to physical objects: spots of ink on paper, or particles of chalk on a blackboard (see, in this connection, *Erkenntnis*, Vol. III [1933]). But even linguists consider the verbal sound the physical side of the word (see, for example, Emile Benvéniste's newest book, *Problèmes de linguistique générale* [Paris: Gallimard, 1966]).

pression," that is, the carrier of a meaning; [3] second, the verbal sound, which seems to be interwoven in a peculiar way with the written sign of the word, is immediately apprehended, again in its typical form, along with the written sign.

When we read a text "silently" (without speaking the words aloud, even softly), our apprehension is normally not limited to simply seeing the graphic form of the writing, as is the case with Chinese characters when we do not know Chinese,[4] or when we see a drawing (for instance, an arabesque) without any idea that it might be a written message. A normal reader who knows the phonetic form of the language well will combine silent reading with an imaginary hearing of the corresponding verbal sounds and the speech melody as well, without paying particular attention to this hearing. When the verbal sound is relatively important, the reader might even pronounce the sound involuntarily and quietly; this can be accompanied by certain motor phenomena. The auditory apprehension of the phonetic form of the words is so closely related to the visual apprehension of the written form that the intentional correlates of these experiences also seem to be in especially close relation. The phonetic and visual forms of the word seem almost to be merely two aspects of the same "verbal body."

As already mentioned, the verbal body is simultaneously grasped as an "expression" of something other than itself, that is, of the meaning of the word, which refers to something or exercises a particular function of meaning (for instance, a syntactical function).[5] When we know the language in question well and use it daily, we apprehend the verbal sounds not as

3. This is the case even when we do not know the meaning (as, for instance, in a foreign language of which we have imperfect knowledge) and thus do not understand the word. The phenomenon of not understanding can occur only where we are dealing from the outset with a written sign and not with a mere drawing.

4. This is the case with all languages whose "pronunciation" we do not know.

5. I use the word "expression" [*Ausdruck*] as Edmund Husserl did in his *Logische Untersuchungen*, 2 vols. (Halle: Max Niemeyer, 1900; 2d ed., 1913); [English translation by J. N. Findlay, *Logical Investigations*, 2 vols. (New York: Humanities Press, 1970)]. Bühler used the same word later in another sense, in which what is expressed is not the meaning of the word in a given language but rather a phenomenon of consciousness or an emotional state of the speaker. In a literary work, words or entire phrases can exercise this new expressive function if they are spoken by the characters in a work, e.g., in a drama. The verbal sounds then gain a new, primarily emotional character, which adheres to them without itself being any physical (visual or acoustic) quality.

pure sound patterns but as something which, in addition to its sound, conveys or can convey a certain emotional quality.[6] As I tried to show in my book *The Literary Work of Art*, this quality, which is intuitively felt, can either be determined by the meaning of the word (or the emotional aspect of the object meant) or can be related to the function of the "expression" of the speaker's emotional processes (fear, anger, desire, etc.). The latter possibility refers primarily to words and phrases quoted in a literary text and spoken by a character in the work, and it is brought about not through the phonetic form of the verbal sound but through the tone in which the words are spoken. This emotional quality often aids in the recognition of the typical phonetic form of the verbal sound when recognition is otherwise difficult.

Simultaneous with and inseparable from the described apprehension of the verbal sounds is the understanding of the meaning of the word; the complete word is constituted for the reader in just this experience, which, although compound, still forms a unity. One does not apprehend the verbal sound first and then the verbal meaning. Both things occur at once: in apprehending the verbal sound, one understands the meaning of the word and at the same time intends this meaning actively.[7] Only in exceptional cases, as when the word is, or seems to be, foreign to us, is the apprehension of the verbal sound not automatically connected with understanding the verbal meaning. Then we notice a natural tendency in us to complete the act of understanding. If we cannot grasp the meaning immediately, we notice a characteristic slowing-down or even a halt in the process of reading. We feel a certain helplessness and try to guess the meaning. Usually it is only in such a case that we have a clear thematic apprehension of the verbal sound in its phonetic and visual form; at the same time, we are puzzled about not finding the meaning, which should be immediately apparent and nonetheless does not come to mind. If the meaning occurs to us, then the obstacle is overcome and the act of understanding flows into a new understanding of the following words. But when we

6. Julius Stenzel once called attention to this possibility. The often-used word "expression" refers here only to the phonetic or written form of the word and is to be differentiated from "word," which encompasses both the phonetic form and the meaning.

7. When we speak about the "word," we are using an artificial abstraction, because in normal reading or understanding of a foreign language we do not concentrate on individual, isolated words; rather, words form for us from the outset only part of a linguistic structure of greater complexity, usually of a sentence. More about this later.

know the words well, it is typical that the verbal sound is noted only fleetingly, quickly and without hesitation; it represents only a quick transition to the understanding of the words or sentences. The verbal sound is then heard superficially and almost unconsciously. It appears on the periphery of the field of awareness, and only incidentally does it sound "in our ears," provided, of course, that nothing out of the ordinary draws our attention to it. It is precisely this fleeting way of apprehending the verbal sounds which is the only correct way for the apprehension of the literary work as a whole. This is the reason one often hears the demand for a "discreet" declamation, to prevent the phonetic side of the language from encroaching too much on the hearer, from coming to the fore.

In the literary work, as we have already mentioned, words do not appear in isolation; rather, they join together in a certain arrangement to form whole linguistic patterns of various kinds and orders. In many cases, especially in verse, words are arranged with primary concern not for the context of meaning which they constitute but instead with regard to their phonetic form, so that a unified pattern arises from the sequence of sounds, such as a line of verse or a stanza. Concern for the phonetic form in arrangement also brings about such phenomena as rhythm, rhyme, and various "melodies" of the line, the sentence, or the speech in general, as well as intuitive qualities of linguistic expression, such as "softness" or "hardness" or "sharpness." We usually note these phonetic formations and phenomena even when we read silently; even if we pay no particular attention to them, our notice of them still plays an important role in the aesthetic perception of at least a good number of literary works of art. Not only do they themselves constitute an aesthetically important element of the work; they are often, at the same time, a means of disclosing other aspects and qualities of the work, for instance, a mood which hovers over the situations portrayed in the work. Thus the reader must have an "ear" for the phonetic stratum of the work (for its "music"), although one cannot say that he should concentrate on this stratum particularly. The phonetic qualities of the work must be heard "incidentally" and add their voice to the entirety of the work.

However, because the disclosure of phonetic phenomena of higher order is connected with the individual phases of becoming acquainted with the literary work of art, it will be necessary to return to the phonetic phenomena in later investigations.

§ 8. *Understanding verbal and sentence meanings*

BUT HOW DO WE KNOW that we "understand" words or sentences? In which particular experiences does this "understanding" take place, and when have we really "understood" the text of a work? Who can guarantee that we have correctly understood and not misinterpreted sentences appearing in various contexts and interconnections? The last question comes to mind immediately, but we cannot answer it until much later.

It is a difficult task to describe or simply to indicate the experiences in which we understand words and sentences, because we normally pay no attention to these experiences. Not all scholars are aware of the difficulties which one encounters here.[8] Thus we will have to limit ourselves in our investigation to rudimentary comments; but even a superficial consideration of the experience of understanding demands an explanation of what the meaning of a word or the sense of a phrase is. Unfortunately, this problem, too, is connected with difficulties and is related to various philosophical problems. Without being able to discuss here the numerous theories which have been advanced since Husserl's pioneering *Logical Investigations*,[9] I want to recapitulate the main points of the concept of the meaning of a linguistic entity which I set forth in my book *The Literary Work of Art*.

The meaning of a word can be considered in two different ways: as part of a sentence or a higher semantic unit or as an isolated single word, taken by itself. Although the latter case hardly occurs in practice, still it is wise to consider it.

Contrary to common assertions, the verbal meaning is neither a psychological phenomenon (in particular, an element

8. Danute Gierulanka furnished a good analysis of "understanding" in the various possible meanings of the word in her book *Zagadnienie swoiśtosci poznania matematycznego* (The Character of Mathematical Knowledge) (Warsaw: Państwowe Wydawn. Naukowe, 1962).

9. The neopositivists caused great confusion in the investigation of the meaning of linguistic formations when they tried to eliminate the entire problem by preaching a physicalistic theory of language. Since the Prague Congress (1934), where I was forced to take a stand against the thesis that the meaning of a sentence is its verifiability, and since the appearance of Alfred Tarski's "Der Wahrheitsbegriff in den formalisierten Sprachen," *Studia Philosophica*," Vol. I (1935), the neopositivists have tried to adopt another viewpoint with regard to the problem of meaning. The "later" Wittgenstein, especially in his *Philosophical Investigations*, was aware of these problems but was unable to find a real solution.

or feature of a mental experience) nor an ideal object. The former view, held by the psychologistic school, was criticized by E. Husserl and G. Frege. In his *Logical Investigations*, Husserl advanced the second view under Bernard Bolzano's influence, but he relinquished it in his *Formal and Transcendental Logic*, although he retained the terms "ideal meaning" [*ideale Bedeutung*] and "ideal object" [*idealer Gegenstand*]. In my book *The Literary Work of Art* I tried to work out a conception of meaning analogous to Husserl's. The verbal meaning, and with it the meaning of a sentence, is on the one hand something objective which—assuming, of course, that the word has just one meaning—remains identical in its core, however it is used, and is thus transcendent to all mental experiences. On the other hand, the verbal meaning is an intentional configuration of appropriately structured mental experiences. It is either creatively constituted in a mental act, often on the basis of an originary experience; or else it is reconstituted or intended again in mental acts after this constitution has already taken place. To use Husserl's apt expression, the meaning is "conferred on" [*verliehen*] the word. What is "conferred" in an intentional mental experience is itself a "derived intention" [*abgeleitete Intention*], as I have expressed it, which is supported by a verbal sound and which, together with the verbal sound, constitutes the word. The word is recognized and used according to what kind of intention it has. The intention can refer denominatively to objects, characteristics, relations, and pure qualities, but it can also exercise various syntactical and logical functions when various meanings enter into relation with one another or when various objects intended by the meanings are brought into relation with one another.[10]

In a living language it is relatively seldom that we consciously confer meaning on a given word. It happens, for example, when new scientific words are formed by means of a definition or by supplying appropriate examples of objects which are to be grasped and named conceptually.[11] Normally one finds

10. It is usually said (especially in neopositivist circles) that the words which have a syntactic function designate other "signs." This is false, primarily because the function of such a word is entirely different from the designative function (the word "and" in the phrase "the dog and his master" does not name these two nouns). In the second place, this explanation completely overlooks the much more important function of such words with regard to what is designated by other words, especially nouns.

11. In connection with this kind of naming, it has become popular in the past few years to speak of "deictic" definitions.

complete words (that is, verbal sounds, together with their meanings) already existing in the languages and simply applies them to the appropriate objectivities.

But when and how do we succeed in finding and thereby actualizing just that meaning which a word has in a given language and in a certain place in the text? [12] Of course it is not seldom that one makes mistakes and *mis*understands this or that word in the text of the work, that is, gives it a meaning other than the one it actually has in that language. This danger in fact exists; but it should be neither exaggerated nor considered unavoidable. Many scholars tend to do just that; they hold a view of the nature of the verbal meaning whereby its correct understanding becomes purely a matter of coincidence. They identify the verbal meaning with the so-called content of a mental act, considering this "content" as a component, a "real part" [*reeller Teil*], in Husserl's sense, of the act. According to this theory, there are in the real external world only so-called physical signs the mental idea of which "combines" with a psychological content through "convention" or random "association." The psychological content, which is naturally always "my own," is supposed to be the meaning of the word, so that the reader of a literary work or the hearer of someone else's speech cannot go beyond the "contents" of his own mental acts. Thus, when two people use the same word, each of them has his own "private" meaning for the (supposedly) identical word, and only the "identity" of the contents they experience accounts for the fact that both use this word with the "same" meaning. From this point of view, the word itself (actually, only the verbal sound—but in this theory the word is equated with the verbal sound) has no meaning at all. To understand in which sense a certain word is being used, one must simply guess what constitutes the content of the speaker's mental act. But the great majority of psychologists maintain that experiences are accessible as objects of cognition only to the experiencing subject. In that case, the correct understanding of the meaning of a word (in short, the understanding of a word) used by another is almost a miracle. Since, according to this theory, understanding is based on a

12. As I have mentioned, I am considering here only those cases of the cognition of a literary work, and in particular of its semantic stratum, in which the reader really knows the language of the work. This restriction obviates the question as to how one learns a language—that is, the sense and the usage of individual words in larger linguistic formations. This latter case should not be confused with the situation of someone who reads a work in a language he fully understands.

completely random association of exactly the same content with the mere verbal sign, it does not consist in knowing the appropriate verbal meaning. Under these conditions, the correct understanding of literary texts, the authors of which are in many cases unknown and often no longer living, seems to be quite impossible. Each literary text would then have to be understood in each reader's own way, and there would be as many ways of understanding the text as there are readers or readings. It would be impossible to achieve real communication through a literary text. But then, how would "intersubjective" science, as it is called, be possible? [13]

Moreover, this theory does not correspond to the actual situation when two people converse in the same language. For example, if I speak with someone about an external state of affairs and he points out to me another feature of this state of affairs, then he is not interested in the concrete contents of my mental acts, just as I am not interested in the contents of his mental experiences. We are both directing our attention to a state of affairs which is exernal for both of us; by its characteristics and details we orient ourselves as to whether we are speaking about the same thing and saying the same thing about it. If something does not tally, we can correct our understanding of the other's speech by reference to the state of affairs; we can then "agree" linguistically that we have established and learned this or that. I take an interest in what the other person is thinking at the moment only if he speaks a language I cannot understand or if he cannot speak at all but I see that he wants to communicate something to me. But even then I do not try to discover the concrete flow of the contents of his mental acts but rather the linguistic sense which he is trying to constitute and communicate to me. I go beyond the concrete contents of his experience in order to grasp the not yet understood sense of the linguistic entity. And trying to grasp the concrete contents of the other person's mental experience would hardly be to the point, since these contents are constantly changing in their transition from the continuously flowing present into the past. Once fixed, however, the meaning of a linguistic entity does not undergo such

13. Oddly enough, those scholars, like the neopositivists, who postulate the intersubjectivity of science as a *conditio sine qua non* are the same ones who, on the one hand, interpret the meaning or sense of utterances psychologically (or interpret them according to their so-called verifiability) and, on the other hand, maintain the impossibility of knowing another's experiences.

changes; it remains identical as a quasi-static unity until a new meaning is possibly conferred on it.

The source of this psychologistic view of the meaning of linguistic entities lies partly in an incorrect view of how word formation comes about and in a failure to recognize the social nature of every language. It is simply not true that each of us forms the meanings of words for himself alone, in complete isolation, "privately." On the contrary, almost every instance of forming words or conferring meaning represents the common work of two or more people who find themselves confronted with the same object (a thing or a concrete process) or in a common situation. The two people attempt not only to gain knowledge about the nature and properties of the object or situation but also to give it an identical name, with an appropriately constituted meaning, or to describe it in a sentence. The name or sentence becomes intelligible for the two persons with reference to the commonly observed object.[14] Suppose that, in a scientific investigation, it becomes necessary to find a new expression for a new concept. The new meaning will become intelligible to others only if it is either brought into relation with or reduced to other, already intelligible meanings. Or it may be placed in an indirect cognitive relation to appropriate objects, thus giving others the possibility of attaining an immediate apprehension (in particular, a perception) of the object in question and of constituting or reconstituting the word meaning relating to the object in view of this object—of constituting, that is, the meaning already intended by the investigator. Then there are means of checking the correctness of the reconstituted meaning and of discovering and removing possible misunderstandings. However great the practical difficulties may be, it is still beyond doubt that the meaning of a new word is always constituted through the intellectual cooperation of several subjects of consciousness

14. The language teachers who have developed the so-called direct method of learning a foreign language have long been aware of this and have devised very subtle methods for teaching their students the meanings of even abstract words without recourse to explicit definitions.

Of course, one must examine further how one comes to the conviction that several persons perceive the same object and are able to assure themselves of its identity. But these are the last important questions in the clarification of the possibility of "objective" knowledge, questions which have not yet been satisfactorily answered. The lack of satisfactory answers cannot, however, make us doubt the intuitive possession of the identical and common world. But the answers would be impossible if we did not have at our disposal a common language, intelligible to all members of the same speech community.

in common and direct cognitive contact with the corresponding objects. The meaning-carrying word originating in this way is thus from the outset an intersubjective entity, intersubjectively accessible in its meaning, and not something with a "private" meaning which must be guessed at through observation of another's behavior. Then, too, words are not fully isolated entities but are always members of a linguistic system,[15] however loose this system may be in an individual case. At any rate, such a linguistic system has certain characteristic qualities and regularities which apply both phonetically and semantically and which are decisive in guaranteeing the identity of individual verbal meanings as well as in determining them. After reference to the direct experience of the same objects, such a linguistic system is the second most effective means for reaching agreement about the identical meanings of words belonging to the same language. Knowledge of a language is not restricted to knowledge of a great many verbal meanings but also pertains to the manifold regularities which govern the language. A word which is at first unintelligible appears together with a sequence of other words, with which it is connected by various syntactic functions or relations established through content. These relations often make it possible to guess the meaning of the word "from context," not only in isolation, as it appears in a dictionary entry, but also in the full form, with the nuances appropriate to this context. All these expedients, well known in philological practice, show that the discovery of the meaning which the word has in context is not impossible when one knows the language relatively well; nor is it so difficult as the psychological theory sometimes maintains.

A living language forms a structured system of meanings which stand in definite formal and material relations to one another and which also exercise various functions in semantic units of greater complexity, particularly in sentences. The structured system of meanings is made possible by the presence of several basic types of words, distinguished from one another by

15. That any given language is a structured system of definite meanings with definite regularities and relationships is the basic assertion of Karl Bühler. Kasimir Ajdukiewicz, the Polish logician, also treated this problem (see "Sprache und Sinn," *Erkenntnis*, Vol. IV, no. 2 [1934]). His concern, however, was not spoken language but the artificial languages of deductive systems. He did not discuss what determines the possibility of an intersubjectively intelligible language. He merely developed the idea of a closed linguistic system, which certainly does not hold for all "languages."

formal elements (form in the grammatical sense) as well as by a different composition of their meaning. We can distinguish three different basic types of words: (1) nouns, (2) finite verbs, and (3) function words.[16] The most important function of the meaning of nouns is the intentional projection of the objects they name. The noun determines its object as to its form (whether it is a thing, a process, or an event, e.g., a tree, a movement, or a blow), as to its qualitative constitution (what kind of object it is and what qualities it has), and finally as to its mode of being (whether it is intended as a real or an ideal or perhaps as a possible object). For instance, the noun "tree" designates a thing in the ontic mode of reality; a phrase like "the similarity of mathematical triangles" designates an ideal relationship among certain mathematical objects; the noun "perceptibility" designates a certain possibility, etc. To each noun belongs a definite purely intentional object which is dependent on the meaning of the noun for its existence, its form, and the stock of material determinations attributed to it. We must distinguish between the purely intentional object and the object, ontically independent of the meaning of the noun, to which the noun can be applied and which, if it exists at all, is real or ideal or what have you in a genuine sense. Of course, there are nouns which do have a purely intentional object without any ontically autonomous object as its correlate, as with the noun "centaur." The purely intentional character of the object is evident.

In contrast to nouns, the function words—such as "is" (as a copula in cognizing something, in a declarative sentence), "or," "and," "to," "each," "by"—do not constitute an intentional object through their meaning; rather, they merely serve to perform various functions in relation to the meanings of other words with which they appear or in relation to the objects of the nouns which they connect. Thus the word "and" between two nouns (dog and cat) joins these nouns together into a semantic unit of a higher order, and as a correlate to this function it creates a certain intentional interdependence of the objects of these nouns. The "and" can also join two sentences, which then cease to be independent and become parts of a compound sentence. Along

16. See *The Literary Work of Art*, § 15. [*Das literarische Kunstwerk* (Halle: Max Niemeyer, 1931; 2d ed., Tübingen: Max Niemeyer, 1960; 3d ed., 1965; English translation by George Grabowicz (Evanston, Ill.: Northwestern University Press, 1973).] One should remember that both nouns and finite verbs exercise various syntactic and logical functions when they are parts of larger formations. These functions are exercised by the grammatical "forms" of the nouns and the verbs.

with the syntactic functions performed by other words—nouns and verbs—through their grammatical forms and their arrangement in the sentence, the functions exercised by the function words play an important role in constituting both sentences and groups of sentences.

The finite verbs, as the most important sentence-forming or coforming element in the language, are just as important in this respect. They determine—although not alone—the states of affairs as purely intentional sentence correlates. In their various forms, in conjunction with the manifold syntactic functions of the function words, they produce a great multiplicity of sentence structures and sentence complexes and, corresponding to them, a multiplicity of sentence correlates, especially states of affairs and their interconnections. Sentences join in diverse ways to form semantic units of a higher order which exhibit quite varied structures; from these structures arise such entities as a story, a novel, a conversation, a drama, a scientific theory.[17] By the same token, finite verbs constitute not only states of affairs which correspond to the individual sentences, but also whole systems of very diverse types of states of affairs, such as concrete situations, complex processes involving several objects, conflicts and agreements among them, etc. Finally, a whole world is created with variously determined elements and the changes taking place in them, all as the purely intentional correlate of a sentence complex. If this sentence complex finally constitutes a literary work, then I call the whole stock of interconnected intentional sentence correlates the "portrayed world" of the work.

But let us return to our investigation of the process of understanding.

When we apprehend a verbal sound or multiplicity of verbal sounds, the first step in understanding it is finding [18] the precise

17. In my book *The Literary Work of Art* I discussed in somewhat greater detail what I merely sketch here. The matter is very complex and demands a comprehensive investigation. I restrict myself here to a very rudimentary indication. If adequately developed, it would lead, on the one hand, to a theory of language and, on the other, to regional ontologies.

18. Normally one should not take the discovery of the verbal meaning to be the object of a separate investigation. Such a thing is possible, of course, but usually occurs only when we are dealing with a completely unfamiliar word or when we consider the verbal meaning from a theoretical point of view, analyze it, or compare it with other meanings. But such a consideration is not necessary in an ordinary reading and understanding of a text; it simply does not occur. When we are dealing with a language we know, we apprehend the appropriate meaning immediately, without making it an object of special consideration. We shall soon explain how this immediate apprehension comes about.

meaning intention which the word has in its language. This meaning intention can appear in two different ways, either in a way characteristic of the word in isolation or in another way, when the word is part of a more complex semantic unit. The meaning of a word undergoes a change, in many cases a regular one, according to the context in which it appears.[19] In particular, it is enriched by specially operative intentions which are performed by the syntactic functions determined by the structure of the corresponding semantic unit of higher order and by the place where the word stands in this semantic unit. In the understanding of a text, the meaning intentions are present in one of these two forms. But whenever the word functions only as part of a sentence, discovering that form of the meaning which the word has in isolation would be neither advisable nor faithful to the text. It is remarkable, however, that in such cases one immediately apprehends the meanings of the individual words in the form they have in context. Usually this apprehension occurs without special effort or resistance; it does not, however, always occur with the same ease. Only in exceptional cases are we oriented toward the discovery of the lexical meaning of words.[20]

The successful immediate discovery of the meaning intention is basically an actualization of this intention. That is: when I understand a text, I think the meaning of the text. I extract the meaning from the text, so to speak, and change it into the actual intention of my mental act of understanding,[21] into an intention identical with the word or sentence intention of the text. Then I really "understand" the text. Of course, this applies only when the work is written in one's so-called native language or at least in a language completely familiar to the reader. Then the text need not be translated into the reader's own language but is immediately thought in the language of the text.[22]

19. See *The Literary Work of Art*, § 17.
20. This lexical form of the verbal meaning is, by the way, only an artificial construct of linguistic analysis and not the original form of the verbal meaning, which in living languages is always part of a linguistic unity. In its lexical form the word almost always has many meanings; it becomes unambiguous when it is used concretely in a larger linguistic unit.
21. Husserl would call this a "signitive act" [*signitiver Akt*]. See his *Logical Investigations*, Vol. II, Fifth Investigation, *passim*.
22. This distinction is usually ignored or insufficiently considered, but it is essential for an apprehension of the work which is faithful to the text. Only when one reads a work in its original language can one apprehend the original emotional character of the words and phrases, the

Only when the language of a work is not immediately intelligible to the reader does he have to search for the meanings of individual words separately, find them (sometimes with a dictionary), and only then, after an appropriate interpretation of the sense, "join" them to form a whole sentence. Thus one sometimes reads old Latin texts without having the ability to think in Latin (in which case the fact that Latin is a "dead" language plays an important role). Basically we then understand the text by translating it into our own language, and we check back only to see whether this translation is correct. Disregarding the fact that a translation of a work is never completely adequate (a problem in itself), the course the reading itself follows is quite different in the two cases compared. In the first case we assimilate the meanings of the individual words in such a way that we immediately think whole sentences. This "immediately" should not, of course, be taken to mean that we think the complete sentences all at once, in one moment, or that thinking the individual words is not necessary to the understanding of the whole sentence. Each time we think a sentence explicitly formulated in words, we need a short stretch of time to complete our thought; and it is also necessary when we think a sentence to traverse in mental acts the verbal meanings which form it. In reading a sentence, the opening words which we understand stimulate us to the unfolding of a sentence-generating operation,[23] a special mental flow in which the sentence unfolds. Once we begin to move with the course of thought which the sentence follows, we think it as a separate whole; and the individual verbal meanings are automatically accommodated into the sentence flow as phases of it which are not separately delimited. The verbal meanings can be so accommodated only if they are immediately thought in those nuances of meaning which they have as parts of that sentence. This is possible only

peculiar language melody, and all the subtle nuances of meaning of the text, which often have no equivalent in another language.

23. I first discussed the sentence-generating operation in my book *The Literary Work of Art.* The peculiar course of this operation and its possible variations have to be worked out more closely. But, even in the rudimentary fashion in which I treated it at that time, the indication of its existence is of great importance for the understanding of the unity of the sentence and for the possibility of the apprehension of states of affairs. Precisely because Franz Brentano, in his *Von der Klassifikation der psychischen Phänomene* (Leipzig: Duncker & Humblot, 1911), found no place for unified operations extending beyond the phase of the immediate present, he was unable to recognize the existence of states of affairs, which then led to his confused theory of "reism."

because the sentence-generating operation consists in filling out a special kind of system of syntactic functions. The functions are filled by the words which make up the sentence. Once we are transposed into the flow of thinking the sentence, we are prepared, after having completed the thought of one sentence, to think its "continuation" in the form of another sentence, specifically, a sentence which has a connection with the first sentence. In this way the process of reading a text advances effortlessly. But when it happens that the second sentence has no perceptible connection whatever with the first, the flow of thought is checked. A more or less vivid surprise or vexation is associated with the resulting hiatus. The block must be overcome if we are to renew the flow of our reading. If we succeed, each following sentence will be understood as a continuation of preceding sentences. Just what is "continued" or developed is a separate problem, the solution of which depends on the structure of the given work. All that is important just now is that there is such a thing as an expectation for new sentences. And the advancing reading simply actualizes and makes present to us what we are expecting. In our orientation toward what is coming and our attempt to actualize it, we still do not lose sight of what we have just read. To be sure, we do not continue to think vividly the sentences we have already read at the same time that we are thinking the immediately following sentence. Nevertheless, the meaning of the sentence we have just read (and, to a limited degree also, that of several preceding sentences), as well as the sound of the words just pronounced, is still peripherally experienced in the form of a "reverberation." This "reverberation" has, among other things, the consequence that the sentence we are now reading is concretized in its meaning, that is, it receives precisely that nuance of meaning which it should have as a continuation of the sentences preceding it. For, as closer analysis shows, the sentences, too, are only to a certain degree independent of other semantic units in the text and receive their full meaning, with its proper nuances, only as parts of a multiplicity of sentences. The meaning of the sentence completes itself and adapts itself to the meaning of the sentences preceding it, but not only to those preceding it. The meaning of sentences which are yet to come can also share in determining the meaning of the sentence we have just read, can supplement or modify it. During the reading this occurs more distinctly when we know from the start the later parts of the work (for example, through a previous reading). On a first reading this is not so noticeable, unless the sentences we have already read are of a kind which enable us to foresee in general outline the meaning of the sentences following. Usually, however, this modification of previous sentences by those which follow displays itself only after reading a series of consecutive sentences. In this case we quickly make a mental survey of the sentences we have already read, the actual meaning of which is disclosed only at this moment, and we think them explicitly again in a new and expanded or connected meaning. Sometimes, however, this occurs automatically, without a special act of explicitly rethinking the sentences. This fact can serve as an argument that the meaning of at least some of the sentences already read does not completely vanish for the reader; rather, he is still peripherally aware of it in the form of a "reverberation" as he reads the succeeding sentences.

In a reading which is properly carried out, the content of the work is organized quasi-automatically into an internally coherent, meaningful whole of a higher order and is not merely a random conglomeration of separate sentence meanings which are completely independent of one another. The various functions of function words, such as "because," "thus," or "consequently," play a significant role in organizing the content of a work into a whole. Interconnections of meaning among several sentences can also be constituted implicitly without the use of such words, through the material content of nouns and verbs. We really understand the content of a work only when we succeed in making use of, and actualizing, all the constitutive elements the text provides and in constituting the organized, meaningful whole of the work in accordance with the meaning intentions contained in the semantic stratum of the text.[24] Of

24. The concept of "content" in contrast to "form" has, of course, a great many meanings. I have also tried to compare the different concepts and, as far as possible, to define them more precisely. (See, among others, "The General Question of the Essence of Form and Content," *Journal of Philosophy*, Vol. LVII, no. 7 [1960].) In the text I make use of one of these concepts, which seems to me the only justified and useful one for the purpose of analyzing a literary work. The "content" of the literary work will be construed as the organized structure of meaning in the work, which is constituted by the semantic stratum. Of course, the "form" in which it is cast also belongs to this "content." The form is merely the way in which the content of the work is organized into a whole. The form of the semantic stratum must be distinguished, on the one hand, from the forms of the other strata and, on the other, from the form of the whole work, i.e., the totality of strata in the structure of the succession of the parts of the work. Each of these concepts can be determined unambiguously. But we must not contrast these various "forms" with the "content" of the work as a whole; rather, we must

course, we do not always succeed, especially when we do not pay special attention to the meaning of individual sentences which we did not understand immediately, and when we do not return to sentences which we have already read and whose meaning must perhaps be corrected. The connections between sentences are also sometimes unclear and hence require special attention. But if even our special attention is of little avail, then, despite all our efforts, we do not understand the text; it contains, as blank spots, a series of incomprehensible sentences, which we do not know how to integrate properly with the rest. But even if we finally overcome all difficulties, so that we can maintain that we understand the whole text, still, this laborious sort of reading hardly reproduces the original form peculiar to the work. The natural flow of successively developing sentence meanings is interrupted by this mode of reading; the dynamic unfolding of meaning in the natural succession of its parts which is proper to the work is affected or even destroyed, and it is almost totally obscured. In a scientific work this often need have no great significance; in a literary work of art, however, at least the aesthetic effect of the work on the reader is seriously modified. And if the work, as a result of its own unclarities and disorder, cannot be read in any other way, then its aesthetic aspect will be seriously impaired. It makes no difference whether the unclarities are accidental flaws or intended features of the work.

One further comment in closing. The declarative sentences in the literary work of art can theoretically be read in either of two ways: as judgments about a reality ontically independent of the work or as sentences which only appear to be assertions. In the first case we refer in our thoughts immediately (directly) to objects (things, states of affairs, processes, events) which do not belong to the work itself and which, in accordance with this understanding of the declarative sentences, exist in reality and are supposed to be in reality just the way they are intended.

---

reserve the concept of "content" for the organized whole of the semantic stratum. The determination of the various "forms" which can be distinguished in the literary work and the explication of their diverse interrelations require a special investigation, which cannot be carried out here. Such an investigation is the only remedy for the hopeless confusion which currently reigns in discussions of the "form-content problem." See my investigation in the second volume of the *Studia z estetyki* under the title "O formie i treści dzieła sztuki literackiej" (On Form and Content in the Literary Work of Art), pp. 343–473. [Also published as "Das Form-Inhalt-Problem im literarischen Kunstwerk," in Roman Ingarden, *Erlebnis, Kunstwerk und Wert* (Tübingen: Max Niemeyer, 1969), pp. 31–50.— Trans.]

When we refer in thought to real objects, we go beyond the realm of being of the literary work, while the objectivities portrayed in the work itself vanish in some measure from the reader's attention. They become "transparent," so that the "ray of vision" of the reader's intention is not arrested by them. In the second case, however, we turn with the intentional act in which the sentence is thought to the objectivities portrayed in the work itself. Thus we remain in the realm of the work itself, without taking an interest in extraliterary reality. This second interpretation of the declarative sentences appearing in the literary work of art is the one proper to it. I shall discuss this subject later. In the following, I shall attempt to describe the experiences of becoming acquainted with, and of apprehending, the literary work of art as these occur when the reader assumes the attitude that the declarative sentences are merely apparent assertions.

§ 9.   *Passive and active reading*

THE ACTIVITIES performed during reading which we have described thus far do not yet exhaust the complex process which we call the cognition of the literary work. Rather, they merely constitute the indispensable means for the performance of a new cognitive operation which is much more important for the cognition of the literary work than the activities previously discussed. This new operation is the intentional reconstruction and then the cognition of the objectivities portrayed in the work.

Any understanding of the semantic units in the literary work (words, sentences, and complexes or structures of sentences) consists in performing the appropriate signitive acts and leads thereby to the intentional projection of the objects of these acts, or the intentional objects of the semantic units. Hence it appears, at first glance, that the understanding in ordinary reading suffices to constitute for the reader the objectivities portrayed in the work. But a closer look shows that this is not the case.

Provisionally, we shall distinguish two different ways of reading the literary work: ordinary, purely passive (receptive) reading and active reading.

Every reading, of course, is an activity consciously undertaken by the reader and not a mere experience or reception of something. Nevertheless, in many cases the whole effort of the reader consists in thinking the meanings of the sentences he reads without making the meanings into objects and in remaining, so to speak, in the sphere of meaning. There is no intellectual attempt to progress from the sentences read to the objects appropriate to them and projected by them. Of course, these objects are always an automatic intentional projection of the sentence meanings. In purely passive reading, however, one does not attempt to apprehend them or, in particular, to constitute them synthetically. Consequently, in passive reading there is no kind of intercourse with the fictional objects.

This purely passive, receptive manner of reading, which is often mechanical as well, occurs relatively often in the reading of both literary works of art and scientific works. One still knows what one is reading, although the scope of understanding is often limited to the sentence which is being read. But one does not become clearly aware of what one is reading about and what its qualitative constitution is. One is occupied with the realization of the sentence meaning itself and does not absorb the meaning in such a way that one can transpose oneself by means of it into the world of the objects in a work; one is too constrained by the meaning of the individual sentences. One reads "sentence by sentence," and each of these sentences is understood separately, in isolation; a synthetic combination of the sentence just read with other sentences, sometimes widely separated from it, is not achieved. If the passive reader were required to make a short summary of the content of what he has read, he would be unable to do it. With a good enough memory, he could perhaps repeat the text within certain limits, but that is all. A good knowledge of the language of the work, a certain amount of practice in reading, a stereotyped sentence structure —all this often results in the reading's running its course quite "mechanically," without the personal and active participation of the reader, although he is the one doing the reading.

It is hard to describe the difference between passive, purely receptive reading and "active" reading because in passive reading we do, after all, think the sentences as we think them also in "active" reading. Thus there seems to be an activity involved in both cases. It would perhaps be easier to contrast these two ways of reading if we could say that, when one reads receptively, one does not think the meanings of the sentences by performing the corresponding signitive acts; rather, one only experiences or feels that they are being performed. By contrast, it is only in active reading that we actually perform the signitive acts. But the matter is not so simple, because in both kinds of reading mental acts are performed. The difference between the two kinds of reading consists merely in the way in which they are performed. It is, however, extremely difficult to describe these modes of performance.

Suppose we assert that in "active" reading one not only understands the sentence meanings but also apprehends their objects and has a sort of intercourse with them. A theory arising from naïve empiricist or positivist realism renders agreement with this assertion more difficult. These realists hold that we can have intercourse with objects only (a) when the objects are real and (b) when we simply find them present before us without our contribution, thus when we need do nothing but gape at what is before us. It is assumed without further ado in this theory that we are presented with objects only through sense perception or, at most, through inner perception. Thus, if we learn about an object exclusively through understanding a few sentences, then it follows that we cannot have immediate intercourse with that object. This contention appears to exclude all cases in which (as in the preponderant majority of literary works of art) we have to do with objects and events which have never existed or occurred in reality.

However, the realist theory is wrong, primarily in asserting that in sense perception we gain knowledge of the things and events of the real world around us only by passive "gaping." On the contrary, in order really to cognize these things, we must perform a series of often complicated and interconnected acts, which demand of us a considerable degree of activity and attentiveness and which, on the basis of the material provided us through a multiplicity of perceptions, finally lead us to the real object we perceive. And only when the object is thus made accessible to us do we have direct intercourse with it as with something which is truly given and self-present. This theory is also wrong in asserting that, beyond the area of sensory or internal perception, we can gain no direct or even quasi-direct knowledge of objects such as those we know only through the understanding of certain sentences. When we are dealing with the objects of a geometrical investigation, for instance, we sometimes gain a direct apprehension of certain states of affairs pertaining in the geometrical objects, as well as of necessary relationships among them, through understanding certain sentences and with the help of specially modified acts of imagination.

When we are unable to succeed at this, we say that we certainly understand the sentences linguistically but that, even when the proof is provided, we are not genuinely convinced that it is really as the proposition in question maintains, nor can we come to clear and distinct awareness of what is "really" being dealt with. Some people express this differently by saying that they certainly "know" what the proposition is about but do not truly understand the sentence, since they obviously derive genuine understanding only from a direct, intuitive apprehension of the corresponding geometrical state of affairs.

Something similar happens when objects are simulated in creative artistic imagination with the help of special acts of consciousness. Such objects are, to be sure, purely intentional or, if we prefer, "fictive"; but, precisely as a result of the particular activity of the creative acts producing them, they attain the character of an independent reality. Once the creative intentionality has thus been actualized, it becomes to a certain degree binding for us. The objects corresponding to the intentional acts are projected in the later phases of the creative process as a quasi-reality to some extent independent of these acts. We take this quasi-reality into account; we must adjust ourselves to it; or, if for some reason it does not satisfy us, we must transform it, or further develop and supplement it, by means of a new creative act.

The reading of a literary work of art can thus be accomplished "actively," in the sense that we think with a peculiar originality and activity the meaning of the sentences we have read; we project ourselves in a cocreative attitude into the realm of the objects determined by the sentence meanings. The meaning in this case creates an approach to the objects which are treated in the work. The meaning, as Husserl says, is only a passageway [ein Durchgangsobjekt] which one traverses in order to reach the object meant. In a strict sense the meaning is not an object at all. For, if we think a sentence actively, we attend, not to the meaning, but to what is determined or thought through it or in it. We can say, although not quite precisely, that in actively thinking a sentence we constitute or carry out its meaning and, in so doing, arrive at the objects of the sentence, that is, the states of affairs or other intentional sentence correlates. From this point we can grasp the things themselves which are indicated in the sentence correlates.

Besides its two linguistic strata, the literary work also contains the stratum of portrayed objectivities. Thus, in order to apprehend the whole work,[25] it is necessary above all to reach all of its strata, and especially the stratum of portrayed objectivities. Even a purely receptive reading discloses this stratum to the reader, at least distantly and obscurely. Only an active reading, however, permits the reader to discover it in its peculiar, characteristic structure and in its full detail. But this cannot be accomplished through a mere apprehension of the individual intentional states of affairs belonging to the sentences. We must progress from these states of affairs to their diverse interconnections and then to the objects (things, events) which are portrayed in the states of affairs. But in order to achieve an aesthetic apprehension of the stratum of objects in its often complex structure, the active reader, after he has discovered and reconstructed this stratum, must, as we shall see, go beyond it, especially beyond various details explicitly indicated by the sentence meanings, and must supplement in many directions what is portrayed. And in so doing, the reader to some extent proves to be the cocreator of the literary work of art. Let us discuss this in greater detail.

§ 10. *Objectification as the transition from the intentional states of affairs to the objects portrayed in the literary work*

THE DIRECT (FORMAL) OBJECTS of sentences are their purely intentional correlates, which are of very diverse kinds and forms and which correspond, in their diversity, to the manifold types of sentences. In particular, there are states of affairs as correlates of predicative assertions, problems as correlates of interrogative sentences, etc.[26]

25. As we shall see, this is only possible in a perspectival foreshortening or distortion. I shall have more to say about this later.

26. I carried out a more detailed analysis of intentional sentence correlates (particularly of the states of affairs) in *The Literary Work of Art*, §§ 20, 28–30, and in the book *Der Streit um die Existenz der Welt*, 3 vols. (Tübingen: Max Niemeyer, 1964–66), Vol. II, §§ 52–54. [A Polish version of this work appeared as *Spór o istnienie świata* (The Controversy over the Existence of the World), 2 vols. (Cracow: Polska Akademia Nauk, 1947–48; 2d ed., Warsaw: Państwowe Wydawn. Naukowe, 1961–62). Volume I has been partially translated by Helen R. Michejda as *Time and*

Any given intentional state of affairs is determined originally and in the most exact way by the meaning of the sentence which projects it. Thus, when we want to indicate in an individual case what constitutes the state of affairs determined by a sentence, the mere thinking of this sentence leads us directly to its state of affairs. We can also, of course, indicate the state of affairs indirectly, "from without," that is, when we go beyond the thinking of the sentence and refer in a new intentional act to the state of affairs of the sentence we have already thought. But this brings about a formal transformation of the state of affairs. The sentences "Cracow, the old capital of Poland, is situated on the Vistula" or "Lord Wołodyjowski defeated the Cossack hero Bohun in single combat" possess an intentional state of affairs which is materially and formally determined by the words appearing in them and by the functions exercised by these words and which cannot be so exactly and explicitly determined and unfolded by other words. But we can denominate the corresponding states of affairs by saying that the first sentence determines "the location of Cracow, the old capital of Poland, on the Vistula," the second, "the defeat of the Cossack hero Bohun in single combat by Lord Wołodyjowski." Each of these states of affairs thereby undergoes a nominalization. The object form is superimposed on the form of the state of affairs and hides or even destroys its original categorial structure. It is a matter of indifference whether there now exist or ever have existed, in the real world independent of these sentences, states of affairs exactly like these purely intentional states of affairs. For our investigation does not deal with facts of the real world, past or present, but merely with what is intentionally projected by a sentence. This does not exclude the possibility that the same sentences might serve as judgments, supplied with an assertive function by virtue of which they refer to materially identical real facts, the existence of which they maintain, whether justly or unjustly. But this has no influence on the existence and the form of the purely intentional sentence correlates; the latter depend solely on the substance of the meaning and the function of intentionality in the sentence. In a literary work of art we are interested exclusively in the purely intentional correlates of the sentences and especially in the states of affairs. In any given work there are pre-

---

Modes of Being (Springfield, Ill.: Thomas, 1964).] I treated the same problems in my "Essentiale Fragen," *Jahrbuch für Philosophie und phänomenologische Forschung*, Vol. VII (1925). Here I shall confine myself to a few examples and rudimentary indications.

cisely as many states of affairs as there are assertions. In a normal reading we make the acquaintance of these states of affairs in the same sequence as that of the sentences projecting them.[27] For the order of the succession of the sentences and of their correlates is identical. At the same time, however, the meanings of the sentences often determine completely different interconnections and a different order among the states of affairs. The description of a thing in several successive sentences projects a multitude of corresponding states of affairs, all of which belong simultaneously to one and the same thing and are causally interconnected or follow one another in accordance with the events which develop in the portrayed world. Each state of affairs reveals this thing from a different point of view or under different circumstances. As we become familiar with the states of affairs during our reading, we gain ever more precise knowledge of the features or progressing fate of this thing.[28] But there are states of affairs in which not one but several things participate. The state of affairs then consists in a whole objective situation. From a series of such situations we learn about the fate of several things which stand in various relations to one another. Thus, in the course of reading, a self-sufficient world of things, people, occurrences, and events, a world with its own dynamics and emotional atmosphere, reveals itself. All this by way of objects portrayed in the work. It is precisely the intentional states of affairs which exercise the function of portraying.

But in order to proceed from the individual intentional states of affairs to the portrayed world, we must accomplish several

---

27. We can, of course, if we wish, read these sentences in a completely different sequence, from the back of the book to the front, for instance. The work demands to some extent, however, that the sentences be read in the sequence in which they appear in the text.

28. An example from Thomas Mann's *Buddenbrooks:*

"Frau Consul Elizabeth Buddenbrook, born Kröger, laughed the sputtering Kröger laugh and tucked in her chin as the Krögers did. She could not be called a beauty, but, like all the Krögers, she looked distinguished; she moved with graceful deliberation and had a clear, well-modulated voice. People liked her and felt confidence in her. Her reddish hair curled over her ears and was piled in a crown on top of her head; and she had the brilliant white complexion that goes with such hair, set off with a tiny freckle here and there. Her nose was rather too long, her mouth somewhat small; her most striking facial peculiarity was the shape of her lower lip, which ran straight into the chin without a curve. She had on a short bodice with high puffed sleeves, that left exposed a flawlessly modelled neck adorned with a spray of diamonds on a satin ribbon." [Translation by H. T. Lowe-Porter (New York: Alfred A. Knopf, 1938), p. 4.]

times the operation of "objectification." It can take any of several forms according to the content of the sentences. The form it takes can result, for instance, from the fact that the content of a state of affairs is set in the formal structure of a feature or condition of the object named by the subject of the sentence, say a person or a thing. When we read the sentence: "Lord Wołodyjowski defeated Bohun in single combat," [29] we can perform one of the possible objectifications and keep in mind only "Lord Wołodyjowski, the victor over Bohun." In what follows, the man characterized thus belongs to the portrayed world of the novel. The objectification can, however, equally well lead to "Bohun, who was defeated by Lord Wołodyjowski." Finally, it can also determine the fact of Lord Wołodyjowski's victory over Bohun. One need not state all this explicitly while reading. The objectification can be accomplished involuntarily, while reading, in simple acts of imagination, with the result that we see Wołodyjowski simply as the victor over Bohun, without becoming distinctly aware of the formal change which has taken place in the portrayed object. Nonetheless, it has taken place; and, as soon as he is mentioned later, Lord Wołodyjowski simply stands before our "eyes" with this particular characteristic.

In this very simple example the process of objectification offers no particular difficulties. In actual literary works, however, we are often dealing with very involved and complicated texts. To accomplish a correct and fairly exhaustive objectification of these texts is a rather difficult task, which we perform only seldom during a superficial reading. It almost always occurs in a very sketchy way and without being carried to conclusion, hence in a way to which a peculiar potentiality adheres. The following is thus to be noted.

Above all, objectification can be performed in quite diverse ways in one and the same sentence complex or even in the same sentence, as can be seen from the example just adduced. In our example the objectification can be accomplished on the basis of the state of affairs in question in at least three different directions. In a specific reading only one of the directions of objectification is chosen (generally involuntarily), according to whatever interest happens to be active in the reader. Other directions of objectification can also be taken into account, either all of them at the same time or only a few of them. For the majority of sentences, especially if they are more or less complex, the

29. H. Sienkiewicz, *With Fire and Sword.*

number of possible or permissible directions and modes of objectification is of course significantly larger. The objectifications are then carried out by the reader in greater or lesser amplitude. It is improbable that any reader, particularly in a single reading, will be able to exhaust the whole multitude of permissible modes and directions of objectification; rather, he will take into account some few possibilities. How much the reader is able to realize from these possibilities depends on various factors, which cannot be completely assessed at present. Above all, it is not entirely clear how the objectification is subjectively performed by the reader. Is it an explicitly performed intellectual operation, or an intuitive procedure, or something which happens involuntarily and automatically and which settles synthetically, as a peculiar sort of deposit of the knowledge gained through reading, upon the portrayed objectivities? All these modes of objectification seem equally possible. Which of them is applied depends on the abilities of the reader but also on the state into which he is transported by the text and thus, to a large extent, on the suggestions proceeding from the peculiarities of the text. We may also ask to what extent objectification absorbs or can absorb the reader, specifically, with regard to whether it can be accomplished during a reading, without interrupting the reading, or whether it demands so much attention that it can proceed only during an interruption of the reading or after the reading, in a special phase of reflection on what has been read. The two latter ways of objectification seem equally possible and are often in fact carried out by the reader in a critical study of literary works. They constitute a special phase in the cognition of the work, a phase which significantly surpasses the cognition taking place in an ordinary reading. We shall consider this later.

To be sure, objectification can also be performed in the course of the reading itself; then, however, it is essentially limited in its effectiveness and range, if there are to be no significant disturbances of the process of reading. Of the many possible directions and modes of objectification, which is usually accomplished involuntarily (although the same holds for an objectification of which one is fully aware!), only specially selected possibilities can be realized in each individual case. And if we want to consider still further possibilities, the reading must then be interrupted or begun anew, which involves the danger of disfiguring the work. The scope of possible objectifications for one and the same work changes considerably from one reading to another and from one reader to another. Consequently, one and the same text can lead to objectivities which have been objectified in different ways and thus give the portrayed world a different appearance. This difference is expressed above all in a different formal structure of the world. Some states of affairs remain in their nonobjective form, whereas others are formally altered in some way and reveal thereby certain things or events of diverse constitution which for the most part participate only in the states of affairs belonging to the sentences, that is, when they constitute the direct correlate of the sentences. Although these differences are of a purely formal nature, they are not devoid of significance for the aesthetic apprehension of the work or for the form it takes in this apprehension. For the objective stratum of the work is then revealed to the reader in different aesthetically valent factors, according to whether the portrayed world appears to be primarily dynamic or static. If this world contains a relatively large number of events, these can, on the one hand, be left in their original form and not objectified; then the portrayed world has a more dynamic character. On the other hand, the processes can be apprehended as objectivities of a peculiar kind, with the result that everything appears frozen, as having already been accomplished. Thus the manner in which the objectification of a work is carried out plays an important role in the concretization of the work and in determining its aesthetic effectiveness.

The objectivities portrayed in a literary work (people, things, processes, events) are not in general immutable and are usually not portrayed in just one temporal phase or in one state but often have very involved fates, participate in various events, and sometimes undergo quite extensive transformations. All this is shown in a multiplicity of states of affairs which portray the same objects in various successive phases. Consequently, the objectification does not end with a constitution of the object in one phase of its being; rather, it is, or at least can be, carried out anew after each new event, after every transformation of the object. The individual objects are not only enriched by new attributes, one after another; they also lose many other attributes and appear later as objects with different determinations than they previously had. They are also constantly entering into new connections and relationships with other objectivities of the portrayed world and are freed from those relationships which had previously been binding. This whole play of events, and all that takes part in it, is portrayed in states of affairs and undergoes this or that mode of objectification during reading. Consequently, it is apprehended as what is "objectively" present in the portrayed world, what takes place there, and what in its totality constitutes this single world. A purely passive understanding of the individual sentences as such and in sequence cannot accomplish this. Only by means of active reading can we petrify to a certain extent all these transformations in the portrayed world and then be witnesses to all its objects and events.

As a consequence of the process of objectification, the stratum of portrayed objects attains a certain independence from the stratum of semantic units. Among other things, it is given a different order from that of the succession of sentences. The sentences referring to a specific person and his fate can appear in the text in a sequence completely different from that of the events in the portrayed world. The whole multiplicity of sentences referring to one and the same phase of an object or objective situation and describing it in various details from various sides, and also in a different temporal perspective, can be scattered throughout the work. The fact that the sentences referring to an objectivity are scattered, however, has no influence on the order of, and the objective relationships among, the corresponding objectivities.[30] The purely objective order in the portrayed world is first revealed in the "objectification."

In order for the portrayed world to attain its independence, it is necessary for the reader to carry out a synthesizing objectification in which various particulars projected by the individual sentences are assembled and combined into a whole. This synthesizing objectification does not simply add facts, one to another, but unifies them. Through the interweaving of facts and details we grasp a unified state of affairs or the form of the object. In connection with this, the reader's operations of objectification become to a certain degree independent of his understanding of the individual successive sentences. More precisely: new acts of synthetic apprehension and of constitution of objects in the portrayed world are founded on the understanding of the

---

30. In this connection we can produce many examples, not only from novels but also from dramatic works. I shall not go into these in detail, since it would require considerable space to analyze any one of them. See, however, Faulkner's novel *Absalom, Absalom!* or Ibsen's *Rosmersholm,* where the so-called exposition extends up to the fifth act, while the so-called action develops on its own, under the weight of events which took place many years before but only "now" come out into the open. In modern novels a special narrative technique has been developed by which the same thing is told several times in a temporal sequence completely different from the one in which it "actually" took place. We shall go into this in greater detail in the next chapter.

individual sentences. In these acts the material furnished by the individual sentences is utilized for the purpose of constituting the stratum of objects. The reader is thus freed from the order of the sequence of the sentences and the states of affairs belonging to them and also from the splitting of a single fact into a multitude of states of affairs. The structure of the work itself demands the reader's realization of this independence if he is to apprehend faithfully the stratum of the portrayed world. Only when the reader is able during reading to rise above the step-by-step understanding of sentences to a total comprehension is the objectification and the correct understanding of the portrayed world achieved. This brings us, however, to new problems, to which we shall return later (see § 16, below).

Only by virtue of the synthesizing objectification do the portrayed objectivities take on a quasi-reality of their own for the reader. This quasi-reality has its own appearance, its own fates, and its own dynamics. Only after this objectification is the reader made witness to certain events and objectivities which he has in some measure intentionally reconstituted, through understanding the sentences and performing the operations of objectification. Having thus become a witness, he cognizes these objects anew, as if they were simply there in front of him, and he is then under their "impression"; he apprehends them then in an aesthetic attitude and reacts to their aesthetically relevant features with appropriate emotions, specifically with a "response to value" [Wertantwort], to use D. von Hildebrand's apt expression. The receptive acts of cognition are here peculiarly intertwined with the creative acts intentionally projecting the reality portrayed. At the same time as he becomes familiar with the meaning of the sentences, the reader intentionally reconstructs the objects belonging to the meaning, in a process of synthesizing objectification. After this reconstruction, he cognizes them again as completed objects found before him and often changes them intentionally in this cognition. In an aesthetically receptive attitude he has an impression of them and perceives the values appearing in them. This latter aesthetic apprehension and aesthetic attitude on the part of the reader are based on the acts of cognition of the literary work of art as well as on other acts, about which we shall soon have occasion to speak.[31]

All this goes beyond the purely passive understanding of the

31. As we shall see, this does not exclude the aesthetic attitude from modifying the course of these diverse operations.

meaning of the individual sentences and requires of the reader not only a special activity but also various abilities which must be adapted to the characteristic structure of the literary work of art. Without this activity and without the proper performance of a synthesizing objectification there will be no constitution of the world of the objects portrayed in the work. And for just this reason there will be no direct cognitive or aesthetic intercourse with this world on the part of the reader. Consequently, there are readers who certainly understand a text in a purely literal way but who still do not know what sort of portrayed world they are actually dealing with. Their aesthetic reactions are either not realized at all, or, if they are, they are not at all adapted to the world revealed in the work.

The process of synthesizing objectification is generally a relatively difficult operation, and its successful performance depends equally upon the abilities and intelligence of the reader, on the one hand, and upon the structure of the stratum of semantic units, on the other. If this stratum is complicated, opaque, and ambiguous in many sentences or sentence complexes, then the objectification can present considerable, sometimes insurmountable, difficulties for even the best-prepared reader. In this case the objectification places such great demands on his penetration, his subtlety, and his ability to unify the scattered particulars into an internally consolidated totality that he simply cannot succeed in accomplishing it. We all know how much effort it sometimes takes to reconstruct exactly and faithfully the world portrayed in a scientific or philosophical work. In the case of literary works of art, a faithful apprehension of the portrayed objectivities can be even more difficult for the reader, since in this case it is a question of reconstructing unique objects, which are often provided with such peculiar attributes that it is almost impossible to determine them precisely by means of everyday language. Thus it is usually a matter of constituting a whole multiplicity of things, persons, processes, and events which stand in numerous relationships with one another. Synthetic, active reading of the text makes this kind of objectification of the portrayed objects easier for the reader because in such a reading the objects are not separate entities but are rather parts of one and the same world. The ordering of this world, its apprehension as a whole, the discovery of the main stream of events and processes which develop in it, feeling one's way into the intangible atmosphere which, so to speak, hovers over the events—all this demands of the reader such effort and such a span of attention and ability for synthesis that we are often (even if not in all phases of the reading) unable to fulfill the task which we are set.

§ 11. *Concretization of the portrayed objectivities*

As I HAVE ALREADY MENTIONED, if one wants to achieve an aesthetic apprehension of the work, one must often go far beyond what is actually contained in the objective stratum of the work in the process of objectifying the portrayed objectivities. One must "concretize" these objects at least to a certain degree, and within boundaries set by the work itself. Let us explain this in greater detail.

The literary work, and the literary work of art in particular, is a schematic formation (see Assertion 7, § 4). At least some of its strata, especially the objective stratum, contain a series of "places of indeterminacy." We find such a place of indeterminacy wherever it is impossible, on the basis of the sentences in the work, to say whether a certain object or objective situation has a certain attribute. If, for instance, the color of Consul Budden-brook's eyes were not mentioned in *Buddenbrooks* (and I have not checked to see), then he would be completely undetermined in this respect. We know implicitly, through context and by the fact that he is a human being and has not lost his eyes, that his eyes are of some color; but we do not know which. There are many analogous cases. I call the aspect or part of the portrayed object which is not specifically determined by the text a "place of indeterminacy." [32] Each object, person, event, etc., portrayed in the literary work of art contains a great number of places of indeterminacy, especially the descriptions of what happens to people and things. Usually there are whole stretches of time in the lives of the persons portrayed which are not explicitly presented, so that the changing attributes of these people remain indeterminate. We merely know through indications in the text that the person existed during this time, but the text is silent about what the person did or experienced. But since, except for the rare cases in which the expressive function of the verbal sounds and the pronunciation are helpful, it is almost exclusively

32. See, in this connection, *The Literary Work of Art*, § 38.

the semantic stratum which determines everything in the stratum of portrayed objectivities, we, as readers, not only do not know what happened in the stretches of time not portrayed, but the events are not determined at all; they are neither *A* nor not-*A*.

The presence of places of indeterminacy is not accidental, the result of faulty composition. Rather, it is necessary in every literary work of art. It is impossible to establish clearly and exhaustively the infinite multiplicity of determinacies of the individual objects portrayed in the work with a finite number of words or sentences. Some of the determinacies must always be missing. One might object that a whole multiplicity of attributes or facts can be intentionally determined by one word or sentence. Thus the number of attributes or facts need not be equal to the number of words or sentences. Second, not everything need be directly determined; much reveals itself indirectly, as a result of the explicit determinations in the text. However, in the first case, the multiplicity of attributes or facts is indeed indicated, but not all the elements belonging to this multiplicity (determinacies, attributes, conditions, etc.) are indicated in their individuality. Thus at least the specific details of these elements remain indeterminate. And the implicit results of what is expressed in the text can determine only those attributes of an object which are constant and necessary. For instance, it follows from the fact that Julius Caesar was a human being that he had all the "normal" limbs. But we cannot deduce anything about him which is not a necessary determinacy; whatever is variable in the concept "human being" is thus indeterminate. We cannot deduce how large his feet were or how high his voice was or how it sounded. If these matters are not specifically indicated in the text, and if no other facts are given from which one could deduce them, then the characteristics of Caesar's body (for instance, in Shakespeare's play) are not determined and thus are simply not present in the objective stratum of the play. There are good reasons why it is not advisable to indicate explicitly as many details as possible about the portrayed objectivities. In consideration of the artistic composition, only some attributes or states of the portrayed persons are important and advantageous for the work, while the rest might better be left undetermined or merely sketched in. One can guess them approximately, but they are purposely left obscure so that they will not have a distracting influence and so that the especially important features will come more to the fore. The choice of places of indeterminacy varies from work to work and can constitute the characteristic feature of any given work as well as that of a literary style or of an artistic style in general. The so-called literary genres can also differ greatly in this respect. My studies of the basic types of lyric poems, carried out in Lvov in 1934–35, showed, for example, that the role of the places of indeterminacy is of great importance for lyric poetry. And the more "purely" lyric the poem is, the less—roughly speaking—is the effective determination of whatever is positively stated in the text; most things remain unsaid.[33]

The presence of places of indeterminacy in the objective stratum of the literary work permits two possible ways of reading. Sometimes the reader tries to regard all places of indeterminacy as such and to leave them indeterminate in order to apprehend the work in its characteristic structure. But usually we read literary works in a quite different way. We overlook the places of indeterminacy as such and involuntarily fill many of them out with determinacies which are not justified by the text. Thus in our reading we go beyond the text in various points without being clearly aware of it. We do so partially under the suggestive influence of the text but partially, also, under the influence of a natural inclination, since we are accustomed to considering individual things and persons as completely determinate. Another reason for this filling-out is that the objects portrayed in the literary work of art generally have the ontic character of reality, so that it seems natural to us that they be clearly and completely determined just as genuine, real, individual objects are. The tendency to apprehend literary works of art in an aesthetic attitude works in the same direction of filling out places of indeterminacy. Of course we cannot say that in every aesthetic attitude there is a dominant tendency to have direct intercourse with concrete, completely determined objectivities. Even the abstract as such and—as has finally been noted [34]—the "incomplete" can be the object of aesthetic experience and aesthetic evaluation. Nevertheless, there are many works which call forth the attitude of apprehending the portrayed reality (world) in the most complete form possible and hence of removing at least some places of indeterminacy. The

33. This topic cannot be treated in greater detail here. A systematic investigation of various types of literary works of art would yield very interesting results as to the role of places of indeterminacy and the relation between what is explicitly determined and what is undetermined.

34. See H. Lützeler's speech on the incomplete in Eastern art, given at the Fifth International Congress on Aesthetics in Amsterdam in 1964.

reader then reads "between the lines" and involuntarily complements many of the sides of the portrayed objectivities not determined in the text itself, through an "overexplicit" understanding of the sentences and especially of the nouns appearing in them. I call this complementing determination the "concretization" of the portrayed objects. In concretization the peculiar cocreative activity of the reader comes into play. On his own initiative and with his own imagination he "fills out" various places of indeterminacy with elements chosen from among many possible or permissible elements (although the elements chosen may not always be possible in terms of the work). Usually the "choice" is made without a conscious, specially formulated intention on the part of the reader. He simply gives his imagination free rein and complements the objects with a series of new elements, so that they seem to be fully determined. Of course, in reality they still contain various places of indeterminacy, but what is determined is as if turned toward the reader and covers the gaps still existing in the determination. How this happens in specific cases depends upon the peculiarities of the work itself and also on the reader, on the state or attitude in which he finds himself at the moment. As a result, significant differences can exist among concretizations of the same work, even when the concretizations are accomplished by the same reader in different readings. This circumstance carries special dangers for the correct understanding of the literary work and for a faithful aesthetic apprehension of the literary work of art. We must pay special attention to it in considering the objectivity or the adequacy of the cognition of a literary work. We shall return to these last problems when we approach the question of the cognition of a scientific work and when we discuss how it is possible to gain genuine knowledge of a (literary) aesthetic object.

But at present we still have to consider the importance of the concretization of the objects portrayed in the literary work for the aesthetic apprehension of the literary work of art—in other words, the role the concretization plays in the transition from the simple extra-aesthetic (or "preaesthetic") apprehension of the work to its aesthetic apprehension.[35]

1. Except for cases in which the literary work of art, on the

---

35. Of course, for the moment we will deal only with the first indications of the problem, because we will not be in a position to analyze the aesthetic experience until much later.

basis of the constitution of its text, demands a certain abstinence with regard to filling out places of indeterminacy, the achievement of an appropriate aesthetic apprehension of a work depends on an appropriate concretization of the objects portrayed in the work.

2. Any place of indeterminacy can be filled out in several different ways and still be in harmony with the semantic stratum of the work. For example, if the text of Shakespeare's *Hamlet* does not indicate the height of the Danish prince or how his voice sounded or what position he assumed when he spoke with Yorick's skull, the reader (or the actor in the theater, a case with its own special problems) can concretize the figure of Hamlet in various ways, can imagine him to be "well built" or somewhat corpulent. Neither concretization conflicts with the text of the work; both are not only possible, but both are also equally permissible, as long as the filling-out is within the scope of the general type whose individual example is indeterminate. From the standpoint of the aesthetic value of the concretized work, however, not all "permissible" concretizations are equally desirable. Within certain limits, this may be rather irrelevant in the case of purely external physical details about the portrayed person. But many places of indeterminacy, for instance those concerning the character of the person, his sensibility, the depth of his thought and of his emotionality, may not be filled out in just any way because the filling-out of these places of indeterminacy is of great importance for the portrayed person. One way of filling-out will flatten the work and make it banal, while another way will give it greater depth and make it, for instance, much more original, as one can often notice in the production of a play. The actor, through his behavior, concretizes the character he plays so as to make it much more interesting and deeper than one would imagine from the text. Although this "interpretation" can lie fully within the bounds of what the text allows, the value of the (concretized) work of art is significantly modified by it. The different concretizations are thus not of equal value, especially since various ways of filling out places of indeterminacy can introduce new aesthetically valuable qualities into the stratum of the portrayed world.

3. The different ways of concretizing the objective stratum necessarily lead to varying concretizations of the whole work. The aesthetically valuable qualities introduced into the objective stratum can bring about new relationships (harmonies or possibly even certain phenomena of discord) among the aestheti-

cally relevant qualities in other strata of the work. The final, aesthetically valuable shape of the work can thereby undergo significant modifications, which can either enhance or detract from the value of the whole work.

4. However, the mode of concretization also shows to what extent a concretization of a work is "in the spirit" of the author's artistic intentions—how close it is to them or how it deviates from them. Either the concretized work is appropriate to and related to the style in which the work was created, in accordance with what is actually present in the work; or it has lost this style because of a certain kind of concretization. There can still be variations among these "stylistically close" concretizations of one and the same work, and they can be either of approximately the same value or of different value. Thus the way the concretization has been accomplished is relevant both from the standpoint of the correctness or faithfulness of the concretization and from that of the aesthetic value. The questions of the adequate aesthetic apprehension of the literary work of art and of its proper evaluation (see Chap. 5) are closely connected with the consideration of the concretization of the work. These questions are usually treated as if there were no places of indeterminacy in the work and as if no concretization were ever carried out. Then these questions are incorrectly posed, and consequently their solution cannot be correct. We can grasp these problems correctly only when we consider the concretization of the work. On the other hand, consideration of the concretization of a work brings up other problems as to the mode of the concretization and its dependence on the atmosphere of the cultural era in which it is carried out, and as to the limits of this dependence. From this point we have a broad view of the problems concerning the "life" of one and the same literary work in various epochs as a historical process in which the continuity of being and the identity of the work are maintained despite all changes.

§ 12. *Actualization and concretization of the aspects*

THE OBJECTIFICATION and concretization of the objects portrayed in the literary work of art go hand in hand with the actualization and concretization of at least a goodly number of schematized aspects. We shall thus turn to the discussion of the reader's constitution of this last stratum of the literary work of art.[36]

The stratum of "aspects" plays a most significant role in the literary work of art, especially with regard to the constitution of aesthetic value in its concretizations. For this reason, the way in which actualization and concretization of aspects take place during reading is of great importance for the aesthetic apprehension of the literary work of art. Moreover, the aspects depend to a far greater degree than the other elements upon the reader and the way in which the reading of the work is performed. In the work itself the aspects abide in mere potential readiness; they are only "held in readiness" in the work. To be sure, they are ascribed in a purely theoretical sense to the objects portrayed by means of the states of affairs. But they are called forth only to an insignificant degree by these states of affairs or the qualities of the objects portrayed by the states of affairs. Usually they are pressed upon the reader to a certain extent by means of other factors in the work which are independent of the states of affairs, specifically by means of certain characteristics of the phonetic stratum. The aspects are that which a perceiving subject experiences of a given object, and as such they demand a concrete perception or at least a vivid act of representation on the part of the subject if they are to be actually, concretely experienced. Only when they are concretely experienced do they exercise their proper function, that of bringing to appearance an object which has just been perceived. Applied to our problem, that means the following. If the aspects are to be actual for the reader during reading and thus to belong to the stock of the work, then the reader must perform a function analogous to perception, since the objects portrayed in the work by means of the states of affairs are not in effect perceptible. This primitive fact suggests the idea of making what is portrayed in a purely literary way at least quasi-perceptible in another, no longer literary, way, e.g., on the stage or on film. If these objects are not to be intended merely in thought, signitively, but rather brought somehow to appearance, the reader must perform a vivid representa-

36. I employ the expression "aspect" here—as was already noted in *The Literary Work of Art*—in a very expanded sense, in which it embraces not merely all the aspects which are experienced by the subject of sense perception but also "aspects" which cause properties and structures of real psychophysical individuals to appear, independently of whether they are experienced in so-called inner perception or in the apprehension of the mental life of others.

tion in reading. And this means simply that the reader must productively experience intuitive aspects in the material of vivid representation and thereby bring the portrayed objects to intuitive presence, to representational appearance. In striving for a faithful reconstruction of all strata of the work and for cognition of it, the reader makes an effort to be receptive to the suggestions provided by the work and to experience precisely those aspects which are "held in readiness" by the work. As he experiences these aspects, actualized as they are in the intuitive material of imagination, he "clothes" the corresponding portrayed object in intuitive qualities; he sees it to a certain extent "in his imagination," so that it almost displays itself to him in its own bodily form. In this way the reader begins to have quasi-direct intercourse with the objects. These merely experienced (hence not objectively intended!) aspects play a role in the reading. They often have a significant influence on the course of the aesthetic apprehension of the work and on the final form the work assumes in concretization. If the reader is concerned—as he certainly ought to be!—with reconstructing and viewing in his concretization the form proper to the work, then he must not proceed arbitrarily in the actualization of aspects. For things and persons should not be merely intentionally projected by linguistic means in the literary work of art; they should also show themselves to the reader in appropriately selected aspects. And the function of the reader consists in lending himself to the suggestions and directives proceeding from the work and in actualizing not just any aspects he chooses but rather those suggested by the work. Of course, he is never completely bound by the work itself; but if he makes himself completely free of it, and does not bother about which aspects the world portrayed in the work would have itself viewed in, then his deviation from the work is almost assured, and an adequate apprehension is out of the question. And even if by chance the concretization of the work should gain thereby in aesthetically relevant qualities and hence increase in aesthetic value, the work would still not be viewed correctly and would sometimes even be grossly falsified.[37]

But it is not just a question of which aspects of a given object are actualized but also of how they arrive at concretization. In the work itself, only schematized aspects are present—certain schemata which remain as constant structures through diverse

37. As actually happens in the modern theater with many classical works, in consequence of the innovations introduced by the director.

modifications of perception. As soon as they are actualized by the reader, they become concrete quite in and of themselves. They are supplemented and completed by concrete data, and the manner in which this occurs depends to a great extent on the reader. He fills out the general aspectual schemata with details which correspond to his sensibility, his habits of perception, and his preference for certain qualities and qualitative relationships; these details consequently vary, or can vary, from reader to reader. In the process he frequently refers to his previous experiences and imagines the portrayed world under the aspect of the image of the world which he has constructed for himself in the course of his life. When he encounters a portrayed object in the work which he has never perceived in his life, so that he doesn't know how it "looks," he tries to imagine it in his own way. Sometimes the work is so suggestive that under its influence the reader succeeds in constructing aspects approximately appropriate to it. Sometimes, however, he involuntarily constructs invented, fictitious aspects, which spring not so much from the work as from his own fantasy. And sometimes he fails entirely in this respect and is unable to call forth any aspects whatsoever. He "sees" nothing of the portrayed object, grasps it only in a purely signitive fashion, and thereby loses the quasi-direct contact with the portrayed world. Despite this, his understanding can be adequate in the sense that in reading he attributes to the objects those, and only those, qualities which can be determined by purely linguistic means and which are indicated in the text. Only at the point where the reconstructed and actualized aspects have to come to the aid of the purely linguistic means of determination in order for the object to be grasped correctly by the reader is the reader who is unable to reconstruct and actualize the aspects also unable to apprehend the objects in their individuality and basically to understand the whole of the work. The actualization and concretization of aspects is often the most poorly developed component in the literary work of art, and it is also here that we encounter the relatively greatest deviations from the content of the work.

To make this point clearer, let us take as an example a passage from a novel by Stefen Żeromanski. In this passage the action takes place in Paris; although this is not expressly stated in these sentences, it comes out in the preceding text.

He wandered through the streets, unable to find the boulevard. He asked a passer-by; the man laughed and pointed out the boulevard, which was only a few steps away. His feet carried him there of their own accord. A myriad variety of colorful flashing neon lights, yellow, deep red, green, blue, and violet, blazing signs, circles, and letters cut into his eyes like splinters of glass. Without knowing what he was doing, he went mechanically into a café on the corner and ordered a cognac.

Since our reader is probably unfamiliar with this novel and is therefore also unaware of the events preceding this scene,[38] we shall ignore the whole psychological state of the hero, whose name is not mentioned in this passage and is not important for us here, and shall direct our attention solely toward the fragmentary description of the boulevard and toward the possibility of actualizing the appropriate aspects. From the preceding text one knows that it is a Parisian boulevard; but there are many boulevards in Paris, so that this information alone is not enough to give us the location of the scene. The comment that the Café Cardinal is situated on a corner does not say much either, since there are many cafés with the name "Cardinal" in Paris. If he knows Paris at all, the reader will probably visually "imagine" some Parisian boulevard in evening illumination. The colored neon lights will flash before him as he reads, and the fleeting sight of a brightly lit street in the evening will be actualized for him for a moment. If by chance the reader is familiar with the inside of that café, then the sight of it temporarily comes to the surface in him; if not, then the interior of some Parisian café or other appears to the reader in his imagination, dimly lit, with many tables and a large crowd in some kind of perspectival

---

38. The passage quoted can serve at the same time as an example of the situation indicated earlier. That is, it is a question of the modification of the meaning of the sentences by the influence of other sentences which precede them. If these preceding sentences lapse for some reason (perhaps, as in our example, because they are simply left out), the reader then understands the sentences which are provided solely on the basis of the words appearing in them and of their syntactic functions. The echo of previous sentences, which augments or modifies their meaning in context, here lapses. Thus our reader does not know whom it is actually about or what the character's mental state actually is. Our reader senses only that the unknown person is already known and that he finds himself in some disturbed state because something has apparently affected him deeply; but what it was, from what realm of life (love, failure, or something else), and in what stage—all this is unknown and is also felt by the reader to be something unknown, something which is distinctly lacking and which would cease to be a deficiency as soon as he became acquainted with the preceding text. In connection with this, the aspects appearing here are essentially impaired and are actually reduced to the visual.

foreshortening. Perhaps the sight of the large lighted window of a café will flash before the reader, and he will "catch sight of" tables and chairs set up on the sidewalk, after which the interior of the café will also briefly appear to him. And, at one of the tables, perhaps the reader will see that stranger who waits with a sad expression for the cognac he has ordered. Other readers will perhaps hear the noise of conversation of the people sitting in the café or the clinking of glasses at the bar, although there is nothing in the text about this; the appearance of acoustical phenomena is, however, very probable, all the same, if one vividly imagines a café in a large city.

From the example just sketched we see the manifold ways in which the aspects suggested by the text can be actualized and how varied the manner of their concretization can be. If the reader is focused more on the psychological state of the hero, then perhaps the external sensory aspects of the real environment in which the hero finds himself will not even be elicited for him. This is all the more probable, as the whole description of the street and the café given here has a thoroughly secondary, accessory character, while the psychological state of the stranger is the main theme.

One can, of course, cite many texts in which the described scenes force, e.g., visual aspects upon the reader with great power and vividness. Among Polish novels, those of Henryk Sienkiewicz furnish a classic example. Compare here, for instance, Ursus' struggle with the bull in the Circus (*Quo Vadis*). After very vivid visual aspects, acoustical phenomena suddenly give expression to the silence which reigns in the Circus when, in the moment of highest tension, Ursus breaks the bull's neck.[39]

39. Take, for example, the following scene from *Lord Jim*, by Joseph Conrad:
"Jim paced athwart, and his footsteps in the vast silence were loud to his own ears, as if echoed by the watchful stars: his eyes, roaming about the line of the horizon, seemed to gaze hungrily into the unattainable, and did not see the shadow of the coming event. The only shadow on the sea was the shadow of the black smoke pouring heavily from the funnel its immense streamer, whose end was constantly dissolving in the air. Two Malays, silent and almost motionless, steered, one on each side of the wheel, whose brass rim shone fragmentarily in the oval of light thrown out by the binnacle. Now and then a hand, with black fingers alternately letting go and catching hold of revolving spokes, appeared in the illumined part; the links of wheel-chains ground heavily in the grooves of the barrel. Jim would glance at the compass . . ." [*Lord Jim: An Authoritative Text*, ed. Thomas Moser (New York: W. W. Norton & Co., 1968), pp. 12–13].

In all these cases the reader is bound by the text to a much greater degree than is the case with works that are lifeless in this regard. He is under the power of the various sorts of aspects which are forced upon him; and, the more he succumbs to them, the more vividly, distinctly, and fully the portrayed world appears to him.

One should not, however, think that vivid and colorful aspects force themselves upon the reader when the aspects of certain things are described in the text of the work. On the contrary, these aspects then become objects which one perhaps cannot even grasp intuitively. In our case it is a question of experienced, not objectified, concrete aspects of things and people, which exercise the function of bringing things to appearance only when the sense of the words and sentences directs the reader's attention to the portrayed things and people and when the mere naming of certain perceptible attributes or sides of things has the result that the appropriate aspects are forced upon the reader at once. Then he sees the things, hears the sounds made by sounding objects, etc. Neither should one think that those parts of the text which describe the perceptible attributes of things with scrupulous accuracy force actualized aspects upon the reader with great power. On the contrary, it can happen that the intimation of a single feature of an objective situation suffices to elicit in the reader a vivid aspect of this entire situation or of the persons and things participating in it. The scene of Ursus' struggle with the bull, mentioned above, can serve as an example. At a certain moment one hears the little bits of coal falling from the servants' torches: so great was the silence in the Circus. To the visual aspects of the Circus, the benches filled with spectators, the arena, etc., are added the aspect of the flickering lights of the torches and the "aspect" of the deep silence of the whole theater in contrast to the soft noise of the bits of falling coal. And in this silence one suddenly hears the crack of the bull's neck breaking.

Works in which the aspects are forced upon the reader with such great suggestive power are much more faithfully reconstructed in their aspectual stratum than works in which the aspects are, rather, determined in an ideal manner and correlated with the portrayed things, without being forced upon the reader. Works which are very rich in intuitive elements of the aspects held in readiness from diverse areas of sensory experience can be falsely reconstructed by the reader insofar as he cannot do justice to the manifold of aspects. Readers are often one-sided; they actualize, for example, visual but not acoustical or tactual aspects. Where it is necessary to actualize aspects from diverse sensory areas, especially from the area of psychological experience, this task often transcends the imaginative powers of the reader. He then actualizes preponderantly aspects from a single sensory region and completely disregards many aspects of other senses. Consequently, the disclosure of aesthetically relevant qualities essential to the work cannot be attained; the aesthetic apprehension of the work remains incomplete and will not do justice to the work.

By means of the actualized aspects the things portrayed appear with a greater plasticity and distinctness, they become more vivid and concrete, and the reader seems to enter into direct intercourse with them. But the aspects actualized in reading are responsible not only for the intensity and richness of the intuitive appearance of the portrayed objects. They also introduce peculiar aesthetically valuable factors, for instance certain decorative factors, into the work. The choice of these factors is quite often closely connected with the mood which prevails in the work or in one of its parts or with a metaphysical quality. The appearance of a particular metaphysical quality, facilitated in this way, forms the culmination of the work and plays a great role in the constitution of the aesthetic concretization of the work during reading.

In view of the manifold ways in which the aspects are actualized and concretized by the reader, the aesthetic apprehension of one and the same work can turn out very differently. Consequently, only some aesthetic apprehensions hit upon the work in its proper form. Even the aesthetic concretizations which are faithful to the work can differ greatly from one another in this respect and allow very diverse aesthetically valuable qualities, and thereby also diverse aesthetic values, to appear. Here again we come up against one of the reasons for the fact that readers—sometimes even highly cultivated and sensitive critics—cannot agree in their evaluations of the same literary work of art. We shall return to this subject later.

The aspects actualized by the reader almost never form a whole continuum but usually make their appearance separately; they are forced on the reader only from time to time and are more or less vividly experienced by him. Where the aspects are separated from one another, a certain stabilization of their contents occurs. And, in reading, the reader also forms certain stereotypes, certain stabilized forms of aspects, which he uses to help him bring objects to appearance. Instead of imagining a portrayed person in different aspects according to circumstances, we often imagine him always in the same aspects, without paying attention to the attributes of this person which have changed in the meantime. This occurs, for example, when long periods in the life of a particular person are depicted in a novel, so that he ages visibly, or would have to age. But in spite of this, the reader imagines this person again and again in the same way, that is, in aspects which have become stereotyped. The same holds true for the aspects of the streets of a particular city, which are constantly imagined from the same standpoint, although they are portrayed from various points of view in the work. Therein lies a further cause of inadequate aesthetic apprehension of a literary work of art, a cause which in this case is purely subjectively conditioned but which exercises its influence on the disclosure or concealment of an aesthetically relevant quality appearing in the work itself.

These comments may suffice to convince us that in this respect the literary work of art can be received in very diverse ways.

§ 13. *Peculiarity of understanding the literary work of art as a poetical work*

BEFORE I TURN to the problems of the apprehension of the literary work of art in the whole interconnection of all its strata and parts, I must refer once more to the problem of understanding its dual linguistic stratum, since special problems present themselves in works of art of this kind, and especially poetical works.

I have already mentioned that, in the literary work of art, the sentences which are predicative sentences in their form and have the external character of assertions are nevertheless only quasi-judgments and should be so read and understood if one does not want to misunderstand the work of art (which, by the way, often happens with a naïve reader). How do we know that we should read a poetical work or a novel in just this way, when

—as happens in ordinary literary language—the predicative sentences in the literary work of art do not, as quasi-judgments, differ in their outer form from genuine judgments? [40]

In logic,[41] as is well known, a special sign has been introduced, the assertion sign, which distinguishes genuine judgments (as logicians say: theses of the system) from those sentences which are not theses but rather mere affirmative propositions (or, in Meinong's terminology, "assumptions" [*Annahmen*]). But such signs have not been introduced in ordinary colloquial language or in literary language. And even if such a sign were introduced for quasi-judgments, the reader, if he did not already know the particular modification of quasi-judgments from his own experience, would know only that he should read the predicative sentences in the literary work neither as assertions nor as pure affirmative propositions. But how would he come to understand them in still another function?

Now poets do not use such special signs. In spite of this, I believe there are certain means in the language of literary works of art which predispose the reader to read the predicative sentences as quasi-judgments. I prescind here from external means, such as the title or subtitle of a work (for instance, *The Magic Mountain: A Novel*). The form of the artistic language itself

40. Käte Hamburger posed this question to me in her *Logik der Dichtung* (Stuttgart: Klett, 1957; 2d ed., 1968). [English translation by Marilynn Rose, *The Logic of Literature*, 2d ed. (Bloomington: Indiana University Press, 1973).] In this book she expressed the opinion that it is necessary to dispense with the theory of quasi-judgments since there is no external, formal distinction, or since none has been exhibited by me. She then introduced another name for the predicative sentences in the literary work of art, whereby she changed substantially nothing, in my opinion, and she made an effort to find a special form of the German past tense which would precisely differentiate quasi-judgments from genuine affirmative sentences. I am not a specialist in the German language and must leave to those who are the question whether there really is such a past form of the German verb. From a purely morphological point of view, however, there appears to me to be no particular difference between the form of the past tense exhibited by Käte Hamburger and the other past-tense forms of the German verb. If this is so, the difference can lie only in a use other than in judgments. This use would then have the result that the sentence in question exercises no "normal" assertive function; rather, its function undergoes a peculiar modification which I believe to be present in what I call quasi-judgments. But then the question posed by Käte Hamburger remains open, that is, how the reader comes to use the verbs in question in just such a way as to understand the literary work of art. See, also, in this connection, my discussion with Käte Hamburger in *The Literary Work of Art*, 2d and 3d eds., § 25a.

41. Bertrand Russell did this in the book *Principia mathematica*, which he published with A. N. Whitehead.

takes the reader out of the normal attitude of reading predicative sentences as judgments and forces him to assume another attitude. It seems to me that there are many such means in language; yet it would lead us far beyond our topic if we wanted to treat in detail their whole multiplicity. Hence I shall confine myself to a few indications.

The means which I have mentioned are to be found in both the phonetic pattern and the semantic shape of the sentences. With the phonetic material it is primarily a matter of choosing words whose sense, phrasing, and composition set them apart from the ordinary speech we use in practical affairs to achieve something with other men in our common real world, and also from scientific language, not only because such words would seem unusual and odd there but, above all, because they would be unsuitable. This is the case, for example, with "lofty" or "great" words where "plain," "simple" words would be appropriate. The former are not at all adapted to the situation in real life and would tend to distract us from this situation. Consequently, they would seem to us inappropriate, useless, and ridiculous. The cadence of the sentences, which differs from the usual speech melody or sentence melody, and the peculiar rhythms which appear also alert the reader to the fact that the language is not being used for normal communication, nor does it aim at the common real world but, instead, evidently exercises some other function.[42] Let us read, for instance, the following excerpt from Rainer Maria Rilke's *Lay of the Love and Death of Cornet Christopher Rilke:*

It began as a feast. And became a festival, one hardly knows how. The high flames flared, voices whirred, tangled songs jangled out of glass and glitter, and at last from the ripe-grown measures— forth sprang the dance. And swept them all away. That was a beating of waves in the halls, a meeting together and a choosing each other, a parting with each other and a finding again, a rejoicing in the radiance and a blinding in the light and a swaying in the summer winds that are in the costumes of warm women.

42. This phenomenon does not appear in all literary works of art, certainly not, e.g., in the naturalistic dramas of the late nineteenth century—for instance, Ibsen's dramas. But there we have other means which bring the reader from the orientation toward the real world and from the carrying-out of genuine judgments. (See, in this connection, my article on the function of language in the stage play, printed as an appendix to the later editions of *The Literary Work of Art.*)

Out of dark wine and a thousand roses runs the hour rushing into the dream of night.*

Even if we did not possess this text as the continuation of other parts of the poetic work by Rilke but rather as a text in and of itself, we would soon notice that it is not a simple report of a real feast occurring at some real time and place. Who would take something of this sort, in a daily newspaper for instance, for a report of an actual ball? It is prose, and yet not the prose of the language of reality. Quite special rhythms, melodies, and even rhymes appear, which one would surely never use in the language of reality, simply because it would be useless and impractical. Anyone "relating" these things would certainly not use these rhythms, this sentence structure, and these rhymes if he simply wanted to furnish us with a report about an actual event. The phonetic phenomena which are present in such a composition obviously have a purpose other than simple information. Moreover, they exercise still further functions, on the one hand, those which are carried out as it were in the realm of the work of art itself and, on the other, those which aim at a particular effect of the work on the reader. Within the work they have the function of creating a particular emotional atmosphere for that which is being spoken of. For the feast described they furnish an emotional character which could certainly be described by other means but not brought intuitively to appearance. The purpose of the use of these phonetic phenomena in the language is precisely to make the emotional character of the portrayed occurrences visible to the reader and to affect him in a certain way. If one only wanted to furnish the reader with a report of a factual event, one could do this in a much quieter and more straightforward manner. The phonetic phenomena under discussion are also supposed to elicit an emotion in the reader, to remove him from the usual attitude of a man involved in practical life, and to move him to a new mode of experience, a mode of experiencing not merely emotion but also an emotional way of seeing and grasping qualities which, to be sure, could also appear in daily life but which elude our attention there.

The peculiarities of language indicated above already make the reader attentive to the fact that he is dealing with something

* From Rainer Maria Rilke, *The Lay of the Love and Death of Cornet Christopher Rilke,* trans. M. D. Herter Norton (New York: W. W. Norton & Co., 1959), p. 45.

other than a report of actual facts. But the meaning of the words employed also alerts the reader that he is not dealing with facts. The meaning of a number of words would be inappropriate if they occurred in a factual report. The words are taken not in their literal meaning but in a metaphorical meaning; they are obviously supposed to point intentionally to something other than they usually do in everyday language. If they were intended to be taken literally, we would be dealing with untrue, indeed ridiculous, assertions. Who could seriously maintain that songs "jangle out of glass and glitter" or that they "jangle" at all? Who would maintain that measures become "ripe" or that there can be a "beating of waves" in halls? If all that were supposed to be taken literally and as a serious report, then we would be forced to say that we were being told some incredible lie, which we can by no means take seriously. It would thus be to no purpose to report an actual event with such inappropriate, untrue phrases, since the only purpose of a factual report is to convince the person who hears it that everything really took place as reported. Obviously a text composed like Rilke's has a completely different purpose if it is meant to be "reasonable" and to be taken seriously, not as a group of true assertions, but as a linguistic formation which is meant to give us the most intuitive grasp possible of a human event by presenting a few prominent features.

Thus, although the sentences in Rilke's text have the external form of statements of fact, and although there is no artificial sign that denies them this character, they are still not read as judgments; it is not possible to do so without their becoming ridiculous. But should we read them as mere "assumptions," in Meinong's sense, which are altogether robbed of every assertive function and are thus strictly "neutral"? This does not appear to be the case either, precisely because the words employed, in their sound, their phonetic composition, and their extraordinary "opalescent" meaning, obviously have a purpose other than just making it possible for us to think certain semantic units the way we do, for instance, in learning phrases in a foreign language in order to become acquainted with them. The purpose here is obviously one of putting the reader in a certain mood, a mood which certainly has a strong emotional color but which is not so strong or serious that the reader really suffers or is really happy. This mood allows the reader to find pleasure in the linguistically projected image of an occurrence in the attitude of beholding it with emotion and admiring recognition. It is not important that something actually happen but only that what unfolds for us—with whatever colors, sounds, movements, and even evident emotions it may have—regardless of whether it is illusion or reality, all appear as attractive. It is not a question of merely understanding certain semantic units but of apprehending and experiencing quite particular intuitively appearing valuable qualities and values which have nothing to do with the truth or falsity of certain sentences. In their opalescent dual meaning, the semantic units, clothed in particular sound material, project an intuitive material, permeated with special materially colored qualities, which allows the reader to apprehend just that qualitative cluster of values which arises as a necessary phenomenon from such intuitive material. That is the reason that, on the one hand, the predicative sentences in the text have the character of *quasi*-judgments and, on the other, that they have the character of quasi-*judgments*. The sentences exercise a certain power of suggestion upon the reader, who is to be made to believe that such a thing as is shown in the image is "possible" and who nevertheless is not to recognize the sentences as actually true and corresponding to real facts. He is also to take cognizance of the sentences as having this character, and the artistic means indicated make such an acceptance of these sentences possible for him.

But this presupposes that they are correctly understood by the reader in their peculiar opalescent or iridescent meaning. The meaning of the words, and consequently the meaning of the sentences is, as I put it, "opalescent." It is almost never the "literal" meaning; that is, "songs jangled out of glass and glitter" is not to be taken in the ordinary meaning of "jangled out of glass and glitter." But the phrase should not completely lose its literal meaning. Through its existence and through its being understood by the reader, the literal meaning should point to something else which is in itself only "similar" and analogous to that which the word originally meant. And, at the same time, it must be clear that it is actually this other analogous thing which is important, while the literal meaning of the word begins to be opalescent as a result of the context, so that the entire phrase becomes only a special means for indicating that other thing which is not named directly. But the function of the literal meaning of a phrase is not exhausted in pointing to this other analogous or similar thing. This pointing occurs in such a way that the aspect of "glass" and "glitter" and of the "jangling" that is characteristic of glass is not lost but should serve only as the intuitive garb for that acoustic characteristic of the songs which is not named directly. And analogously, when Rilke mentions the "beating of waves in the halls," we are not dealing with a genuine "beating of waves," such as we can actually observe on the beach, but with a similar characteristic of the movement of the people dancing in the halls. This characteristic of the movement with which we are actually dealing here is not named directly and determined in a purely conceptual way, so that it is not given to the reader in its pure, proper form, although the reader does have the feeling that he intends it in the final result. This trait, proper to the dance movement, takes on to a certain extent the intuitive character of the "beating of waves" which is suggested by the literal meaning of the phrase; and it is the literal meaning which brings it to appearance through the peculiar opalescence of the meaning of the phrase. Thus both meanings, the literal meaning and the metaphorically used "actual" meaning with which we are really concerned, have their function, and both play an indispensable role in constituting the events portrayed in the work.

In the last few years a great deal has been written, especially in the literature on aesthetics in English, about the "metaphor." I do not here intend to treat exhaustively the subject of the metaphor with respect to its peculiar nature and its function. This belongs to a broader presentation of the general theory of the literary work of art, which is not part of our present undertaking. We are concerned here merely with pointing to the particular character of the understanding of the semantic stratum, or the language, of a literary work of art. This understanding is essentially different from the understanding of a scientific work, for example, or of texts which merely provide information concerning actual states of affairs, as is the case, say, with newspaper items. First of all, in a scientific work or in a factual report we encounter genuine judgments which exercise the ordinary assertive function; here we are dealing with quasi-judgments. But, second, we are dealing in a literary work of art with a kind of thinking of the semantic units which is completely different from that found in the reading of factual reports or scientific works. In these latter kinds of literary works we are dealing with an unambiguous act of thinking the verbal meanings or the meanings of the sentences, which are employed, not in a metaphorical sense, but only in the sense proper to the words in the given national language. Every "opalescence" and every indirect "double-rayed" act of intending what is actually being dealt with in a scientific work is out of place there. The "actual" meaning is apprehended and intended directly and in a "single-rayed" way. But in a literary work of art in which such "metaphorical" turns of phrase appear, a direct, single-rayed understanding would be out of place. The "literal" but metaphorically employed sense of the word is certainly understood in the literary work of art, but it is only a means for thinking another meaning along with it. This other meaning leads us directly to what is only suggested by the metaphor, if the other meaning is actually and centrally intended or if its intention is fulfilled along with that of the literal meaning. But this other meaning is only brought into view, suggested, by the "metaphorically" employed sense, not, however, thought in its true content. This constitutes a quite peculiar act of thinking along with the meaning which is contained in the dual stratum of the language of the literary work of art. The act of thinking along is characteristically opalescent, "double-rayed" in the intending of the verbal and sentence meanings, but it is nevertheless supposed to attain its conclusion and culmination in a clear opinion concerning that which the poem is "actually" about. The "real" content of the poem is determined by a detour via the metaphorical way of speaking and, considered more precisely, can only be determined and intended in this way. This "opalescent" understanding or thinking along with the language of the poetic work of art carries with it special difficulties, which are not always overcome by the reader, especially not always immediately on first reading. For "behind" the words which are used and which must be understood first, it is necessary to look for another meaning, and not just any meaning but a very particular one. The other meaning is certainly suggested to the reader by the metaphorically employed word or phrase, but usually not with sufficient clarity or the necessary force to enable him to hit upon the "actual" meaning behind the words effortlessly and then carry out this meaning with full activity without at the same time losing sight of the literal meaning and ceasing to think it as well. It is easy for the reader to fail in the face of this difficult task, and he can fail in various ways. The worst way is when the reader either fails completely to notice the allusion of the "nonactual" metaphorically used meaning or else notices it but interprets it in a direction other than the one with which the poem actually deals and thus misses the "actual" intended meaning of the poem. Then it is not so much a case of not understanding the work as of misunderstanding it. A different danger threatens when the "actual" ultimate meaning is understood but, at the same time, the nonactual, metaphorical meaning, used at first as a means of arriving at the "actual" meaning, is then allowed to lapse completely; the result is that the nonactual meaning can no longer perform its function of aiding the intuition of what is apprehended, and the poem is then not apprehended in an opalescent, "double-rayed" way but rather is transformed into a purely conceptual, "intellectual" configuration.[43] The poetic quality as such then vanishes completely from the field of vision, and the question arises whether the work in question can still be apprehended as a work of art in this case.[44] This sometimes happens to literary scholars who want to teach their readers about the "content" of, say, a lyric poem, and thereby turn it into a philosophical theorem or interpret it as a report by the poet on his amatory experiences. This is one of the central points and chief dangers of the "art of interpretation" about which Emil Staiger once spoke (in *Die Kunst der Interpretation*), but concerning which he had little to say in his introductory essay, which was intended to determine the nature of this art.[45] And the

43. We can raise the question whether this scintillation and opalescence of the meaning of the actions and sentences are also preserved, for instance, in the naturalistic drama or in a contemporary novel, which indeed, as has frequently been emphasized, are written in plain, everyday language (see, for example, the dramas of Ibsen, *Buddenbrooks* by Thomas Mann, or novels by Zola). This would have to be studied in detail in individual works. If it should not be confirmed, it would be necessary to look for other artistic means, which decide that even in such literary works of art no genuine judgments, but only quasi-judgments, appear. It is to be noted that even the most ordinary-seeming turns of phrase which are used in them are yet only an imitation of people's daily mode of speech (we can easily persuade ourselves of this if we compare the artistic prose of a novel with phonographic recordings of actual conversations or speeches). But then we would have to consider whether particular traits of the composition of large parts of a work (e.g., individual chapters or acts) are not an indication that the whole is nevertheless intentional art and not simply a factual report, whereby it is immediately revealed that the sentences appearing in the work do not relate to real facts, transcendent to the work, but only to a "reality" simulated with their help and that they are also ambiguous: they apparently postulate that they relate to a genuine reality but determine only an intended, "portrayed" world, which only makes the claim of simulating a genuine reality. Even in this case the reader must do justice to this particular instance of the "scintillation" of the assertive units.

44. That is, of course, a complicated question, which can be answered only if we take into account several other points of view—e.g., the possible appearance of aesthetically relevant qualities, which constitute the aesthetic value of the work. It can thus be attacked only much later.

45. See, in this connection, Emil Staiger, *Die Kunst der Interpretation* (Zurich: Atlantis, 1955), pp. 9–33.

genuine problem of "interpretation"—that many interpretations are possible for one and the same work of art and that these arise from diverse understandings of the dual stratum of language, many of which are permissible within limits set by the text—was not touched on by Staiger at all.

But only later shall I be able to go into these various problems in critical epistemology, and especially also in critical aesthetics, concerning the "correct" and "incorrect" understanding of literary works of art (and of lyric poetry in particular). For the present we are concerned only to give a descriptive analysis of what occurs or can occur in reading, in order, on the one hand, to indicate something of the specific nature of the behavior which takes place in the reading of a literary work of art and, on the other hand, to collect material in preparation for our further considerations.

§ 13a. *The combination of all the strata of the work into a whole and the apprehension of its idea*

WE HAVE NOW DESCRIBED in a preliminary fashion the complex and closely interconnected subjective operations by means of which the reader obtains a view of all the strata of the work and produces a particular concretization of it. Of course, we have not yet considered those complications which arise, on the one hand, from the quasi-temporal structure of the literary work and, on the other, from the necessarily temporal process of reading the work. We shall take this problem up later.

As we have seen, we become acquainted with the literary work of art in several different operations, all of which must be carried out at the same time. The interconnection of these operations has the consequence that the strata of the work with which we become acquainted in this way are not isolated formations but appear together from the start in various more or less close connections.[46] Despite the variety and quantity of operations, their simultaneous performance constitutes the first, indispensable step in apprehending the whole work, especially where its aesthetic apprehension is concerned. There are two reasons for

46. How close this connection is depends on various properties of the work. But the mode in which the work is apprehended in the reading has an influence on how close this connection appears to the reader. This must be investigated later.

this. First of all, the strata, not so much despite as because of their heterogeneity, are adapted and adjusted to one another as parts of a single whole. Such a whole is—as one usually and not quite correctly says—organically constructed. It is something other and more than an agglomeration of unconnected, loosely stacked strata. Second, the literary work, since it consists of several successive parts (see Chap. 2, below), is again not a series of loosely connected, unrelated formations but consists of parts or phases which in various ways influence one another, determine one another more closely, and lead to an internally closed whole or, rather, can be discerned only in this whole. In both of these respects new difficulties arise for the apprehension of the work as a whole. Many of these difficulties are such that the final apprehension of the whole in a single sweep becomes impossible. I shall begin with the first group of these difficulties.

Even acquaintance with all the individual strata of the work is not yet sufficient for the apprehension of its totality. The operations which must be carried out to this end vary according to whether we are trying to apprehend the work itself in its schematic form and with a preaesthetic attitude or whether we are trying to view it as the object of an aesthetic experience in an aesthetic concretization, in light of the aesthetic values embodied in it. Not until later will I be in a position to analyze the distinctions which are of importance here. For the moment I must confine myself to describing, at least in crude outline, those operations or functions which underlie these two modes of cognition of the literary work of art as a kind of skeleton, although they undergo certain modifications in each of these modes.

First of all, however, I must take up at least briefly the so-called organic structure of the literary work of art.

There has been considerable talk of this "organic" structure of the work of art—especially in those circles which have been influenced by vitalism or by Gestalt theory or, finally, by W. Dilthey. So far as I am aware, however, no one yet has explicated in detail the concept of "organism" or "organic structure" which is employed in this context or has shown which properties of the individual elements of the literary work of art lead to such an "organic structure." In connection with the second question I shall take the liberty of referring to my book *The Literary Work of Art*,[47] in which I made some comments on

47. Ten years after the appearance of the first Polish version of *The Cognition of the Literary Work of Art*, I treated exhaustively the problem

this subject. Consequently, I would like to occupy myself here briefly with the first question.

What do we observe when we are dealing, not with a mere complex, an agglomeration, of loosely connected, basically unintegrated elements, but with an "organism"? It seems that many different features are decisive in this connection. I should like here to indicate several of them.

1. An "organism" does not merely exist but also performs or should perform a particular main function, to which various other functions, performed by its individual organs, are subordinated. This main or basic function of the organism consists in maintaining the individual life, in which, at the same time, the survival of the species is made possible and which in this connection serves the continuation of the species in its descendants. The functions subordinated to and serving this basic function are those of nutrition and, particularly, of obtaining nourishment, of adjustment to the conditions under which digestion and elimination of waste products are accomplished, and various functions of the central nervous system, etc., which among others consist in relaying to the living being indispensable information about its environment and in permitting it to react in various ways to the stimuli which the environment exercises on the organism. The peculiar trait which belongs to the essence of the organism is the hierarchy of various functions which are adapted to one another and in various ways are dependent on one another and which are all, in the final result, subordinated to the one main function. The fulfillment of this main function constitutes the "meaning," the *ratio,* of its existence, its "determination."

2. The hierarchically ordered system of functions of the organism is closely related to the structure of the organism, which is adapted to them. Every organism is a system of organs, the form of which enables them to fulfill the individual, subordinate (subservient) functions of the organism. The main function, however, is fulfilled, not by the individual organs, but only by the whole organism. The individual organs determine one another, supplement one another's functions, and aid the other

---

of the "whole," and, in particular, I analyzed the form of an "organic whole" in my book *Der Streit um die Existenz der Welt.* It must be noted, however, that one can speak of an "organism" only metaphorically in connection with works of art, so that the form of an "organic structure" in a literary work of art deviates in various features from the form of an organism in the genuine sense, as applied to living things.

organs in fulfilling their functions. Every hypertrophy or hypo-function of an organ results in certain disturbances in the functions of certain other organs. These disturbances can either be compensated for, or else they can result in certain injuries, above all to the affected organ. But the cooperation of the various organs is so extensive that, if they are not too serious, injuries or abnormal functioning of one organ can be compensated for by the cooperation of other organs. We then talk of the "self-regulation" of living organisms. But if the disturbance in the function, or the damage to the structure, of the organ in question is so significant that it cannot be overcome by self-regulation, then this has an effect on the function and also the form of the other organs and results in a dangerous disturbance or even in the destruction of the equilibrium among the functions of the organism. But as long as the disturbances and injuries of the organs can still be overcome, or as long as everything runs without disruption, a remarkable equilibrium prevails among the functions of the organism, which is the essential feature of the organic structure and the result of the mutually adapted functions of the organs. No organ of the organism is self-sufficient, and, as a result, each perishes after separation from the organism. Nor may it be separated from the whole of the organism unless it is a "double organ," like the lungs, or an organ which can be artificially replaced. This seems to be contradicted by the fact that various organs have been separated experimentally from living organisms and have then continued to exist for some time and even to function in their own way. But one forgets here that these extracted organs were immediately transplanted into an appropriately selected milieu which permitted them to continue to exist and to function.[48] There also are no organs or elements in the organism which are fully isolated and which are thus completely independent in their form and their functions from the other elements of the organism. But the organs do seem to be so differentiated from one another in their functions that they are not in general disturbed in their functions by the functions of other organs as long as the influence of the latter functions remains within the

48. But it is well known that, if this new milieu is a foreign living organism—e.g., in the case of a kidney transplant—this experiment fails in the great majority of cases because the new organism feels this organ to be "foreign" and strives to eliminate it. Only a new modification of the receiving organism weakens this resistance of the organism and can, it appears, lead to a new equilibrium in the latter. How this comes about in detail is no longer our concern.

bounds of the "normal." There is a hierarchy among the diverse organs of the organism, not only in the sense that their functions are ordered upwards or downwards of each other and that they have a greater or lesser significance for the function of the organism, but also in the sense that the sphere of influence of one organ is greater than that of another organ. As a result, a disturbance or cessation of its function also has more extensive and more damaging influence on the other organs than a failure on the part of a less influential organ.

3. Though the fate of individual organisms may vary according to the circumstances of their lives, a certain typical course of life is manifested in all organisms: upon the phase of development and formation follows the phase of culmination (*akmē*) and then the phase of aging and decline. The finitude of life appears thus to be no accident but is the natural product of the organism's performance of its functions, e.g., the effect of a collection of waste products in particular organs which do not contribute in a positive way to their function but instead lessen their efficiency and gradually weaken the organism's general strength of resistance in the battle of life. I do not feel qualified to judge whether talk of the natural atrophy of the "vital force" is justified or to judge whether the teleological or the purely causal conception of the structure of the organism and its functions is correct. The answer to these questions is in any case of no importance to the problems which interest me here.

The above observations are doubtless not sufficient for a systematic analysis of the nature of an organism,[49] but they are quite adequate for our purposes. It is clear that the concept of organism can be applied to the literary work of art or to the work of art in general only in a metaphorical sense and by way of approximation. It is not, of course, a living organism and also has no ontically autonomous being. It owes its existence and its form to the creative acts of consciousness and other acts of the author. Nonetheless, it does have certain characteristic traits which permit us to see in it an analogue to an organism, specifically as follows.

49. This is the chief task of a general theory of the organism. Since the time when I wrote this book (1935–36), various extensive studies have been published on this subject (e.g., Ludwig von Bertalanffy, *Theoretische Biologie* [Berlin: Geb. Bornträger, 1932; 2d ed., 2 vols., Bern: A. Francke, 1951]; Karl E. Rotschuh, *Theorie des Organismus* [Munich: Urban & Schwarzenberg, 1959], etc.). But all of them go beyond the set of problems which is important to us here.

1. Above all, we must consider here the fundamental heterogeneity of the individual strata of the literary work of art. Their determinations are of such kind that they are distinctly adapted to one another. Yet none of the strata is independent of the rest in either its being or its determinations. Just as a hierarchy of organs exists in an organism, in which some organs are more and others are less dependent on other organs, so there is also a stratum in the literary work of art which depends least of all upon the rest: the stratum of semantic units. But even that stratum is not completely independent of the stratum of phonetic formations; and in its various relative determinations it depends on the stratum of portrayed objects, although the latter derives its being from the semantic stratum. In the literary work there is an interconnection of strata in structure and function which is analogous to the mutual influence of various organs in an organism. This is not, however, so clear in the literary work as in a living organism, since the literary work, as a completed formation, is unchanging. In radical contrast to a living organism, the mode of being of which consists in the performance of its inner processes, no alterations or processes occur in the literary work of art. Neither the strata of the work nor any of its parts are organs with specific activities to perform. The "influence" of one stratum or one element on other strata manifests itself only in the ontic dependence of the latter on the former, as well as in the presence of certain relative determinations which have their foundation in the common appearance of various sorts of elements in the whole of the work. Only when we pass from the work itself, as a schematic formation which is viewed in isolation, to its concretization, which is reconstructed in the process of active reading, are we able to see it as an unfolding process in which various factors of the work or of its concretization begin to assume the appearance of life, of effect, of function. Some elements perform certain functions with respect to other elements, and, at the same time, the whole concretized work of art performs one main function. In the work itself, however, it is more accurate to speak of the "role" of elements in the work with respect to other elements and to the whole work. Of course, the concretization of the work (or the concretized work) and its elements perform the appropriate functions only when its constitution, or at least the constitution of its individual phases, has taken place. And for just this reason the operations of the reader I described earlier, which lead to the constitution of the particular strata of the work, cannot

reproduce the totality of the work even in individual phases. We must let the particular functions of the elements of the work develop so that the work can show its "organic" face.

2. These diverse "functions" of the strata and parts of the work constitute the second factor which permits us to see an analogy between the work or its concretization and an organism. It is not only their heterogeneity that plays an important role in this but also their mutual adaptation and the degree of their subordination under the main function, which is carried out by a particular literary individual in its concretization. At least in the creative intention of the author, who is, incidentally, not always successful in fully realizing it, every literary work of art exercises a particular main function proper only to itself. It exercises this function in itself to a certain degree only potentially, and the function becomes actual in an adequate concretization. Thus the literary work of art closely approximates an organism in that both have a primary function. The work of art is also something which does not simply exist but which also has a "meaning," a *ratio,* for its existence, a "determination."

With the possible exception of very extreme formalists, all literary critics appear to feel this. But there has never been a unanimous recognition or satisfactory clarification of the question as to what kind of function the literary work of art performs or has to perform or what the product of that performance is. On the contrary, very one-sided if not outright false views prevail on this subject. Of course, what kind of main function a particular individual work of art performs (e.g., *Hamlet,* a single lyric poem, or a novel) is a problem which is one of the tasks of literary study. It is, to be sure, seldom posed and even more seldom solved in a satisfactory way. For us, however, only the general problem is of importance here. If we grant that there is a main function proper to every literary work of art,[50] we still must determine the general type of this main function. Present conceptions are greatly divergent in their answer to this second question. This is partly connected with the fact that there are literary works which present themselves as literary works of art without really being such in fact; partly it is connected with the

50. That there is such a thing as a specific main function of the work of art, and in particular of the literary work of art, appears to belong to the essence of the work of art or, better, to its idea. If an entity is so formed that it excludes the existence of such a main function or the possibility of its realization, this circumstance excludes that entity from the domain of works of art from the outset. Even this is not clearly seen by everyone.

fact that one and the same literary work of art can in fact be concretized in various ways and that not all concretizations are suited to actualizing the primary literary function of the literary work of art.[51]

For the most part, we find two different conceptions of the main function of the literary work of art. (1) The main function of the work is supposed to consist in expressing the spirit of the author (the "poet") or else his thoughts, his psychological makeup, or, say, his attitude toward reality and, along with that, his individual world view, and more of the same. (2) The literary work of art is supposed to express an "idea." Both these conceptions usually have a character which is not purely theoretical. They are used, as it were, as guidelines by which literary works of art should be explicated, interpreted, indeed even read. The history of literary study in the twentieth century provides numerous examples of this. This is all the more important since there are reasons for rejecting the first conception as false and for viewing the second as ambiguous at best. The second conception is usually given a false interpretation. But with an appropriate interpretation, it can be seen as true.

Ad 1. It is undoubtedly true that every literary work of art, like all other products of human activity, displays a series of properties or elements whose appearance in the work stands in a relation of more or less functional dependence not only to general characteristics of its creator but also to characteristic features of his psychophysical makeup and his individual psychological life. This applies, for example, to certain peculiarities of the language of the work, e.g., to particular turns of phrase which are used, the particular sentence structure, characteristic properties and juxtapositions of portrayed objects, to their mode of portrayal and the choice of aspects in which they are presented to view, etc. All this can throw a certain light on the psychological occurrences which have taken place in the author in the forming of the work or on various features of him as a psychophysical organism. Consequently, in our treatment of a literary work of art we can use all these features of the work in order to discover this or that about the author. All this information about

---

51. Thus we are here forced for the second time to speak of an appropriate or actual concretization of a literary work of art, since there can also be "inappropriate" concretizations, those which are in some sense "false." What this means and what properties a concretization of a literary work of art must display in order to be "appropriate," "correct," and not "false" will be the subject of a later study (see Chap. 5).

the author which we can gain with the aid of the work (but need not gain, as if it forced itself upon us irresistibly) is always based on material which is present in the work but is often especially singled out from the rest of the work. And it concerns something which is not contained in the work itself and thus even less in its concretization.[52] Even if it is true that the literary work of art can be used for such purposes of information, it is at the same time not true that it is intended to perform this informational function. Whoever maintains that the work of art has such an immanent determination as part of its essence because it *can* be used by us for this purpose is committing just as ridiculous an error as someone who maintains that ancient Greek war chariots were designed primarily to give classical philologists information about the life and psychological characteristics of the ancient Greeks. The fact that many, indeed very many, literary scholars use literary works of art to gain a more or less probable knowledge about their authors testifies to nothing more than that they have not become conscious of their actual task. We need not reproach them for directing their chief interest to the characteristics of the author. Every scholar may, of course, occupy himself with whatever happens to interest him and seems important enough to him for him to share the results of his investigations. My reproach is not directed against this at all. I am only concerned that the scholars I have in mind believe that they are investigating a literary work of art, whereas they are actually doing individual psychology, usually without having sufficient training in this area and without applying the proper methods of research. Herein lies the principal misunderstanding of this whole trend of scholarship. Its proponents do not attend to the fact that one must read the literary work of art in a particular way, a way which is not at all appropriate to its essential nature, if one is to use it as an aid to knowledge about its author. They treat literary works of art as diaries of their authors, as letters of a particular kind to the reader, in which the author

52. This is a completely trivial fact. And there would be no reason whatsoever for emphasizing it, especially here, were it not so often maintained that the author is somehow present in his work, constitutes its essential form, or at least comes to concrete appearance in his work. (All these assertions, which degrade the literary work of art to a mere "expression" of its author, I consider basically false; but I cannot occupy myself with this in an exhaustive fashion here. Incidentally, this expression theory of the work of art was still very fashionable at the time when this book was written in Polish. Today, when I am writing the German version [1966], this theory already appears to have lost much of its force.)

wants to inform us about his fate in a way that is more artificial than artistic. In doing this, the author is too clever to speak about himself directly; he always speaks indirectly, through the subterfuge of certain "images," and thus allows the reader to sense the truth about him, which he does not dare to state directly. Sometimes, of course, there are actual confessions of an author, such as the memoirs of Oscar Wilde, which also possess artistic value and consequently also belong to the realm of "literature." But those are quite special cases, and, moreover, we immediately recognize them as confessions. Even in the case of works of the purest lyric poetry which demonstrably stand in close connection with the individual experiences of the author, these still were not created as confessions, as data about the author himself, and hence are not to be read as such. And even when a love poem was first composed as a special letter to the beloved and also was read as such by her, it loses this function as soon at it is read only as a poem, as a particular work of art for its own sake. And it also loses this function as soon as it is published by the author in a collection of poems. So as soon as the reader reads this poem as a means of informing himself about its author, he feels himself to be a psychologist and not a literary receiver. He reads it as a psychological document, not as a work of art, and he overlooks the main literary function proper to it.

Ad. 2. What does it mean when one asserts that the main function of the literary work of art lies in "expressing" an "idea"? As we have said, this is understood in very different ways. Most frequently, we encounter the opinion that the literary work of art expresses an assertion, a "truth." This assertion is usually understood as a thesis about something which is present in the real world or which, for some reason or other, should be present or take place. Consequently, many literary scholars either try to extract such an assertion from the text of the work itself—for example, by citing sentences which are uttered in the work by some portrayed person or else by the author himself, and openly —or else they are concerned to construct such an assertion on the basis of the text. In both cases this assertion is ascribed to the author himself and given out as his opinion. In the process it is not noticed that these means not only falsify the text of the work, in which such assertions (judgments) do not even appear, but also that views are foisted on the author which are often quite foreign to him. And when such an assertion maintains the presence of a fact in the real world, one often begins to dispute with the author about the truth of that assertion. When, on the other hand, the assertion has the form of a postulate, a program, or a norm, one often reproaches the author with doing an injustice in representing such a program or, as one also says, such an "ideology."

There actually are various literary works which are usually considered "literature" and which are "polemical"; that is, they contain certain statements which, as appears from the text, are meant to persuade the reader that this or that fact exists or ought to exist in the reality independent of the work. This appears to speak in favor of the foregoing conception of the "idea" of the literary work. The polemical effect of a work is more covert and indirect when the objective stratum of the work contains fictional circumstances which are chosen and presented in such a light as to force on the reader a certain conviction about a reality existing independently of the work. Such a purpose is then expected of all literary works of art, indeed it is even demanded that they contain it; and many works are criticized for showing no trace of such a "purpose."

The circumstances under which the various national literatures developed have also contributed to making this conception of the literary work of art, and its social function in the epochs of development, predominant. This is true, for instance, of Polish literature, in both the time of Romanticism and the epoch of so-called Warsaw Positivism, in the long years in which the Polish nation had no independent state. At that time literature had assumed various functions which were not at all proper to it as a particular art and which it was able to exercise with a certain success only when its works were genuine works of art. But even then their artistic aspect became less important, and they were not appreciated in a way which did justice to their artistic character. Then the appearance of Stanisław Przybyszewski and the so-called Young Polish literature in the last decade of the nineteenth century, with the motto "L'art pour l'art," brought about a change of atmosphere and restored to literature the character of pure art. And precisely that made it evident that the conception of the "idea" of the literary work of art as a true proposition which the work expresses could not be maintained.

Further, we must take note of the following. From the fact that many literary works have a "purpose," even when they are otherwise genuine works of art, it does not follow at all that all genuine literary works of art have such a purpose and that we should conceive of them in this light. This only shows that many authors have used their works for an extra-artistic purpose and perhaps have adapted them to it. But even the most significant personal or social ends cannot convert works which are not works of art into works of art or lend them an artistic value when they do not possess it in themselves. When we value a work highly in spite of the "purpose" which it may have, we do so not because of the social or ethical values which it may embody but because it embodies certain specifically artistic or aesthetic values or leads to the appearance of such values in concretization. This is especially evident in works of art from a past epoch, whose "purpose" has long become fully irrelevant and tends to disturb rather than to promote the aesthetic apprehension of the concretized work, if we still notice it at all in reading. But if its appearance does not have a negative effect on the structure of the work and does not make the aesthetic apprehension of the work more difficult, then it does not obliterate the artistically valuable features of the work. Only when this is the case can we apprehend the work in its specific main function, the one which is appropriate to the work of art.

If, therefore, the aforementioned conceptions of the chief function of the literary work of art are to be set right, it is necessary to understand the "idea" which is supposed to be "expressed" by the work of art in a completely different way. First, however, another comment on the turn of phrase that this "idea" is supposed to be "expressed" by the work of art. It appears to be incorrect because it presupposes that the "idea" does not belong to the literary work of art, is not contained in it, but rather is only supposed to be "expressed" or somehow "mediated" by it, as a structure foreign to the work, as some second object. Independently of the question as to whether the work actually "expresses" something distinct from itself, we must first consider whether there might be something which we could conceive of as the "idea" of the literary work of art *in* the work itself or in that which is determined by it and belongs to it in an essential way. If there is such an "idea" *in* the work, it could then be encountered in a proper apprehension of the work, either in the work itself or in an adequate concretization. It would be encountered in such a way that we would have apprehended the work completely only when this particular factor had been made evident. Various points must still be discussed in this regard.

Above all: the primary function proper to the literary work of art consists in enabling the reader who has the correct attitude toward the work to constitute an aesthetic object which belongs to the aesthetic objects permitted by the work and to bring to appearance an aesthetic value which is appropriate to the work. The function of its elements or properties should be subordinated to this chief function if the work is to achieve its highest effectiveness. In any case, they are such that they contribute essentially to its fulfillment and determine the course it takes in a positive or negative way. All other functions which the literary work of art can perform in the cultural, or especially in the moral, atmosphere of a community, regardless of whether it has a positive or negative moral effect on the individual reader, are secondary and not specific to the literary work of art, however significant they may be in other respects and however much they can endow the work with new positive or negative values in addition to its artistic or aesthetic value. Neither the literary work of art nor, in general, any work of art, so far as its property of being a work of art is concerned, is called upon to perform these other functions; and if it does not exercise them, this is no shortcoming. If, on the other hand, it does not perform the chief function proper to it, then it does not fulfill one of the tasks pertaining to its determination and is defective as a work of art, even if it still belongs to "literature." It is then a work of art only by presumption and not in its essence, or at least it is only a "bad" work of art.

The point of view which I represent will probably be branded as "idea-free aestheticism." [53] That is to say, the prevailing opinion both here and abroad is that one is recognizing nothing but "mere technique" in a work of art whenever one regards all moral, social, or political tendencies of the literary work of art as completely dispensable, as having nothing in common with the work of art. But this opinion reverses the true state of affairs and only arises from an inability to discover the "idea" of the literary work of art in the actual sense, and to determine it conceptually, and from a false, or in any case completely inadequate, conception of the literary object and its value. People are usually blind to aesthetic values or seek at least to deny their existence, or to relativize them, or to "reduce" them to other values. Once we succeed in overcoming this failing, even in a merely preliminary fashion, we shall see that the position of

53. During the writing of this German version, I am reading Etienne H. Gilson's book *Introduction aux arts du beau* (Paris: Vrin, 1963). [English version: *The Arts of the Beautiful* (New York: Scribner's, 1965).] This book is a series of statements which agree well with the point of view I represent. Gilson would probably be quite surprised to be accused of "idea-free aestheticism."

"idea-free aestheticism" which I have just assumed is very far from treating the literary work of art only as a collection of technical means and from denying all "content," as is often said. But this means that we will be forced to occupy ourselves with the aesthetic experience and the aesthetic object, among other things.

The "idea" of the literary work of art in the actual sense appropriate to the essence of the work of art can be determined here only in a very general way. It is completely different for every work of art, and whatever content it has in any given case can be clarified and conceptually determined, as far as that is possible, only on the basis of a particular analytical (although ultimately synthesizing) consideration of the individual work of art and of the aesthetic concretizations that are possible and appropriate to it.

But in general we can say the following. The "idea" of the literary work of art is a "demonstrated," synthetic, essential complex of mutually modulated, aesthetically valent qualities which is brought to concrete appearance either in the work or by means of it. The aesthetically valent qualities lead to the intuitive constitution of a certain aesthetic value, and this value forms a whole, in intimate unity, with the basis on which it is founded (the literary work of art itself). At least in the case of great and genuine works of art, this whole is unrepeatable, "unique," and inimitable. It is revealed to the reader in an adequate aesthetic concretization of the work, which is not to say that it is then actually apprehended in its full peculiar nature.[54] This qualitative complex, which culminates in the value given in intuition, endows the work of art in concretization with an evident "organic" unity of structure. The qualities contributing to this complex (and in particular the aesthetically valuable qualities) vary in the literary work of art according to the variety of its individual strata. In well-constructed and truly valuable works of art there is a hierarchy among these qualities which exhibits an order of its own. Only some of the qualities (or perhaps only a single one) serve as a kind of center of crystallization for the qualitative whole; the others play the part either of founding the primary value or of augmenting it to some extent. They form a sort of accompaniment, so that the central quality, the final value constituted, which is qualitatively

54. There are various other possible states of affairs which must yet be analyzed.

determined in itself, can come to concrete appearance and also to full effectiveness in a proportionately clearer and more express way. There are, however, various types of literary works of art; and, among the really great masterpieces, every work forms—if we may put it so—a particular, unrepeatable "type" of its own. Thus we cannot say in general and in advance which particularly valuable qualities of this "crystallization center" form the value-bearing core of the individual work of art. There are works, for instance, in which peculiar kinds of aesthetically valuable emotional qualities form the value-bearing core of the qualitative synthetic whole, qualities which come to appearance in certain interpersonal situations in the portrayed world or characterize a person involved in a tragic conflict or, finally, appear in the form of a metaphysical quality.[55] Then they can be made immediately intuitable to the reader, but not only through the portrayal of certain interpersonal situations; for they can also be forced on the reader by the method of portrayal, by the choice of appropriate qualities in the verbal sounds and phonetic phenomena of a higher order, by the dynamics of the sentence structure and the sequence of sentences, by a characteristically selected manifold of aspects in which the portrayed objectivities are brought to appearance. But there are also works in which the peculiar factors of the dynamics of temporal perspective of the time portrayed in the work, or of the temporal structure of the work itself in the sequence of its parts, constitute this aesthetically valuable core; and there are others, again, in which the aesthetically valuable core is founded above all in the particular qualities of the melody of the verse, etc. Now this value-bearing qualitatively determined core of the whole of the literary work of art can also be conceived of as its "idea" in the narrower sense.

If the work is well constructed, then it has for the most part only one such crystallization center in its correct concretization. The supplementary aesthetically relevant qualities are then subordinated to the constitution of this center. The individual elements of the work (or one of its strata or phases) or its particular structural factors then perform various kinds of functions which should work together to disclose the "idea" of the work of art in the narrower sense, as well as to supplement or perfect it through relevant qualities appertaining to it, by means of which an essential harmony of all the aesthetically relevant qualities comes about. But it appears possible that there can be literary

---

55. On metaphysical qualities, see *The Literary Work of Art*, §§ 48–50.

works of art (and perhaps works of art in general) with several such "crystallization centers," which cannot be brought into harmony and consequently lead to no one unified whole. Such works then lack the internal wholeness of the work of art with its one value-bearing core. This is not to say that such a work of art is then altogether devoid of value; for even the form of the work of art that leads to no strict unity can contain a special charm, which characterizes it positively. But it is not then possible to speak of a single unified idea of the work of art. Finally, there are also literary works which are devoid of an "idea" in the sense that, although various factors are present in their content which could possibly constitute an "idea" (or which purport to be capable of so doing—for this reason the work has the character of a work which is supposed to be a work of art, or was attempted as such), no intuitive demonstration of an essential inner connection of harmonious, aesthetically relevant qualities comes about. The whole content of the work then consists of an agglomeration of various individual features and motifs, which can be aesthetically valuable in themselves; but the work exhibits no "organic" structure, so that, in a sense, it disintegrates. It is not capable of performing the primary function of the literary work of art.

In the light of these cursory remarks, what does it mean that the operations of the reader which are supposed to lead to the constitution or reconstitution of the individual strata of the work do not suffice to apprehend the whole of the work? It means, above all, that they do not suffice to disclose the "idea" of the work in the meaning we have given above. Only the appearance of the "idea" discovered in the work or, more precisely, in a concretization which does the work justice (and we shall return to this problem later) discloses the work for the reader in its final "organic" structure. For this purpose one must, during reading, catch or sense the ancillary functions contained in the work and allow them to unfold through an appropriate attitude. I speak about "sensing" or "catching" these subordinate functions of the elements and factors in the work, because it is not a question of making them the object of an investigation but rather simply of actualizing them in reading and thus using them to bring about the disclosure of the "idea" immanent in the work. Only then will the final, peculiar, unique, and simple value-bearing quality of the whole of the work manifest itself directly as a unique, unrepeatable, inimitable individual.

Aside from the conditions which the work itself must fulfill if the "idea" is to be present in it (this is a problem which belongs to the theory of the literary work of art itself and hence cannot be considered here), the reader must fulfill certain conditions if the "idea" of the work is to disclose itself in a concrete way. Not only must he have the proper sensibility, an openness and a susceptibility to the various kinds of qualities appearing in the work or in its concretization, especially for the aesthetically relevant qualities. He must also exert himself with a special effort which is necessary for an emotionally established apprehension, a perception of that final (finally resulting) quality of the aesthetic value which is constituted by the work. This effort will also bring about a perception of the essential qualitative relationship of several cooperating, harmonizing, aesthetically relevant qualities on which that final value is based. The disclosure of the "idea" of the work demands of the reader, who is involved in performing the multitude of operations described above, another special activity in addition to all this. He must exploit the "sensed" manifold of aesthetically relevant qualities in a synthetic way if he is to arrive at the intuitive revelation of the "idea" constituted in them, of the self-present aesthetic value of the concretized work of art, and if the aesthetic experience is to reach its conclusion in the final contemplation of this "idea." A certain gift is required in order to feel and to see what in the work of art, if it is a genuine work of art, is peculiar, unrepeatable, and is that for which there exist no "models." Nor can we instruct anyone concerning this with words alone, unless we pass from the words themselves to a particular kind of perception of the value-bearing qualitative complex, to a vision of the finally constituted form of the value quality of the aesthetic value of the work. The reader must then to a certain extent work along with the author, use his work to become a codiscoverer of the peculiar value quality which the author originally had in mind in creating his work and which made possible the realization of all those conditions in the work itself (insofar as the work is "successful") which are necessary for the concrete appearance of the value quality, though they alone are insufficient to bring it to appearance. Not many readers are capable of making the effort required to attain this final vision during every reading. They know then only the cold, value-neutral, and somehow dead skeleton of the work of art. They have intercourse with something which lacks the resultant simplicity and individuality of the fully concretized work of art.

The great difficulty—and hence the great rarity—of a perception which encompasses the whole of the literary work of art is especially evident when the reader is dealing with a great masterpiece. This seems paradoxical and for that reason improbable. True masterpieces have the greatest power to dominate the reader (the receiver), and they seem to have the ability to put the reader into the state of a cocreative emotional sensibility through which the adequate aesthetic apprehension of the work of art can most easily be accomplished. Nor is this to be doubted. But, on the other hand, every great masterpiece is generally distinguished by such a thoroughly integrated "organic" structure that overlooking or incorrectly apprehending any detail, even a subordinate one, can or even must result in a concretization which gives only a disfigured torso of the work instead of a specifically structured whole. The essential and unique character of the work of art is then not grasped by the aesthetic apprehension.

As we have seen from the course of the investigation so far, the totality of acts and experiences which are necessary to the reconstruction of the literary work is quite extensive and contains several different functions which the perceiving reader must perform simultaneously or at least in close succession and direct connection with one another. It is thus extraordinarily difficult to carry out all these acts and experiences in such a way that there are no distortions or imperfections anywhere, in any phase of the reading, and so that the harmony of the strata and the polyphony of the aesthetically relevant qualities appearing in them are nowhere affected or changed. Although masterpieces are often distinguished by a particular simplicity, transparency, and crystal-clear harmony of structure, at the same time they tower far above the average level and constitute something quite unusual and unique. Their faithful and complete apprehension requires of the reader that he raise himself above the level of his averageness and orient himself toward values which are evident only through great concentration of apprehension and of his mental life in general. Masterpieces also demand of the reader a certain "freshness" of feeling and of experiencing. This involves not only a sensitivity to the unusual and to that which is quite new because it is extraordinary but also a readiness of the reader to make himself independent of the systems of values previously recognized by him and from the influence of the stereotyped multiplicities of aesthetically valent qualities which he frequently encounters. In the face of the absolute originality of every masterpiece, freshness of feeling and inner independence are quite necessary for a faithful and correct apprehension; but they are rare, and hence a correct apprehension is also something extremely rare, especially among readers of high aesthetic culture. Their culture often makes them unfree. On the other hand, there is no substitute for this high aesthetic culture when it comes to the discovery of the extraordinary character of the masterpiece. Thus a series of very different factors has the result that precisely the great masterpieces of literature are very hard to apprehend adequately.

§ 14. *Influence of the composite nature of the apprehension of the literary work of art on the form of its concretization*

IN READING, there are a multiplicity and variety of experiences and acts of apprehension which the reader must perform almost simultaneously if the reading is to do even approximate justice to the many strata and the many forms of literary phenomena in one and the same literary work of art. As a result, the reader does not give the same active attention to all the acts he performs, nor does he perform all of them with the same requisite vividness or thoroughness. Consequently, many details in the various strata and phases of the work undergo more or less significant distortion in concretization. Many details of the structure of the work may be omitted or incompletely constituted in concretization; or else they may be overconstituted, developed too prominently; or they may even be falsified. Then the equilibrium of structure present in the work itself and required in its concretizations is upset, especially the equilibrium among the aesthetically valent qualities. One-sidedness of the reader's type of imagination may lead to certain distortions in the stratum of aspects; a weakened sensitivity to certain aesthetically relevant qualities may rob the concretization of those qualities; an insufficiently subtle empathy with the psychological situation of the portrayed characters may change the content of the stratum of portrayed objects to its disadvantage and thus prevent certain metaphysical qualities from appearing. We cannot perform a detailed investigation of all these different possible cases here. But it is certain that these deviations in the concretization from the form demanded by the work itself has, or at least can have, a detrimental effect on the reconstitution of the polyphonic harmony of the aesthetically relevant qualities and hence also on the constitution of the finally resultant value of the concretization as an aesthetic object. The constant, unavoidable variation in the reader's concentration of attention, the change in the center of his attention, his limited ability to divide and distribute attention correctly—all this is of special importance for the way the concretization of the work, which unfolds during reading, is formed and transformed. Variations in concentration and a change in the direction of attention are determined only to a limited degree by the properties of the literary work of art; to a large extent they are independent of it. As a result, not all details of the work appear in concretization with sufficient clarity and distinctness. Sometimes a certain act, e.g., understanding the semantic stratum, will be accomplished with greater activity and concentration of attention; sometimes an act of vividly perceiving the aesthetically valent qualities or of actualizing and concretizing the aspects will be performed with greater concentration. When this happens, the other strata of the work are grasped only peripherally, so that they become blurred on the edge of the field of awareness. During reading, we are usually absorbed in apprehending the objectivities portrayed in the work, which then seem to occupy the foreground of the concretization. The details of the semantic stratum, such as the peculiar sentence formation and the way the meanings of the sentences are interrelated, will then hardly be grasped for themselves because, in reading, one generally only passes through them to reach the portrayed objects. In order to grasp the whole of the work adequately, we may actualize the meaning intentions only in order to turn directly to the objects. Consequently, in a concretization which is formed in this way, the literary work of art appears as if in perspectival foreshortening, with a peculiar distortion and an excessive enlargement of certain strata of the work and, at the same time, a stunted realization of the other strata.

Just the opposite kind of perspectival foreshortening in the concretization of a literary work occurs when the reader takes a "philological" attitude during reading. The main interest is focused on the "language" of the work, on the purely phonetic phenomena as well as on the peculiarities of the semantic stratum. The reader heeds and considers primarily the diverse modes of expression, the sentence construction, the way sentences are joined, the vocabulary, and the various stylistic peculiarities. This gives philologists pleasure. In their opinion, the value of a work is decided mainly by whatever occurs in the dual stratum of language; for them, what is present in the other strata, the polyphonic harmony of all the strata and the aesthetically relevant qualities contained in them, has rather secondary importance. Thus the kind of reading which often accompanies a philological attitude does not produce a full and vivid constitution in the concretization of the work. The peculiar polyphonic harmony of the concretized work is disturbed and undergoes a characteristic "perspectival foreshortening" which is inadequate to many works. We do not deny, of course, that there are literary works of art in which the two strata of language, with their aesthetically relevant qualities, actually do play a decisive and very important role for the whole of the work. In the case of such works, the "philological" way of reading is perhaps justified. But, generally speaking, literary works of this type constitute an exception among works of belles-lettres; they tend to be works of decadence or of the baroque style. When they are read with attention focused on the strata of portrayed objectivities, they show an emptiness and poverty both in "ideological" substance and in the polyphony of the aesthetically relevant qualities present in them. But the works of art which contain a rich polyphony of such qualities can never reveal their own artistic character if they are read in the "philological" way, because in this kind of apprehension they sacrifice just those elements which constitute the most important factors in them and which belong to their essential nature.

These examples will perhaps suffice to indicate what we mean by so-called perspectival foreshortening.

These "foreshortenings" result from the contrast between the richness and complexity of the literary work of art, on the one hand, and the relatively limited and narrow consciousness and abilities of the reader, on the other, which, incidentally, vary from case to case but which can never surpass a certain upper limit. But the literary work of art is often so rich and its structure so complex that the work itself exceeds this upper limit. It is as if the genuine literary work of art—considered now independently of its length and what kinds of demands it makes on the reader with regard to its apprehension in all its consecutive parts—is too rich to be apprehended immediately in its whole abundance, even by a very gifted reader. That is the first, merely formal result of our consideration of the various operations performed during reading, when they are confronted with the structure peculiar to the literary work of art. We will not be able to consider until later what further conclusions we can draw from this and what possibilities are opened up for an epistemological investigation of the cognition of the literary work of art accomplished in the operations we have discussed.

For the moment, just one more remark: the not accidental fact that the literary work of art is, so to speak, beyond the possible reach of the operations performed in reading is the best demonstration that the work transcends the experiences of consciousness and thus may not be "reduced" to them; in particular, it may not be "psychologized." An analogous "transcendence" to those mental acts which are performed by the author in the creation of the work should be determined in special analyses; this alone would definitively overcome "psychologism" in the theory of the literary work of art. But such an undertaking surpasses the theme of this book.

2 / Temporal Perspective in the Concretization of the Literary Work of Art

§ 15. *The structure of the sequence of parts in the work*

THERE ARE STILL OTHER perspectival "foreshortenings" in which the literary work of art presents itself to us. They are essentially related to its structure and are thus independent of the variable and accidental circumstances of the reading, although the reading can cause certain secondary modifications in them. Thus they are quite different from the perspectival foreshortenings already discussed. That brings us to a discussion of the assertion that becoming acquainted with the literary work takes place, and must take place, in a multiplicity of temporally consecutive phases which are synthetically connected with one another. In relatively short works, for instance in a lyric poem, the phases can form an uninterrupted continuum; but in longer works interruptions in reading are practically inevitable, and this is not without effect—often disadvantageous—on the apprehension of the work.

Each literary work of art, and each literary work in general, has a certain "extension" (length) from its "beginning" to its "end." [1] The great majority of works consist of a title and a multiplicity of "consecutive" sentences. [2] In the relatively rare

1. See *The Literary Work of Art*, Chap. 11, §§ 54–55. [*Das literarische Kunstwerk* (Halle: Max Niemeyer, 1931; 2d ed., Tübingen: Max Niemeyer, 1960; 3d ed., 1965). English translation by George Grabowicz, *The Literary Work of Art* (Evanston, Ill.: Northwestern University Press, 1973).]
2. This "sequence" of the parts of the work—which after all possesses all its parts, in a sense, at once, with none of them earlier or later with

cases in which a single sentence constitutes the whole work, the sentence consists of a multiplicity of words or semantic units of a higher order (e.g., subordinate clauses)[3] which stand in a certain sequential order and which in reading can never be concretely thought in a single moment. This applies also to a series of sentences. These too are arranged in a very definite way in a finished work, as are all units of higher order consisting of sentences, e.g., individual chapters in a novel or individual scenes or acts in a drama. This order cannot be changed without causing great changes in the construction of the work, and sometimes the rearrangement of sentences can bring about the destruction of the work, especially of its unity of meaning and of the artistic whole itself. The reason for this is primarily the fact indicated in the previous chapter, that in many, if not all, cases the meaning of the individual sentence is not fully determined until it stands in connection with other sentences which precede or follow it. This connection is at least partially determined by the place which the sentence occupies among other sentences. A different arrangement of sentences often destroys the connection among them or at least changes or blurs this connection, because the rearranged sentences then usually receive a somewhat different meaning.

As a short example of this, I offer the following, which was intended as part of a larger whole, as a continuation of an earlier situation which is unknown to us:

> . . . As a result, the father was enraged at his son's behavior. He gave him several hard blows. And after he had chastised him for his lack of family feeling, he went about his business. . . .

When we read these sentences, we think that the son probably behaved defiantly and disobediently toward his father, so that the father became angry, hit the son, and then continued with what he had been doing. The father doesn't appear in a particularly good light in this passage; in any case, he doesn't use the correct and appropriate pedagogical methods.

Let us rearrange the sentences.

---

respect to the others—presents a special and very difficult problem, which I have tried to solve elsewhere. The solution is not important here, because in reading we are concerned with a concretization of the work and, in concretization, the parts of the work are actually in a temporal sequence.

3. Of course, there are one-word sentences, but we need not consider this exceptional case here.

. . . He gave him several hard blows. As a result, the father was enraged at his son's behavior. And after he had chastised him for his lack of family feeling, he went about his business. . . .

This rearrangement changes the meaning of the sentences, and the situation portrayed in them is hence also changed. Most importantly, instead of two people, we now have three people to consider: the son, who hits someone, the person he hits, who seems to belong to the family, and the father. The son is now the one who hits, and the father is angry at him, but for a different reason than before, because he doesn't chastise him for defiance but rather for his unjust behavior toward a close relative. And so forth.

Any literary work can provide us with examples of such changes as a result of the rearrangement of sentences. The rearrangement of the individual parts of a literary work of art produces other changes in it as well, in its composition, in the dynamics of its unfolding events, in the tempo of the smaller or larger units of thought developed in it, etc. These changes, which are derived only from changes in the order of parts in a work, can also have a great effect on the literary work, especially when they concern those characteristics of the work which determine its artistic and aesthetic value.

But as soon as the order of the sequence of parts is determined in the work, that dictates to the reader the order in which he has to read those parts. In reading, the order of sequence of parts in the work itself becomes the temporal sequence of the phases of reading, as well as the temporal sequence of the parts of the concretization. The reading must be performed in a process which has temporal extension. Initially it seems as though one could faithfully apprehend a work just by becoming acquainted with its parts in the same order as that in which they follow one another. It would seem that any deviation from this order in reading—if, for instance, someone were to read the work backwards, chapter by chapter—would lead to a concretization differing greatly from the work itself. However, closer consideration shows that, even if one observes the order of sequence of parts in reading, there is a certain inevitable difference between the concretization and the work itself. This difference is especially important for the aesthetic apprehension of the literary work as a work of art. I should like to indicate some of its features here.

I shall consider primarily two different phases of the cognition of a literary work of art: (*a*) the phase during reading and (*b*) the phase after reading.

§ 16. *Becoming acquainted with the literary work of art during reading*

IN REALITY, one can read one and the same work in quite different ways. It would be extremely difficult to describe them all. For the purpose of simplicity I shall consider only the case in which a given work is read for the first time from beginning to end without interruptions and without rereading parts already read. Of course, this is possible only with relatively short works.

When we read a work sentence by sentence and perform the operations described earlier in each phase of the reading, only the part of the work we are now reading is immediately and vividly present to us. Its other parts (the "earlier" and the "later") certainly do not disappear completely from the field of our actual awareness, but they are no longer present in that vivid way unless we perform special acts to recall them. The scope of the phase vividly present to us cannot be determined for all works and all readings in the same clear way. The scope is quite different and variable and depends primarily on the type of consciousness the individual reader has, on the structure of the work itself, and especially on the way the sentences are constructed and the way they are interrelated.

The reader's present moment—as I think Bergson first pointed out—can have a greatly varying "extension" and is never a "temporal point," as one usually says under the influence of the physicalistic, mathematical conception of time. But the scope of the phase of the work which is vividly present must be contained within the limits of the "extension" of the reader's present moment.[4] Sometimes it encompasses a single sentence, sometimes several related sentences in succession, sometimes only a fragment of a long, complicated sentence, especially if the sentence in question is syntactically opaque. Usually the

4. I shall not discuss the variations in the actuality of the immediately present phase within the reader's present moment, because this encompasses states of affairs which are quite various, complicated, and difficult to describe.

scope of the vividly present phase is identical with the semantic unit, the sentence.

In the course of reading a work, it is always a new part or phase which is immediately vivid and present to the reader. Each phase passes from the state in which it was still unknown to the reader and announced itself only in a vague way, if at all, into the state of being immediately present, and then changes immediately into the form of being already known but no longer actual or vividly present. But it doesn't immediately disappear completely from the reader's field of vision. It distances itself in a peculiar way from the always new present moment of the reader and sinks slowly into the horizon of the past, although it itself is never completely obliterated, nor does it pass in a genuine sense. One could say that the reader distances himself from it but that it itself continues to exist, even for the reader, although he perhaps no longer remembers it explicitly. One can compare the reading of a literary work with visiting a country, but with the crucial difference that the "country" of the work is not real and that a certain amount of effort is demanded of the reader to maintain the work in a certain changing actuality.

The part of the work we are just now reading is immediately, vividly present to us because at just the moment of reading we are actively performing those signitive acts which constitute the meaning of the sentence (or group of sentences) in its concrete unfolding. It is also present to us because we vividly imagine that the stock of verbal sounds and the various phonetic formations and phenomena of higher order in the concrete details which appear one after the other are "sounding in our ears." The objectivities portrayed in the phase of the literary work of art present to us appear to us clothed in concrete intuitive aspects. It is as if we were direct witnesses to what is just now happening in the objective stratum of the work, as well as to everything which appears in that phase in the other strata of the work. How can we be witnesses to the events portrayed in the work when, in dealing with a purely literary work, we do not actually perceive these objects and events in the strict sense of the word? This is a matter which demands special discussion. But such an analysis of the various possible modes of having consciousness of the objects with which we enter into relationship would far surpass our present investigation. In any case, it is impossible to be satisfied with the stereotyped view that the reader simply "imagines" the objects when he reads. One would at least have to say that there is a particular way of "imagining" which makes the "imagined" object present to us. Husserl speaks of a "presentification" [*Vergegenwärtigung*] which, though different from the "presentifying" [*Gegenwärtigung*] which takes place during perception, is definitely related to it. That there really is such a presentification when we "imagine" the objects in the present phase of reading is seen most clearly when we compare the phase of the work present to us with the parts we have already read which still remain in the scope of our awareness even though we do not direct ourselves to them in special acts of thought or imagination. Of course, we can focus on them in such acts, but usually this does not happen unless there is a special reason for it.

Although we are already distanced from the parts of the work we have read and from the objectivities portrayed in them, we not only have the feeling that they continue to exist, but we also retain them, or at least some of them, in more or less active memory. There are factors in both the work itself and the circumstances of the reading which allow some of the parts already read to be retained in active memory.

Doubts as to whether there really is such an active memory and even as to the possibility of such active memory probably arise because not every stratum of the work is remembered in the same way. The phonetic stratum is remembered primarily in the form of an echo of characteristic rhythms and other phonetic formations of higher order. The concrete sounds of the individual words tend to disappear from the reader's field of awareness, although many especially strong words, or words which have an emotional effect, can echo in a more vivid way. In the parts of the work already read and hence "past," the sentence meanings which the reader developed explicitly as he was reading them appear as complete units of meaning, as if apprehended in a summarizing intentional act; in this form they are retained in active memory. Such summarized, "shortened" units of meaning are often formed not from single sentences but from whole groups of sentences. As the reader keeps them in active memory, smaller or larger groups of sentences will be condensed into a relatively simple meaning—for instance, into the meaning of a state of affairs which was presented "earlier" (in the part of the work already read) in great detail. For instance, as we read the last chapters of Thomas Mann's *Buddenbrooks,* a sentence or a name from the scene when, long ago, Johann Buddenbrook was elected senator echoes in our memory without a special act of remembering on our part.

I stated that the reader "summarizes" certain sentences or groups of sentences already read in a "special way," because this summarizing or condensation of the meaning usually comes about to a certain extent automatically, without special attention on the part of the reader to these sentences and without a special summarizing operation. Such an operation is certainly possible; but then the reader explicitly turns his attention back to the parts of the work already read, and that results in a new actualization of those parts. But this special act is not necessary in order to keep them in active memory; moreover, it would disturb the progress of the simple reading with which we are here concerned.

The meaning "condensed" in this way can also take on other forms. It can simply be the meaning of an especially important sentence, which automatically stands out in its context. Or a new sentence (or even just a word) which does not actually appear in the work can sometimes represent extensive parts of the work for the reader in condensed abbreviation. It is striking that this abbreviated meaning is formed without the reader's conscious intention. It seems to form itself.

I have stated that we retain a condensed meaning in "active memory." That does not mean that in reading we perform a special act of remembering directed at this meaning; nor does it mean that we have a certain "disposition" toward performing such acts of remembering, as many psychologists might be tempted to assert. Both cases can of course exist from time to time, but usually they do not. At least when we are dealing with active memory, which is a special mode of consciousness, they never do. So far as I know, the phenomenon of "active memory" has not yet been exposed or discussed in psychology or in the phenomenology of consciousness,[5] perhaps simply because it is always present and we are accustomed to it. We become clearly

5. It is not to be confused with Husserl's concept of "retention." Retention is an experience whose objective domain is still completely within the reach of the vivid present even though it concerns what is "just" past or passing. And retention helps constitute the vivid present (see Edmund Husserl, *Vorlesungen zur Phänomenologie des inneren Zeitbewusstseins,* ed. Martin Heidegger [Halle: Max Niemeyer, 1928]; [English translation by James S. Churchill, *The Phenomenology of Internal Time-Consciousness* (Bloomington: Indiana University Press, 1964)]). "Active memory," on the other hand, takes us beyond the domain of the actual present. It is one of the ways in which the past, or past things and events, are constituted for the subject. It seems that we can retain many facts in active memory which are relatively remote from our present moment.

conscious of it only when it becomes noticeable for some special reason. An elucidation of this special function of consciousness would require extensive analyses, which cannot be carried out here. We can only say quite provisionally that it is a kind of peripheral feeling, which has no more precise content than that something has happened which is closely connected with our present moment (for instance, the first part of a sentence which has been begun and is being thought further) and which has a certain continuation in the present or else detectable consequences in what is actual in the present. This involuntary feeling of what is already past can either resolve itself in an explicit act of remembering performed on what is thus felt, or it can simply die away. In the latter case, all memory knowledge of the past event or of an objectivity already submerged in the past vanishes, and a special new act of recollection must be performed in order to "call to mind" what is past and to gain a new knowledge of it. Except for pathological cases (for instance, when one is slightly intoxicated), the consciousness of the actual present is always bound up with the active memory of many facts or objectivities which are already past. One way this is shown is that things which are retained in active memory affect our behavior in our present moment, or contribute as a distinct motif to the determination of what we have just apprehended, even if we do not always take them into account.

The active memory of the condensed meaning of the parts of the literary work which have already been read thus constitutes only a particular case of active memory in general, albeit with the difference that what is retained in active memory from the literary work belongs not to the real world but to the special sphere of the literary work. The vividness of active memory decreases, the "earlier" the part of the work is to which it refers, or the earlier that part is read, and the less important that part is for the whole of the work or for the part now being read. Then active memory is as if extinguished, so that those early parts of the work disappear completely from the reader's field of awareness at some point as the reading continues. Individual readers can vary greatly in this respect, according to the type of memory each has and the external circumstances under which the reading is carried out, which permit greater or lesser concentration on the reader's part and produce in him a more or less lively interest. However, the following fact is important for the remainder of our investigation: in longer literary works, no one can ever retain all the parts already read in active memory; on the other hand, the reader is always conscious, in the way already indicated, of certain fragments of the work in abbreviated, condensed form. What has already been read never disappears immediately and completely from the reader's field of consciousness, except, of course, in pathological cases.

The reader retains in active memory the phases of what is portrayed in the objective stratum of the work in a way that is analogous to, and closely connected with, the way in which he retains the corresponding phases of the semantic stratum in active memory. After we have already learned something or other about the portrayed objects (things, people), they are no longer explicitly present to us clothed in aspects. We have only a more or less nonintuitional memory knowledge of them, primarily only a knowledge about what happened to them in the parts of the work already read, what events they participated in, and how they changed as a result of them. In this case, too, there occurs a peculiar condensation and abbreviation of the phases of the objective stratum which have already been read. The reader retains in active memory only the culminating phases of events, the most important characters, etc., or else facts which somehow concern him personally, such as those which produce certain feelings in him. The facts and objects retained in active memory during the reading are constantly changing, not simply because the multiplicity of facts portrayed keeps growing, but also because, as the reading progresses, other processes, events, or characters often assume a significance for the reader which is different from the significance they seemed to have in the earlier parts. A fact which in itself does not seem very important at first is revealed in the course of further events as a turning point of the developing action or as an event which has more important effects than other events. Then the fact forces itself upon the reader and is suddenly called back into active memory.

In general the reader seldom retains the past phases of all strata of the literary work in active memory. Usually there is a characteristic narrowing (limiting) of the concretization to some of its strata. For the most part, the stratum of portrayed objects is predominant.

In contrast with the immediate, vividly present phase of the work, we have those of its parts which the reader has not yet come to but which he is constantly approaching in the course of the reading. They too exist in some way for the reader, although in general he does not know them at all. Sometimes, because of the dynamics of the work, parts which the reader is approaching announce themselves with rather clear and definite features. Certain "coming" events announce themselves in outline; sometimes several possibilities announce themselves at once. Their announcement, however unclear and indefinite it may be, colors in a peculiar way the events we witness during reading. But only further reading can give us positive knowledge of whether and to what extent the events announcing themselves take place. "Surprises," sometimes consciously prepared, are not without importance, especially for the aesthetic apprehension of the literary work of art: something appears in the objective stratum of the work, or in the other strata, which could not have been foreseen. Or else something which was prepared and expected does not occur. The preparation of such a surprise occurs through certain artistic means, by which something indicated in the text as possible and threatening suddenly does not happen after all but is replaced by its opposite. There are special artistic effects in such a surprise; and it is not without significance for the aesthetic apprehension of the work that these surprise phenomena be apprehended by the reader in their correct role, which is important for the development of the work.

The other strata of the work do not generally announce themselves, even in a merely schematic way, although exceptions are possible. In poems written in regular verse forms, e.g., in a classical octave, the repeated rhythm can so affect the reader that he comes to expect the return of the same rhythms and "hears" them approaching to a certain extent, without needing to see the graphic form of the verse.

But independently of the way in which the coming parts of the work announce themselves to the reader and of what features of the work can and do so announce themselves, the reader is always aware of the phenomenon of progression to new parts or phases of the work and sometimes also of the phenomenon of the constant decrease in the parts of the work which are still unknown. The phenomenon of the constant increase in the parts already read is also perceptible. This is what gives the process of reading the character of a movement which unfolds in a certain tempo and with a characteristic dynamism.

The part of the work we are now reading is thus constantly surrounded in concretization by a double horizon (if we may use Husserl's expression here): (*a*) of the parts already read, which sink into the "past" of the work, and (*b*) of those parts which have not yet been read and which are unknown up to the present moment. This double horizon is constantly present as horizon, but it is always being filled by different parts of the work. Its existence has a constant influence on the constitution of the content of the part of the work now being read, even though the kind of influence often changes. This matter was discussed in § 8 with regard to the semantic stratum of the work. But this influence is more or less clearly evident in all strata of the literary work in the phase of the work being read. However extensively this phase of the work is determined, primarily by its own content, nevertheless its concrete form would look different if it followed, not the phase it does follow, but a different, "earlier" phase of the work, or if it were the beginning of the work or were simply read as the first phase of the work. Many of the events occurring in this phase would then be incomprehensible or would take on a different meaning. Their role or importance, their internal dynamics, what they express, would then all be different. The schemata of aspects forced on the reader by the text would also be concretized differently, and this would result in essential distortion and warping of the polyphonic harmony of the aesthetically relevant qualities. The concretization of the part of the work we are reading is often functionally quite dependent on the parts of the work already read and even more on the way in which the parts already read were concretized. In many cases the concretization of the part of the work being read is also functionally dependent on the "later" parts of the work, which are vaguely and imprecisely indicated or anticipated; this dependence is most noticeable in the objective stratum.

On the other hand, from the point of view of the "later" phase (the phase being read), the parts of the work which the reader already knows, especially the events portrayed in them, often present themselves in another form from the one in which they showed themselves in their self-presence when they were being read. We have already discussed the possible forms in which these "earlier" parts are retained in the reader's active memory; but the reader can also call them to mind in special acts of remembering. In both cases we see the phenomenon of perspectival foreshortening, which, however, is completely different from the phenomenon discussed in § 14. We have to do here with the quite characteristic, but thus far scarcely investigated, "temporal perspective." The phenomena which appear in the concretizations of literary works of art during reading are only a special case of "temporal perspective" in general. Thus it will serve our purpose to investigate temporal perspective in a broader sphere.

§ 17   *The phenomena of "temporal perspective"*

THE PRESENCE OF ACTIVE MEMORY, of voluntary and involuntary memories which occur from time to time, and the orientation of the subject of consciousness toward the future and the fact that our lives are directed toward it: all this has the result that we always experience our present moment as a phase integrated with the unified whole of time. We live in phenomenal time, of which, by the way, there are different varieties, such as monosubjective ("private") time or "intersubjective" time, which can be common to us all or only to a certain community but which is still phenomenal time. It has nothing in common with time measured by clocks, though in a particular cultural milieu it is correlated with clock time and thus acquires new aspects. This phenomenal time, in all its varieties, is filled out by events and processes which take place in it and which are ordered according to the two dimensions or temporal categories of simultaneity and temporal disparateness.[6] In principle, phenomenal time can be extended infinitely in two different directions. Actually, however, it is limited in the sense that the temporal

6. See, especially, Edmund Husserl, *Vorlesungen zur Phänomenologie des inneren Zeitbewusstseins*, as well as §§ 81–82 of his *Ideen zu einer reinen Phänomenologie und phänomenologischen Philosophie*, Vol. I, in *Jahrbuch für Philosophie und phänomenologische Forschung* Vol. I, no. 1 (1913); see also Vol. III of *Husserliana, Edmund Husserl: Gesammelte Werke* (The Hague: Martinus Nijhoff, 1950). [The second and third volumes of the *Ideen* were published posthumously in *Husserliana*, Vols. IV–V (1952). English translation of Vol. I by W. R. Boyce Gibson, *Ideas: General Introduction to Pure Phenomenology* (New York: Macmillan, 1958; New York: Collier Books, 1962).] Certain of Bergson's examinations are also relevant here. A new edition of Husserl's *Vorlesungen*, mentioned above [edited by R. Boehm (The Hague: Martinus Nijhoff, 1966)], and other studies of time, such as that by Hedwig Conrad-Martius, *Die Zeit* (Munich: Kösel, 1954) and various investigations influenced by Heidegger, have appeared since 1936, when this book was written. But I do not believe that I need to change the assertions I make in this chapter. What I have done here could at most be supplemented and developed in greater detail. But what has been said in the analysis of temporal phenomena and temporal perspective is still valid and of importance for the literary work of art and the mode of its apprehension.

phases themselves and the events taking place in them come to concrete appearance in a finite temporal domain which is clustered in a peculiar way around the present moment. The temporal phases appear as concrete phenomena because, as Bergson has shown, they are qualitatively determined in a peculiar way. Strictly speaking, this applies only to the present moment and to the temporal phases which have already been experienced. The temporal phases of the approaching future, on the other hand, announce themselves either as empty temporal schemata which seem merely to be thought rather than being phenomenally present to us; or else, when we are expecting certain coming events, we imagine them in the form of only vaguely indicated qualities of the temporal phases. As a result of this phenomenal vagueness, a temporal phase which merely indicates itself qualitatively is not clearly and definitively integrated with phenomenal time. Usually, as soon as such a vaguely indicated temporal phase becomes the actual present moment, its qualitative determination is completely different from what it seemed in mere anticipation; and this is true even when the expected events have actually come about.

Both the phases of past time, which we have already experienced, and the phases of the approaching future appear in their intuitively apparent qualitative determinations only in a relatively limited area around the actual present moment. They are almost always closely related to the events and processes which have taken place or are taking place in them and which we more or less directly perceive or merely imagine. In the realm of the past, these are either events or phases of processes which we reexperience in special acts of remembering, or else they are facts which are still within the domain of active memory. Both lie within the bounds of the time of our individual lives and are usually less frequent, the closer they get to the beginning of our conscious life. Only with the help of information received from others can we know something about things which happened "earlier," before our birth. By means of such information, the past is extended to include arbitrarily large temporal periods, with an unlimited open horizon into the past. But however rich and detailed all the knowledge that we receive from others about the past may be, it still cannot evoke in us the intuitive, original givenness of the qualitative determination of the temporal phases in question. To a certain extent we choose a formal temporal schema for the events which are reported and try, in a purely conceptual way, to fit them into it, although it is never actually filled by them. The schema in such a case has many gaps, for two reasons: first, because the events are missing in many phases (at least for us, to whom they are completely unknown); and second, because we do not construct it conceptually in all its phases. Only when we think it necessary for some reason do we bridge those gaps mentally by making mental connections among the phases of the schematic time with the help of relations and dependencies among the facts related to us. For this purpose we often use only certain formal schemata of such interrelationships, thus strengthening the merely schematic character of the reconstructed time. The temporal schema is then in principle unlimited and constitutes, on the one hand, an extension of our filled past time and extends itself in an analogously schematic way into the future. The time which we really experience and fill is thus fitted into this one schematic time.

The temporal perspectives of which I propose to speak appear (*a*) in phenomenal, qualitatively determined time and (*b*) in the formal temporal schema, but only where the events we learn about occur relatively close together in one period of schematic time and obviously succeed one another.

But what is "temporal perspective," as I call it, and on what is it based? It constitutes an analogue of spatial perspective. In the latter we are given the spatial determinations and order of material things under aspects in which the spatial determinations are systematically distorted and transformed, but in such a way that, when we concretely experience them under the aspects, the relevant things are given with the "objective" spatial determinations which appertain to them. That is, we believe that we are seeing them in the flesh in the relevant perception, although we are actually experiencing only those distorted, "foreshortened" forms in the contents of the aspects. If we perceive a regular cube of a certain size and at a certain distance, then, as is well known, we experience one or several overlapping aspects in whose content an entity with only three surfaces appears. The surfaces have the form of rhombuses; they seem to be distorted in space and are much "smaller" than the size we attribute to the cube in perception. Parallel lines which in space are directed toward the horizon appear in the content of the aspects to be running together, etc.[7]

7. Of course, in ordinary perceptions directed at things we are not aware of the content of the aspects we experience, but we can become aware of this in a peculiar kind of reflective experience without losing sight of the perceived thing.

We often speak of perspectival deceptions which are to be corrected and which actually are somehow corrected when we ascribe to the things we perceive their "true" spatial properties and attributes, those which actually appertain to them. But of course there is no deception, because when we experience the aspects on which our perceptions are based, we by no means mistakenly believe that the cube has, for example, only three surfaces in the form of rhombuses. On the contrary, the "objective" form—the form of the cube—is intuitively present to us in perception even when we are experiencing such aspects. And there is a possibly strange but still necessary regular correlation[8] of the one "objective" form which appears as the determination of the perceived thing with a multiplicity of forms which are perspectivally distorted and experienced in the contents of the appropriate aspects. Only when, under the influence of an aspect or a multiplicity of aspects, we ascribe to the perceived thing a different spatial form (from that of the cube, for instance) in the conviction that we have actually seem this form (as, for example, in the case of the stick partially submerged in water and appearing to be bent) can we speak of a perspectivally based deception.

As I have stated, temporal perspective constitutes an analogue of spatial perspective. In perception, but also in the memory of certain processes in time and of the temporal phases in which they occur, there appear strange distortions and transformations of their "temporal form" in the "temporal aspects" under which they come to givenness. When we experience these distorted and transformed temporal forms immediately under their aspects, in intuition we attribute the appropriate "undistorted" temporal forms to the perceived processes and temporal phases. One should not speak of "deceptions" in this case either. There would be particular deceptions of temporal perspective only if the merely experienced "distorted" temporal forms were attributed "objectively" to the perceived events and their temporal phases. Of course, that does happen sometimes; but we are interested only in the question of how and whether the deceptions which arise from temporal perspective are to be discovered and

8. One might question whether the correlation is really necessary and might refer to the fact that the Chinese use a completely different "perspective" in their pictures than the Europeans. In this connection one could also mention the differences between immediately seeing the mountains on the horizon and seeing a photograph of them. But these are all special phenomenological problems which we cannot treat of here.

removed, since we are undoubtedly dealing with a situation different from the case of spatial perspective, where the discovery and elimination of such deceptions is possible and easy.

Spatial perspective manifests itself primarily in the experience of the aspects of spatial, material things which are perceived visually. The only processes we need consider are the motions of material things in visually perceived space. Even then, the motions themselves are not subject to perspectival foreshortening, so that we can speak of perspectival foreshortening of motions only in a secondary, derived sense. On the other hand, other processes we perceive are not subject to spatially perspectival changes in their aspects. In contrast, however, all processes, even objects enduring in time, are perceived in a temporally extended multiplicity of aspects of the things involved in the processes.[9] As a result of active memory and of recollections, not only do the already experienced phases of the multiplicities of aspects appear under "temporal aspects" of their own —as if these were aspects of a secondary, higher order—but also the processes and things which come to appearance under these aspects show themselves directly in specifically temporal aspects. Special phenomena of temporal perspective appear in the content of these aspects.

I should like to indicate some of these here.

1. The most obvious phenomenon of temporal perspective is perhaps the abbreviation of temporal phases (as one usually and incorrectly says) and of the processes which are developed in them. Temporal intervals in the past usually seem shorter in memory than they seemed while they were actually being experienced. We are speaking, of course, of the phenomenal length of a temporal interval, just as it presents itself in experience, and not of length in the sense in which a temporal interval is judged to be "longer" or "shorter" according to the number of "objectively" measured seconds.

The phenomenal abbreviation of temporal intervals can be

9. As long as there is no interruption of the process of perception, these multiplicities constitute *de facto* a continuum of aspects, in which one aspect flows continuously into its successor. The individual aspects are basically merely the passing phases of a process. Nonetheless, we usually speak of "aspects" as if they formed certain independent units (as if they were separate from one another like the cinematographic frames of a continuously unfolding process). We speak in this way in order to simplify the analysis of the contents of the individual aspects; but it is unquestionably an abstract, formal transformation of the concretely unfolding continuum of aspects, which to a certain degree also distorts this continuum materially.

greater or less, according to circumstances. The way in which we remember a past occurrence or past processes plays an important role here. There are two main ways of remembering past processes: either we apprehend a whole temporal interval and what happened in it from the standpoint of our actual present in a single act of remembering, all at once (for example, as we call to mind in one act the long period of World War I); or else we transport ourselves in memory back to the beginning of the period in question and, in the process of remembering, progress as it were simultaneously with the remembered period by calling to mind the successive events and processes phase by phase.[10] In the first case we certainly know from the outset that World War I, viewed objectively, lasted over four years and that it was very long for us once, when we were living through it. But the way in which we now call this time to mind all at once causes it to seem much shorter than the time we once experienced and also shorter than when, for instance, we first call to mind the assassination of the heir to the Austrian throne and, starting from that point, follow the development of the events of the war in memory, as we once experienced them phase by phase. The temporal interval which is filled with the recollection itself of course also becomes longer when we transport ourselves back in time; but this lengthening has nothing to do with the phenomenal lengthening of the remembered temporal interval. We are hardly aware of the stretch of time filled with acts of recollection.

The "length"[11] of the remembered temporal interval also depends on how many details of an event we pursue in memory. The more exact the recollection is and the more it goes into the details of the past event, the longer the temporal period seems in which it took place. This length also depends on what we remem-

10. In active memory, only the first way of experiencing past events or occurrences obtains. Thus we have, for example, an extreme summarization and abbreviation of the parts of a literary work of art that have already been read.

11. I am using quotation marks to indicate that this "length" is essentially different from the length of a spatial segment, for instance a line, and that it is not a "spatialization" of time, as Bergson, for example, asserts. But colloquial language, which we must use here, has no special word for "length" of time. Only physical time is subject to geometrical analysis, especially time considered as the fourth dimension of four-dimensional space. But in the original experience of concrete, qualitatively determined time there is a special phenomenon of the "length" of duration, and this "length" is then itself a qualitative determination of the temporal phase itself and also of whatever it is that lasts "so long."

ber. Temporal intervals which were filled in experience with boring, monotonous action and which seemed very long to us at the time* appear very short when they are remembered. The awaiting of a decision which at the time was very extended seems so short to us now, when we remember it, that it tends to disappear completely from our life.

2. But there are also other phenomena which are directly opposed to the ones just described: temporal phases which are experienced under extreme nervous tension, which are full of intense action, seem very short while they are being experienced and immediately thereafter.[12] In later recollection, however, this same temporal phase seems much longer, especially if we remember along with it the whole course of events. But these are relatively rare cases.

But there is still the peculiar case when the present moment seems very long to us—if we may use that word here—for example, in moments of very great danger, when we experience or observe in amazement what is happening with the most intense concentration, ready to undertake immediately whatever might be necessary to save ourselves. In recollection, this "long" present appears as a "momentary" event, just as it was actually only a single present moment when we experienced it.

In consideration of the phenomenal length of past and recalled temporal intervals, which depends on such diverse factors and which differs according to their effect, we cannot assert as a general rule that temporal intervals seem shorter, the further removed they are from our actual present.

That is true in many cases, but it is by no means always true. Here there is no analogy with spatial perspective, in which more distant objects always, according to a universal rule, appear "smaller" than those which are "near," where this "nearness" can vary greatly.

* Here we have omitted an untranslatable pun on *lang* (long) and *Langeweile* (boredom).—Translators.

12. Bergson, especially, emphasizes this, and he established his theory of the *tension de la durée* in connection with it. It seems to me, however, that he went much too far. But war experiences perhaps bear the most effective witness to the fact that there actually is such an abbreviation in direct experience and a certain—if we may use the term—condensation of the experienced temporal periods. A colleague told me once how the approximately ten-hour bombardment of a fortification of which he was commander in the siege of the stronghold of Przemyśl in 1914 seemed very short, about "half an hour." He became aware of the passage of time only when his servant brought him supper that evening, after an entire day of bombardment.

3. Changes in the "dynamics" of processes. Not all processes have a dynamic character. For instance, it is not present in processes which consist in a monotonous repetition of the same movements. The dynamic character or, as is often said, the "dynamics" of the process (especially of an action) manifests itself where the process develops in a series of qualitatively different phases and where an intensification of strength exerted is evident and leads to a culmination in which the climax, like a special event in itself, is contained. Every battle, for instance, and every fight, even if broken off without a decision, has a pronounced dynamic character. After a phase of preparation, of appraisal of the opponent's forces and of a first test of his power of resistance and of the resources which he has at his disposal and can bring into play, there follow increasingly frequent and violent attempts to overcome the opponent, which ultimately lead to a maximal intensification of attacks and counterattacks and a total engagement of forces on both sides. The culminating phase, the phase of highest tension in the battle, lasts until the forces of one side either effect a breakthrough or suffer a collapse. Then the battle abates or is interrupted suddenly because one of the parties takes flight. The variations in the exertion of the forces, in the way the attacks are carried out, etc., give the whole process of the battle a dynamic character. Of course it can vary greatly according to the course of the whole event and the kind of event which is being developed "dynamically." Whether it is a battle involving masses of people or a duel, a physical fight between two people or merely a game of chess, in all cases the characteristics of the dynamics of the process appear or can appear. Even the course of an infectious disease is marked by various dynamic characteristics, as are some natural events, such as a thunderstorm or a fire, a flood or the eruption of a volcano.

In the realm of art, the phenomenon of the dynamics of a process unfolds primarily in music and literature; but even in works of architecture and painting it is present, perhaps in a modified sense.

When we observe or actively participate in an event which is just developing, we pass through all its phases, or we participate in them; and in the process we also perceive those details which decide the character of its dynamics. But in general our attention is held by the continual emergence of new present phases of the process, and we do not so much perceive the characteristic features of its dynamics as endure them. Only when the process is over and we make ourselves aware retrospectively, in active memory or in an act of recollection, of its characteristic features, do we notice the stock of its dynamic properties in a peculiarly stabilized form, as if they were petrified. The dynamics of the process develop while the process is being vividly apprehended, coming into being along with the process itself. In recollection, however, a temporal distance arises between the act of remembering and the process recalled, a distance which allows us to survey the whole process in its phases; the process then takes on the form of something which has already happened, which has become static, which is fixed for all time. From this perspective, its dynamic properties no longer appear in the process of becoming but rather as something already complete. Thus they lose much of their freshness, vitality, and impact. There are, incidentally, many ways of apprehending the dynamic character in recollection, according to the way in which the recollection takes place or is accomplished. The most solidly petrified form of the dynamics of a process is evident when we recall the whole process in all its phases at once, in a single act of remembering. In a static apprehension we see the "petrified" dynamics of the process. They appear in a synthetic, condensed form. In such a case we may apprehend the specific character of the dynamics most clearly, but we no longer feel the pulsing of the dynamically developing process, we no longer tremble in the phases of tension, nor do we follow the change of tempo and the culmination of the process. To the extent that we survey the individual phases of the process in recollection from beginning to end, we lose, to be sure, the comprehensive view of the dynamic form, the distinctness of its synthetic appearance, but we then feel more clearly the pulse of the characteristic factors of its dynamics which succeed one another in the individual phases of the process; in a sense we experience their actual unfolding again. We can also remember an event by imagining first the culminating phase at the zenith of dynamic tension, for instance in the decisive phase of a battle, and then extending the recollection by looking backwards and forwards from the culminating phase. We thus complement the original recollection and reveal the whole dynamics of the process. They then appear in a different perspectival foreshortening and transformation. They have neither the fluid form of developing dynamics nor the form of "petrified" dynamics but are something different and quite peculiar.

I have treated these modifications of the dynamic character in somewhat greater detail because they play a large role in the literary work of art. Thus it is important to note how they can be apprehended in reading a literary work of art. I shall return to this subject later.

4. The phenomena of temporal perspective we have described help us to become aware of the special phenomenon of temporal distance. It has nothing to do with the temporal remoteness of an event (with the character of its "age"). We can recollect the same process or event from a varying temporal distance. This distance is relatively greatest when we are looking for an event in the past which, although we already know that it has occurred, has not yet been localized at a certain moment in remembered time and has not forced itself into our memory. At most, we think of it as being in the past, but it has not yet appeared at any qualitatively determined place in past time. As soon as it comes to that, the distance of this temporal place from our present is determined. But this distance is diminished and is made more precise when we succeed in intuitively recalling that event with its own characteristic features and when this occurs in a single act of recollection in which the whole process or event is apprehended in a single ray. Then we can bring the remembered event ever closer to our present moment either by recalling its features at random or by following its whole course in memory from beginning to end. But even in the latter case we can imagine the individual phases as more or less distant from our present according to our success in seeing them, vivid and in a sense self-present, in recollection. It is not a question of the multitude of details which manifest themselves phenomenally but rather of their emergence into intuition from the dark medium of the past. Absolute proximity is out of the question. If that were possible, what is simply remembered would become something perceived; but there is no genuine return to the past. In this state of affairs is expressed a very specific transcendence of what is remembered as opposed to everything which is accessible to inner or outer perception. Even the greatest effort on the part of memory cannot conquer this transcendence. The term "self-presence," which we have employed several times in connection with what is remembered, is to be taken with a grain of salt and cannot be identified with the self-presence of the perceived object. What is called to mind again, no matter how distinct and close to us it seems, always presents itself under the aspect of something perceived at one time and now no longer perceived. In many cases this aspect can have in itself the quality

of the moment in which we originally perceived what we now remember, but this is not always so. We can distinctly apprehend something we remember as something we once "really" perceived and witnessed but still not succeed in accounting for when we perceived it. This is not because we could not say, on the basis of memory, under what circumstances it occurred, since we can recall these circumstances; but the situation we remember still does not have the qualitative character of the original moment. Even when someone, for example, gives us the exact date of the event which we remember, it will not help much until we suddenly feel the quality of the past moment, which quality, however, is still not identical with the intuitive and exact apprehension of the place this moment occupies in the past that is available to our memory. Only when this, too, occurs can we clearly localize the event in our phenomenal past. The temporal distance can thus be greatly diminished even if the point at which the event occurred (presents itself as having occurred) belongs to our distant past.

But there are still two other ways in which we can remember something. We can bring a past event or process close or place it at a distance in such a way that our immediate feeling is that we remain in our flowing present moment and retain our "now" as a center of observation without being aware of its constant change into a new now. On the contrary: we feel as if we were remaining always in the same present moment.[13] But we can also forget our constantly changing present, as if we were experiencing nothing at the moment, and bring ourselves more or less close to past events; the extreme form of this mode of remembering is that we transport ourselves back into the past events. Then it is as if we really returned to the past and left our real present without "feeling" that this present is always in the process of becoming a new present and that we are thus irrevocably becoming more and more removed from the past event. If we may make a comparison with spatial perspective, it is as if, in the present, we were to step up to something removed from us in order to see it better or else bring it closer to ourselves by means of binoculars. Its visual aspects change in a particular, regular way, but we experience these aspects only when

13. This phenomenon is especially evident when we are recalling different phases of a process or series of events simultaneously and comparing them with regard to their sequence or their temporal position, or when we are considering events which have recurred often.

we take an attitude of perception toward the thing itself. Nonetheless, the set of details given us varies with different distances, so that the experience of a certain series of aspects is not without influence on the form of the perceived thing. It is the same with the phenomena of temporal perspective. The phenomenon of temporal distance is not without consequences for the way in which an "objectively" existing past event, now remembered at some remove, appears to us. In the case of spatial perspective, we can reverse the modifications we notice in the perceived thing as a result of perspectivally foreshortened aspects by perceiving the same object again at close range. We have still other means of checking our visual perceptions by calling on the perceptions of other senses. In the case of temporal perspective, we do not have these possibilities. Thus the changes in the form in which an event can be remembered have a much greater importance for the knowledge we can gain about the past under the aspect of various distances. A past event or process or a phase of past time must always be recalled from a temporal "point of view" which is at a greater or lesser phenomenal distance from what is being remembered and which, moreover, is constantly shifting. As a result of the change in the "point of view," the process or event remembered shows itself, as it were, from different sides. Sometimes one phase of the event and sometimes another is recalled more distinctly, while the other phases seem to disappear into obscurity. They become less distinct, more vague, or visible only in certain of their features; thus their temporal extension becomes shorter in a phenomenal sense. To each point in time, or at each zero point of the act of recollection, where a certain temporal interval and the events occurring in that interval are brought into conjunction with each other, there belongs a certain temporal "aspect" or a whole stock of "aspects" of the recalled event which we can also call foreshortenings through temporal perspective.[14] No past event or process can be remembered in a way which is completely free of the interference of the aspects of temporal perspective, not even when we apprehend a whole process in a "single-rayed" act of recollection and limit the point of view of our apprehension to our present moment, in other words, when the distance at which what we remember appears is as great as it can be. Even in such a case this

14. Of course, all the phenomena of temporal perspective which we have discussed belong to the content of such a "temporal aspect"; the phenomena occur in various combinations, and different phenomena of this perspective predominate at different times.

process appears under a greatly condensed and synthetic temporal aspect.

5. The temporal distance we have just discussed is not to be confused with the quality a remembered event may have of belonging to the distant past (*ancienneté*). Besides the change in temporal distance, there is the independent phenomenon of the constant sinking into the past which is inalterably bound up with the duration of the psychological subject in time. Even when we bring a past event closer to us in memory in the way we have described, thus diminishing its temporal distance, we still have the peripheral awareness that it is constantly and inevitably sinking deeper and deeper into the past. It becomes more and more "past," more *ancien*.[15] New facts, processes, etc., which are present to us now or are already past are always intervening between the past event and our always new present. This intervention is constant and inevitable, even if it does not always have the same tempo and although the sinking of events into the past seems to be diminished phenomenally when we remember the events and when we put ourselves back into the past. For our present moment, which is "flowing" and always new, exhausts itself to a certain extent in our remembering, in our "living with the past." No new "contents" or experiences from the world around us seem to unfold. But even this developing actual present, which almost exhausts itself in recollections, changes into a new past; and a new present emerges, as it were, from the one which is passing away, only to pass away itself in turn, separating us more and more from the "old" event, which becomes ever more "past" (*plus ancien*). Of course, it maintains the same qualitatively determined place in past time, without shifting in it; it can neither overtake "later" events nor be overtaken by "earlier" ("older") events, but with all of them it sinks deeper and deeper into the past, becomes "older" and more "past" than it was a moment ago. The continuous change in this characteristic of one and the same event while its temporal relations to the other events "surrounding" it remain the same happens quite independently of whether we are aware of the event or not, but it is more clearly evident when we recall the same event several times. This is a new factor of temporal perspective:

15. Unfortunately, there is no German word to correspond to the Polish *dawny* or the French *ancien*. The Polish word also has the comparative *dawniejszy* (*plus ancien*) and the superlative *najdawniejszy*, *bardzo dawny* (*très ancien*). To speak of "being old" [*Altsein*] in German is not the same thing.

the phenomenon of "sinking further and further into the past," of "becoming ever more past," if we may so formulate it (which is, of course, different from the sense of "past" which, as the mode of being of the "no longer actual," characterizes equally all events and processes which have happened, regardless of when they happened). As a necessary consequence of the accumulation of constantly new actualized present moments, this phenomenon of "sinking into the past" is inevitable and irreversible and has thus absolutely no correlate in spatial perspective. Even when a thing (such as a galaxy) has moved steadily away from us over a long period of time, there remains in theory the possibility of a return, a new approach to us. In the realm of phenomenal time such a return is, strictly speaking, impossible.[16] If it were possible to relive our life without losing our memory of our first life, then that would be a second, later life, in relation to which the first would sink further and further into the past. Even if we were to begin to live our life backwards from a certain moment (as in *Der Zauberlehrling* [*The Sorcerer's Apprentice*], by Hanns Heinz Ewers), with a new adulthood, a new youth, a new childhood, just the way we once lived them, then that would all be phenomenally "later" than the life we lived "forwards," and the first life would sink further and further into the past as we lived the second. It is not the phases of time which are reversed in this situation but merely the sequential order of what happens in the new time period. This absolute impossibility of a return in time makes us still more clearly aware of the phenomenon of events sinking into the past, becoming more and more "past," and allows us to distinguish between this phenomenon and that of temporal distance. This phenomenon is also a cause and a factor of the transformation of the temporal aspects under which one and the same event or process can appear in recollection.

6. But there is still another peculiar phenomenon of change in a past event when we recall it several times. This phenomenon also belongs to temporal perspective and is related to the phenomena we have already discussed. In a certain sense, it is also much more important than those phenomena. It is a peculiar change in the qualitative determination of past events. That may seem strange and will perhaps be pronounced impossible by many readers, because we generally think that what hap-

16. This, of course, has nothing to do with the problem of "recurrence" in world history. In history it is a question of the return of a cycle of world events in a new temporal epoch; it is not a return to the past.

pened once and then passed necessarily remains exactly the same for all time. "Remains" is not a very apt expression, because we are speaking of something which, once it has happened, can no longer "remain." "To remain" means to be identically the same and actual in constantly new present moments; but what has once happened no longer exists in a new present moment. But apart from this linguistic inaccuracy, there are two distinctions to be made. On the one hand, there is that which is actual in a present moment and as such attains the final form of its being and determination in that present. As such, it no longer actually exists but, as a result, is no longer capable of changing.[17] On the other hand, there is the qualitatively determined phenomenal past,[18] which in some sense exists, although in a different, no longer "actual" way, and which comes to appearance in appropriate acts of consciousness. Each of us has this kind of past (although "we" can also have a "common" past

17. This present moment, or what is contained and present in it, can be apprehended cognitively only from the point of view of the same present moment (which, by the way, is doubted in various circles). But as soon as the content of the present moment is completed, completely formed, in a present moment, and passes with the passing present moment, it is cognitively accessible only in active memory or in an act of recollection, across the past which constitutes itself in these experiences and which manifests itself under the various temporal aspects or "perspectives" we have described. The question whether it is possible to reach the no longer existing present moment and its contents in this indirect way and to apprehend it cognitively is one of the central concerns of epistemology, especially when one considers that the phenomena of temporal perspective always create interference. This would be the standpoint from which to develop the problem of historical knowledge, which was solved somewhat too hastily by so-called historicism, which goes back to Wilhelm Dilthey and which led to a complete relativism. In order to decide whether we have to come to such a conclusion, we would have to analyze in greater depth the phenomena of temporal perspective discussed above and think through their implications in the framework of a critique of knowledge.

18. About ten years after the first edition of this book, I treated the problem of time as a mode of being in Volume I of my book *Der Streit um die Existenz der Welt*, 3 vols. (Tübingen: Max Niemeyer, 1964–66). [A Polish version of this work appeared as *Spór o istnienie świata* (The Controversy over the Existence of the World), 2 vols. (Cracow: Polska Akademia Nauk, 1947–48; 2d ed., Warsaw: Państwowe Wydawn. Naukowe, 1961–62). Volume I has been partially translated by Helen R. Michejda as *Time and Modes of Being* (Springfield, Ill.: Thomas, 1964).] I paid special attention to the problem of the mode of being of what is past. I cannot develop the problem further here. For a discussion of the problem of the past and of past events and occurrences, see the interesting article by Nicolai Hartmann in the *Kantstudien* for 1938. [There are no *Kantstudien* for 1938. I was unable to find this reference.— Trans.]

as soon as a genuine community is constituted).[19] The events and processes contained in this past which constitutes itself phenomenally are by no means "set" and immutable, once and for all. This is true in a double sense. First of all, this past is not closed so long as we are still consciously alive, because new events are always being added to it. These new events have an influence on what is already contained in the past. Second, what appears in the past is not immutable in its concrete form but is subject to certain changes, without our conscious, deliberate contribution.[20] It is not immutable primarily because one and the same past fact is constantly being clothed in new temporal qualities; for example, it is always sinking further back into the past. In addition, however, it also acquires other determining factors by always appearing in a somewhat different past and surroundings because of added new past events and new acts of remembering. There is a peculiar "temporal contrast" which is a sort of inversion of the "sequential contrast" familiar from psychology. Whereas in "sequential contrast" the later phenomenon acquires many new characteristics because it follows another phenomenon, in our case a past fact acquires new features it did not previously have because other events have occurred after it.

For example: the way certain events in our youth become "insignificant" because they are followed by other, much more important events. When we were young, they seemed, and were, quite significant and occupied all our attention and our power of feeling. "Today," when we are older, the same events are nothing more than an episode, and we are perhaps amazed that they could have moved us so deeply once. And what is more: not so long ago, perhaps a year ago, we saw those events in a still different light. We felt their essential connection with our actual life, with our personality, although they had already lost much of their color. Today they are not just insignificant; they have even become foreign to us, possibly even incomprehensible.

These are generally known facts; we do not need to discuss them at length. There are, however, other facts that are less familiar and more peculiar. To be sure, these also arise from temporal contrast, but they transcend the realm of merely rela-

19. The relationship between what is no longer present and what manifests itself in the past is a basic ontological problem which cannot be treated here.

20. Our deliberate wish to change something once it has happened is completely impotent. The changes of which we are speaking happen without our wishing to change anything, as if of their own accord, although they are not independent of what happens later in our life.

tive factors. Often it is only on the basis of what happens after an event that we learn that both it and our behavior were basically different from what they seemed at the time when we were witnessing them in our present moment and, indeed, not just in relation to their role or significance in our life but in their essential determination. What happened later, and which "today" also belongs to the past and lives only in our memory, reveals, for example, certain essential, decisive motives of our actions which "at that time" were still hidden, of which we were not fully aware or which we even repressed. This revelation causes a change in the essential character of our actions. What appeared to us at that past moment to be a defense against someone else's attack reveals itself as a disguised attack. What we at that time experienced as a victory over ourselves turns out to be an unacknowledged flight from danger. What we thought to be genuine love for a person, binding for our whole lifetime, is "now" unmasked as a merely apparent love, which we in some way intended, although we did not admit it, to save us from another love that was genuine but hopeless, etc. "Today" we know it with certainty, having seen what happened later. And it can prove to be the case that once, in this past moment, we were not feigning this love which was really only apparent. On the surface of our past life that was love. Something else lay hidden in the depths, but, because it was unrevealed, it did not exist for us in a practical sense. Only a later experience, which today also belongs to the past, brought to the surface the hidden forces affecting our life and our actions and, by revealing what was previously hidden or not admitted, modified our past in an essential way. The past is stamped with a different character and is thus thoroughly changed.

The examples above do not merely indicate the changes in our past because of temporal perspective; they also show us a reason for distinguishing the once-actual present from our past. The once-actual present no longer exists; it was once, and, if it were possible to apprehend it immediately, without any temporal perspective, it would still be as it once was. It is only our past which has changed, because of new events which once were not yet part of the past and at that time had not yet appeared in any present moment. Only later, or "now," do they really occur and have an inestimable influence on the reshaping of the past.

7. One more remark to conclude our investigation: facts (events, processes, objects enduring in a phase of time) can appear in recollection under various aspects, depending on whether

and how much we expand our recollection. By "expanding" a recollection I mean recalling facts which were simultaneous with the event we first remembered and which characterize it more closely or show it from a different side. Usually we remember only a particular detail from a whole objective situation, a detail such as a certain form or state of affairs. Only this further recollection of the circumstances or of other details of the same objectivity permit us to "fill in" more exactly and completely what we remembered originally. It can thus assume a different character, not only in the realm of relative determinations but also in its essential core, which was first in shadow, unnoticed or not clearly distinguished. We can thus not only change the scope of what is recalled in this manner; we can also let the primary intention of our memory wander over various details or elements of the total situation. Many new details can be rescued from oblivion and can appear in new clarity. At the same time, the spatial perspective in the remembered section of the world changes, so that the same spatial objects appear in memory under various aspects and perspectival foreshortenings. But as soon as certain details in the total situation receive better "lighting," other details and circumstances usually move into the background and sink at least partially into the obscurity of what is remembered only incidentally. The whole remembered situation is always surrounded by a horizon of obscurity and vagueness, out of which it moves, as it were, for just a moment into the cone of light cast by memory, soon to sink again into the twilight of what is only incidentally remembered. These vacillations in brightness, clarity, and precision of the objectivities appearing in recollection proceed during the course of recollection (and during the whole continuity of a wave of recollection); they thus fall within the concrete qualitative time of what is remembered, and they essentially modify and influence the phenomena of temporal perspective described above. The vacillations are much greater than in the realm of immediate perception, but in both cases they are unavoidable and play an important role in determining what the acts of consciousness can yield for cognition. In the realm of perception this kind of vacillation is important for the way these objectivities are later remembered or can be remembered, although it cannot be said that what is perceived only in twilight and imprecisely must necessarily be remembered in the same way. The same is true of the breadth and possible expansion of the recollection. This too seems to be conditioned by the breadth of the perception which goes before. But it also seems possible that something can occupy a central place in recollection and can appear in full light although it was apprehended only peripherally and in semidarkness in perception. It often happens that in the process of remembering we suddenly say: it just occurred to me that such and such was in fact the case, although I didn't notice it in the process of perception. Thus there are various possibilities which should be considered in detail but which surpass the main theme of our investigation.[21]

The manifestations of temporal perspective which we have sketched above occur primarily in cases of recollection of past facts. To a certain extent they also occur within the scope of active memory, but I cannot discuss these problems here. The events given in recollection under the "foreshortenings" of temporal perspective need not be finished events. In a process which is still developing at the present moment, the phases which are already past appear in analogous manifestations of temporal perspective, although we do not imagine them in special acts of recollection and although they are encompassed in part by active memory and even by retention. Further: every process is perceived as a process only because the phases which have just passed come to givenness in active memory or in recollection in the manifestations of temporal perspective. If both active memory and recollection were extinguished and our perceiving consciousness were limited to the actually present phase of the "now," it would be doubtful whether the process we just perceived would still present itself as a process. To a certain extent, we can see evidence of this in anomalous cases; for example, in mild alcoholic intoxication the scope of the actual present becomes obviously smaller in the direction of the past because

21. So far as I know, no one has ever investigated, from the standpoint of a critique of knowledge, what memory (in its various modes) can yield for cognition. Nor has anyone considered to what extent the cognitive yield of memory is important, to a certain degree perhaps even decisive, for the knowledge obtained in perception. These problems are especially significant when it is a question of remembering facts which, once past, can never again be given to perception, in cases, that is, of unique events, such as the occurrences and events in a man's life. The way in which they are "retained" in memory or recalled (or can be recalled) and to what extent memory can give us knowledge about real (past) facts are decisive for what a man is "now," in his present moment, and for how he acts in this present. These problems are also important for the elucidation of the way in which we gain knowledge of the literary work of art; but there the circumstances are somewhat different, in that the same work can be read and apprehended several times. We shall return to this question in later chapters.

retention is weakened and active memory and recollection are also largely extinguished. In an extreme case it does not seem impossible that a process would then take on the shape of a multitude of events quickly succeeding one another. But this is only an approximation of what is really the case, because, even in the condition of mild intoxication, the present, or the consciousness of the present, never becomes a "punctual" consciousness, limited to discrete points of time. This latter seems to be merely a fiction forced on psychologists by the pressure of the mathematical-physicalistic concept of time. If it ever really came to this extreme case, both action and genuine perception would also become impossible.

The manifestations of temporal perspective in the earlier phases of a process which we are still perceiving in its later phases is of particular interest to us, especially when we are considering the act of reading a literary work of art without interruption and without returning to the parts of the work already read. But a return to earlier parts of the work is often involved in the reading of longer works. Thus it will be necessary to discuss it. For the present, however, we can close our general consideration of temporal perspective and return to the problems concerning this perspective which arise during the reading of a literary work of art.

§ 18. *Temporal perspective in the concretization of the literary work of art*

THE MANIFESTATIONS (phenomena) of temporal perspective appear in two different spheres in the concretization of the literary work of art. On the one hand, the events and processes portrayed in the work appear under various phenomena of temporal perspective. On the other hand, temporal perspective also applies to the individual phases or parts of the whole work, or of its concretization, which have already been read. Thus there occurs a peculiar "crossing" of the two applications of temporal perspective; and this crossing often produces manifestations of it which are quite complicated and difficult to foresee,[22]

22. This is especially important for the author during the stage of composition of the work. For the phenomena of temporal perspective possess in general a high level of aesthetic relevance, as we shall show,

because both applications are conditioned to a great degree by the reader's behavior during reading.

The phenomena of temporal perspective can be present in the portrayed world of the work in various forms and in various modifications. Their selection depends primarily on the mode of portrayal of the objects, and especially the events, belonging to the portrayed world and thus ultimately on the construction and the sequence of the sentences contained in the work and partly also on the phonetic phenomena in the language of the work. To this extent the phenomena of temporal perspective are determined by the basic structure of the literary work of art and accordingly belong to the work itself, in a more or less potential form, although they can be unfolded fully only in a concretization of the work. To the extent that the reader submits to the demands of the work, he is under the influence of the temporal perspectives predetermined by the text and comprehends the portrayed events and processes under these perspectives. The most important role in projecting the temporal perspectives is played by the various temporal forms of the finite verbs which function as main or subordinate predicates (predicates of subordinate clauses). As we know, the work can be written in the present tense or in various past tenses of the verb. Sometimes the future tense is also used. Usually, in the novel for example, the past and present tenses are used alternately. Situations and events are described in the past tense, whereas the sentences uttered by the portrayed characters are usually written in the present. The present tense is often used, too, to describe, for instance, certain things or people. This gives them a semblance of permanence, of being beyond time, as if they were not subject to change. Sometimes, especially in lyric poetry, the poem seems to present its so-called *pointe* as being beyond time. The present tense predominates in the drama and in many lyric poems. If a book is written consistently in the past tense, we read it—regardless of whether the action described is localized in a specific historical time—with an attitude related to the one we take in remembering past events. But there are widely differing possibilities here.

The tense of the verb does not alone suffice to determine whether the portrayed events seem to lie in the past or in a special present. An artful use of the different past and present

---

and must thus be taken into account by the author as an important factor in the artistic or aesthetic effectiveness of the work of art.

tenses, united with a vivid and plastic portrayal and the emphasis of many details of the events, can cause events portrayed in the past tense to show themselves to the reader under the aspect of a vivid present. The reader seems to enter the portrayed past and feels, when the temporal distance is reduced to a minimum, like a witness to the portrayed events. The reader takes a peculiar recollective-perceptive attitude. The temporal distance shrinks so greatly that the reader's return to the time of the described events allows him to observe these events, so to speak, from the same temporal phase in which they are developing. The reader then seems to move along with the stream of the time portrayed, primarily or only incidentally, in the work by passing in reading to constantly new and "later" events; while those which were "earlier" and are already known sink into the past,[23] and these "earlier" events begin to present themselves to the reader under various phenomena or "aspects" of temporal perspective. And the phenomena of temporal perspective can be concretized in various combinations and syntheses.

In many works, the past tense of verbs is used in such a way that the portrayed objects, and especially the events, appear predominantly at a great temporal distance. Then the reader cannot "enter" the past; he observes the events portrayed in the work from the point of view of his present,[24] because he learns about them under a considerable shortening of the temporal phases in which they occurred. Processes which develop over long periods of time, which are of a very complicated nature and contain many diverse phases, are not described in their full course, phase by phase and from the point of view of the cor-

23. We have to take into account a double past, if we may use such an expression: first of all, the past of the "reality" portrayed in the work and of the time portrayed along with this reality; second, the past of the temporal structure of the work itself.

24. It is not so easy to say exactly what "his present moment" is. It seems to be the present of the reading, a phase, therefore, of the time the reader experiences in reality. But, on the other hand, the time of reading seems to some extent to be lifted out of the flow of this time. The concrete life of the reader stands still; he fictively enters the time of the portrayed events as if his learning about these events took place in the same temporal flow as the events themselves, albeit at a much later moment, and the temporal phase of the reading either does not count or else strangely shrinks to a single present moment. It coincides in a peculiar way with the temporal structure of the concretization of the work. And only later, when we return from reading to our concrete, active life, do we fit this temporal phase of reading somehow into the course of our life again, although it does not really belong there. I shall return to this problem in my discussion of the aesthetic experience.

responding temporal phase, but are portrayed very "summarily," as an undifferentiated unity (whole). A period of time is sometimes described in a single sentence. A complex process will simply be mentioned with the statement that it took place. Many and multifarious events will be summarized in a short report, so that we do not see at all their unfolding, realization, and change. We can "see" them only at a great temporal distance, if at all; we remain in the present of the "narration" itself,[25] which is by no means identical with the present of the reading, although the reader often identifies it with that present. As a result of the great temporal distance, we hardly notice that the quality of belonging to the distant past of the individual "earlier" and "later" events changes, in reading, through the transition to constantly new events. Everything seems equally "old," equally "past," and equally far removed from the temporal phase of the narration. In this case the reader does not take the "recollective-perceptive" attitude mentioned above; rather, a purely recollective attitude prevails, of course with the fundamental difference that the reader is generally in a "passive," "receptive" attitude, because those "memories," or "what is remembered," are forced on him by the narration. Other phenomena of temporal perspective which appear in this case are the shortening of the intervals of portrayed time and an appearance of torpidity and completion in the dynamics of the developing events, to the extent that the phenomenon of dynamics can be detected at all. Everything seems rather to move with equal slowness and calm.

Sometimes the one and sometimes the other kind of temporal perspective predominates in literary works. For each type of perspective there is a corresponding mode of reading, which is, to a certain extent, forced on the reader. Usually, especially in the novel, the two types of presentation are interwoven. The more "important" events are generally told from close up; the rest are portrayed from a great distance. Incidentally, this change of temporal distance has a special compositional significance for the structure of the whole work and forms an effective means of constituting the specific aesthetically relevant qualities in the concretization of the work. If these qualities are to be constituted

25. The "present" of the narration, which is, of course, a flowing present, constitutes a problem in itself and is especially prominent where the so-called narrator himself belongs to the portrayed world and shapes his narrative from the standpoint of this world. It is by no means true, incidentally, that every novel has a narrator portrayed in the work itself and belonging to the world portrayed in the work. But more about that later.

and revealed in the concretization, the reader must have a fine sense for the changing temporal distance of the portrayed events. Only then does the portrayed world acquire plasticity and a certain three-dimensionality as a result of the intermittent emergence into the foreground and recession into the background of various events.

To make more clear what we have just stated, we shall give several examples from the novel *Lord Jim,* by Joseph Conrad.

The first chapter of this novel gives us a good example of the change in temporal distance. On the first few pages we learn various details about the character and the earlier life of "Lord Jim." In a rough sketch we see not individual events but whole series of events which were repeated several times in Jim's life and which are ordered according to their type. They are mentioned only to emphasize some character trait of the "hero." Upon entering the portrayed world, we find ourselves in an unspecified moment of portrayed time about which we know only that it is somehow much later than the narrated events, which are shown at a relatively great temporal distance. This distance is a result of the sketchiness of the portrayal and of the constant use of the iterative in the narration.[26] We are always given almost simultaneously a multiplicity of similar facts which take place at different moments. Thus we cannot grasp any truly unique event in itself. As readers we must place ourselves in a sense outside the concrete, unidirectional flow of events and cannot place ourselves mentally in any given moment, in order from there to move along with the stream of events and regard them from close up. For instance:

> On the lower deck in the babel of two hundred voices he would forget himself, and beforehand live in his mind the sea-life of light literature. He saw himself saving people from sinking ships, cutting away masts in a hurricane, swimming through a surf with a line; or as a lonely castaway, barefooted and half naked, walking on uncovered reefs in search of shell-fish to stave off starvation. He confronted savages on tropical shores, quelled mutinies on the high seas . . . [p. 5].*

26. At least this is the case in the Polish translation. It is not important whether the translation is faithful to the English original or not on this point; if not, then the phenomena which I indicate do not appear in the original. In the German translation they are hard to find, since German has no true iterative and no true imperfect.

* All quotes from Joseph Conrad, *Lord Jim: An Authoritative Text,* edited by Thomas Moser (New York: W. W. Norton & Co., 1968).

Suddenly the temporal distance changes radically. A "scene" is described in its different phases at very close temporal proximity. From a certain moment on we must in a sense become part of the course of events and move forward with them by observing them one after the other; but even here there are still some relatively minor changes in the temporal distance.

> "Something's up. Come along."
> He leaped to his feet. The boys were streaming up the ladders. Above could be heard a great scurrying about and shouting, and when he got through the hatchway he stood still—as if confounded.
> It was the dusk of a winter's day. The gale had freshened since noon, stopping the traffic on the river, and now blew with the strength of a hurricane in fitful bursts that boomed like salvos of great guns firing over the ocean. The rain slanted in sheets that flicked and subsided, and between whiles Jim had threatening glimpses of the tumbling tide, the small craft jumbled and tossing along the shore, the motionless buildings in the driving mist, the broad ferry-boats pitching ponderously at anchor, the vast landing-stages heaving up and down and smothered in sprays. The next gust seemed to blow all this away. The air was full of flying water. There was a fierce purpose in the gale, a furious earnestness in the screech of the wind, in the brutal tumult of earth and sky, that seemed directed at him, and made him hold his breath in awe. He stood still. It seemed to him he was whirled around.
> He was jostled. "Man the cutter!" Boys rushed past him. A coaster running in for shelter had crashed through a schooner at anchor, and one of the ship's instructors had seen the accident. A mob of boys clambered on the rails, clustered round the davits. "Collision. Just ahead of us. Mr. Symons saw it." A push made him stagger against the mizzen-mast, and he caught hold of a rope [p. 5].

And one more passage:

> Jim felt his shoulder gripped firmly. "Too late, youngster." The captain of the ship laid a restraining hand on that boy, who seemed on the point of leaping overboard, and Jim looked up with the pain of conscious defeat in his eyes. The captain smiled sympathetically. "Better luck next time. This will teach you to be smart" [p. 6].

And so on, till the end of the chapter.

This whole scene certainly took place much earlier than many of the events described before it (for example, the details about Jim's duties as a commercial agent in different ports).

Nonetheless, this scene is portrayed at such a small temporal distance that we almost become eyewitnesses to what is "just" happening. Only occasionally does the temporal distance become greater because a certain temporal phase, such as the description of the storm, is given in shortened form; but then what is portrayed again comes very near. The vacillation of the temporal distance does not permit us to see the events unfolding (taking place) as we would experience them in the present. Some temporal distance, however small, still remains. But precisely because it is small, the relatively insignificant differences in time between what was "earlier" and what came "later" are more obvious. It is possible to determine almost exactly the order of temporal succession of the portrayed events.[27]

The method of indirect narration often employed by Conrad serves also to emphasize the "oldness" (*dawności*) of the portrayed events in relation to the present moment of the narration itself and to set in plastic relief significant differences in the "age" of the portrayed events. A perspective thus opens on "earlier" and "later" events, where the "earlier" events are in a sense visible through the "later" ones. Let us recall Marlow's narration of the conversation with Jim in the front gallery of the restaurant. The conversation takes place just after the adjournment of the first session of the Inquiry about the officers of the *Patna* and before Jim is sentenced. In this narration, four different time periods are interwoven in a strangely artful but also natural way: (1) the phase of Marlow's narration itself; (2) the phase of Marlow's conversation with Jim in the restaurant; (3) the phase of the first part of the Court Inquiry, which has already taken place; and (4) the period of the incident on the *Patna* and of what has happened from the time Jim left the ship until the landing in Aden. From time to time, what will happen after the conversation—the coming decisive session of the Court—shines through the narration. On the other hand, certain intimations about Jim's father open a perspective on a period which is much earlier still. The first time period above seems to be much, much later than the other time periods which are mentioned. It forms

27. In close connection with the increase or decrease in temporal distance appear analogous changes in the vividness and clarity of the aspects presenting themselves to the reader under which the portrayed objects come to appearance. Sometimes they are as distinct in their content as if we were actually perceiving these objects in reality. When the temporal distance becomes greater, the aspects flow into one another, become unclear, and disappear quickly.

the constantly new, unfolding present of Marlow's narration, although, at the moment in which it begins, it is already given in the past tense; but the result of the extensively quoted words of Marlow is that we are witnesses to this narration in all its successive phases. The first of the time periods mentioned above is "later" than the second; the second is "later" than the third; the third is "later" than the fourth. The beginning of the fourth period connects with the story of the *Patna* presented directly in the earlier chapters of the novel. But while we hear Marlow's story, we actually place ourselves in the second time period, and only Jim's words, quoted by Marlow, cause us to think ourselves back into the earlier periods. Thanks to Marlow's conversation with Jim, by virtue of the vividness of Jim's narrations woven into the conversation, of his memories, and finally of what we know already from the earlier chapters of the novel, the whole story of Jim is in a sense concentrated in the second of the above time periods. Various incidents and past events well up again in his memory, allowing us to witness these events and to return to Jim's tragedy, experienced anew by Jim. The fact that the incidents took place at different times, their interconnection despite this, their bearing on what will happen later in Jim's psyche, Jim's visible involvement in the unified flow of time, the dynamics of the events and the strength of their influence on later events: all this causes time in its very diverse perspectives to take on the form of a concrete phenomenon, to be peculiarly colored in the individual phases, and to constitute a reality closely connected with what happens in it.

It is not possible to treat all the details of the story here; only a sentence-by-sentence analysis of the story could clearly show the whole abundance of manifestations of temporal perspective which unfold in the story, a task which has not yet been carried out.

The following two texts will serve as an example of "entering" the past and of bringing the past up to the present.

The first text is from the novel *Jealousy and Medicine* by Michał Choromański, the second is a poem by Leopold Staff.

> His wife and the surgeon were left alone together. She remained silent, as before, and this wordlessness had a more exciting effect on him than all the perverse caresses he knew. Besides, the surgeon was under the impression she had said something, but this was while her husband was still there. She had brought out something utterly stupid, which had no sense whatever, one of those hopelessly banal paradoxes in which she delighted and

beyond which her intelligence could not aspire. She had said something of this kind: "The hundred per cent man possesses the lowest percentage of virility," or "a woman only gives herself to someone she doesn't love." This was most awkward and the surgeon looked at Widmar with an embarrassment obviously shared by the other.

"Anyway, I'm not interested," declared the surgeon, holding his hat on. His eyes were filled with dust: the moon was quivering in the yellow, forbidding sky. Dr. Tamten rubbed his eyes and growled:

"What an infernal wind. . . .

"But when Widmar snapped his cigarette-case and gave me a sideways look, I felt something unpleasant might happen, and in self-protection put my hand in my pocket. As to women's brains, I'm not in the least concerned; I think a woman has more interesting organs."

In this way he went on with his musings, sensual, licentious, and, what is worse, a little affected and insincere in the face of his idols. As he stopped in front of the hospital gate, a young house-surgeon rushed up to meet him, the sides of his white gown blowing up in the wind. Surgeon Tamten tried to ignore his assistant and hurriedly pursued his thoughts still further, before anyone could hinder him. "I knew perfectly well that this man would strangle me with his hands, in spite of the sincere understanding we undeniably feel for each other."

The surgeon still wanted to recall something, something which had seemed to him important and which should not be delayed, but he had not time enough. The assistant had jumped on to the cab [pp. 30–31].*

In reading the first two sentences of this passage, we have the impression that the author is presenting the scene in the salon directly and that this scene is the present to which we are witnesses in reading. But as soon as we learn that the woman had said something "while her husband was still there," we realize that the first two sentences were also thought by the surgeon in recalling a past scene and that the surgeon is returning in memory to the earlier situation, when there were still three persons present in the salon: the woman, her husband, Dr. Widmar, and the surgeon, Dr. Tamten. The following sentences

* Michał Choromański, *Zazdrość i medycyna,* 2d ed. (Warsaw: Gebethner & Wolff, 1933); English translation by Eileen Arthurton, *Jealousy and Medicine* (London: Willow Press, 1946). Page numbers in the text refer to this edition. American edition, translated by Eileen Arthurton-Barker, *Jealousy and Medicine* (New York: New Directions, 1964).

portray the situation in greater detail. But it is still not clear from the standpoint of which present moment the scene in the salon is recalled. The sentence: "Anyway, I'm not interested," is the first to define the present moment in which the surgeon's recollections take place. The following two sentences give further details of what is happening "now." In this present moment the surgeon continues his recollection, until he returns to the scene in the salon. In his memory it is so vivid that he completely leaves the present and enters the past. Still more: he tries to keep the present at a distance from his awareness, he shoves it away when the assistant appears and returns once more to the past in order to spend just one more moment there. He lives in the past; the present passes by without a trace until he is forced by the march of events to turn at least partly toward it. But even then he notices in the present only some details and carries out his duties mechanically, singing softly and cheerfully: "Rebecca, oh Rebecca, dear, what luck's in store for us two here?" (p. 31).

Just the opposite situation is portrayed by Leopold Staff [28] in the following poem:

I strike you, sorrowful chord of the soul—
You play me the quiet of evening, the smell of mown hay.
I remember the white house, two maple trees,
Summer evening, bird singing sweetly in the branches.
This remains of those happy days:
Two trees, a bird singing—nothing, and yet so much, so much. . . .

Here is the present moment in which the lyric "I" of the poem lives. It is filled with the memory of a long-ago past which is called into the present by the aid of insignificant details. It expresses itself in the melancholy awareness of what has remained from the past. The irrevocably lost happiness, its negligible but still precious traces retained in memory, and the sadness at a loss which cannot be made good emotionally determine the present of the lyric "I" in which it pronounces the words of the poem. It is not as if the lyric "I" entered the past. On the contrary, the past is revived for a moment, like an echo summoned to the present, and merges with what is happening "now." It shows the poet's great artistry that this past, although sketched from afar and only in a few insignificant details, still obtrudes

---

28. An important lyric poet of the so-called Young Polish literature. He lived from 1878 to 1962. [Our translation—R. A. C., K. O.]

upon the reader with its specific, very vivid emotional coloring and forms the necessary background for the unfolding melancholy in which it becomes effective. Although we live this present along with the lyric "I" and experience its full emotional content, we are not limited to it but rather gain a view of the past life from the standpoint of the present and experience the present as an echo of the past.

The following poem by K. Wierzyński ("Journal of Love") will serve as an example of the portrayal of a present in which all perspectives into the past and future disappear:

> Your lips wander, your lips move,
> Like two rosy birds they touch me lightly,
> Touch my eyes, like two blessed lights,
> Your lips have taken me, your lips possess me.
>
> Like a shameful confession, like mad whispering,
> I repeat your countless lips in my mouth.
> From the smile at the corners to the taste on the tongue—
> Your lips kiss and the world disappears.*

We will not attempt an analysis of this poem; we will only consider the phenomenon of time and the mode of its apprehension. Like almost all genuine lyric poems, this one portrays an actual "now." [29] The lyric "I" is so submerged in this "now" that all perspectives on past and future disappear. All that remains is the actual emotion of delight which is expressed in the attitude of the lyric "I" in this moment. It is grounded in the formation and assertion of the sentences constituting the poem. It is not so much what is said in the sentences as the assertion itself, as a form of discharging a feeling and thus also a way of disclosing the unnamed feeling to intuition; the assertion and the emotion together constitute that actual self-contained present created in the poem, which we have to experience in its peculiar, unique form and in full qualitative determination. But we cannot "ap-

* Our translation.—R. A. C., K. O.

29. The many analyses carried out in my advanced seminar in 1934–35 show that the characteristic feature of at least a certain kind of lyric poem consists in their being a mode of behavior of the lyrical subject itself within the scope of a single present moment, which is qualitatively determined by an experience concentrated in it. This present moment is, at the same time, as it were, lifted out of the flow of time, or else it is not localized in the temporal flow, not even when a past or a future is indicated in the experience of the lyrical subject, from the standpoint of the present. In Poland, Julius Kleiner showed still earlier that the present plays a special role for lyric poetry. I shall return to the problems of lyric poetry.

prehend" it from a distance, through contemplation or observation of a life-situation offered us "objectively"—as would be the case if someone were to tell us about an analogous situation— but rather through the removal [30] of all distance separating us as readers from the lyric "I" during reading and by the realization of precisely that "now" which is created, simulated, in the poem. In a proper reading there should be no distance, no duplexity, between the "now" of the poem and the "now" of the reading. The "now" of the poem is determined exclusively by the semantic content of the sentences forming the poem and, as one can see from the text, is set in no particular temporal flow; it is not at all localized in time. In other words, because of just this lack of a unique, fixed position in the real flow of time, the poem can be concretized, so to speak, in any present. For exactly that reason, if the two "nows," that of the poem and that of concretization in reading, are to coincide, the "now" of reading must in a sense be lifted out of the flow (course) of our normal real life and must allow itself to be determined by the content of the poem's present in order to become the "now" of the present projected by the poem with all the fullness of that "now." The reader, as a particular psychological subject, must, in other words, not only identify with the lyric "I" expressing itself in the poem; he must feel for a moment as if he were such an "I" experiencing and expressing himself as the lyric "I" does; he must become the lyric "I" in fiction. Only then will there be a concretization of the poem which will be close to the poem itself, and then a full, direct, undistanced aesthetic apprehension of the resulting concretization will also be possible.

As we see, there is a great difference between the attitudes of the reader which we described earlier (which are determined by the work being read), and the temporal perspectives which come to view through them, and the attitudes and temporal perspectives pertaining to the reading of lyric poetry. Earlier, it was sometimes seen as essential that the reader leave the sphere of his actuality and enter the fictional past of the work; here the reader's complete submergence in the fictional now of the poem is necessary, and every real or portrayed past and future disappears.

If we regard submergence in temporal change, with the

---

30. It is incorrect to speak of "removal," since, as a result of the art of literature, this distance disappears by itself or, better yet, is never present at all.

attendant full resonance of the past and announcement of a future, though only in the context of the emergence of the actual, constantly changing present, as an essential feature of time or of duration in time, then we could say that the present created in the poem above and forced on the reader is outside time. This view is true in one respect: the present projected in a poem is peculiar to it and different from the present we witness, for example, in a drama in that, in a poem, the resonance of our perspective on a given past and a future is missing. But it would be incorrect to speak of "nontemporality" or "extratemporality" because the "now" as such is itself a "temporal category." What is peculiar about the "now" of this poem is that its horizons—to use Husserl's term—are indeterminate or empty.[31]

But there is a kind of lyric poem which one could call, if not extratemporal, then, in a sense, supratemporal without abandoning the claim that in this kind of poem, too, a "now" is projected. This is the case in a kind of philosophical poetry. For instance, let us read the well-known "Closing Piece" from Rainer Maria Rilke's *The Book of Pictures* (I think we could find many such examples in the *Sonnets to Orpheus*, but they are much more complex):

> Death is great.
> We are his
> with laughing mouth.
> When we think ourselves in the midst of life,
> he dares to weep
> in the midst of us.*

Here, too, the lyric "I" speaks, thinks this thought and experiences it at the same time, submerged in an unnamed meditation and quiet feeling; all this constitutes a concrete present moment of its life. This poem, too, is an attitude of the lyric "I" expressed in a single moment. But what is said does not constitute a unique, unfolding, concrete, filled present moment of human life, as did the earlier poem; rather, it is something which in a sense hovers above all present moments, as the eternal fate of man, which is there even when one is not thinking about it, when the actual now is filled by various events seemingly quite the opposite of death ("We are his / with laughing mouth").

---

31. We shall soon give other reasons why we cannot speak of extratemporality here.

* From M. D. Herter Norton, *Translations from the Poetry of Rainer Maria Rilke* (New York: W. W. Norton & Co., 1938), p. 147.

The hovering over every present moment of something which "dares to weep in the midst of us" gives the whole poem, despite the filled present moment of the experiencing lyric "I," the stamp of a certain supratemporality. The same is true of Goethe's poem "Wanderer's Night-Song II":[32]

> O'er all the hill-tops
> Is quiet now,
> In all the tree-tops
> Hearest thou
> Hardly a breath.
> The birds are asleep in the trees;
> Wait; soon like these
> Thou too shalt rest.*

Let us discuss drama for a moment. Whether read or seen, drama allows the reader (the spectator) to follow a constantly new present moment of events which are in the process of developing—not a present into which we have to project ourselves as into a past time, but a present which is constantly being realized anew in the course of the drama, which is always in the process of becoming actual. It is this feature of moving along with the constantly new present that characterizes the spectator of a drama insofar as he submits to the demands of the work. But the present of a drama is not that of a lyric poem. There are, of course, many varieties of drama, and we cannot discuss them all here, since all these considerations would serve simply as concrete examples to illustrate our case. Let us say, then, without committing ourselves, that on the one hand there are explicitly historical dramas, such as Shakespeare's histories, and then there are plays which are not historical dramas, in the sense that they do not present an individual story which is explicitly located in history, however much they might bear the traces of historical time and might then be located in time after all, by literary scholars. In such a nonhistorical play, while we follow the developing action, on which we primarily concentrate, we thereby grasp a constantly new "now" which is filled and determined by what is happening at the moment. But this "now"

32. Philologists often say that an "eternal truth" is expressed and make an effort to reduce this "truth" to a so-called philosophical theorem. But then they have abandoned the poem and have made of it nothing but a trite little treatise.

* Translated by Henry Wadsworth Longfellow in *The Permanent Goethe*, edited, selected, and with an introduction by Thomas Mann (New York: Dial Press, 1948), p. 16.

is at the same time one phase woven into the course of the time portrayed with the story presented in the drama. The changing situation presented in every new now allows the spectator to apprehend the now in itself, directly and without any distance, in the events which are happening. It is always surrounded, on the one hand, by a past which has already gone by and, on the other hand, by a future which is announcing itself, sometimes threateningly, sometimes hopefully. The events already past (part of which were shown, part only mentioned in conversation or revealed by the behavior of the characters) are either kept by the spectator in active memory or recalled; they then appear in some manifestation of the temporal perspective. This incidental givenness, this resonance of the past events, is not without consequence for the further direct apprehension of what is happening "now." As much as the spectator may be shaken by what he sees, as much as his sympathy may thereby be aroused, as much as he is drawn, in a sense, into the action or swept along by it, he still remains merely a "spectator" until the end of the portrayed events. He remains outside the portrayed world and thus also outside the time of that world. In drama, therefore, we never experience the kind of closeness, the living ourselves into the portrayed present, that we have in the experience of a lyric poem. Nor is there such a limitation of the portrayed present to itself alone, because the present in the drama not only constantly renews itself but is also only a passageway, a phase of a time which is unfolding and constituting itself as a course of time. The temporal distance described above, which is often characteristic of the mode of appearance of past events and of the events portrayed in a novel, is missing in the apprehension of events which are just taking place. But there remains, if we may so put it, a distance of apprehension or of perception which cannot be eliminated in the drama. This latter distance disappears, however, in a lyric poem, as in the one by Wierzyński discussed above. The "now" of the poem and the "now" of its receiver coincide in all their qualifications and in what fills them as if they were one and the same "now." It must not be forgotten, either, that the fullness of the receiver's experience becomes dim in a peculiar way on the periphery of the experience.[33]

33. Of course I do not deny that the poem by Wierzyński can be read and conceived of in a quite different way as well. For instance, we could read it in such a way that the temporal distance and the perceptual distance are both preserved and also without touching in any way the real difference between the reader and the lyrical ego. I grant it,

A natural objection is the following: the time in which the poem is read is, despite the poem's shortness, surely not "a single moment." Surely several seconds pass before we finish reading the poem. When we read the last words of the poem, the moments in which we began to read the poem are already over and thus belong to the past. Then how can one speak of a single now of the reader which is supposed to be made to coincide with the "now" of the poem? Nor can we say about this "now" that it constitutes a single present, because even the poet or, if we prefer, the lyric "I," will certainly not be able to pronounce his words, spoken in rapture, "in a single moment."

Although this objection rests on a misunderstanding, I mention it here because it will allow me to discuss another way in which temporal perspective manifests itself in the literary work of art. But what is this misunderstanding?

I mentioned earlier that one must distinguish between phenomenal, qualitatively determined time and time measured by the clock, especially physical time. Both Bergson's observations and the later, much more extensive investigations by Husserl of experienced, filled time justify us in considering this distinction. When I speak about a "now" or a present moment, I am not concerned with time measured in seconds or fractions of seconds. The moments of phenomenal time, if they are to be compared with clock time at all, must be regarded in this comparison as temporal phases [34] which, when measured, can be "shorter" or "longer." The concretely experienced "moments" differ from one another because of their different qualitative, unique, and, as Bergson rightly states, unrepeatable coloring. This coloring is clearly determined primarily by what fills the moment, that is, by what is happening in the experiencing subject's sphere of experience. The coloring is also determined in part by a certain echo of what has just passed and an announcement of what may be coming. But two factors are decisive in making it a single moment, a single now: first, uniform qualitative coloring; second, the actuality of everything which has this coloring and fills the now, although it is framed by retention and protention. It is a single temporal unit, and only as such does it

---

but I then disregard the question whether such a different way of reading can constitute a faithful concretization of the poem. I am merely concerned with the fact that it is possible to read the poem in the way I have tried to demonstrate in the text; this is not possible with works of a different type.

34. Although this does not tally with experience!

sink into the past, acquire the quality of having "just" been, and then remain in a sense incidentally present in active memory; after it has sunk into the past, it can be "recalled" only with the help of a special act. But then it is already something which has lost its self-presence forever and thus is transcendent to the act of recollection, however vividly we may remember it. This former "present" which has become past is subject to the temporal perspective we have described. But in all the modifications in which it appears again, this moment always appears as a single identical temporal unit.

In the poem by Wierzyński we discussed, the "now" is filled by the whole psychological situation and attitude of the lyric "I" expressed or portrayed in the text. This determines the uniform coloring of the "now." Because the coloring is uniform and encompasses the whole temporal phase in which the poem unfolds, it is a question here of only a single now, a single present, and not of a temporal flow in which we can distinguish several qualitatively determined units of time. This does not exclude the possibility that there are various elements in this temporal unit, such as the preparation and the culmination of the emotion being discharged.

As long as we apprehend this poem in the (admittedly somewhat one-sided) orientation toward what belongs to what is portrayed or expressed, without paying attention to other sides of the poem, which reveal themselves in a full aesthetic apprehension, then everything we have just said about the temporal structure of the poem is valid. But it must be supplemented. The poem we are discussing, like all literary works of art, is a many-layered formation. In the analysis carried out above, we considered only one of its strata, and that only from its temporal aspect. The phonetic stratum and the stratum of semantic units were not considered; nor was the fact that this poem consists of several sentences, which must be read in a shorter or longer phase. When we read the second verse, the first verse has already been read and is retained in active memory as soon as we understand the whole poem and apprehend it aesthetically. The phonetic formations and phenomena such as rhyme and the speech melody of the line are also developed in the temporal phases of the reading. Both, the semantic units of the sentences and the units of the lines, allow the temporal flow of reading and the appearance of the poem with regard to the sequential structure of its phases to emerge as rhythmical.

Let us lay aside the question whether the "length" of the

poem permits us to read all its sentences within the scope of our single present or whether the sentences and phases at the beginning already pass beyond this scope or even, in longer poems, must necessarily pass beyond it by the time we apprehend the last words. As already indicated, this depends to a great extent on the span of the reader's present. It can vary from reader to reader and even for the same reader, according to his concentration and the level of exertion of his consciousness at the moment. But if the first lines or words are beyond the scope of our present moment when we come to the end of the poem, then they must sink into the past—however "close" a past it is —and then appear in the garb of temporal perspective, insofar as they still resonate in the reader's consciousness. That cannot be without influence on the formation of the poem. With the shortness of the successive sentences, which are closer to emotional outbursts than to calmly formed thoughts, with the repetition of certain phrases, they introduce a factor of unrest into the poem, a lack of self-control in the face of this overwhelming emotion, which breaks through the barrier of silence. The sound of these individual, forcibly expelled words and the sentences tossed out at random form a complement to the content of what is portrayed by means of them and supplement it in a peculiar way by adding their own unrest to the fullness of dynamics and emotion. By apprehending how they follow one another, how some are dying out while others are just emerging and beginning to be heard, we supplement the now of the rapture with a factor which harmonizes with it and with the violent emotion of the lyric "I." The reader identifies himself for a moment, in imagination, with the thus-formed lyric "I." It is obvious how important it is in this case for the constitution of the poem as a whole that the "earlier" phases of the poem be retained in active memory in their peculiar temporal perspectives. A diminution of the active memory and the replacement of the function it performs by special acts of recollection would call into question the whole of the poem as revealed in the concretization and threaten to destroy it.

It is very important, of course, even with much longer works of art, to retain the earlier phases of the (concretized) work in active memory or else, if it is necessary, to recall them in all their strata, no matter in which temporal structures the events and processes in the stratum of portrayed objectivities come to appearance. The longer a work is, the richer becomes the multiplicity of the different phenomena of temporal perspective in which the earlier phases of the concretized work appear. It cannot be stated in general which phenomena will pertain in individual cases, since they are quite diverse and can appear in a varied selection. Here we are merely concerned with indicating the particular group of phenomena which are significant for the apprehension, particularly the aesthetic apprehension, of the literary work of art.[35] When we consider the way in which the reader retains the "earlier" phases of the (concretized) work in active memory or recalls them, we must take into account, in some selection or other, all the phenomena of temporal perspective discussed above. In moving along with the new phases of the work which are revealing themselves to us, we "see" the previous parts of the work under constantly new phenomena of temporal perspective, usually in a selection which is at least partly determined by the content of the part of the work we are just reading. These changes in our way of "seeing" what we have read reveal not only the dynamics of the work itself (and not merely of the events portrayed in it) but also the type of its unified structure, which is based in the peculiarities of its composition. We perceive (or in a sense experience) these features of composition [36] during the course of the reading, but not always in the same way. The way we perceive the features of composition is dependent on both the work and the reader's receptivity and his openness to the structural peculiarities of the work.

We can state as a result of these observations that, as we slowly progress from beginning to end of a work in reading, we apprehend the concretized work from a constantly new temporal point of view but always under a temporal aspect which corresponds both to the standpoint and the attitude assumed by the reader and to the part of the work we are presently reading. No one of these aspects, of these temporal perspectival "foreshortenings," alone can make the whole work of art present to us in its actuality during reading. Each of them reveals only a single

35. Herder was the first German philosopher to see these temporal phenomena of the sequence of parts in the literary work; at least he mentions them in a polemic against Lessing, without, however, analyzing them in greater detail (see Herder's *Kritische Wälder*). In later times, Fr. Th. Meyer, in his *Poetik* [I was unable to find this reference.— Trans.], has been the only one to point them out, but he, too, did not further explore the phenomena of temporal perspective and their role in the aesthetic apprehension of the literary work of art.

36. These features of composition can be apprehended conceptually only through a scientific analysis of the work, which would go beyond both ordinary reading and the aesthetic apprehension of the work.

fragment of the work in a "foreshortening." Only in the succession of all the parts of the work during reading do we obtain the whole system of its temporal aspects, which, if we could have them all at once, would be able to give us the totality of the work of art in a single aesthetic apprehension. But this possibility is excluded by the very nature of the literary work of art as an ordered sequence of parts. The literary work of art can reveal itself to us in reading only in a temporally unfolding continuum of phenomena of temporal perspective, if, of course, reading is not interrupted, which always happens when we read a novel. Thus it is not permissible to demand the kind of apprehension of a work of art which would be completed in a single "now" and encompass all its phases and strata. Such a demand would only prove that one had neither apprehended nor understood an essential feature of the literary work of art.

§ 19. *Cognition of the literary work of art after reading*

IT MIGHT PERHAPS BE SAID that we know the work from all sides only at the moment in which we have finished reading and still have a vivid impression of the work. I shall discuss later what can be done after the reading of a work to bring about a better and different apprehension than is possible during the (first) reading. But the opinion that it is better or easier to apprehend a work from all sides after the reading is an illusion. If we keep the work in active memory directly after reading, or if we still recall it vividly—we sometimes speak of "reexperiencing" the work—then we naturally have it in only one temporal perspective, from a definite point, namely, the end of the work. This aspect of the work has certain advantages over those we have in the course of the reading; it gives us, at least in principle, the whole work. We know that there are no more parts to follow, that nothing is missing, which is, of course, important for our understanding. In theory, everything should have been explained at this point. But when we consider temporal perspective and the aspect of the work from the end, then this aspect does not render the work in any more adequate way than any earlier aspect. At any rate, we cannot remove the various perspectival "foreshortenings" which may be present, and it is perhaps only more difficult to survey the whole of the work under the aspect of the end. Moreover, the so-called impression the work makes on us in the moment we finish it and under which we live for a time is simply an echo of the perception just past (an experience of a peculiar kind). No part of the work is itself present to us any longer in actual apprehension, whereas, during reading, at least one phase was always present to us. And we must make a special synthetic effort to apprehend what is already past, in order to achieve a résumé of the whole work.

But it must be admitted that the aspect of the work which we have, or at least can have, after finishing our reading plays for various reasons an important role for the cognition of the work, not merely because we have already become acquainted with all parts of the work in the direct experience of reading, but also because we now have within our field of experience the definitive ordering of the objects portrayed in the work and of the sequence of parts in the mode of portrayal; we know, too, how all the strata of the work are coordinated with respect to one another. Thus it is only at the end of reading that the reader possesses not just all the (raw) "material"—if we may express ourselves in such a way—but also the "material" as it is arranged, once and for all, with all the internal relations which exist among the diverse components of the work. Knowing this allows the reader to begin a further cognitive effort on the work and enables him, in particular, to perform analytic and synthetic acts of apprehension, on which a deeper knowledge of the work depends. These cognitive acts which are (possibly) performed after the reading must be subjected to a special analysis. They are quite diverse and can follow various courses, depending essentially on the peculiar characteristics of the work itself and on the attitude, the interest, and the capabilities of the reader. But all these acts presuppose that the person trying to perform them has really completed the first reading of the work; we have tried here to describe some features of this reading. Without it we have no experience of the work, and any acts of cognition or observation which would relate to the work are without an object. It is necessary to return again and again to the results of the reading, especially when some details of the work are forgotten or were never clearly apprehended in the first reading. The cognitive processes unfolding after reading allow us to see such gaps and refer us back to the work itself. Without this return to the work and without rereading it, one cannot progress in the effort to understand the work in its own peculiar construction and in its specific details and to apprehend it synthetically. Reading brings us to the source, to the work itself. All judgments made about the work must be measured against what is given in the work or what can be gained from it. To be sure, it can be claimed that becoming acquainted with the work during reading, when the individual parts of the work first constitute themselves for us, is merely the beginning, the preparation for the cognitive operations which are later to be performed on the work itself. But this "preparation," as the phase in which one gains experience of the work, is not only indispensable but is also irreplaceable, since it is decisive for all cognitive operations which might follow upon it. Of course, we can read the work again, as a whole or in part. But despite its possible shortcomings, the first reading has the advantage over all following readings that it decides in large measure whether one will succeed in a correct apprehension of the work at all. The first reading is particularly important for literary works of art, which are perceived in an aesthetic attitude and which make possible the constitution of the aesthetic object. Later this may become more clear. For the time being, we must be satisfied with what we have indicated here.

One final remark. The fact that the literary work can be brought to appearance only in a multiplicity of successive aspects which flow into one another and cannot be apprehended all at once, in a single act—just as a statue cannot be seen from all sides at once—is perhaps the clearest proof that the literary work of art is transcendent to both the diverse acts of apprehension performed during reading and the multiplicity of aspects under which it comes to givenness. It is something toward which our acts of consciousness are directed, which they try to apprehend, successfully or unsuccessfully, but which is always beyond these diverse processes of consciousness. Now one can see clearly that the theory according to which the literary work of art is supposed to be contained in the "mind of the creator" or the "mind of the reader" is fundamentally false. That theory could arise only in an atmosphere in which people knew nothing about the nature of the literary work of art. They simply read the individual works without becoming aware of what kind of objects they were dealing with and what really happens in reading. I have tried to give a first indication of what takes place in reading. But we are only at the beginning; we must still overcome many difficulties and elucidate many obscure points.

3 / Remarks on the Cognition of the Scientific Work

§ 20. *On the difference between the scientific work and the literary work of art*

BEFORE I PROCEED to further questions, I must make a few remarks about the cognition of a scientific work in contrast to the cognition of a literary work of art.

In *The Literary Work of Art* I tried to establish the structure of the "literary work" in a very broad sense. The particular cases of the literary work are, on the one hand, the literary work of art (the work of belles-lettres) and, on the other hand, various works in the medium of language, among which the scientific work is most prominent. An essential feature of the scientific work is that it is intended to fix, contain, and transmit to others the results of scientific investigation in some area in order to enable scientific research to be continued and developed by its readers.[1]

If it performs other functions in the process, these are not essential, and it performs them almost incidentally. But the literary work of art is not primarily intended to form and fix scientific knowledge in concepts and judgments, nor does it serve to communicate the results of scientific research to others. And should it accidentally happen to do so, then that goes far

---

1. See, in this connection, *The Literary Work of Art*, pp. 328–30. [*Das literarische Kunstwerk* (Halle: Max Niemeyer, 1931; 2d ed., Tübingen: Max Niemeyer, 1960; 3d ed., 1965), pp. 350–52 (3d ed.); English translation by George Grabowicz, *The Literary Work of Art* (Evanston, Ill.: Northwestern University Press, 1973).]

beyond its proper function. The literary work of art does not serve to further scientific knowledge but to embody in its concretization certain values of a very specific kind, which we usually call "aesthetic" values. It allows these values to appear so that we may see them and also experience them aesthetically, a process which has a certain value in itself. If in a particular case the literary work of art is unable to embody these values for some reason, then the whole supply of transmitted knowledge of one sort or another which may be present in it is of little help. The work is a failure and only appears to be a work of belles-lettres. What we have just said holds also when the work manifests no aesthetic values but does express important philosophical or psychological insights; it is still no work of art. And, conversely, it is a mistaken undertaking to examine and interpret literary works of art as if they were disguised philosophical systems. Even if literary works of art sometimes perform other social functions or are used in the performance of such functions, that adds nothing to their character of being works of art, nor does it save them as works of art if they embody no aesthetic values in their concretization.

From this fundamental distinction in function between the scientific work and the literary work of art it follows that the former has a completely different structure from the latter, although both are "literary works" in the broadest sense. This difference in structure can be summarized as follows.

1. All assertions in a scientific work are *judgments*. They may not all be true, they need not all be true, but all claim to be true. As judgments they allude to means of confirmation which are supposed to show that claim to be justified and which are either found in experience, outside all written scientific works, or are contained in proofs which are themselves literary, that is, given in conceptual language. If a scientific work does not refer back to means of confirmation, then it can still transmit certain results of cognition; but it becomes much more difficult to verify the assertions made in the work, and the functional value of the work becomes less.

By contrast, literary works of art (or at least works that claim to be works of art) contain no genuine judgments. As I have tried to show elsewhere, they contain only quasi-judgments, which make no claim to being true, not even if their content out of context could be judged with regard to its truth value. Even then they do not function in the literary work of art as true sentences in the logical sense.

There is an analogous difference in the two types of works between sentences which have other linguistic structures. Thus, for example, interrogative sentences in a scientific work are genuine questions which are seriously posed concerning an existentially autonomous sphere; that is, they demand an answer. They also claim to be "correct," although it sometimes becomes apparent that they are incorrect; for instance, they may contain a false formulation of a problem.[2] Such questions, however, do not appear in the literary work of art. That does not, of course, exclude their being posed by the persons portrayed in the literary work of art, but then they retain this function only in the framework of the portrayed world. By the way, the same applies to sentences uttered as judgments by a portrayed person. These, too, claim to be true only within the framework of the portrayed world, where they themselves are merely "portrayed assertions" and do not belong to the basic text of the literary work of art.[3]

2. To be sure, a scientific work, like a literary work of art, also has a stratum of "portrayed objectivities." Here, too, these are intentionally projected by the sentence meanings. The meaning intentions of these sentences normally pass through these objectivities and aim at corresponding (analogously determined) objectivities in a sphere of being which is independent of the scientific work, e.g., in the real world. They thereby claim to determine these objects by their meaning in just the way that the objects actually are in themselves. Therein lies the claim to truth of judgment sentences in every scientific work. It has its source in the assertive function of the judgment sentences. The projected, merely portrayed objectivities in the scientific work constitute, to be sure, a formation which necessarily arises from the intentionality of the sentence meaning; but at the same time they are only an involuntary by-product, which is not noticed at all in the correct reading[4] of a scientific work. The function of the scientific work consists in directing the reader's intention, realized in the understanding of the sentences (judgments), to the objects which are transcendent to the work. These objects are supposed to exist of themselves, independently of the work,

2. In this connection, see my "Essentiale Fragen," *Jahrbuch für Philosophie und phänomenologische Forschung*, Vol. VII (1925).
3. See *The Literary Work of Art*, § 26.
4. Precisely how a scientific work is read correctly and how it can yet be read otherwise is a question to which I shall return immediately.

and to be determined exactly as the meaning of the judgment sentences in the work shows.

3. At first glance we would perhaps be inclined to maintain that the objectivities portrayed in a scientific work function primarily to depict the transcendent objects which correspond to them in an autonomous sphere of being. This is, however, not true. In order really to perform this function, they would have to be given to the reader in reading just as in a literary work of art. But this is not normally the case. "Normally," that is, when the scientific work is read as it should be read. But how do we read it when we apprehend its function correctly? We read it as a multiplicity or a connected group of judgments which assert something about certain objects independent of the work. That is, we realize the meaning content of these judgments from the outset in such a way that we turn, in the intention we have from the work, directly to the ontically independent objects and seek to apprehend them in the light of this intention, in both their qualitative determination and the mode of being which is ascribed to them by the assertive function. In this attitude, the purely intentional, merely portrayed objectivities are, as I once expressed it, "transparent" for the reader. They do not even appear in the reader's field of vision. Consequently, they are not compared with the ontically independent objectivities, nor do they have the function of "depicting" or "representing" these objectivities.

There are, however, moments in the reading of a scientific work when they are seen and also apprehended. That happens when we either do not understand something or begin to doubt whether the sentences in the text are really as true as they pretend to be. Then we try to become aware of what constitutes the "conception" or, as we say, the "thought" of the author. And then we concentrate our attention either on the meaning of the sentences themselves or on the intentional correlates which correspond to them. We read the sentences anew and attend to all the words employed, as well as to their syntactic interconnections, etc., in order to check on our understanding. In the second case, when we begin to doubt the truth of the sentences, we seek to apprehend the sentence correlates and, in particular, the states of affairs; we perform the previously described operation of "objectification," after which we finally attempt to apprehend clearly the objectivities projected by the sentences just as they are intended or as they have been constituted on the basis of the completed (checked) objectification. The portrayed objectivities then either stand out clearly and unequivocally, or they contain certain obscure points or double determinations, as it were, or else they do not constitute any comprehensibly consistent whole at all. And only when this work of apprehension and understanding of the portrayed objectivities appears to be relatively complete do we begin to confront the product which we have obtained with a "reality" in order to check the correctness of the opinion—which is a consequence of the assertive function—that "such a thing" exists in a sphere ontically independent of this work. Only at this moment does the "depicting" function which is allotted to the portrayed objectivities appear. Its effectiveness is tested in the confrontation with "reality." In this process we must, of course, go beyond the scientific work in question and establish a direct contact with reality on our own. The way in which this occurs depends on various circumstances. It can, for instance, involve referring back to appropriate relevant experiences or an appeal to facts which other scientific works recognize as already known and indubitably existing. The comparison achieved in this way between the portrayed objectivities in the work and those given to us in some way which is independent of the work can lead to various results. Either the portrayed objects are recognized as a correct, faithful picture of "reality," or they are rejected as fiction or error by appeal to "experience." Finally, we may be obliged to correct or elaborate on the results of previously gained experience on the basis of facts in the work which we at first doubted. We thus gain a "more correct" experience by a new attempt. We can then also see that the newly gained experience confirms the work's claim to truth.

All these operations and attitudes on the part of the reader and the corresponding modifications in the function of the portrayed objectivities are absent when we simply read the scientific work in an ordinary way and, realizing the meaning intentions of the judgments, refer them directly to the objects transcendent to the work. These operations are absent in another way when we are dealing with a literary work of art. The reader's attention is immediately directed at the portrayed objectivities in their depicting function. Consequently, they appear from the outset in their own peculiar character and present an independent reality to the reader, just as if they were themselves that reality. But once they become quasi-present to the reader, given the proper attitude on his part, they constitute the object of an aesthetic apprehension, and their aesthetically relevant qualities are enjoyed to the full by him. After that, any comparison with a transcendent "real" reality ceases. For the objectivities portrayed in the work itself appear as this presumed reality.

4. As has already been noted, aesthetically relevant qualities can appear in the various strata of a scientific work and can even lead to the constitution of specific aesthetic values. But they need not be present in this work at all, and they represent, if they are present, a dispensable luxury. Sometimes they can even hinder the work in the performance of its proper function by making the reader's approximation to the transcendent reality brought to cognitive apprehension in the work more difficult. In a literary work of art, on the other hand, these qualities constitute not only an essential element but in fact the most important element in the work of art as brought to aesthetic concretization. Their polyphonic harmony is the aesthetic value of the work of art; when they are missing or do not lead to any harmony, ending rather in a qualitative conflict which cannot be resolved in any higher harmony, then the work in question is either entirely without value or else has a negative value [*Unwert*], and any further good qualities it may have are still unable to save it as a work of art. And to be a valuable work of art is, after all, its "determination."

5. But what about the stratum of aspects in a scientific work? Aspects can appear in a scientific work, but in general they need not be present in it at all. Whether they are there and held in readiness in the proper place depends above all on the domain of the objects which are treated in the work. It can be about objects which belong to the sphere of things perceived by the senses, for instance, works of art brought to appearance. But the objects can also be of the kind that are not perceivable at all or even imaginable. This is the case in some areas of mathematical investigation. Then the schematized aspects do not, and indeed cannot, appear in the work. The scientific work in question then has only three strata. But where aspects are held in readiness by the peculiar characteristics of the dual stratum of language and by the kind of objects determined in it, and where they are also concretized by the reader, two kinds of things can occur. Either they perform an auxiliary function in the cognitive apprehension of the objects to which the sentences refer, or else they do not. In the latter case they are dispensable and could cease to exist without damage to the work. But they

could also disturb the reader in gaining knowledge of the work. Then it would be better if they were not present at all or at least were not actualized by the reader. But if they do perform an auxiliary function, they can help the reader "imagine" the objects referred to more easily and thus also help him understand the work more precisely or understand the situation which is supposed to prevail in the sphere of being which is transcendent to the work. Sometimes, therefore, works which concern basically unperceivable and also unimaginable objects, as, for instance, in microphysics, are intentionally so written in form and content that they employ "models." That is, in place of the objects which they are actually dealing with, they specify other objects, which are, however, isomorphic to these in certain respects. These other objects have the advantage that they are at least in principle perceivable and that their portrayal holds predetermined and in readiness a multiplicity of schematized aspects. With the help of these aspects the reader is then better able to "form a picture," by analogy, of the situation that is actually under discussion and thereby to perform the acts of actual understanding of the text and also to proceed to the apprehension of this situation itself. Then the presence of the corresponding aspects in the scientific work is justified, although they involve their own dangers to the proper employment of such works. But even when they are present, they play a completely different role from the role they play in the literary work of art. In the latter, to be sure, they also serve to help "form a picture" of the objects, not as "models" of other objects which are transcendent to the work but rather as the independent "reality" which is being portrayed in the work of art itself. But this is only one function of the aspects, to bring out another stratum of the same work. That function is by no means the whole reason for their presence in the work of art. Their most important function is that their content makes visible new aesthetically valent qualities. Thus the aspects participate in the constitution of the polyphonic aesthetic value of the concretized work of art, enrich that value, and concretize the harmony of aesthetically valent qualities. It is a deficiency or a flaw in a literary work of art if the aspects held in readiness are not present or appear only very rarely and then have few aesthetically valent qualities, or if they introduce discord into the harmony of these qualities. On the other hand, the absence of the stratum of aspects in a scientific work is completely unimportant, except in the special case already mentioned, where it has a share in the cognitive function of the work.

6. Finally, the same holds for the metaphysical qualities, which often play a very great role in the literary work of art; in the scientific work—except, of course, where they constitute the object under discussion!—they are quite dispensable and can be a distracting factor when they do occasionally reveal themselves. But when they themselves are the theme of discussion in a scientific work, they play a completely different role from the role they play in a literary work of art. In any case they are not there to contribute to the aesthetic value of the scientific work, and it is not so important that they reveal themselves and produce a certain emotion in the reader. They are there only to be recognized in their peculiar nature and to be conceptually grasped, where this is at all possible. That is, of course, completely different from the purpose of their presence in the work of art.

We could point out still more differences between a scientific work and a "literary" work in the narrow sense. For example, we could show different types of scientific works and try to determine their peculiar characteristics. But what we have said is sufficient for us to regard the distinction between these two basic kinds of "linguistic" works as established.

§ 21. *The understanding of the scientific work and the perceptive apprehension of the literary work of art*

IT IS REMARKABLE that until now there has actually been no theory of the cognition of the scientific work. This is all the more remarkable because the answer to the question about how science is possible as a system containing intersubjectively verifiable results of scientific cognition depends on the solution of the problems which crop up with regard to the cognition of the scientific work. Science so understood develops gradually in a historical process by means of the research of individual scientists and by the registering of their results in scientific works. It is indispensable to the origin and further development of science that scientists understand one another and agree on the results already attained and on questions which are still open or doubts which may arise. Only in this way is any supervision possible; only in this way can results be proven true or false, where this is necessary. Mutual understanding is, of course, achieved in part in oral discussions and in part in written works, but both come down to the same thing. Assertions and theories which are merely spoken are basically also linguistic (or "literary") works, although they have not been set down on paper. It is necessary to the existence and continued development of science that we become acquainted with the content of these works, first, because we must all apprehend the same linguistically formulated results if the process of checking results (of proving truth or falsity) is ever to be put into operation and to be meaningful (otherwise we simply "talk over one another's heads"). Second, however, it is only with the aid of scientific works that we can learn what has already been accomplished by others in the science in question and how this came about. This can aid our own cognitive efforts and supplement our ignorance in cases where we would not accomplish anything on our own. All our present scientific cognitive labor is only a continuation and augmentation of science which has already been created, and scientific works only unburden the memory of mankind. Without the existence of the whole scientific literature, not only would every advance in science and human culture be delayed, but it would also be impossible to maintain the level already attained. It is also highly important that scientific works be not merely available but also that they be read and understood in precisely the sense which is contained in their sentences and groups of sentences.[5]

5. One might be tempted to formulate this sentence differently. Namely: It is important that the scientific work be understood in precisely the sense which its author gave it (which was intended by its author). But such a formulation leads us astray, taking us from our problem to the question of the agreement of the mental experiences of two human beings, as if there were no identical system of meaning— precisely the scientific work itself—between them, and as if this work were only a stimulus which sometimes, it seems, fails to work; but then there is no means of proving its capacity in this regard. That is a regression to the psychologistic-positivistic line, according to which the scientific work is only ink on paper. This road does not lead to a solution to the problem. The neopositivist reduction of the phonetic stratum of sentences to flecks of ink, and of their meaning to its "verifiability," also fails to solve the problem. (See, in this connection, my article "Der logistische Versuch einer Neugestaltung der Philosophie," *Akte des VIII. internationalen Kongresses für Philosophie* [Prague, 1934]; also "L'Essai logistique d'un refonte de la philosophie," *Revue philosophique,* Vol. LX, nos. 7–8 [1935].)

But then it is equally important to know in what way an understanding of the scientific work takes place and how a faithful and exhaustive apprehension of the meaning of the sentences in the work can be attained by this mode of procedure. It is also extremely important to study what dangers and difficulties stand in the way of the correct understanding of a scientific text and whether they can perhaps be removed and, if so, how. For if it should turn out that it is not possible, even with the greatest exertion and most extreme caution, to unearth the meaning of the sentences of a scientific text and to actually understand them in an unambiguous way, then the possibility of obtaining identical cognitive results in the research of different scientists would be left to good fortune.[6] And in any case there would be no question of mutual assistance in research and consequently no question of any real progress in the development of science.

In order to take the first step in solving the problem before us, it will be useful to make ourselves aware of the differences between cognition of the scientific work and cognition of the literary work of art. That there are indeed such differences appears to follow from the dissimilarity of the two types of works.

When we read a scientific work for scholarly purposes (and not, say, to enjoy its style, composition, or clarity of thought), we ultimately want to attain, through its mediation, to a knowledge of those objectivities to which the judgments in it refer; we want precisely that knowledge with which the work is supposed to provide us. Our interest in the scientific work is thus much more limited and much simpler than the interest we have in reading a literary work of art, particularly in the aesthetic attitude. The structure of the latter is much more complicated and richer than that of the scientific work. Many of the elements and factors of the scientific work are insignificant when it is read for information. In particular, any aesthetically relevant qualities which happen to be present in the stratum of phonetic formations in the scientific work are completely irrelevant. They are usually ignored in reading, too, even if they somehow show

6. This danger would be inescapable if the psychologistic conception of the literary work were correct. Consequently, it was of fundamental importance to me to first make clear the structure of the literary work. But even the exhibition of such a structure of the literary work, which I believe I have clarified in outline, does not suffice to solve the problem which we are now facing.

themselves vividly. The exclusive function of the phonetic stratum in the scientific work is as a means for determining meanings of words and sentences, and otherwise it plays no part in the work. Since the verbal sounds and the phonetic phenomena are known to fluctuate greatly and, with varying intonation, can lead to the determination of a meaning different from what was foreseen, it could seem advantageous to leave the phonetic stratum out of the scientific work entirely and to replace it with characters fixed unambiguously once and for all. These characters would be symbols for concepts, as positivistic mathematical logic, for example, has postulated but has never actually carried out.

A faithful translation of truly great literary works of art hardly seems possible, whereas with scientific works a "good" translation is not impossible, though it may often be difficult. That fact indicates that the living natural language, with its phonetic material and numerous stock phrases, is able to accomplish more than artificial scientific symbols, and also more than another natural language, which in turn has at its disposal other possibilities for forming thought. Aside from various extra-semantic functions which corresponding words in two living languages can perform analogously, and which can sometimes function rather as distractions in scientific languages, it is often very difficult to find words in two different languages which have exactly the same meaning or the same ambiguity. The subtle shifts in the meaning of individual words in turns of phrase, which even in a scientific work can be of invaluable service, can hardly be grasped in a purely conceptual way, so that it would be difficult to bring them into relief by means of artificial symbols. Not all words can be strictly defined with regard to their meaning, as the logistical attempts at the creation of formalized languages have clearly shown. It is an illusion to think that the phonetic stratum in the scientific work could be so constituted that every ambiguity could be removed and replaced by an unambiguously fixed stratum of graphic symbols.

From these remarks, however, we see what is involved in the "correct" apprehension of the scientific work. The words appearing in it should be precisely noted as regards their sound (or their printed symbols) and should be employed, with whatever in them is essential to the unambiguous determination of the meaning, for the understanding of the work. Anything else that is still present in the way of verbal sounds and that can perform this or that function may simply be ignored in reading, and actually should be ignored. Noticing the artistic function of the phonetic phenomena, for instance, can distract from the attempt to understand the scientific work correctly. In general it is important to free oneself from the influence of the aesthetic-emotional attitude in order to give free reign to purely cognitive functions with respect to the objects treated of in the scientific work. The situation of the aspects which may be held in readiness in a scientific work is analogous, unless the aspects perform a particular cognitive function in the work. In general, we do not need to actualize them or even to pay attention to them in reading a scientific work. Nor is it necessary to apprehend any aesthetically relevant qualities appearing in the content of the aspects in reading the scientific work. The same holds for all aesthetically relevant qualities which can appear in a scientific work. In this respect the function of reading a scientific work is considerably simplified, and it seems much easier to read such a work than to read a literary work of art. Nonetheless, there exist special difficulties, which we must discuss in a preliminary manner.

The main task for the reader is the correct and exhaustive understanding of the stratum of semantic units in the work. The difficulties under consideration vary greatly according to the work and also according to the area of knowledge with which the work deals and, finally, according to the state of knowledge in this area. The difficulties can be very great or they can be insignificant, but they never disappear. In a literary work of art, the ambiguity of individual words as well as of whole sentences can be intended and can often be a means of portrayal. Much is said in similes, metaphors, and figurative or pictorial language. These linguistic phenomena are by no means a flaw in artistic form; they can, on the contrary, often play a thoroughly positive, even an indispensable role in the work. But the ideal of a scientific work is a text which is as unambiguous, "rigorous," and precise as possible. That means, above all, that it must have a stratum of semantic units which is constituted in an unambiguous way. And much, if not everything, must be staked on realizing this ideal to a high degree. But basically it can never be fully realized. There always remains, as stated, a trace of ambiguity. Consequently, the reader, even one who wants to follow the intentions of the work, is almost never forced to understand the work in a specific, completely unambiguous way. If he is uncritical, or if he is influenced too strongly by his own linguistic habits, he will automatically read the work with the interpretation which comes to his mind in reading and will not even suspect that the text may contain ambiguities which open up the possibility of understanding it differently. Hence this manner of reading can lead to crass misinterpretations. If the reader is critical enough and sensitive to multiple interpretations, he is often faced with the necessity of deciding which of the possible interpretations of the text have been read into it by him. In scientific works written in a good and responsible manner, one of these interpretations is usually distinguished as the "most probable." But in order to find it and also to decide in favor of it, the reader must look for reasons why it is really the "most probable." There are various ways and means of finding these reasons. For example, one can investigate the peculiarities of the language of the work (particularly of the scientific terminology for the area of knowledge in question) or of the language of the author. One can consider other sentences in the context or the consequences following from each of the possible interpretations. One should especially consider the contradictions which would be avoided by another interpretation. What course this may take in the individual case can only be shown in a particular work. But one thing is certain: even if we succeed in reaching a decision by these means and in selecting the "most probable" interpretation, this choice is usually made with the aid of an understanding of the other parts of the work (or of other works) and can be recognized as correct only to the extent that these other parts have been correctly and unambiguously understood (in the event, of course, that they are intelligible at all). The correctness of the reader's decision is conditioned by the correctness of his understanding of the other parts of the work (or of other works). This procedure, or the attempt to resolve a noticed ambiguity, only shifts the problem of the unambiguous understanding of the text of a scientific work from the understanding of one text to the understanding of other texts. Is it ever possible, by means of this circular process, to reach the solid ground of unambiguous understanding? Further, it is clear that the reading of a scientific work cannot take the same course as we demanded for the literary work, namely, a straight and uninterrupted running-off of all phases of the work from beginning to end. What was undesirable with reference to an adequate aesthetic concretization of the work of art and an undisturbed aesthetic apprehension of this concretization has no disturbing effect in the cognition of the scientific work. On the contrary, it seems advisable to make interruptions, to read individual passages repeatedly if necessary, to juxtapose and compare different parts of the work in order to avoid the threat of ambiguity or misinterpretation. The meaning immanent in the work is not simply encountered but rather must be worked out in operations which are sometimes complicated and difficult. Thus a certain distance arises between the reader and the text of the work (that is, the dual stratum of language). But this does not mean that the semantic units of the judgments become, or even ought to become, objects of cognition. There are certainly phases in which we consider how the meaning of the sentence in question or the meaning of a whole set of connected sentences should be understood. And then it occurs temporarily that it is the meaning toward which our attention is directed, and the meaning itself thereby becomes an object to a certain extent. But as soon as a decision is reached as to how it is actually to be understood, the meaning is absorbed, as it were, into the intention of the mental act and is quite simply thought. Then the assertive function of the sentence is thought along with the meaning, so that what is intended, the relevant state of affairs or the object revealing itself in states of affairs, becomes the actual object toward which the understanding of the reader is directed. This object is then an object (state of affairs, thing, event, etc.) existing in a specific ontic sphere and transcendent to the work. Hence a successful understanding of the semantic units in the dual stratum of language in the scientific work takes the reader beyond this work to a "reality."

We do not always succeed in removing all the ambiguities we notice in the text. There are often cases in which the reader clearly recognizes, by means of a critical and analytical reading, which ambiguities are present and which readings of the text are possible in view of them but still does not succeed in choosing the "most probable" interpretation. Then there is no other recourse than to confirm that the work is ambiguous in a particular passage and to be clearly aware what different readings the text allows. And it is then advisable, in further reading of the work, to keep those possible interpretations in mind and to check how the interpretation of the further parts and, finally, the interpretation of the whole work appear when one takes into account the unresolvable ambiguities. The attitude of the reader toward the reality determined by the work is then noteworthy. He can no longer think of it as existing fully determined in itself. The judgments which were formerly simply made, formed (or, more precisely, made, formed, at the suggestion of the work), are now made with some reservation. The stratum of merely portrayed objects, which becomes completely transparent in the case of judgments simply read and formed at the suggestion of the work, then begins to emerge in its ontic character, which appears in the content of the portrayed objects. This stratum then reaches toward an ontically autonomous sphere of being but is yet not fully posited there. The transcendent sphere of being begins to distance itself; it is not actually capable of being apprehended, although the sentence meanings and assertive function are still directed at it. The judgment sentences formulated unambiguously in the work nevertheless allow the reader to get a foothold in this reality which is transcendent to the work and —already independently of the work—to seek in it facts which could allow him to emerge from the uncertainty and ambiguity which have arisen. For the intellectual impulses which he has received from the work often allow him to cognize on his own the facts existing in the relevant sphere of being more easily than he could without the aid of the work. This is only natural, for every scientific work actually serves to facilitate precisely this independently performed cognition. It also often happens that we are already familiar with at least some of the facts stated in the work from other sources or from our own experience, and then we read the work from the outset in the light of those facts; consequently, we understand it more easily. This has its advantages, of course, but it also has its drawbacks. The advantages lie in the fact that it is then easier to understand the work during reading. Almost every scientific work (with the exception, perhaps, of some philosophical works) is today an advance in the cognitive mastery of a particular sphere of being. The language of the work is taken over extensively from other works in the same field. It makes use of a series of established terms for concepts and complexes of concepts and is partly re-formed and partly augmented in only a few details, e.g., by the introduction of new terms, by making some concepts more precise, by rejecting previously assumed sentences as false, etc. Of course, all this is of little help to the reader who is reading the book in question with no preparation. One understands a scientific work only if one has mastered its technical language; often, of course, this is not sufficient, and it is also seldom possible on the sole basis of the work in question. The work only helps the reader to apprehend the changes which the language undergoes as a result of new scientific advances. One must learn for oneself what has preceded the developments in the work.

From the work itself the reader learns only that further development of research which is indicated in the work; he thus increases his own knowledge of the relevant area of being.

There are many dangers in this process, above all the danger that the work read may be misunderstood by the reader under the influence of the language of a branch of knowledge which he has previously mastered or under the influence of facts he knows from experience. This can occur in various ways. The reader's prior knowledge, having become automatic, often has the result that unimportant shifts in the meaning of individual expressions which are based on the new cognitions in the work remain unnoticed by the reader. The sentences are then understood in a language no longer present in the work. The facts newly discovered in them are often not precisely apprehended in their peculiar nature and novelty because one would have to perform new free acts of cognition in order to achieve this apprehension, and these acts of cognition are obstructed by the automatic prior knowledge. Thus the facts newly portrayed in the work are given a different interpretation, or are simply rejected, in the light of the previously recognized theory. The difficulty of a correct understanding of scientific works which are really creative and demand of the reader that he apprehend something new lies in the fact that on the one hand he must have complete mastery over his prior knowledge, but on the other hand he must have the strength to free himself from the burden of transmitted factual material and from linguistic habits and be intellectually receptive to the new things that the work offers. In order for the reading of such works to be really successful, however, the reader must still have the strength to maintain his intellectual freedom in relation to what is newly offered after he has apprehended it with as much penetration as possible. He must still be able to discover facts which permit him to check the new knowledge critically by an independent search for the corresponding facts in the relevant ontic domain. Such an attitude on the reader's part is especially useful in the case of philosophical works which contain in seminal form a revolution in the intellectual atmosphere of the time.

Direct contact with the facts in a domain of being which is independent of the scientific work is made easier for the reader from the start in such a work by the following facts. The sentences appearing in a scientific work are genuine judgments, which refer with their meaning intentions directly to states of affairs transcendent to the work itself. These states of affairs are grounded in a domain of being which is ontically independent of the work and in most cases is also existentially autonomous. If the reader follows the meaning of the text and makes the judgments at the work's suggestion, he immediately finds himself in a domain of independent objects and is then able to cognize them with the help of his own acts of experience. On the basis of the factual material he has found, he can then, on the one hand, understand more clearly the sentences read and, on the other hand, find in them the point of departure for further research. The scientific work does not actually fulfill its intended function if it does not bring about the necessary investigative attitude in the reader and does not help him attain to an existing reality beyond the work itself. This kind of assistance is simply absent in the case of a literary work of art, since there is no such corresponding ontically independent domain for that work. The sentences appearing in the literary work of art cannot assume the function of leading the reader to such a domain. And anyone who, in reading a literary work of art, seeks such a domain of facts ontically independent of the work is making a great mistake. The proper function of a literary work of art lies in making possible for the reader an appropriate aesthetic concretization of an aesthetic object. In reading a scientific work, the reader does not fulfill the task before him if, after he has understood it as precisely as possible, he does not know how to go beyond it to the corresponding "reality" and if he does not linger upon it with his investigating gaze in order perhaps later to return to the work and then accept it or reject it or else only then reach a correct and deeper understanding of it.

But if we want to apprehend a literary work of art faithfully, then knowledge of certain objects existing outside the work which are in some way similar to the objectivities portrayed in the work or which are supposed to be somehow "depicted" by the work are of no help in the effort to understand fully and correctly the sentences of the work. This also holds for the "historical" literary works of art (as, for example, "historical" novels or dramas). Here the reader's main task is to apprehend the meaning of the words and sentences in the work of art faithfully, and as completely as possible, exclusively on the basis of their own content. To be sure, our prior knowledge of the objects existing in reality and similar to the objects portrayed in the work cannot be completely without significance. But in reading a literary work of art, this prior knowledge can often be the source of false suggestions or—even worse—it can lead the reader to read the work of art not as a work of art but as information concerning a certain reality.[7] This unfortunately often happens with naïve readers, who are not mature enough for an aesthetic apprehension of the work. But it is worse when, as happens even in some circles of literary study, literary works of art are read and "interpreted" in this way and are even evaluated from this standpoint. The world portrayed in the work of art then either disappears altogether from the reader's field of vision, or, if it is apprehended, it is only attended to in order to be compared with a reality. Then a value is attributed to the work only if the objectivities portrayed in it agree with that reality. The aesthetic apprehension of the work of art itself and the aesthetic value response to it do not then occur at all. The considerations of literary works of art carried out from this point of view, interesting as they may be for other reasons, contribute little either to their aesthetic analysis or to the understanding of the essence of literary art. Just as the literary work of art is not read as a work of information, and in particular not as a scientific work, so the scientific work must not be treated as a work of art. This sometimes happens to philosophical works, as if they did not have to achieve knowledge of a world independent of themselves but were rather mere "conceptions," "world views," of certain peculiar poets. In order to apprehend a literary work of art faithfully in its proper form, regardless of whether it is a "historical" work, in which the portrayed objectivities legitimately perform the function of "depicting," or a work whose structure makes it clear that it is not such a work, it is necessary to tear ourselves away from the familiar extraliterary reality and submerge ourselves in the microcosm of the work of art with all its strata and to reconstruct it in such a way that all its points of artistic excellence are utilized for the constitution of a faithful aesthetic concretization. And for this reason it is often much harder to apprehend faithfully the world portrayed in the work, and all the rest of the elements of its many-layered and

7. It has become fashionable lately to treat works of art in general as information (as Max Bense does); but this problem would have to be treated in a special study. It is only to be noted here that the fashionable concept of "information," in the sense of "information theory," has been so expanded as to include everything possible, even, for instance, the members of a causal relationship, with the result that any application of it to the literary work of art, for example, becomes so vague as to be practically meaningless. Moreover, we would have to elucidate just what it is that we are being informed about in a literary work of art.

many-phased totality as well, then to understand the assertions of a scientific work. The whole process of becoming acquainted with a literary work of art is fundamentally different from that of understanding a scientific work.

This is also apparent from the following details, which we must yet discuss. The faithful apprehension of a literary work of art takes place through experiences which are much more complicated than those through which the understanding of a scientific work takes place. All those factors which in the former case are of the greatest importance to aesthetic apprehension have no part in the understanding of scientific works. This applies especially to all the aesthetically relevant qualities which constitute aesthetic value but which are totally unnecessary to the scientific work and its essential function, should they by chance appear in it. We do not need to occupy ourselves with them in reading the work; if we did, it would tend to have a disturbing effect. The simple apprehension of the meaning of the judgments appearing in it could suffer as a result. The aesthetically relevant qualities could place the reader in an emotional attitude which could not help but influence his acceptance or rejection of the assertions contained in the work. This clashes with the essential function of the scientific work. The cognition of such a work is nothing other than the correct understanding of its stratum of semantic units and, through that, the cognition of the "reality" (in the proper sphere of being) which is transcendent to and intended in the work. Anything else which may occur during reading must be subordinated to this fundamental task.

One further point: it is important for the constitution of a faithful aesthetic concretization of the work that the order of succession of its parts be preserved. Any alteration of this order, for example by a transposition of its parts, affects the characteristic traits of its composition, often produces completely different dynamic effects, and alters the appearance of specific phenomena of temporal perspective both within the framework of the events in the portrayed world and in the sequence of the parts in the work as a whole. All this has, or at least can have, an influence on the actualization of aesthetically valent qualities and consequently also on the constitution of the aesthetic value founded in them. Sometimes even apparently insignificant alterations or an insufficient apprehension of certain details of the work of art can prevent it from being constituted at all in the final aesthetic form which is proper to it or which adequately expresses its artistic essence. In other cases its positively valuable aesthetic qualities come to appearance only in an incomplete form. The equilibrium of the qualities in the whole of the work of art can become shaky as a result and can lead to the constitution of various flaws in the work. Lengthy interruptions in reading, the repetition of certain parts of the work during reading, referring back to parts which have already been read and have sunk into the phenomenal past—all this disfigures the aesthetic concretization of the literary work of art and its aesthetic value. But this exercises no disadvantageous influence on the apprehension of the scientific work. On the contrary, it often aids in its correct and deep understanding. Schopenhauer once said that one must read his work *The World as Will and Idea* twice in order to understand it correctly. One might correct that to "several times," with repeated reading of individual parts, with comparison of various assertions, etc. Cursory understanding by rapidly running through the sentences can succeed only with very superficial works. For the most part, understanding is not to be attained without the correct apprehension of the logical and material connections among the individual assertions and the correct evaluation of their logical function and their degree of cognitive importance. For with the possible exception of the deductively written systems in mathematics or logic, scientific works are not generally written in such a way that they always preserve the logical order of sentences in their presentation and shape the logical structure of the investigation through this order. This is especially the case with those authors who already have much knowledge in the domain of being in question and in their works provide only fragments of what they have to say in this area. Then only certain central theses—often of a very sketchy nature—are provided, and the reader must himself fill in the rest, either from other sources or on his own. But it is precisely the emphasis on the logical connections among the assertions, as well as the verification of their formal correctness, for instance the correctness of the arguments they present, which helps the reader to understand the scientific text better. This is often not as productive in the reading of a literary work of art, because there strict logical connections among the sentences need not always exist or be preserved. And a certain "illogic" can sometimes be employed as an artistic means. The reader of a scientific work, however, is often forced to make himself independent of the sequence of sentences and to rearrange them on his own in the sense of their logical order. It is often only then that the significance of certain assertions can be judged and that certain details which may have been ignored can be brought to the fore. In this way we can approximate the theoretical unified whole which the work itself provides only in outline. To be sure, we thereby go beyond the actual form of the work in question. This causes no harm, however, since it is actually demanded by the work itself. We are, after all, supposed to go beyond its contents and further develop the cognition begun in the work and carried only to a certain point. Indeed, every scientific work constitutes only a phase in the great process of research and can never provide a comprehensive knowledge which embraces the whole of a theory. It opens up new horizons of problems and points to new courses for the investigation to take. If it does not do this, it is somewhat unfruitful. None of this is true for the literary work of art. It is a whole in itself; and if it opens up certain horizons to the reader, it does so only in the sense that there are points of departure for possible concretizations which are still, however, true to the work. An attempt to go beyond the work of art in the way that is possible and permissible with the scientific work would lead at best to completely new literary works of art, and these would by no means be a continuation of the work of art in question. The work of art—in the present case, especially the literary work of art—is not simply the high point of a creative process but is also its completion, in which it comes to a conclusion and rest. The work, if it is successful, is the embodiment of the artistic form which simply hovered before the author's mind. Beyond this completion there is no possible continuation, such as is certainly possible and quite natural in the case of a scientific work.

Perhaps these sketchy comments will suffice to convince us that we do and should behave differently in reading a scientific work for scientific purposes than in reading a literary work of art, a reading which leads to the actualization of an aesthetic concretization of the work. Perhaps these comments will also be of significance for those who occupy themselves in a scientific way with literary works of art. They can serve as a warning to these scholars not to read works of art as we read scientific works about literary works of art. Precisely as scholars dealing with literary art, they must not be merely scientists. They must read literary works of art as aesthetic receivers, as literary consumers, and in a certain phase of their dealing with the works they must also be artists themselves. That is, they must be able to feel themselves into the course of the poetic creation and thus be able to understand the finished work of art in its artistic intentions and in the means which lead to the realization of these intentions. In this way they can inform themselves about the artistic accomplishments of the work of art which they are investigating. Only after they have already constituted an aesthetic concretization of a work of art on the basis of a reading performed during the aesthetic experience can they make this work of art and the concretization obtained from it into an object of their scientific investigation, an object of special, new, often very complicated efforts at scientific cognition, which must to a certain extent be undertaken on the basis of the aesthetic experience of the concretized work of art.

The next chapter will permit us to treat of these questions in somewhat greater detail.

4 / Varieties of the Cognition of the Literary Work of Art

§ 22. *Outlook on further problems*

THE PRECEDING EXPOSITIONS had the task of sketching in a preliminary way a schema of the first acquaintance with the literary work of art. They constitute only the beginning of the investigation of the problem. It was necessary to carry them out under a number of simplifying conditions in order to get our bearings in the multiplicity of experiences and phenomena which come to light in this area. It is too early to set aside these simplifying conditions at this point, since we would then find ourselves in a tangle of complicated and varied facts and processes which we would be unable to master at this stage. Thus the following deliberations will also yield certain results which must also be seen as idealizations or preliminary "approximations." Such a procedure seems to be natural and unavoidable whenever one investigates a basically unexplored field. Once more, however, it must be emphasized that we are not doing psychology here. I do not dispute that the actual reading of literary works of art proceeds in very diverse ways and is often disturbed or even broken off by external circumstances, although there is still a lack of empirical psychological research in this area, so that we may still assert nothing about how the individual reading proceeds in reality. What I am seeking to show is merely that the simplifying conditions given above allow us to trace a general schema of the reader's modes of procedure in becoming acquainted with literary works of art and that this schema determines the limits of the possible variations in actual readings, insofar as no disturbing influences essentially modify their course.

Our further reflections will be carried out in two different ways. We shall (*a*) continue the descriptive analyses and (*b*) pose the problems of an epistemological investigation, that is, an investigation which attempts to gain at least a preliminary clarity regarding the possible cognitive value of the results obtained in the various modes of cognition of the literary work of art. It is chiefly a matter of sketching the epistemological problems which, on the one hand, concern the results of the cognition of the literary work of art as regards their truth value or objectivity and, on the other hand, relate to these cognitive operations as regards their ability to achieve such results. Such an investigation would lay the first foundations of a critically oriented epistemology of the mode of cognition of the literary work of art and of the literary work in general. Only on this basis can we raise the question of the "possibility" of literary studies, on the one hand, and, on the other, of aesthetics as a study of the experience of works of art, a question which is often decided negatively without exact formulation and precision of the basic problems.

Let us add a few further introductory remarks.

The descriptive investigations must distinguish, above all, the different possible typical varieties of cognition of the literary work, particularly the literary work of art. There are two sources of difference in modes of cognition. The first source of possible difference lies in the reader's adopting very different attitudes with regard to one and the same work and consequently conducting himself in different ways with respect to it. His behavior varies with the different goals which he hopes to realize. The second source of differentiation of his conduct lies in the fundamental differences between literary works in general and literary works of art in particular. These differences force the reader, or the literary scholar, to employ different ways and means of gaining knowledge of the work. Of course we are concerned here in both cases with the typical differences and not with those which can appear from work to work and from reader to reader. Sometimes both kinds of typical variations intersect and then lead to multiple complications in the course of cognition of the literary work which can scarcely be surveyed here. We must therefore adopt some simplifications and abstractions here as well. Unfortunately, the investigation of the basic types of literary works of art has not yet been concluded.[1] Thus it will be necessary for now to postpone those investigations which deal with the diversity of modes of cognition which are connected with the differences among the basic types of literary works of art; we must confine ourselves to the variations of cognition of the literary work of art which arise from the basic types of possible attitudes of the reader (or scholar). I shall occupy myself here, however, only with two different attitudes of the reader, specifically with the attitude of the scholar, who reads the work for the purpose of scientific knowledge and investigates it in one way or another, and with the attitude of the reader who is concerned above all with bringing the work through a reading to the actualization of an aesthetic concretization in order to enjoy it aesthetically in this concretization and to contemplate it. This contrast seems to be important, for it is related to the basic epistemological and methodological problems of literary study as a study of works of art of a quite specific kind. We shall see that the cognition of the literary work of art for specific purposes of research can also be accomplished in two basically different ways: in a "preaesthetic" and an "aesthetic" way. In the first, the literary work of art itself in its schematic form constitutes the main object of study; in the

1. Almost forty years ago, when I gave my readers *The Literary Work of Art* [*Das literarische Kunstwerk* (Halle: Max Niemeyer, 1931; 2d ed., Tübingen: Max Niemeyer, 1960; 3d ed., 1965); English translation by George Grabowicz, *The Literary Work of Art* (Evanston, Ill.: Northwestern University Press, 1973], I hoped that my general conception of the literary work of art would furnish literary scholars with a tool which they could use to attack, among others, the problem of the so-called literary genres or basic types of literary works of art. My expectations have been fulfilled only to a relatively limited degree. Still, several studies have appeared which try to take up this problem from the standpoint of general literary studies and which, it seems to me, come to results which agree with my view. The authors in question did not, to be sure, refer to my book; but a certain similarity in the aim of the investigation can be noted. These results seem to me to be present above all in Emil Staiger's *Grundbegriffe der Poetik* (Zurich: Atlantis, 1946; 2d ed., 1951) but also in a number of works about the novel (among which I include Käte Hamburger's book) and, finally, in many of the investigations by Polish literary scholars (which are, of course, unknown in the West). Among the last group, Julius Kleiner, Manfred Kridl, and Kasimir Wyka deserve mention. I should also mention the preparatory formal work done after the war in Poland at the Institute for Literary Study of the Polish Academy of Sciences, as well as the studies published in the journal *Zagadnienia rodzajów literackich* (Problems of Literary Genres), edited by Stefania Skwarczyńska. Nonetheless, the state of scholarship and of the problems which I have developed here is still far from the point where I would be able to refer to concrete results and to use them as a starting point for the related epistemological investigations.

second, however, the object of study is its concretization actualized in aesthetic experience. Later we shall see that there must be a phase of reflection in literary study in which both attitudes, and the procedures connected with them, must necessarily be brought into connection. It is only from this phase that there arise quite specific problems of literary art (of artistic effectiveness), as well as various further problems in connection with the scientifically based evaluation of the (individual) literary work of art and the legitimacy of this evaluation. But for the moment these are very distant prospects of the problems we have to treat. Even the cognition of the literary work of art which is accomplished merely for the purposes of aesthetic consumption can be accomplished in two different ways, which must also be considered here.

Only when the descriptive considerations have led to relatively satisfactory results and the lacunae which we have necessarily left until now have been eliminated will we be able to approach the epistemological problems of the cognition of the literary work of art. I hope that we shall be successful in formulating here at least a few basic problems of the critique of the cognition of the literary work of art as a specific kind of work of art. The solution of these problems will have to be left to the future.

§ 23. *On various attitudes in the cognition of the literary work of art*

WE READ LITERARY WORKS OF ART with very diverse attitudes. Some read them only to kill time and to amuse themselves in the process. Others read them simply because they want to have commerce with certain peculiar objects which we call "works of art." They believe that works of art are gifted with quite peculiar capacities and with equally peculiar characteristics which we call values and, in particular, aesthetic values, and they strive to come into contact with them and to obtain enjoyment from that contact. It is not this enjoyment, however, which constitutes the actual goal which we want to attain in reading. This enjoyment is only a kind of special gift which we receive because we do justice to the work of art in direct contact with it. There are, however, also readers who are scientists in their basic attitude and who read literary works of art in an attitude of "investigation" and want to attain in this way a true and well-grounded answer to the question of how the work is structured, to which genre it belongs, etc.

I shall not occupy myself any further here with how literary works of art come to be known by readers who merely want to amuse themselves without caring what it really is which gives them enjoyment. Since they undoubtedly read, they probably have to perform the majority of the cognitive acts which we tried to describe above. But they do it merely fleetingly, imprecisely, and idly, simply in order to progress and to find out how the story ends. They look up the "happy ending." Since they care nothing about a faithful concretization of the work of art or about the value which comes to appearance in it, but only about their own experience and the experienced pleasure, their concretization of the work usually takes on a very imperfect and distorted form, which, however, satisfies them and gives them enjoyment. They could just as well employ other means of experiencing such enjoyment; the work is degraded to a mere tool of pleasure. The preponderant majority of readers, to be sure, belongs to this type of "consumer," but they can be of interest only to the psychology or sociology of the mass consumption of art. They play no role for our purposes, except, perhaps, at most as an example of how literary works of art should not be read, since such a reading does them an injustice.

But we must examine the characteristic features of the acquaintance with and cognition of literary works of art in readings which (1) serve the purpose of investigation or (2) are carried out in an aesthetic attitude. In both these cases the literary work of art or its concretization ceases to be a mere tool for some other end and becomes the main object of the reader's activity, particularly of his acts of consciousness. In Chapter 1 I attempted to characterize those experiences which play an essential role in both modes of cognition of the literary work of art. Now we are concerned with working out the modifications which result from the different attitudes of the reader.

Above all, it is necessary to characterize the two attitudes of the reader which are here being contrasted. They constitute only particular possibilities within the two general attitudes which a person may assume in his contact with the objects which confront him: (a) the purely cognitive or "investigating" attitude and (b) the "aesthetic" attitude. Both are distinguished from the "practical" attitude, in which a person sets out to change or effect something in the world. This is not to say that these three attitudes are the only ones which a person can take toward life.

We usually say that we can assume any of the (three) attitudes to one and the same object. For example, if someone closes a business deal by the purchase of a picture by one of the old masters, he does so in a "practical" attitude. Similarly, when he hangs the picture on the wall of his study, his attitude is "practical." But when he wants to investigate whether or not he was cheated by the seller and has acquired a forgery, he assumes a cognitive, "investigative" attitude and makes an effort to gain knowledge of a series of properties and characteristic traits of the painting which he has purchased. Finally, when he reposes on a sofa, is sunk in "contemplation," and attempts to view the work in its totality in its artistic form, only then does he assume the "aesthetic" attitude and, in the fulfillment of the "aesthetic experience," discover the picture in its full individuality and also in the value belonging to it which has been brought to appearance. The same thing is supposed to be the object in all these three fundamentally different experiences and different attitudes of the person in question, although these experiences and attitudes differ in their goals. Specifically: in the practical attitude, the buyer wants to effect by the aid of certain psychophysical activities a new state of affairs in the real physical or psychophysical world. By his purchase of the picture he wants to create a new legal state of affairs; and when he hangs the picture on his wall, he wants to create a new physical state of affairs. In the investigative attitude, on the other hand, he does not want to create any new states of affairs in the world; in particular, he does not want to "do" anything with the object of his interest, the picture, since he merely wants to become acquainted with it or gain knowledge of it. Indeed, if it turned out that this object had suffered any alterations as a consequence of his cognitive activity, in consequence of the completion of certain cognitive experiences, he would come to the conviction that he had not succeeded in simply "cognizing" this picture. Put differently: the cognition and also the knowledge attained should apply to an object which we encounter in a real world ontically independent of our act of knowing when we begin to cognize it. The goal of this cognition is to acquire a knowledge, or, if we will, a number of true sentences, relating to this object which we have before us and which our cognizing has left untouched, and determining it in one way or another, ascertaining it in its being, all exactly as it is in itself. Finally, in the aesthetic attitude, as it is often believed, a few of the objects which we cognize are used as peculiar stimulants in order to produce strange experiences in us which are somehow enjoyable or pleasant. And here, as we are aware, the points of view diverge. The dispute is over the nature of these experiences. Some simply speak here of a sensuous enjoyment, which is supposed to be strangely "connected" with certain "mental images"; others say it is a matter of "contemplation"; still others speak of "empathy" or of some kind of feelings, particularly of "autopathic" feelings, which accompany the content of certain mental images, and so forth. The aesthetic object is from this standpoint, as before, an object which we find before us, just as those objects are which are subjected to some action or cognition. It is supposed to belong to the real world and to be itself real, as is, for example, a physical thing, quite apart from whether it is simply a "natural object"—like, for instance, "beautiful mountains" or "a beautiful old oak"—or a physical thing made by an artist, perhaps a block of marble. According to this conception, it is distinguished from other real things in that it has or only appears to have certain particular features which we usually designate by the words "beautiful," "handsome," "charming," "pretty," etc., which, however, are supposed to be nothing but the ability of the object to produce certain experiences (feelings, sensations, and so on) in the person perceiving it. Often the passive character of the aesthetic experience is emphasized in the process, and it is described as if it were a momentary experience.

I do not have the intention of carrying out a critique of the many different conceptions of the "aesthetic experience" here. This would take up too much space and carry us much too far from our main subject. On the other hand, an attempt to give the positive characteristics of the aesthetic experience as well as its correlate, the aesthetic object, seems to me indispensable. I shall confine myself to the main points.

§ 24. *The aesthetic experience and the aesthetic object* [2]

IT SEEMS TO ME that the fundamental error of all previous conceptions which I have alluded to in the preceding section lies in the assertion that the same thing which constitutes an element in the real world and at the same time an object of our actions and our cognition is also the object of an aesthetic experience. There are undoubtedly circumstances which seem to justify this conception. Have we never had the experience of drawing back the curtain from our window on an early spring morning and suddenly seeing the trees in our garden, which have blossomed overnight, shimmering in the bright sun against the blue sky? We are dazzled and quite delighted by the magnificent bloom of the fruit trees in the early spring morning. What pleases us so in this? Is it not certain real things which we encounter in the world around us, which we see before we experience this delight at the true wonder of their beauty and which we also continue to see when the wave of feeling and pleasure has already abated? And is it otherwise, one might ask, when we wander through the halls of the Louvre in Paris and all at once, from afar, catch sight of the *Venus de Milo,* snow white against a dark background, in all her slenderness and agility and with the charm of her barely indicated movement? Is what pleases us not just a block of marble which is simply formed in a particular way? What does our admiration refer to? The fact that this shaped block of marble is the work of an artist does not seem to change in any way the fact that what pleases us can be known by us in a purely cognitive, investigative attitude, as when we

2. A short résumé of this section constituted my lecture at the Second International Congress on Aesthetics in Paris in the year 1937. My lecture was also published at that time in the reports of this congress (see "Das aesthetische Erlebnis," *IIe Congrès International d'Esthétique et des Sciences de l'Art* [Paris, 1937], I, 54–60). An English translation of the Polish version of this section, as it appeared in the book *O poznawaniu dzieła literackiego* (The Cognition of the Literary Work of Art) (Lvov: Ossolineum, 1937), was published in the journal *Philosophy and Phenomenological Research*, Vol. XXI (1960), under the title "Aesthetic Experience and Aesthetic Object." The text reproduced here is somewhat expanded; the original conception, however, has remained unchanged. ["Das aesthetische Erlebnis" is also published in Roman Ingarden, *Erlebnis, Kunstwerk und Wert* (Tübingen: Max Niemeyer, 1969), pp. 3–7. —Trans.]

establish the mass of the statue or observe exactly the surface of the marble in order, for example, to assess the damage which it has suffered in the course of time.

The facts just adduced are undoubtedly true, and yet the theory which is advanced on the basis of such facts appears to be erroneous. The fact is merely that we begin with the perceptions of a real thing in many cases such as those just adduced. The question, however, is whether, proceeding from a real object, we also remain with it when the aesthetic perception (apprehension) takes place in us and, second, whether this proceeding from a particular real object (e.g., a block of marble) is indispensable in every aesthetic apprehension.

The fact that we are pleased by objectivities which are completely fictional, conceived by us in our imagination, which were thus never perceived by us and can never be perceived, proves that the second of the questions just asked must be answered in the negative. We can, for example, conceive of a very tragic interpersonal situation about which we are certain from the beginning that it never took place and which we have also never experienced or perceived in our relations with other people, and nevertheless we can assume a positive or negative aesthetic attitude toward it. Any literary work of art can provide further examples. Literary works of art do not exist as physical or psychological or psychophysical objects. Among physical things there are merely books, that is, in their present form, pieces of paper with colored signs (printer's ink) bound together in volumes. But a book is not a literary work of art; it is only a material tool (means) for giving a stable, relatively unchanging real foundation to a literary work of art and in this way providing the reader with access to it. Among psychological states and experiences appear only acts of reading, which were described above, or various mental acts and mental images which refer to a specific literary work of art, have it as their object, but are not literary works of art themselves. In spite of this, however, literary works of art or their concretizations can be objects of aesthetic experiences or at least objects on the foundation of which, with the proper aesthetic experiences, specific aesthetic objects are constituted, provided the constitution attains a certain conclusion in the experiences. In connection with our second question, it can be doubted whether, in reading or hearing a literary work of art, we must not after all have to do at first with a real thing or process, with printed signs on paper or with the concrete phonetic material. At first glance it seems that we really often do have to do with a real thing. But we do not need to, since we could very well read the work by the aid of merely imagined written signs. Second, there is the question of the degree to which we really sensibly perceive and must perceive the individual paper and the individual flecks of ink themselves in the concrete reading of a printed book. Are we not rather immediately disposed to apprehend the typical forms of the printed "words" or the typical verbal sounds, without bringing to consciousness what the individual written signs look like? [3] We do not, therefore, have to begin every aesthetic experience with the perception of an individual real thing in order to make the transition to another, no longer real, object.

The example of "reading" proofs leads us to suppose that, even where the whole process of the aesthetic experience begins or seems to begin with a sense perception (a simple seeing) of a real thing, the reality of this thing and the apprehension of its reality and individuality are not at all indispensable to the completion of the aesthetic apprehension or to the unfolding of the whole aesthetic experience or, finally, to the direct contact with the aesthetic object. Suppose that when we perceive the block of marble which, according to the general conception, is the *Venus de Milo,* we are subject to a strange deception or illusion. We would then of course be convinced that we were perceiving this block of marble as something real, but this would be just an illusion; "in reality" there would be no such real thing in that hall of the Louvre, or else there would exist something completely different from what is (ostensibly) perceived by us. Would an aesthetic experience then be impossible? To this we must answer: as long as only the phenomenon of the Venus de Milo continued to exist, nothing would change in the conditions of an aesthetic apprehension. The same traits of the concretized work of art would be given us, and we would feel at the proper moment the same admiration. The reality of the perceived physical object (the marble block) and the apprehension of this reality are thus not at all necessary for the unfolding of the aesthetic experience. Normally there is also no question of an explicit apprehension of the reality character of the marble block and its individual

---

3. We can convince ourselves of this, for example, in proofreading, where we so often "overlook" errors. That is, we immediately focus on the typical features of the verbal sign and do not even apprehend the strictly individual features in our perception. Thus, in the simple reading of a literary work there is no real transition from the individually perceived thing to the no longer simply perceived, "seen" word type; rather, we apprehend typical verbal forms immediately.

characteristics. And even if this reality character and the individual traits of the stone were apprehended, neither this reality nor these traits would constitute the reason why something pleases or displeases us. Otherwise, all objects appearing clearly in their reality character would be "beautiful," "handsome," "charming," "graceful," etc., for us, which is by no means the case. On the contrary, the distinct apprehension of the reality of the block of marble disturbs the free unfolding of the aesthetic experience, the object of which is the Venus de Milo. For we must basically leave the block of marble behind in a peculiar way, we must forget it to a certain extent, in order to achieve the unfolding and the free continuation of the aesthetic experience, in which the Venus would not merely be constituted but also felt as beautiful.

This does not suffice, however, for us to maintain that in no case of aesthetic apprehension of an aesthetic object and of disclosure of its beauty or ugliness do we remain with the real thing, with the perception of which the aesthetic experience began. It could be that, although the mere reality of the perceived object for itself alone is not necessary for the appearance of the aesthetically valuable features of the perceived object and does not result in or influence the appearance of these features in any way, still there might be other determinations of the real object which are both source and object of the aesthetic experience. This opinion is held by those scholars who consider the objects of aesthetic experience and apprehension to be simply certain particularly constituted, real, sensibly perceivable things. Everything depends, they say, upon this particular constitution, and beyond this nothing else need be considered.

In order to decide this question, let us note above all what we do when, in a purely cognitive attitude, we seek knowledge of a real thing with the help of appropriate sense perceptions or experiences. Second, let us note what we do when an aesthetic experience takes its course in us and brings us to a peculiar object which is somehow aesthetically valuable for us in direct experience of a particular kind. We shall not succeed in making this clear, however, so long as we hold fast to the rather widespread prejudice according to which the two activities or attitudes here contrasted are just certain momentary experiences which differ from each other only in that, in the second case, a "feeling" of pleasure or displeasure attaches to the momentary, immediately passing sense perception, whereas in the first case there is no such feeling.

Cognition of a real thing in sense perception (or cognition

merely aided thereby) and the so-called aesthetic experience, which we shall immediately consider, are both temporally extended events which develop in multidetermined phases and in the course of which several distinct acts of consciousness are performed.[4]

The block of marble which we know today as the *Venus de Milo* can be cognized in the investigative attitude only by way of performing, before all else, a multiplicity of sense and, in particular, visual perceptions, which often follow directly upon one another but which need not necessarily so follow. These perceptions, however, must not—as Max Scheler once maliciously maintained—be a mere "gaping." Rather, they must be so intelligently directed and concentrated on the block of marble that we make ourselves conscious in performing them of what kind of thing we are dealing with and how it is constituted. In doing so, we must take note of the way in which the object is given in its constitution and under what conditions it is given. For this mode of givenness entitles us to recognize that the determinations in which the object is given really belong to it as its attributes.

There appear, therefore, in the process of cognition not merely perceptions but also certain judgments in which the results of perception are combined and conceptualized and in this way brought to the consciousness of the subject of cognition. The results of various perceptions of the same block of marble must then be compared with one another and perhaps combined, in which process the objective and subjective conditions under which the relevant perceptions took place are taken into consideration, since they have an influence on the cognitive evaluation of these results. Here it is a question, for example, of the kind of lighting in the space in which the block of marble is situated, of the appearance of other objects (things) in the field of vision, and of the environment of the perceived thing, which can produce at least certain apparent characteristics in the perceived thing by being observed with it.[5] The factors which influ-

---

4. The aesthetic experience has predominantly been considered a momentary experience, but there has been no lack of indications that it lasts a length of time and develops in several phases. In what follows, however, I should like to show something more, namely, that insofar as it develops undisturbed, it consists in its typical course of several meaningfully connected phases which succeed one another in a particular order.

5. We remember how the room looked in which the *Venus de Milo* was once exhibited. At that time the walls were covered with red cloth,

ence the content of what is given in perception do not even need to be certain things appearing in the field of vision; there can, for example, be disturbances, moods, or feelings appearing accidentally in the perceiver. The presence of such disturbances, etc., is by no means produced by what is given in perception, but it does have an influence on the content of what is given. The consideration of all these codetermining circumstances has the purpose of assessing the role which they play in the course of perception and in the appearance of certain determinations in the object given to perception. The motives which guide us in this—which, for example, are constantly taken into account by physical scientists in the observation of certain things or events or in the performance of scientific experiments—are, on the one hand, the desire to attribute to the object under cognition no features which appear in perception as properties of the object but which owe their appearance to the circumstances in which the object is perceived and do not have their basis in the constitution and nature of this object itself. On the other hand, we wish to determine the properties which can justifiably be attributed to this object. There are then two different possibilities. Either some determinations are visibly given as properties of the object; then they should be attributed to the object, if their givenness does not result from certain circumstances of perception (or of some other mode of cognition) which are variable (external to the object) but rather shows itself to be independent of these circumstances and founded solely in the object to which they belong. Or else they are not given in any perception of the relevant object itself; then, however, we have the right to conclude, on the basis of a series of carefully performed perceptions, that they constitute a factor independent of all the circumstances accompanying the perception, a factor which represents the necessary and sufficient condition for the appearance of a particular quality as a characteristic of this object among the data of the perceptions of the thing in question.[6] In this case these determinations should be recognized as characteristics of the object in question. As long as it proceeds regularly, the whole process of

which contrasted in a very unpleasant way with the color of the statue. Now the *Venus* stands in a room of neutral color, which forms an unobtrusive background for the work of art. In the evening the artificial light seems too harsh. But these circumstances I have just considered are significant only for an aesthetic consideration of the Venus, which cannot be identified with the block of marble.

6. For instance: the property of the reflection of certain waves (or rays) and of the absorption of other rays of this kind.

cognition, composed of many different acts of cognition, is then guided by the idea that the results of cognition gained in it are accommodated to the object of cognition and that all those elements are eliminated from it which arouse even the slightest suspicion that they originate in some factors foreign to the object.

The situation is quite different in the relatively complicated process which, for the sake of brevity, I shall call the "aesthetic experience."

Anyone who has been in Paris and has observed at close range the block of marble which allows us the apprehension of the Venus de Milo knows that this block has various real qualities which are not only not considered in the aesthetic experience which results in giving us the Venus de Milo but which would even noticeably disturb us in the aesthetic experience if they were considered. Consequently, they are as if involuntarily overlooked. For example, the "nose" of the *Venus* has a dark speck which interrupts and disfigures its uniform surface. The stone also evidences a certain roughness, indentations, and even small "holes" on the "breasts," which seem to have been eaten out by the water, an "injury" to the left "nipple," etc.[7] We overlook all this in the aesthetic attitude in which the apprehension of the Venus takes place. We behave as if we did not notice these details of the stone, as if we had seen the form of the "nose" in a uniform color, as if the surface of the breasts did not reveal any damage. One might perhaps be inclined to say that, although we actually see the smooth, somewhat gleaming, yellowish-white surface of the block of marble, it is as if we did not see it, as if we somehow forgot that the "body" of the Venus would not, after all, be so blindingly "white" as the marble, that it would not have such a gleaming surface, etc. We overlook what does not suit our conception of the "living body of a woman," indeed of a "goddess"; and without bringing this clearly to consciousness, we supplement those elements which are in keeping with the form of the "living body of a woman." These elements are not merely thought (although one would like to say it is precisely "in our thoughts" that they are there) but come somehow to vivid appearance and join harmoniously with the totality of other elements constituting the form of a woman's body. In the course of

7. Already, when we speak here of a "nose," of the "breast," of an "injury," it is clear that we have gone beyond sense perception of the block of marble. We have left this block behind and have already somehow arrived at the Venus.

the aesthetic experience exactly those factors are added which play a positive constructive role in maintaining the possible "optimum" of the aesthetic "impression" and which bring about (or at least help to bring about) the appearance of that form of the aesthetic object which brings aesthetically relevant qualities and aesthetic values to the relatively highest degree of prominence in the given circumstances.[8] In cognizing the block of marble in the investigative attitude, it would be thoroughly out of place to overlook the damaged spots and in their place to put qualities which are not present. This would amount to a conscious or unconscious falsification. In aesthetic perception of the Venus, however, this is not only thoroughly proper but even, if we may so put it, "advisable." And it occurs, strange to say, in a way which we did not at all intend, as if by itself. And it by no means occurs, as one might perhaps want to interpret it, because we persuaded ourselves that all those details which we overlook are, after all, only "later damage," which we consequently "overlook," from which we may "abstract," because it was not present in the sculpture as it came from the hand of the artist. Such a conception of this state of affairs would be justified only if we wanted, as art historians, to learn on the basis of the current condition of the statue (the stone) how it was originally, when it left the hand of the master. Then we would have to consider especially the missing arms of the *Venus* and somehow imaginatively restore them; this has actually been attempted in various and singularly unsuccessful efforts at reconstruction. But that is not what we do at all. For both the manner and the basis of "overlooking" some details and "adding" others in the aesthetic attitude and in the aesthetic apprehension of the Venus are completely different from the study of the "sculpture" just described. The details "overlooked" disturb us somehow, although they are not distinctly, "thematically" apprehended by us in their proper character and in their role as a disturbing factor. They are noticed only incidentally and in passing, and we feel or, if one pre-

8. In his *System der Ästhetik,* 3 vols. (Munich: Beck, 1905–14; 2d ed., 1925–27), Johannes Volkelt speaks of a "supplementation" [*Ergänzen*] in the aesthetic experience of "real sensations" [*wirkliche Empfindungen*] by "represented sensations" [*vorgestellte Empfindungen*]. He speaks in this connection of an "empathy" [*Einempfindung*] and of a "seeing in addition to what is there" [*Mitsehen*]. It seems to me that both are closely connected with the facts I have described here. Whether it is justified to speak of "represented sensations," whether it can be a question of "sensations" at all, we shall not discuss here. (See *System der Ästhetik,* I, 117 [2d ed.].)

fers, "sense" to a certain extent the obtruding disturbance as a disharmonious factor which threatens to undermine the developing unity and harmony of the object. We then disregard this disturbing factor to a certain extent. In all this, however, the object whose harmony and unity are endangered is not the block of marble itself, the stone, but rather, already, the Venus. For a block of marble, it would represent no "disturbance" to have a darker fleck in a particular place or a shallow indentation on a semispherical curve. Hence these facts are somehow connected: that it is not the stone but rather already the Venus which is given to us and that the disturbing details are "overlooked," since we disregard them or even apprehend in their place something almost completely different, as if we were seeing it. And because the form of the Venus is already given to us, we may speak of "hands" and "breasts," of the "head" and the "glance" of the Venus. And we may speak of them because we already apprehend this by seeing. We see the living body of a woman, although at the same time it is not really alive, a fact which peripherally we somehow do know, although we are inclined to forget it in almost the same way as we forget what we disregard or "overlook." That it is precisely Venus is, of course, something we, as modern Europeans, do not see. If we say so and also to a certain extent believe that we apprehend Venus, that occurs because we have already obtained certain information from the art historians, of course, who in the museum kindly tell us everything which appears necessary to them in their art-historical and didactic attitude. But how it was when the tradition of Greek religion or, more generally stated, the ancient Greek way of life was still quite alive is something we can no longer reexperience today. We can now only presume that this female form was indeed somehow the image of an individually determined goddess. One could say that even then some "information" that it is supposed to be "Venus" was surely necessary. But it was certainly not a question of this purely intellectual art-historical information which we are given today, without which we cannot come into contact in any way at all with "Venus" but which was scarcely necessary and useful to the ancient Greeks. They were reared in a living religion and mythological tradition and lived in it. As soon as this tradition makes its way to us, we too, in viewing the *Venus de Milo,* have the impression that we are dealing with an embodiment of a mythical goddess, although we do not see this immediately in the portrayed female form. But, however that may be, the *Venus de*

Milo is undoubtedly given to us as a young woman, and this is not the result of some secondary, conceptual knowledge (of some "information," as it is now fashionable to say) but of the fact that the statue has a particular bodily form which gives us cause to see a particular female body and, more, a particular woman. This total form is meaning-determining for the appearance of the woman, specifically because it is not at all characteristic of the marble. It stands in no relation to its general nature and is obviously artificially imposed on it from without. On the other hand, it is precisely a "female form," characteristic of the feminine body. This interpretation is forced on us immediately, at first glance. It is decided to some extent automatically that we intuitively apprehend the form of the female body in the spatial form of the stone, so that we then obtain the right, secondarily, as it were, to speak of the head, of the (missing) arms, of the breasts, of a particular movement of the entire body. We see that we are given a particular female body. And not just a body. To a certain extent we see still more in the aesthetic experience; we apprehend "Venus" in an intuitive way, but now that means only that we apprehend a particular woman in a particular situation and physical position and in a psychological state which shows clearly in the facial expression, in the glance, in a very particular smile, etc. At the same time, however, it is not a real female body and also not a real woman. We can imagine that if we caught sight of a real woman with such severed (let us say, already healed) arms, we would certainly feel a strong repugnance or disgust or, finally, sympathy for the poor woman. In the aesthetic perception (apprehension) of the *Venus de Milo*, on the other hand, nothing of the kind is to be found. Something quite remarkable occurs here. We can neither say that we do not see the arm stumps at all nor that we see them quite distinctly, direct our attention toward them, and underscore to a certain extent the presence of this defect or else somehow restore the missing arms in our thoughts.[9] In the aesthetic attitude it does not disturb us that the arms are missing. As is well known, it has often been asked whether it would not be better if these arms were not broken off. But in what respect "better"? Certainly

---

9. Both are, of course, possible, and we would certainly do them if we had the task of scientifically describing the statue in its present state or of making sketches for a "reconstruction" of the work in its original state. The remarkable thing is, however, that we do not do these things at all in the aesthetic attitude.

not for the block of marble, which has surely already lost its material value as a block. But, in the same degree, not for the Venus as a woman. One is not thinking of that at all, even if it really is better to have sound arms than severed ones. But certainly "better" for the formation of an aesthetic object coming to constitution in an aesthetic experience. And, more precisely still, "better" in reference to a value of a specific kind which comes to intuitive apprehension in the aesthetic experience and finds its foundation in this object. However much the opinions may differ as to what would be better, it is worth noting that there will be many who will answer this question with a resolute "no." Without being precisely focused on the defect of the "missing" arms, we also do not completely overlook their absence, but we see it only secondarily. We apprehend above all an intuitive character of positive aesthetic value of the whole form of the Venus; the arms do not prevent us from seeing directly the pure line of the body and the peculiar slenderness of the whole form, which shows itself especially when we catch sight of the statue from a distance and are struck by the subtlety and agility of the scarcely suggested movement of the body. The arms would bring yet a further accent and a new movement into the whole. This would have as its result a complication which is not present in the present state and the lack of which permits us to concentrate in peace on the form of the female body (it would be false to say: of the "trunk," although it would be anatomically correct).

Be that as it may, all that is certain is that the basic situation in which we come to consider what would be "better" is neither the plain sense perception of a block of marble nor the perception of a living real woman nor, finally, the cool contemplation of an art historian, who observes precisely the details of the "work of art" dragged up from the sea in order to describe it "scientifically" and who also, for the most part, relies merely on sense perception. It is rather that situation in which we weigh what would be better for the aesthetic form of the work of art. For this situation, sense perception constitutes only a basis,[10] albeit an indispensable basis, for further experiences, which receive a certain support from it and which finally lead to the apprehension of the Venus de Milo as an object of a particular aesthetic experience. As a correlative statement we can say that

10. As I shall show in the following, this basis undergoes an essential transformation in the course of the aesthetic experience.

the object of this aesthetic experience is not identical with any real object.[11] It is just that some real objects, constituted in a certain way (in particular in sculpture: things), serve as point of departure and basis for the constitution of certain aesthetic objects in the course of an experience unfolding in the aesthetic attitude. The form and various visible traits of these real objects which serve as point of departure and basis are not completely irrelevant and arbitrary if there is to be an experience in which a particular aesthetic object is constituted. The creative artist seeks to give the real object precisely that form and to bring to appearance those traits which, with the appropriate attitude on the part of the beholder, fix guiding principles for the constitution of an aesthetic object (an object anticipated and in a certain sense foreseen by the artist). Herein lie those "mysteries" of art which we are able to solve only after the work of art has already been created. But this is a theme which we cannot develop here. For the time being, all that is important is that the experience in question is not a momentary experience, realized at once and immediately extinguished, but a process which unfolds in a multiplicity of successive experiences and modes of behavior of the aesthetic beholder and which must, so to speak, fulfill particular functions in its individual phases. In order actually to bring the Venus de Milo to full givenness in aesthetic experience and to behold the values grounded in it, it does not suffice to look fleetingly at the block of marble and perhaps already at Venus from a single point of view and then calmly turn away, convinced that we have already "seen" everything. As soon as we reach the point where we see Venus, or the female form, we must view it from different sides and also from different points of view, in varying perspectival foreshortenings. On the basis of the essentially modified [12] sense perceptions which take place with the change of perspective, we must apprehend in each

11. The conception that the aesthetic object is not a real thing is emphatically defended by Johannes Volkelt in his System der Ästhetik. It also appears, for instance, in Rudolf Odebrecht's Grundlegung einer aesthetischen Werttheorie (Berlin: Reuther & Reichard, 1927). Thus the assertion just made is nothing new. But neither has very much been accomplished with this mere statement. Above all, it must be shown how this object comes to be constituted in a special experience and is brought to concrete appearance and, second, how it can be more closely described in its general form.

12. Modified insofar as the final form of the physical thing (e.g., the block of marble with a particular spatial form) is not simply given, but rather another subject is, so to speak, imputed to this spatial form—not a dead block of marble, but a living woman.

new phase of the unfolding experience the visible details of the whole, as well as this whole of the work of art itself, which disclose the aesthetic values and also give them a particular effect. And only when we have succeeded in concretizing these values in intuition and in attaining synthetically to the final unity of the whole can we give ourselves over in a quite special emotional contemplation to the magic of the visible and felt beauty of the finally constituted aesthetic object.

In individual cases, this whole, often very complicated, process can take place in very different ways.

But let us prescind from this here and attempt to apprehend generally in these manifold variations the most important traits of the structure of the aesthetic experience which remain constant.

1. In contrast to what one frequently hears, the aesthetic experience is not a mere experience of pleasure, which stirs in us as a kind of reaction to something given in sense perception. The reasons for considering this experience as actually momentary and relatively simple are only apparent. They arise from the fact that the aesthetic experience is often not completely unfolded, for quite incidental reasons. It is interrupted before the constitution of the aesthetic object is achieved, and consequently the culmination of the experience is also missing. Certain professional habits or artificial preparations keep it from developing in its whole course; it begins to unfold, so to speak, only from the middle on, after the aesthetic object has already attained to givenness.[13] Thus it is, for example, when we view a picture which we have already seen a number of times and have learned to see as it once constituted itself for us in an aesthetic experience as an aesthetic object with quite specific properties. The source of the conception of the aesthetic experience as momentary can also lie in the circumstance that it has been subjected to analysis only in its final, concluding phase. On the other hand, the constant reduction of the aesthetic experience to pleasure or enjoyment is only the expression of the primitiveness of the psychological treatment of the whole problem. The question why this experience is called an "aesthetic" experience is not even asked, although Baumgarten, for example, must already have had it in mind.

Incidentally, the length, as well as the complexity, of the

---

13. Ostap Ortwin, an important Polish critic and literary scholar, brought this to my attention.

aesthetic experience can vary greatly, and it depends on the kind of object with which we are dealing—whether it is a more or less complicated or even a simple object—and on whether the object itself unfolds in several temporal phases—as, for example, a musical or a literary work of art—or whether, at least in principle, it can be apprehended "at once," as, for instance, a picture (although in fact there is never such a thing as a momentary apprehension of a picture). Sometimes even a simple chromatic quality or the particular constitution of a tone (e.g., its timbre) can become the object of an aesthetic experience which is relatively simple and usually passes quickly; but even this experience is no momentary and simple feeling of pleasure or displeasure.

2. If an aesthetic event begins with pure sense perception, then it is a most interesting and at the same time a most difficult task to clarify wherein the transition from the perception of a real object (thing) to the aesthetic experience consists, that peculiar change from the natural attitude of practical life or from an investigative attitude to the aesthetic attitude. What produces this change of attitude? What happens when, instead of occupying ourselves with the various concerns of daily, practical, or theoretical life, we interrupt its "normal" course (often quite suddenly and unexpectedly) and begin to occupy ourselves with something else, which to some extent does not appear to belong to our life but which nevertheless enriches it in an unsuspected way and gives it a new, often very deep, meaning?

It is possible that this change comes about in different ways for different people and that it is completed in very different ways according to circumstances. But perhaps it will not be too far from the truth if I point to the following—as I believe—essential elements:

In the perception of, say, a real thing, we are struck by a peculiar quality, or a multiplicity of qualities, or, finally, a particular Gestalt quality (e.g., a color or a harmony of colors, or a quality of a melody or of a rhythm, etc.) which not only draws our attention to itself and concentrates our attention on itself but, in addition, does not leave us cold. It is somehow not a matter of indifference to us and affects us in a particular way.[14]

14. What kind of quality that is cannot be said in advance, since that sometimes depends not only on the quality itself but also on the predisposition of the perceiving subject. In the discussions about the aesthetic experience which took place in my advanced seminar at the University of Lvov in 1935–36, Frau Łuszczewska-Romahn pointed out that this is

This specific quality which attracts our attention and affects us produces in us a quite peculiar emotion, which, with a view to its role in the aesthetic experience, I shall call the "original emotion" of this experience. For it is the actual beginning of the specific event of the aesthetic experience, although it must not be forgotten that it is already the result of the affection to which we succumb by virtue of that quality which strikes us.

As stated, the quality strikes us, forces itself upon us, grips us, or however one wishes to put it. By these expressions I want to indicate that the reception of the quality is passive and, in this phase of experience, transitory as well but that the quality itself, on the other hand, is distinguished by a peculiar aggressiveness in relation to us. At the same time, both it and its presence are such that, if the aesthetic experience were interrupted in this phase, we would not be able to answer the question as to what kind of a quality it was. We receive, rather, only a sensation of it which brings us out of our equilibrium; we experience it too strongly to be able actually to apprehend it.

The original emotion, which develops from this reception of that quality, is not, however, that "pleasure" about which one often speaks to the point of boredom in various reflections on "aesthetics." At its very beginning, in the moment in which it arises, it is nothing but an excitement resulting from that quality which struck us or forced itself upon us in the perceived object. Without making ourselves conscious in the first moment of what kind of a quality it is, we feel that it attracts us, that it wants to move us to advert to it in order to possess it in a direct contact (as by touch). In this excitement there is contained at the same time the element of a certain generally pleasant surprise at the appearance of the originally exciting quality, or rather surprise that the quality is precisely such a one, that there even is such a thing, although we have not yet had time to attain to a distinct, intentional, and conscious apprehension of it. To express this at first in a metaphorical way, it touches, rouses, or excites us in a peculiar way rather than being given to us. This excitement is transformed into a peculiar transitory state of being in love with

usually a quite specific kind of Gestalt quality. In this seminar I developed for the first time my conception of the aesthetic experience which is summarized here, and I owe to my coworkers and friends of that time who participated in the seminar my deepest gratitude for many a critical comment. The war, which broke out a few years later, and the following years had the result that, of the study group, which then consisted of thirty people (in which several professors, art critics, and also several young postdoctoral students took part), only a few remain alive.

it, which in a further phase of the original emotion passes over into a more articulated, delineated emotional experience in which the following original elements can be distinguished: (*a*) the emotional, direct intercourse with the received quality, which intercourse is still in the process of developing; (*b*) a certain hunger for the possession of this quality and for intensification of the enjoyment which the intuitive possession of it promises; and (*c*) a growing striving for satisfaction from this quality, for lasting possession of it.[15]

Therefore, although the original emotion is, in its basis, undoubtedly an emotion, distinct elements of desire appear in it, specifically, of a desire which is directed toward the original quality affecting us and, at first, toward beholding it but then, however, to possessing it and enjoying its magic to the full. When we are dealing with this phase of the experience, the often-repeated talk of "pleasure," of "pleasant" feelings, and so forth, in connection with the investigation of the aesthetic experience amounts not only to a trivialization [16] of the problem but

15. Of course, all the expressions used here are metaphorical and have something of a poetic character. This is only the result of the peculiar nature of the phenomena appearing here, which cannot be named directly because language has not yet found such specialized designations. Nor are they meant to determine the phenomena under discussion conceptually; they should merely rouse the reader's sensitivity to these phenomena and direct his attention to them or move him to pay attention to such elements in analogous situations in his own experience. It is a special linguistic technique which is supposed to be helpful in detecting these complicated experiences but is not meant to perform the function of a definitional determination. No purely conceptual determination can help us here. What exercises a determining function here is only the fact that various factors in the experience of the original emotion are pointed out which should then, with the help of the metaphorical expressions, be vividly experienced by the reader in his own experience, through his own effort, and should be singled out of the whole experience. A certain ambiguity and imprecision in these metaphorical expressions even has the advantage that, within the imprecise bounds of the meaning, there is room for the different variations of the experience which can occur in individual cases. It is not impossible that someday we shall succeed in carrying the description further and in replacing the metaphorical expressions with vivid ones taken over from a creative language—expressions which will exhibit neither the ambiguity nor the imprecision of meaning which our metaphors still have. At the beginning of an analysis of experiences which we usually just have and perform without reflection, because we merely submit to them and are not trying to elucidate them, it is not possible to proceed otherwise.

16. It is a "trivialization" because (1) the expression "pleasure" or "a pleasant feeling" is so vague that it actually explains nothing and (2) in any experience, even a purely intellectual one, we can find something "pleasant" or "unpleasant." Thus, pointing out that there is an element of enjoyment or pleasure in the aesthetic experience does not teach us

also to missing the phenomenon we want to apprehend. For even where an element of pleasure appears in the original emotion, it is not characteristic of it and also does not exhaust this experience, all the less since an element of displeasure or discomfort can also appear in this emotion (if we actually want to mention such vague terms). For the original emotion is full of inner dynamism, of a kind of unsatisfied hunger which appears when and only when we have already been excited by a quality but have not yet succeeded in beholding it in direct intuition so that we can be intoxicated with it. In this condition of being unsatisfied (of "hunger") we can see, if we will, an element of discomfort, of unpleasantness, but the characteristic quality of the original emotion as the first phase of the aesthetic experience does not consist in this unpleasantness but in inner unrest, in being unsatisfied. It is an original emotion precisely because from the elements present in it are developed both the further course of the aesthetic experience and the formation of its intentional correlate, the aesthetic object.[17]

3. But let us consider, above all, the direct consequences of the original emotion for the further development of the aesthetic experience. These branch out in various directions. Specifically:

a. The appearance of the original emotion in a person's

---

either anything essential or anything characteristic about this experience. Many objections have been raised against considering pleasure an essential element of the aesthetic experience. See, for example, Richard Müller-Freienfels, *Psychologie der Kunst,* 2 vols. (Leipzig and Berlin: Teubner, 1912; 2d ed., 3 vols., 1922): "I emphasize that these feelings of pleasure merely accompany consciousness and are not themselves the essence of the aesthetic experience. If it were only a question of pleasure, then we would have to call certain substances like opium or laughing gas the highest aesthetic values" (2d ed., I, 6). [My trans.—R. A. C.]

17. In the first volume of his *System der Ästhetik,* Johannes Volkelt writes: "Especially if seeing and hearing are expressly accompanied by the feeling of sensory freshness, then seeing and hearing will be joined by a certain desire for this freshness, a certain surrender to it. It is thus a matter of the direction of our striving as determined by our disposition. We feel ourselves inclined to look, we feel ourselves lovingly disposed toward looking" (1st ed., I, 89). [Our trans.—R. A. C., K. O.] It seems to me that Volkelt has in mind here nothing other than what I call the "original emotion." But Volkelt did not succeed in analyzing it more closely; neither is he aware of the importance of this emotion for the aesthetic experience. Consequently, I adduce Volkelt's text here only as a certain fortification of my description of this first phase of the aesthetic experience. The first to notice an element of "being in love with" the quality first appearing, as well as a certain desire in the aesthetic experience, was Plato. See, for instance, his expositions in the *Phaedrus.* These elements appear, I believe, primarily in the original emotion of the aesthetic experience.

stream of consciousness produces, above all, a certain check in the preceding "normal" course of experiences and modes of behavior in regard to the objects surrounding him in the real world. What he was occupying himself with a moment before at once loses its importance, becomes uninteresting, a matter of indifference. Therefore he abandons, perhaps only "for a moment," those occupations in the course of which that quality which produced the original emotion obtruded upon him. How often does it not happen that perhaps, in walking along a rather dangerous mountain path, we are paying primary attention to the path itself and not to the beauty of the landscape. And suddenly we look up and are overpowered by the view. We then pause involuntarily. The details of the path upon which we climbed to the peak have suddenly become uninteresting to us. We no longer have time, so to speak, to pay attention to it; something else "draws" us. We submerge ourselves in the contemplation of the mountains or of the views which open up on a valley. It is the same when, in conversation about certain very important concerns or about certain theoretical questions, we are suddenly transported into the original emotion by the sight of, or by a particular expression of, a beautiful woman passing by; then we interrupt this conversation, unable to continue it.

With this "check" is connected a certain diminishing or even extinguishing of the actual experiences which relate to things and affairs of the real world. A certain narrowing of the field of consciousness relating to this world takes place, although we do not lose the involuntary feeling of its presence and existence, and we continue to feel that we are in the world. Nevertheless, our conviction of the existence of the world, which constantly colors our actuality, is shifted, to a certain extent, to the periphery of our consciousness or loses weight and force. In the later phases of the intensive aesthetic experience there can emerge the strange but well-known phenomenon of quasi-forgetfulness of the real world. This is directly connected with the change in a person's attitude which takes place as a consequence of the original emotion. I shall soon return to this subject.

The "check" which we have been talking about can be strong or weak, long or quickly passing, according to the strength of the original emotion and the preceding interest in the events of real life. If this strength is not great, and if at the same time the affairs of daily life are sufficiently important, the further phases of the aesthetic experience do not take place. After a quickly passing check in our activity, we return to daily life. A certain disorientation in the situation of our life which then appears is the best evidence that such a check has taken place, although we do not necessarily have to be conscious of it. If, however, the event of the aesthetic experience continues to develop, then the check of the "normal" course of daily life lasts longer; and either a full unfolding of the aesthetic experience or a new, stronger attraction of the concerns of daily life is needed if we are to return to this life. The phenomenon of "return" is very characteristic. That is, we usually resume the concerns and activities which were interrupted by the original emotion and return to the attitude of daily life. This latter fact is the best indication that the original emotion leads to a change in a person's attitude. The phenomenon of the "check" is only an external expression of this change. The return to the concerns of earlier life is often accompanied by discomfort, by a feeling of the pressing weight of life, from which the original aesthetic emotion had, to a certain extent, freed us. Much less frequent, by contrast, is a feeling of satisfaction at standing once again in the midst of concrete active life. There are, however, very different possibilities here, and the mood with which our active life is once again attacked depends greatly on the nature of the original emotion in question and on the state in which we found ourselves before the beginning of the aesthetic experience.

b. The influence of the original emotion extends further, however. As indicated earlier, the phase of our actual present moment (of the now) is always "framed" by an echo of the experiences of the immediate past or by events which stand in more or less intimate connection with the given present moment, as well as by perspectives on the unfolding proximate future. The original emotion causes the echo of the immediately preceding experiences to be significantly deadened and the perspective on the coming future of our real life to be eliminated or weakened.[18] Our new present moment, which is filled with

18. Of course, this occurs only when the original emotion came about unexpectedly. Under the mechanized conditions of our present life, specific hours are set aside for aesthetic experiences. We go to the theater or a concert at a specific time of day and are prepared from the outset to have an aesthetic experience "now" and to give ourselves up to the enjoyment of art. Thus we expect these experiences before they really begin to take place. If our expectations are actually fulfilled, which is of course often not the case, then the developing aesthetic experience is connected with the phase of expectation and the phenomenon of a check does not occur. But this fact must not be adduced as an argument against the description of the course of the aesthetic experience we have given here. For in the case just mentioned we ourselves interrupt the course of

the original emotion and with the further phases of the aesthetic experience which develop out of it, loses thereby any distinct connection with the immediate past and future of our daily life. It then forms a self-contained unit of life which is set off by itself and is only later inserted into the course of our life, after the aesthetic experience is past. On this quality of being set off, or, better, this separation of the aesthetic experience from the course of daily life, rests what Stanisław Ossowski in his analysis of the aesthetic experience calls "life 'with the moment' " or "in the moment," [19] which he considers to be the chief characteristic of the aesthetic experience. As we can see, this separation from daily life is only one element which can be derived from the original emotion, and it is connected with its other consequences, which we shall discuss shortly. This separation (or quality of being set off) is not, however, characteristic only of the aesthetic experience.[20] An analogous isolation from the continuous stream of daily life, as well as an immersion and a limiting of oneself to the present moment, can also be produced by other powerful experiences. A very concentrated, purely theoretical reflection on a problem which strongly moves us leads to an analogous immersion in the immediate present and to its exclusion from the course of other interests. This of course manifests itself above all when the reflection relates to very abstract problems which have no connection at all with the real world, e.g., in certain mathematical or philosophical reflections.

c. The original emotion produces in us a radical change in attitude, namely, from the natural attitude of active life to the specifically aesthetic attitude. This is its most important function. It has the result that one passes from the attitude which

---

our occupations intentionally, we ourselves check it, and it is also we ourselves who weaken the echo of the preceding experiences precisely in order to give ourselves up without disturbance to aesthetic contact with the work of art. What the original emotion otherwise effects of itself is here produced voluntarily but also, precisely because of this, artificially. Perhaps this is the reason why, if we prepare ourselves for the appearance of an original emotion, it fails to appear or, if it appears, is robbed of that original force and freshness which characterizes it when it is produced unexpectedly by a particular quality which moves us. The mechanization of life is a disorganizing or demoralizing factor for our self in this case as well.

19. See Stanisław Ossowski, *U podstaw estetyki* (Basic Problems of Aesthetics) (Warsaw: Państwowe Wydawn. Naukowe, 1935), pt. 4, pp. 259 ff. Ossowski, incidentally, speaks only about the elimination in the aesthetic experience of the attitude of orientation toward the future and does not take into consideration the weakening of the echo of the past.

20. Ossowski also ascertains this, incidentally.

focuses on facts in the real world, which are either in existence or are to be realized, to an attitude which focuses on intuitive qualitative formations and the achievement of a direct contact with them. In both sense, or inner, perceptions which are interwoven with the course of our practical interests and activities, and in perceptions which are performed for purposes of pure research, we are focused on what really is, on actual things and states of affairs. What we perceive and how it is structured are certainly not unimportant in this connection—and our efforts to discover the object are guided by our understanding of its nature and structure. In the final result, however, we are interested in the fact that something so constituted actually exists as it exists. Our cognitive operations reach their high point in that affirmation of the real or ideal existence of certain facts or things. Normally, all our cognitive or practical activities are performed on the basis of a general belief, held by us constantly in the natural attitude, in the existence of the real world in which we ourselves also exist.[21] But when the original aesthetic emotion takes place, this belief is, to be sure, neither questioned nor suspended nor removed from the realm of our usual beliefs but is forced to the periphery of our consciousness and weakened in actuality. For, as a result of the original emotion, we are focused not on the fact of the real existence of these or those qualities but on these qualities themselves, on their Gestalt, if we may be permitted to express it thus. Their factual appearance in a real object as its determination becomes a matter of indifference for us. In particular, it does not matter much to us whether the thing in which a quality appears which affects us aesthetically really is as it appeared to be before the original emotion affected us or whether it was mere illusion. The mere appearance of this quality fully suffices for our beholding it in its specific nature and consequently for the generation of the original aesthetic emotion. Under the influence of this emotion, sense perception, among the data of which we found the aesthetically affecting quality, is modified in an essential way. Specifically, (*a*) the experiencing subject either does not take

21. See Edmund Husserl, *Ideen zu einer reinen Phänomenologie und phänomenologischen Philosophie*, Vol. I, in *Jahrbuch für Philosophie und phänomenologische Forschung*, Vol. I, no. 1 (1913); see also Vol. III of *Husserliana, Edmund Husserl: Gesammelte Werke* (The Hague: Martinus Nijhoff, 1950), §§ 27–32. [English translation of Volume I by W. R. Boyce Gibson, *Ideas: General Introduction to Pure Phenomenology* (New York: Macmillan, 1958; New York: Collier Books, 1962).]

cognizance of or involuntarily neutralizes[22] the belief, contained in the act of sense perception, in the real existence of the object through which that quality appeared, and (*b*) the quality which originally appeared as a feature of the thing given in the relevant perception is now freed to a certain extent from this formal structure; it remains, for a moment, pure quality in order to become, in the immediately succeeding phases of the aesthetic experience, a center of crystallization for a new object: the aesthetic object.

This transition from the practical to the aesthetic attitude is perhaps the most thoroughgoing change in man's psychological attitude. It is consequently no wonder that the aesthetic experience is separated from the course of our daily life and that it inhibits our practical occupations to such a degree. The phenomenon of forgetting the world manifests itself here; and either the aesthetic experience must come to a close, or there must be a strong attraction from without in order for that "return" to "real" life, of which we spoke earlier, actually to occur.

But we must not for this reason suppose that the aesthetic experience is a purely passive, inactive, and uncreative "contemplation" of a quality (or, as Max Scheler once said, a gaping), which is in this respect opposed to "active" practical life.[23] On the contrary, an aesthetic experience constitutes a phase of a very active, intensive, and creative human life; it consists, however, of "activities" which produce no changes in the real world about us and also do not "aim" at doing so. I shall later attempt to show this. It will then also become clear that the whole process of aesthetic experiencing contains within itself, on the one hand, phases of a special activity but, on the other hand, also elements of passive receptivity, of a certain torpidity and immobility in contemplation and admiration.

4. The original emotion contains within itself, as already indicated, a demand for satisfaction by the quality which originally excited us and for continued possession of it in immediate contact with it. Thus it passes over—without completely disappearing—into a phase of aesthetic experiencing in which the

22. For this reason Husserl tends to treat the aesthetic experience as a "neutralized" experience. But this is incorrect, as will be shown in later expositions. For a moment of existential positing occurs in the last phase of the aesthetic experience, and this moment is completely different from the moment of ontic positing with respect to a thing given in perception.

23. The passivity of the aesthetic experience is maintained by Oswald Külpe, among others. Johannes Volkelt contradicts him in this.

intuitive apprehension (the perception) [24] of that quality which produced this emotion is predominant. After the phase of the emotion, which dominates us for a moment, follows the return to the quality which aroused us. Although the apprehension of it takes place in some cases on the basis of the earlier perception, the previously described modification of this perception has the result, above all, that the relevant quality now steps into the foreground and is apprehended much more distinctly and in greater fullness than in its first appearance. In addition, the quality (and not the thing in which it appears) now becomes the object of apprehension; it finally begins to be set off from its surroundings. Since we now apprehend it after having previously experienced the original emotion, and because it always excites (moves) us, the quality conceived in the apprehension acquires certain new, secondary traits: it satisfies our desire to "see" it; it appeases that desire, at least to a certain extent; and in connection with this it also becomes—in popular language—much more "beautiful" than it was before, it acquires a certain vitality, a charm and a magic, which we scarcely suspected before. We satisfy our hunger with it to a certain extent. The quality which appears in this light and enchants us now becomes a particular value for us, specifically, a value which is not coolly judged but is only directly felt by us. This produces a new wave of emotion in us which is actually, in this case, a certain form (mode) of pleasure, of joy in this quality, in the sight of it or in its self-presence. It intoxicates us and delights us, for a moment, the way the scent of a beautiful flower intoxicates us.

Almost every delight, every instance of sating ourselves with something, conceals within itself a germ of new longing and desire. Thus, even this second phase, of emotion in direct contact with the object which excites and delights us, does not usually constitute a conclusion of the aesthetic experience (although it is also possible for it to do so).[25] A new feeling of being

24. Since the original emotion does not have to arise against the background of outer or inner perception, it is not always a "perception" in the strict sense of the word. If the quality producing it is merely imagined, then the return to it also takes place in an act of imagination in which we make an effort to apprehend this quality as clearly as possible. It is then not a simple act of imagining but a particular form of apprehension (of perception) in the imagination. It relates, of course, to the act of imagination and not to its shifting content.

25. When it actually does constitute a conclusion to the aesthetic experience, it is a sign that we are dealing with a very primitive aesthetic object, e.g., with a rich color or with a simple contrast of colors. Even

unsatisfied can arise for two reasons. Either the quality grasped in aesthetic apprehension is of such a kind that it demands supplementation, or there appear in the apprehension of it completely new qualitative details of the object in which the relevant quality first emerged; these details are, moreover, of such a kind that they harmonize with the originally given quality and enrich the whole of the given object. Then a new development of the aesthetic experience sets in, which can often be very complicated and manifold; it can develop into either of two different situations. Either the original emotion and the quality which appears in the beginning stimulate us to a completely free constitution of the aesthetic object, without our remaining in further contact with the objects surrounding us, or this quality is a detail in a work of art which has as its physical foundation of being a real thing (a painting, a building, etc.) so formed by the artist that the perception of it puts the observer into the aesthetic attitude, allows him to behold a multiplicity of aesthetically valent qualities, and moves him to reconstruct the corresponding work of art and to constitute a particular aesthetic object. I shall not consider the first case in further detail here, for what is involved in it is the creative behavior of the artist. But it will be useful to occupy ourselves a little with the second case.[26]

In the return to the quality which produced the original aesthetic emotion, we encounter anew the thing or the work of art in which that quality originally appeared. This quality continues to manifest itself in it, although, to be sure, in a manner which differs, insofar as the original perception has been modified in the meantime in the way suggested above. Since we are now focused exclusively on qualities and on a desire to enjoy the sight of them and their presence, either we notice a certain inadequacy or a need for supplementation in the quality itself, or else new details of the work of art now obtrude of themselves. In the first case it could be, for example, the beginning of a developing melody, the continuation of which announces itself, or the particular expression of a human face which was not itself apprehended, or the general outline of the façade of a Gothic cathe-

---

such simple aesthetic objects are possible, although their value may not be very high.

26. These two cases have, however, much in common. In the second, the aesthetic observer, in apprehending the artist's work, attains to a sort of creative cooperation with him. By this I mean that the observer must also develop a certain creative attitude in order to arrive at the aesthetic concretization of the work and thus to an aesthetic object.

dral, which seems to demand to be filled in with specific details. Then we ourselves look for those missing qualities which present themselves for completion of the analyzed whole. Sometimes the previously given object or the relevant work of art is unable to provide that quality whose lack we feel and whose discovery could form a new qualitative harmony which we only surmise. Then we are called on to make an effort, sometimes a very demanding one, in order to discover with vivid imagination that missing quality or a whole cluster of qualities which help to provide the foundation for that quality. Let us suppose we have succeeded in this. Then there are still two possibilities.

a. The mental image of that supplementing quality is so vivid that, without our being conscious of the fact, it is stamped on the work of art which has been brought to appearance. We then see the work (or hear it, etc.) under the aspect of the harmony of qualities which has thereby come into being (among which qualities only one, i.e., that given originally, was forced on us by the work of art). If, in doing this, we overlook the deficiences which may perhaps be present in the work of art, then a perfecting of the work takes place. For we then constitute an aesthetic object whose qualitative, aesthetically valent content is richer than that which was suggested by the work of art itself. At the same time, the very fact that a certain multiplicity of harmonious qualities is stamped on a physical object (e.g., a block of marble) has the result that the latter appears to be the bearer of these qualities. We forget that the physical thing, the work of art, and the aesthetic object are three different entities. The fact that we are not conscious of the essential modification of the perception involved is partly responsible for this. The thing, the work of art, and the aesthetic object being constituted appear to be the same. We become convinced that the thing itself possesses those aesthetically valent qualities and the qualities of value which are constituted in it; we are convinced that we simply perceive them in the thing. On account of this, we believe that we apprehend the thing itself as "beautiful." This view is also the source of those false theories of which we spoke at the beginning of these deliberations. And only the analysis just completed shows that this is not the true state of affairs.

b. The mental image of the supplementing quality is not vivid and concrete enough to lead to this quality's being stamped on the work of art. This new quality (or, in the further phase of the experience, even a whole set of connected qualities) can, to be sure, harmonize well with the originally given quality and form with it a "well-rounded" ["*gut abgeschlossen*"] [27] qualitative whole; but the details of the work of art which we see at the same time not only do not contain it at all but do not even harmonize well with it. For two reasons, therefore, it does not happen in this case that the newly imagined quality is stamped on the work of art which we see (or hear). The divergence of the work of art from the merely imagined qualitative harmony presents itself to our eyes as an inadequacy or a mistake. Consequently, a negative emotional reaction takes place in us as a response to the work of art (already apprehended in a modified perception). The work does not please us; it shocks us; it is not fully ripe; and so forth. It can be said that actually, in this case, two different aesthetic objects are constituted: a vividly imagined object, with a full (completed) qualitative harmony, and a second, which is apprehended on the basis of perceptual data and is "not fully ripe," "ugly," or "bad." We have then a strangely compound, divided aesthetic experience, which contains two different emotional responses [28] to the constituted and conflicting aesthetic objects. The experience can end with this dissonance; it can also lead to rejection or condemnation of the "ugly" work of art, from which can develop an immersion in the contemplation of the aesthetic object formed in imagination. Or the aesthetic apprehension, being completed in perceptual beholding, of the "not fully ripe," "ugly" work of art can predominate and completely supplant the observation of the merely imagined aesthetic object. Then the whole experience concludes with a final constitution of the aesthetic object of negative value and with an emotional response to value appropriate to it.

The consideration of the second case brought us close to the situation in which—after our return to the originally given quality—the encountered work of art imposes its further details upon us itself; in particular, it imposes further qualities, which produce in us a new wave of aesthetic excitement, which we have described as the original aesthetic emotion. Since this case is of particular interest to us, let us suppose that when, having experienced the original emotion, we return to the intuitive apprehension of the quality which first excited us, we do it with the attitude of forming the aesthetic object—to which we hope

27. This is an expression which the Polish psychologist Władysław Witwicki (1878–1948) introduced for the Gestalt qualities.
28. We shall soon speak of the "emotional" response.

to press forward in the further course of the aesthetic experience —in such a way that it is as close as possible to the work of art which provided us with the original emotion. Then we do not wait passively for this work of art itself to impose new aesthetically moving qualities on us, but we make use of the possibilities provided by the work of art and seek in it sides and details that allow us to apprehend new qualities in harmony with the quality which first attracted us.

This demands an attentive consideration of all sides of the work of art [29]—always as modified by the original emotion— hence a consideration in which we focus solely on the qualities, and particularly the aesthetically relevant qualities, and do not pay attention to their "function," so to speak, of determining a real thing. Instead, we look in the work of art for qualities which form a qualitative harmony [30] with the originally given quality. This cannot be done all at once or in such a way that one can say from the outset at which qualitative harmony we shall finally arrive. Not all at once, because the work of art, e.g., a picture or an architectural work, must be viewed from different sides and also from different points of view, and the qualities provided in each phase must be adjusted to one another both within a single phase and in the sequence of phases. This even occurs in the case of a picture. Even if we succeed in the first moment in apprehending the whole of the picture, this does not suffice for its aesthetic apprehension. But as soon as we begin to occupy ourselves more closely with it, we notice its various parts and details and notice them from various points of view. The first impression is thereby not merely supplemented but is also checked and perhaps corrected and is, in any case, combined synthetically into a whole. It is the same with the contemplation of other works of art. In the case of works of literature or music there is, in addition to the complications mentioned earlier, the circumstance that both their contemplation and the

29. In this phase there appears what Johannes Volkelt regards as the indispensable condition of the aesthetic experience, as in his assertion that "perception must first of all be accompanied by sharpened attention" (*System der Ästhetik*, 1st ed., I, 88). [Our translation—R. A. C., K. O.] Of course, there can be no talk here of an "accompaniment" by sharpened attention. On the contrary, it is a matter of a particular mode of perception or, in more general terms, of observation. Volkelt is also unaware of the fact that this perception has undergone an essential change as a consequence of the original emotion.

30. We shall soon discuss this harmony.

concretization which takes place in it unfold in time and consequently force the perceiving subject to perform particular synthesizing operations. Thus various kinds of harmonies of "aesthetically relevant qualities" are present here, which condition and supplement one another in various ways and consequently demand quite specific modes of behavior from the perceiving subject in order to be constituted and apprehended in their multiplicity and in the final harmony resulting therefrom.

5. In this process of apprehension there occurs at the same time a forming of the apprehended qualities in two different, albeit connected ways. Specifically, (a) in categorial structures and (b) in structures of qualitative harmony.

Ad (a). If the quality which produced the original emotion in us, e.g., slenderness of line, is of a spatial form that the human body can possess, then we comprehend it in perception as the form of the human body, although, purely visually, we have before us only a piece of marble. To the quality of the relevant figure we add the corresponding fictional subject of attributes, e.g., the human body, and not the subject of attributes which that form possesses in reality (i.e., the block of marble or a piece of canvas covered with paint). Something similar also appears in other areas of "representative art." We impute to the given qualities, so to speak, the formal structure of a subject of attributes, which is materially determined in its nature in a way suggested to us by the apprehended quality. It is precisely thereby that we leave the realm of real perceived things (of the given block of marble, the canvas, the building), which form the physical foundation of the work of art (of the *Niobe,* of Rembrandt's self-portrait, of Notre Dame in Paris, etc.), and (involuntarily and under the influence of the quality affecting us aesthetically) substitute for the real subject of attributes, which has vanished from the field of vision, a completely new subject of attributes which is selected so as to be the bearer of the qualities just given us. Or, to put it another way: this bearer is determined in its material (in its constitutive nature) by the multiplicity of qualities given to us and apprehended by us, as well as by the connections existing among them. Since, as soon as it is created by us in imagination, this new subject of attributes begins to appear even in the concrete qualities apprehended by us, it assumes the character of a particular object which is present to us. And correlatively: upon the phase of categorial forming of the object which is portrayed in the work of art follows the phase of perceiving (of receiving) the object by the aesthetically experiencing subject, as well as the phase of the varied emotional reaction to the imagined quasi-existing object.

Here, in the process of imputing a new subject of attributes to the given qualities, takes place what Theodor Lipps probably has in mind when he speaks of "empathy" [*Einfühlung*] and of "aesthetic reality" [*aesthetische Wirklichkeit*] as a correlate of empathy.[31] This is especially evident when we impute a psychological or psychophysical subject to the qualities given us. We then "empathize" into those qualities not only this subject but also his definite psychological states and acts, precisely those acts and states whose "external expression" (e.g., the shape of lips closed for smiling) appears among the qualities we are given. We are struck by the phenomenon of this expression; when it is apprehended in emotional sympathy, it leads to "empathizing," e.g., the joy or joyful admiration of the person we have imagined, into the perceived phenomenon and transforms it thoroughly. But as soon as the act of empathy is performed, there takes place that strange direct intercourse or companionship with the imagined person and his condition. Feelings arise in us which are very similar to the feelings we would have if we were close to such a person and his states in reality—feelings of rejoicing with him, admiring with him, hating with him, etc. Everything is almost as if this imagined person and his life existed in reality. These acts of emotional coexperiencing are the first form of the emotional response of the aesthetically experiencing subject to the constituted aesthetic object. But there is yet a second form of this response, which stands in close connection with another forming of the structure of the qualitative harmony in the content of the aesthetic object. We shall now proceed to a description of this second form.

Ad (*b*). As soon as the aesthetic object exhibits not just one quality but a multiplicity of qualities, they do not appear in random grouping but rather form a harmonious whole, a qualitative harmony. We shall now discuss what this means.

A. Each of the appearing qualities has a greater or lesser effect on the others. This effect expresses itself in a qualitative transformation, in a certain displacement of the quality in one

---

31. Lipps means by "empathy" [*Einfühlung*] very diverse phenomena and subjective activities, which he does not distinguish from one another. It is not possible to sort this out here. I should like, however, to emphasize that, when I speak of "empathy" here, I mean only one kind of the facts which Lipps covers with this expression.

direction or the other. This "influence" is generally reciprocal. A given quality appearing with a given multiplicity of other appropriately arranged qualities is not exactly the same as if it were to appear with a different (and possibly differently arranged) multiplicity of qualities or if it were to appear all by itself, if that were possible.

The simplest examples of such qualitative transformations are to be found in the domain of colors. It is well known that in order to obtain a spot of color with a rich and vivid tone it is necessary to choose an appropriate background, one which does not weaken the luminous power of the color. All cases of so-called (simultaneous) contrast belong here, but not only these.[32]

It must be noted that all these transformations of the quality of the color take place within the framework of its identity. Only a radical alteration of lighting can lead to such a transformation of color that it is no longer the same color.

B. Formally, the qualitative harmony is distinguished by the fact that the qualitative factors appearing in it belong to the whole of the harmony in the sense that they lose their absolute particularity and independence.

C. The reciprocal modification of the qualities appearing together can lead to the appearance of a completely new quality, which is, so to speak, built on the foundation of the factors modifying one another. This quality cannot then be identified with any of the "founding" qualities or with the relations among them or, finally, with the fact of the appearance in common of many qualities in a whole. For it is, in relation to the elements founding it, a new quality, the appearance of which is conditioned by the simultaneous appearance of many different factors modifying one another in a particular order. To give only a simple example: When two notes, C and E, sound together, there then appears, along with the full qualitative determination of these notes, also the specific quality of the major third, which is sharply distinguished, for example, from a minor third or a fourth—a quality which is here independent of the absolute pitch of these notes and depends only on their relative difference in pitch. This new quality constitutes a kind of clasp which unites the qualitative elements founding it into a whole, by giving the whole a qualitative stamp peculiar to itself. I call it the "quality of harmony"; after Ehrenfels, it is usually called "Ge-

32. Of course, we ought to abstract here from the psychophysiological interpretation of these phenomena. All that matters here is the pure description of what appears as a given in direct experience.

stalt" or "structure" or even "totality." [33] It is distinguished by the fact that it does not conceal the founding qualities, as well as in other ways. Therefore, everywhere it appears, we have to do, not only with it, as with something absolutely simple and unified, but always, in addition, with a qualitative multiplicity which is sometimes very rich and which flows together, a multiplicity which, despite the unification with all its founding qualities, nevertheless "registers." Even with the same unifying quality, as experience also teaches, the qualitative harmony can nevertheless be different. But not just any multiplicity of qualities leads to the constitution of a harmony and its quality; which general regularities must exist among the manifold qualities for there to be harmony has not yet been elucidated.

D. Special groupings can exist among the qualities that found a specific quality of their harmony, and these groupings lead to the constitution of various parts of the whole. Within the framework of such a part, the connection among the qualities founding it is much closer than among the qualities which belong to different parts of the whole. As a result, Gestalt qualities of higher and lower levels are constituted, and these, again, are connected with one another, etc. Without losing its unity, which is preserved by the determining highest quality, the whole is then distinguished by a special organization, which can be of various kinds while nevertheless preserving the final quality which is stamped on the whole. This "organization" of a qualitative harmony is what can be called "structure" in the strict sense. It must be distinguished from the quality of harmony, from the "Gestalt."

The formation in direct apprehension of such a qualitative harmony with this or that structure can also depend in many cases on the behavior of the aesthetically experiencing person. Particularly, the organization of the whole often takes this or

33. Actually, Bergson was the first in modern philosophy to allude to the existence of such Gestalt qualities in his *Essai sur les données immédiates de la conscience* (Paris: Alcan, 1889) [English translation by F. L. Pogson, *Time and Free Will* (New York: Macmillan, 1959)], although he did not introduce this name for them. Today the word "Gestalt" or "Gestalt quality" is not understood by everyone in the same way. It is also taken in a wider sense than the quality of harmony specified here. On the other hand, the existence of "Gestalten" is denied by many, in particular by positivists of various origins. A still greater ambiguity distinguishes the expression "structure," from which the whole movement of so-called structuralism, for instance in general linguistics, suffers. I cannot occupy myself with this here but will simply attempt to avoid these terms.

that form—with the same multiplicity of founding qualities—according to the course of the aesthetic experience and the operations of consciousness performed in it. The realization of the organization of a qualitative harmony, where this is possible at all, constitutes that second process of the forming of a qualitative harmony which was mentioned above.[34]

The constitution of an organized (structured) qualitative harmony with a finally determining quality is the final goal of the whole process of the aesthetic experience, or at least of its final creative phase. The categorial formation of the aesthetic object is subordinated to its structure (see *sub* [*a*]). That means: the categorial formation should be carried out in such a way that we achieve as rich and valuable a qualitative harmony as possible. This harmony, and in particular its determining quality, is—if we may put it so—the final principle of the constitution and existence of the aesthetic object. The work of art helps us (in the case discussed) in this constitution by furnishing us with the guidance of the highest quality and the structure of the aesthetic object. This either leads to the constitution of a precisely determined qualitative harmony, or else it provides the foundation for a multiplicity of possible qualitative harmonies permitted by the work of art and suggested to the perceiving subject. Whether any of these possible qualitative harmonies is actually constituted in an aesthetic object, and, if so, which, depends on the course of this experience and the operations of consciousness performed in it.

The formation of such a qualitative harmony by the experiencing subject often occurs only with the help of an extremely difficult process. This is especially the case when the work of art fails to help the perceiving subject sufficiently on the basis of its attributes. Then he is himself compelled to add to the composition either the missing elements or parts of the harmony to be constituted or their coordination. It sometimes happens that we feel the absence of these elements and indeed sense the highest quality of the harmony but are yet unable, at

---

34. In the circles of aestheticians of music, there is often talk of the "structuring" of tonal complexes. But such talk supposes that this structuring constitutes something—precisely the "structure"—which is imagined by the subject without any *fundamentum in re*. In my opinion, however, the structure is either sufficiently founded on the elements of a qualitative harmony or else finds in it a necessary but not sufficient condition, which must then be augmented by the subjective behavior of the aesthetically experiencing subject; but it is only augmented and not freely created by the subject.

least at first, to behold the missing quality in intuition and consequently are also unable to constitute the final form of the harmony and, on the strength of that, to apprehend it. For it is only when the constitution of the aesthetic object has been completed that the final phase of the aesthetic experience begins, which constitutes a special kind of culmination of it.

6. The preceding phases of the aesthetic experience are all distinguished by the fact that three kinds of elements stand out in their relatively compound structure: (*a*) emotional (aesthetic excitement, the original emotion, emotional reaction); (*b*) active, creative (formation of the aesthetic object); and (*c*) passive, receptive elements (the apprehension of the harmonizing qualities already disclosed). The individual phases of the experience are interwoven in various ways with these elements, so that now one, now another of the elements predominates. This whole segment of the aesthetic experience is characterized by a restlessness of investigative seeking, by an instability distinguished by a changeable dynamism. In contrast to this, the final phase of the aesthetic experience manifests a certain calmness. On the one hand, there is an immersion in a more restful reflection, in the contemplation of the qualitative harmony in the aesthetic object, as well as in the reception of the individual qualities which have become visible. On the other hand, and in accord with this, there begins what I referred to above as the second form of emotional response to the constituted qualitative harmony. That is to say, feelings begin to stir in which the acknowledgment of the value of the aesthetic object, the mode of admiration befitting it, takes place.[35] Experiences of this kind, such as, for example, pleasure, admiration, delight, enthusiasm for something, are all expressly emotionally determined acts. Max Scheler speaks here of "intentional feeling" [*intentionales Fühlen*] in contrast to the pure "emotions" [*Gefühle*] in which, simultaneously with a direct intentional relation to something, there is expressed some form of esteem for it. For just this reason the acknowledgment takes place in an act of feeling. It consti-

---

35. The word "acknowledgment" [*Anerkennen*] should not be taken here in the sense in which it is employed by various theorists (e.g., Franz Brentano) in the theory of judgment as acknowledgment of the existence of a fact (in contrast to "rejection" [*Verwerfen*]). The sense which is involved here appears, for instance, in the phrase "he turned to him with words full of acknowledgment," with the difference that it is not a question here of a purely intellectual judgment of a value but a question of an experience in which the emotional factor essentially predominates. One gives someone acknowledgment, admiration for something, etc.

tutes our fitting "response to the value." D. von Hildebrand speaks here with justice of a "response to value" [*Wertantwort*].[36] It grows out of the contemplation of a directly given value.

Only in direct intercourse with the aesthetic object is an original and vivid response to its value possible. We can, of course, coolly "judge" the value of something, i.e., make a judgment about its (aesthetic) value by making use of the proper professional criteria without having had the corresponding aesthetic experience and without ever having constituted and beheld a qualitative harmony in the aesthetic object. People who have a great deal to do with works of art and who have almost become accustomed to them are "spoiled" to a certain extent and cannot be so easily delighted by something. They develop a technique for orienting themselves by certain secondary features of the work of art, whether or not it possesses a value, without ever having beheld this value and without ever having known the value quality at all. From the secondary features they notice, they infer purely intellectually that the work of art in question can lead to the constitution of a valuable aesthetic object. They judge the work of art with regard to its containing certain possibilities for the constitution of aesthetically valuable objects. The judgment of the value of a work of art is in this case a purely intellectual act, no less intellectual than the judgment that, for example, a certain tree is an oak. The difference consists only in what is being predicated of an object. Such a merely inferential judgment of the aesthetic value of an object no longer belongs to the aesthetic experience. It may be false or it may even be correct; but the experience which essentially grounds it, which shows it to be legitimate, lies in the final phase of the aesthetic experience and is in particular contained in the emotional acknowledgment of the value of this aesthetic object, which is based on the beholding of its qualitative harmony. Only judgments grounded in this emotional acknowledgment are actually substantiated, confirmed, demonstrated. The judgments passed, often with great skill, by professional critics are in general only indirect judgments, not of the value of the aesthetic object, but of the work of art as a means (tool) which, given the aesthetic experience, can lead to a positively valuable

36. See D. von Hildebrand, "Die Idee der sittlichen Handlung," *Jahrbuch für Philosophie und phänomenologische Forschung*, Vol. III (1916). Hildebrand is concerned primarily with ethical values, but the concept of the response to value can be taken widely enough to be applied also to the emotional acknowledgment of aesthetic values.

aesthetic object. The reason why professional critics, even when they are not mistaken in their judgment of works of art, are capable of saying so little about the essential substance of the aesthetic objects appertaining to the works lies in the fact that they are often no longer able to have a complete aesthetic experience. This shows itself as soon as they try to describe the works of art, which they have judged correctly, as ostensible aesthetic objects. The value of the aesthetic object is not the value of a means (tool) to something which lies outside itself and to which another value would be attributed. If it exists at all, it is contained in the aesthetic object itself and is founded in its qualities and in the qualitative harmony constituted in it. If we acknowledge it and do it justice in acts of emotional response, we stand in the closest relationship with the aesthetic object in question and allow ourselves to be determined exclusively by it. Afterwards, after the completion of the whole aesthetic experience, when we have gained a certain distance from the aesthetic object intuitively present to us, we can ascribe a value to it in a judgment; we can also make judgments about this value or compare it with other values and order the value-bearing objects in series of values. But all this happens no longer in the aesthetic attitude but in an investigative, cognitive attitude, to which we return when we coolly seek to make ourselves conscious of what was given to us in the aesthetic experience and when we want to determine conceptually the result of this experience.

Doubtless, one should not disdain the judgmental evaluation of an aesthetic object. It has reference to a part of what appeared in the aesthetic experience under the form of the directly beheld and simultaneously felt qualitative harmony. To experience something aesthetically, and in particular to contemplate the qualitative harmony in intuitive apprehension, is not yet to know (in the narrower sense of the word) what the aesthetic object in question is, how it is constituted, which qualities appear in it, and which immanent value they constitute in it. In order to obtain this knowledge, it is necessary to return to the attitude of investigation. On the one hand, it is necessary to maintain the already constituted aesthetic object in actuality by further intercourse with the founding work of art, which meets with no insuperable difficulties in the case of pictures, sculpture, and works of architecture but is not so easy in the case of literary and musical works. On the other hand, it is also necessary to keep the content of the value response, as well as the results of the acts of apprehension relating to the aesthetic object, as long as possible in active memory. Both manifestations of the investigative attitude enable us to make the relevant value judgment, or judgment about the value of the constituted aesthetic object, with clear knowledge about the state of affairs furnished by the aesthetic experience. We can also try to call on memory and with its help revive the form of the previously constituted aesthetic object. Finally, we can try to build a new experience on the aesthetic experience we have already had, in which we direct our attention toward the constituted aesthetic object and bring its details and, in particular, its value to clear apprehension. One must, in other words, seek to rationalize to a certain degree what has been constituted in the aesthetic experience in order to capture in concepts what is saturated with emotional elements and to determine it predicatively in strictly formulated judgments. Whether the knowledge only postulated here is actually capable of being realized, and, if so, to what extent, must still be considered. All that is certain now is that this is not possible without the aesthetic experience which forms the foundation and which, especially in its final phase, constitutes a mode of practical aesthetic knowledge. Thus, whoever begins the study of works of art with the purely investigative attitude suitable to the cognition of a real object, without trying first to restore the sometimes fairly complicated work of art which is built upon it and without, at the same time, setting himself the task of constituting in the aesthetic experience an aesthetic object founded in this work of art in order to learn something from it, will never be able to gain knowledge of aesthetic values. On the other hand, aesthetic experience alone will not furnish him with this knowledge. It merely gives him a concrete experience, which, like any other concrete experience, must be apprehended conceptually in its results, as far as that is possible.

Of course, not every aesthetic experience ends with a positive emotional response to the value of the aesthetic object revealing itself to us in it. The final conclusion of this experience can also be formed by a negative emotional response in the form of antipathy or abhorrence or even revulsion. Of course it can also happen that there is no value response at all, although the aesthetic experience did actually begin. A negative response to value comes about when a negative value is constituted. But this negative value can rest on various things. It can rest on the fact that the aesthetic object does not form any unified qualitative harmony, which would be held together by a final quality. Then it actually does not form any genuine totality but is rather tossed together out of aesthetically valuable qualities which are insufficiently harmonious, which do not require one another, or which even make the demand that they not participate in one and the same whole. Then the aesthetic experience gives rise to neither contemplation of the final aesthetically valuable quality of the harmony nor any satisfaction by means of this quality. Nor does it then give rise to the intimacy, fervor, and warmth of the relation between the experiencing subject and the aesthetic object which characterizes the culmination of an aesthetic experience which ends positively. We can say, rather, that here there remains a distinct distance between the experiencing subject and the aesthetic object. The act of judgment (in contrast to "acknowledgment") increases this distance still more and forces the experiencing subject to reject the object and to occupy himself no further with it. This distance also appears in other cases of aesthetic experiences which end with a negative response to value, specifically when the negative value does not rest on the disorganization of the structure of the aesthetic object but is constituted by a "negative" quality, e.g., by a repellent ugliness or poisonous hideousness. The aesthetic object so constituted is then often very actively rejected. This rejection can, incidentally, go hand in hand with acknowledgment, perhaps even with admiration, of the artistic excellence of the work of art which was able to make this hideousness stand out so crassly.[37] We then say: it is ugly and repulsive, but it displays this ugliness masterfully.

In both cases, positive and negative, there is a constitution of the aesthetic object. But, as we have said, the aesthetic experience can take such a course that this culminating phase of a response to value does not occur at all. The aesthetic experience, although it began and unfolded for a time, dissipates to a certain extent or runs off in a certain emptiness, becomes an object without any face or character, which says nothing, and which we simply let drop and coolly pass over for other activities. There

37. In the art of the twentieth century there are many examples of works which are able to constitute this kind of aesthetic object, and at the same time there is an expressed preference for this kind of aesthetic experience. We seem to enjoy experiencing acts of rejection or condemnation of ugly objects. This does not prove that these negative values are transformed into positive values, as the relativists would claim, but merely that the response to value is not identical with "pleasure" or "enjoyment." I shall return to this subject immediately.

can be various possibilities for this lack of a response to value. It is possible, on the one hand, for no aesthetic object to be constituted at all. A real object which was intended by the artist as a work of art is then completely irrelevant to us aesthetically; we pass it by without any aesthetic excitement, since the original aesthetic emotion does not begin at all. If we did not have at our disposal external information that the object in question is supposed to be a work of art, it would never occur to us to occupy ourselves with it aesthetically. We then sometimes judge such a "work of art" negatively, by criticizing it; but we do so unjustly, since it warrants no aesthetic judgment whatever but only indifference. Only a negative judgment of the artistic defects of the miscarried work of art would be appropriate, but that is another problem, which we cannot deal with here. But it is also possible that a work of art has produced an original aesthetic emotion in us, so that the aesthetic experience begins to develop. In the aesthetic object which is being gradually constituted, many further relevant qualities then appear; but finally everything gradually dissolves, and from the aesthetically relevant qualities coming forward, here and there, no aesthetic value results. This sort of thing often happens with literary or dramatic works or with miscarried films: we begin to look on with interest; we also begin to experience the original aesthetic emotion; this or that seems good or interesting to us, but then it is revealed as only a cheap spectacle, a product manufactured for the masses, who do not want to experience anything aesthetically but are looking only for "something to pass the time." Then we stand up and leave the hall in disappointment. The aesthetic experience has simply been extinguished, although the aesthetic object had already begun to be constituted.

Before I conclude these deliberations, one further thought, which has already been touched upon. The aesthetic experience unquestionably contains in its entire course, and especially in the positively developing culminating phase, certain elements which are pleasant for the experiencing subject. It also produces in the experiencing subject certain further pleasant, even joyful, states or, on the contrary, unpleasant states of aversion. It is unquestionably a great delight to have intercourse with an aesthetic object of high value, seeing it directly and admiring it. But whoever sees in this delight the main and essential element of the aesthetic object is actually passing it by completely and occupying himself only with a resultant phenomenon of the aesthetic experience, a phenomenon, incidentally, the production of which is not limited to the aesthetic experience. There are many different ways of putting ourselves in this state of pleasure or delight which have nothing in common with art and with the aesthetically valuable. Whoever passes by the aesthetic experience and the aesthetic object in such an uncomprehending way is also not capable of understanding the essential function of the aesthetic experience. It consists, on the one hand, in the constitution of the aesthetic object and thus in the "realization" of quite specific values which can be concretized only in this way and, on the other hand, in the realization of an emotional-contemplative experience of the harmony of aesthetically valuable qualities and thus also of the values founded in it. The performance of this essential function enriches the world belonging to man by specific values which cannot be replaced by anything else; it also enriches human life by a kind of experience which opens the door to those values and, finally, also endows man himself with an ability which belongs to his constitution as a human person.

Whoever does not understand this particular function of the aesthetic experience and does not suspect that there even is such a thing and, in the hope of experiencing aesthetically, focuses on the attainment of a certain pleasure or delight does not actually know aesthetic values at all and is basically not worthy to behold these values. He usually fails also to attain to the constitution of the harmony of the aesthetically relevant qualities and obtains only a certain pleasure from his own experiences, in particular from the feelings of pleasure which are often just a way of having emotional contact with the objects portrayed in the work of art (for example, in a novel). One is pleasantly moved by the vicissitudes of the "hero," one is erotically excited, one becomes ardently interested in the realization of certain social, ethical, or religious ideals, etc.; but all this has nothing in common with the original aesthetic emotion and the values revealed in the aesthetic experience.[38]

7. The final constitution of the aesthetic object with a positive emotional response to value leads to the appearance of a further element in the culminating phase of the aesthetic experience. I have already discussed the modification, under the influence of the original aesthetic emotion, in the perception of

---

38. See, in this connection, the very pertinent statements by Moritz Geiger in his essay "Vom Dilettantismus im künstlerischen Erleben," in his book *Zugänge zur Ästhetik* (Leipzig: Der Neue Geist, 1928).

an object which functions as background for the appearance of that first aesthetically valuable quality which moves the experiencing subject. At that time I mentioned that I regard as false the conception according to which the aesthetic experience is "neutralized." It is now time for me to account for this.

In the aesthetic experience there appear various "thetic" moments, as Husserl would say; that is, moments of assuming the existence of something. The first group of these relates to the objectivities portrayed in the work of art, in particular in the literary work of art, and is related to (even if not identical with) those existence-assuming moments which appear in the cognitive experiences and, in particular, in the perceptions of real objects. But such existence-assuming moments, moments assenting to the existence of something, appear only in some aesthetic experiences, in direct aesthetic contact with works of sculpture, representational pictures, or literary works. Hence they are not altogether indispensable; they are absent, for example, in the aesthetic apprehension of works of pure, non-representational music. But when they do appear in an aesthetic experience, they enrich it and influence its course in a way quite similar to that in which a many-layered aesthetic object that also possesses among its strata the stratum of portrayed objects is richer in a certain sense than, e.g., a one-layered abstract picture. But these special "thetic" moments appear here as a peculiar variation of those moments of acknowledgment of existence which appear in every apprehension of a real object, especially in the whole domain of sense experience. To be sure, we do not believe in all seriousness and without qualification that the objects, people, fates, battles, victories, and defeats portrayed in a novel or in a drama actually exist, but we behave as if we were pretending to ourselves that we believed in them completely and absolutely. At the same time, we fail to a certain extent to admit to ourselves that we are only pretending, acting "as if" they were real. It is a very peculiar variation or modification of belief, of conviction of the reality of a thing, and is very hard to describe in its peculiar nature.[39] But we know this variation of conviction quite well. The appearance of this variation of

39. Hans von Vaihinger had this modification in mind when he wrote his book *Die Philosophie des Als Ob* (Berlin: Reuther & Reichard, 1911). [English translation by C. K. Ogden, *The Philosophy of "As If"* (New York: Harcourt, Brace & Co., 1924).] However, he expanded this concept so greatly that very diverse phenomena were included in the domain of "as if."

conviction or of the moments of existential acknowledgment in the aesthetic experience constitutes another consequence of the original aesthetic emotion, one not considered until now, and is closely connected with the categorial formation of the substance of the aesthetic object, in particular with the supplementation of the corresponding pure qualities by the subjects of attributes determined by them. The quasi-reality of the things, people, and events which are portrayed in the aesthetic object constitutes the intentional correlate of these modified "thetic" moments.[40]

Although this variation of conviction can appear in a natural way in an aesthetic experience, it is nevertheless not characteristic of this experience and is also not itself specifically aesthetic. It does not appear in aesthetic experiences which relate to the nonrepresentational (one also says, incorrectly, "nonobjective") arts, such as pure music, architecture, and abstract painting. On the other hand, there exists in every aesthetic experience which has reached the point of concretization of an aesthetic object (of positive value) an element of existential acknowledgment which concerns the whole aesthetic object for which the harmony of aesthetically valuable qualities is constituted. Just like the existential acknowledgment of reality, it is an element of an acknowledgment (Husserl always says "positing" [*Setzung*]) of being, which one must not, however, identify with real being. Although the aesthetic experience is creative, insofar as it leads to the constitution of a completely new object, which extends not only beyond any real being but also beyond the work of art which founds it, it is at the same time in a certain sense an experience of discovery. For following the suggestions originating with the perception of the work of art, it leads to the discovery of certain necessary connections among the pure qualities, in particular among the aesthetically valuable qualities. And after these have been apprehended, it leads to the grasping in imagination of the qualitative harmonies embodied in the aesthetic object. In particular, aesthetically valuable Gestalt qualities are stamped on the aesthetic object in the aesthetic experience with the help of the aesthetically valuable qualities suggested by the work of art. But as soon as this course results in a

---

40. Consequently, the affirmative sentences appearing in the literary work of art are neither genuine judgments nor "assumptions" [*Annahmen*], in Meinong's sense, but only quasi-judgments. In order to read them correctly in this modification, one must either go through the original aesthetic emotion or focus artificially upon this particular mode of reading from the start.

completed constitution of this object, which is perceived in the succeeding phase by the aesthetically experiencing subject, there emerges in the aesthetic experience a specific element of existential acknowledgment which consists in the conviction that there actually is such a harmony of aesthetically valuable qualities. Its possibility is demonstrated in the concretized aesthetic object. Something is seen to be possible there whose presence was neither expected nor suspected. But as soon as we find ourselves confronted in the constituted aesthetic object with such a harmony of aesthetically valuable qualities, we are overpowered by a certain admiration that "such a thing" is even possible, i.e., such a harmony, contrast, rhythm, melodic line, etc. This possibility is "realized" [41] in the aesthetic object, shown *ad oculos*, in an aesthetic experience combining elements of creativity and discovery. We then see that there is such a thing. And in the establishment of the "existence" of this something is contained just that element of existential acknowledgment, of conviction, which was already mentioned. Of course, this "existence" is no real existence; it is, rather, the ideal existence of a necessary and essential interconnection among pure qualities—here, specifically, pure, aesthetically valuable qualities. And precisely in the discovery of the possible harmony of aesthetically valuable qualities "realized" in a concretum there consists an essential relationship between an aesthetic experience and an experience in which the effective cognition of a necessary ontic connection is attained. And, analogously, there appears, both in the latter experience and in the last phase of a successful aesthetic experience, an element of existential acknowledgment in the domain of pure, ideal qualities, in particular the aesthetically valuable qualities of different particular qualitative interconnections and harmonies.

We cannot here discuss what the talk of "ideal existence" is supposed to mean, since complicated existential-ontological and epistemological problems open up here which essentially go beyond the subject of our reflection. [42] Here we are only concerned

41. We put the word "realized" in quotations here because we are not and cannot be dealing with a reality in the true sense, since no aesthetic object, although brought to givenness on the foundation of a real object, is "real" in the true sense of the word. But the word "realization" has yet another meaning which leads us to use it here, specifically the meaning of something "being fulfilled" which is at first only potential, intended, planned, and as such is only thought.

42. I attempted to analyze only a part of these problems in the first volume of my book *Der Streit um die Existenz der Welt,* 3 vols. (Tübingen:

to indicate that the element of existential acknowledgment is the last phase of a successful aesthetic experience and is different from and completely independent of the element of existential acknowledgment of the real world surrounding us and even from the modified element of existential acknowledgment of the objectivities portrayed in a work of art. This element changes (or enters) into an element of confirmation or fortification of the existence, e.g., of a qualitative harmony. One could also interpret it as an element of postulating, of demanding, that the qualitative harmony continue to exist, that it be made somehow permanent. It is closely connected with the element of acknowledgment of value which we pay it in the emotional response to value. The state of affairs is different in an aesthetic experience in which the emotional response to value is negative. It is there combined with the element of conviction regarding the impossibility, and hence regarding the nonexistence, of a harmony of aesthetically valuable qualities or regarding the impossibility of its "realization" in a particular aesthetic object. It can be, too, that we sense and seek this qualitative harmony but, in an unsuccessful aesthetic experience, come to the conviction that it "cannot be realized," at least not with the help of the aesthetically relevant qualities appearing in the aesthetic object in question. But it can also be the case that the aesthetic object results in the "realization" of a qualitative harmony with a resulting negative termination. Then, along with the negative emotional response to value, there is contained at the same time a postulative element of the cessation of existence of this resulting value quality, the element of demanding that it "never again" be "realized" or that its realization be made impossible.

This, then, is a sketchy outline of the basic elements of the aesthetic experience. It contains certain simplifications and idealizations designed to enable us to exhibit the skeleton of this experience. In actuality, in particular in practical contact with works of art of various kinds, there are different variations of the aesthetic experience as a whole, as well as of its individual phases. Its formation depends on the structure of the relevant work of art, on the psychological peculiarities of the experiencing

Max Niemeyer, 1964–66). [A Polish version of this work appeared as *Spór o istnienie świata* (The Controversy over the Existence of the World), 2 vols. (Cracow: Polska Akademia Nauk, 1947–48; 2d ed., Warsaw: Państwowe Wydawn. Naukowe, 1961–62). Volume I has been partially translated by Helen R. Michejda as *Time and Modes of Being* (Springfield, Ill.: Thomas, 1964).]

subject, and on the changing circumstances under which the aesthetic experience develops. The aesthetic sensitivity of the experiencing person, his emotional and intellectual type, his general and aesthetic culture, etc., all play a great role in this. It is the task of special investigations of the subjectively oriented branch of aesthetics to work out the several possible varieties of the aesthetic experience. We cannot examine them here. There can also be no doubt that the descriptions given here require supplementations in the working-out of details, as well as a series of critical studies of the difficulties which result from the general schema of the course of the aesthetic experience.

§ 25. *Is there a specifically "literary" experience, or does it belong to the aesthetic experiences?*

IN THE 1930s Władysław Tatarkiewicz made the assertion that one should not delimit only one kind of aesthetic experience but that one should rather distinguish two fundamentally different types of so-called aesthetic experiences (in the broader, previously advocated sense). Specifically, (*a*) aesthetic experiences in the narrower sense, which are supposed to take place exclusively in contact with works of art capable of being perceived by the senses, thus with works of sculpture, painting, architecture, and also music, and (*b*) "literary" experiences, which appear in contact with literary works of art. The former are supposed to be distinguished from the latter by a sensory immediacy *par excellence*. Certain things are supposed to be directly given in them upon the "appearance" of which we "concentrate" (which we "contemplate"), while the other experiences refer by means of language and imagination to objects which are not directly given to us. "In poetry only the word is given us directly; aesthetic concentration can thus be directed only at the word, but the word . . . is rather a mediator, a sign which is supposed to suggest absent things and to elicit them in thought." The literary experience "is an indirect intuition and contact with things, in contrast to the direct contact which appears *sensu stricto* in the aesthetic attitude." [43]

43. See Władysław Tatarkiewicz, "Skupienie i marzenie" (Concentration and Dreaming), *Marchołt*, Vol. III (1935); also *Skupienie i marzenie:*

If Tatarkiewicz's conception is correct, reasonable doubt could arise as to whether the assertions made by us in the preceding section concerning the aesthetic experience are to be applied to experiences which we have in contact with literary works of art. Hence we must weigh this conception critically.

It is doubtless necessary to distinguish between different variations (kinds) of aesthetic experience. The aesthetic experiences which we have in contact with literary works actually differ in many respects from the aesthetic experiences which take place in us in the apprehension of a sculpture, a picture, or an architectural work. I myself once indicated some elements which are characteristic of the experiences in which we have contact with literary works of art (a fact which Tatarkiewicz probably overlooked).[44] Incidentally, both the conception of the literary work of art previously presented by me and the course of the reflections in this book thus far are the best evidence that I recognize this distinction. But, in agreeing, I must pose two questions. First: Are these distinctions so important that they allow us to assume no general type of aesthetic experience and that they effect a kind of compartmentalization of aesthetics, as Tatarkiewicz, at least in some of his writings,[45] seems to demand, or do they only apply to certain secondary elements which would be admissible as specific elements within one genus of the aesthetic experience? Second: Should we distinguish between aesthetic and nonaesthetic experiences within the domain of "literary" experiences?

Our answer to the first question should, I believe, be along the lines of the second of the alternatives indicated. In the

Studia z zakresu estetyki (Cracow: M. Kot, 1951). See also "L'Attitude esthétique, poétique et littéraire," *Bulletin international de l'Académie Polonaise des Sciences et des Lettres* (1933). The third attitude is supposed to be that "dreaming" which is supposed to be possible in contact with works of art.

44. See *The Literary Work of Art*, p. 211 (*Das literarische Kunstwerk*, p. 223). This distinction, incidentally, was formerly emphasized very strongly. See, for example, among others, Friedrich Bouterwek, *Aesthetik* (Leipzig: Martini, 1806); Friedrich Theodor von Vischer, *Aesthetik*, 3 vols. in 5 (Reutlingen and Leipzig: C. Mäcken, 1846–57); Eduard von Hartmann, *Philosophie des Schönen*, pt. 2 of his *Aesthetik*, 2 vols. (Berlin: C. Duncker, 1886–87); Theodor A. Meyer, *Das Stilgesetz der Poesie* (Leipzig: S. Hirzel, 1901).

45. Tatarkiewicz's standpoint is, incidentally, not completely unambiguous in this respect. Sometimes he speaks as if he wanted to assume two kinds of the aesthetic experience; at other times he shows a distinct tendency to limit the concept of the aesthetic experience exclusively to experiences which we have in contemplating works of art which are capable of being perceived by the senses (?).

reflections carried out in the preceding section I tried to indicate those elements of the aesthetic experience which are essential for every aesthetic experience and which at the same time do not exclude the differences existing between the experiences taking place in contemplation of works of art given in sensory immediacy and the aesthetic experiences in the reading of a literary work of art.[46] For they are quite independent of these differences.

Neither the original aesthetic emotion nor the consequences produced by it (in particular, the change of attitude, the constitution of the aesthetic object as a qualitative harmony, and the various modes of response to value) by any means presuppose that the work of art, which forms the point of departure for the constitution of an aesthetic object, with the work of art as foundation, must be perceivable "by the senses" [47] and cannot be made intuitive in various acts of representation (or of imagination). Tatarkiewicz's assertion that the object of the "aesthetic" experience in the narrower sense established by him is simply given to us in sense perception cannot, however, be corroborated. The analyses which I have carried out here show that, even in the contemplation of a picture or a sculpture, normal visual perception—a perception, that is, such as that which we perform when we are trying to cognize a real thing, hence, in particular, the physical foundation of the work of art—takes a different course from the one it takes when we are using it as a preliminary operation in order first to apprehend the work of art in question and then to apprehend it in the aesthetic attitude. It is also insufficient for the realization and course of the aesthetic experience. My investigations also indicate that the aesthetic object is actually given to us in the final phase of the aesthetic experience (specifically, on the basis of acts of perception or imagination and signitive acts); but in order for this stage even

46. To be sure, I made use there of examples of contact with "visually" given works of art, but only in order to increase the range of examples and to indicate that the assertions concerning the aesthetic experience were by no means limited to experiences which we have in contact with literary works of art.

47. The existence of numerous theories of "empathy" advanced in Germany from Fr. Th. Vischer to Theodor Lipps and Johannes Volkelt in order to solve the problems which the aesthetic experience posed at that time for scholars is proof that this "sensory" perceivability of certain works of art is to be taken with a grain of salt. That does not mean that I advocate these various theories of empathy. All that is "perceivable by the senses"—even in all "plastic" art—is merely the physical thing which constitutes the ontic foundation of the work of art, hence the "painting" in contradistinction to the "picture."

to be reached, the aesthetic object must first be constituted in the manner described above; thus it is never an object which we simply encounter as given in mere sensory perception of it. And indeed, this is true quite independently of whether we have to do with a sculpture, a picture, a building, or with a literary work of art. In order to apprehend the work of art, we must always go beyond the sense perception which serves as point of departure and beyond the real things given in sense perception and, through a transition to the aesthetic attitude, allow the aesthetic object to be constituted. In aesthetic contact with a work of art whose physical, visually perceived foundation stands in a much closer relation to it than is the case with a literary work of art, the importance of sense perception for the course of the aesthetic experience is much greater than it is for the aesthetic experience of a poetic work. It is consequently also correct that the qualities with which the aesthetic experience is furnished by sense experience constrain us much more in aesthetic contemplation than is the case in the aesthetic apprehension of a poetic work. Furthermore, we do not need to be so active there as we do in contact with a literary work of art, where, for example, the constitution of the objects portrayed in it and the actualization of the manifold aspects in which they appear impose upon us a much more extensive and complicated task than is the case, say, in observing a cathedral or listening to a Beethoven sonata, where these functions either lapse entirely or are at least much easier to perform. But all these are only differences of degree among the variations of the aesthetic experience. They should be neither overlooked nor underestimated, but they do not entitle us to limit the concept of the aesthetic experience in the way that Tatarkiewicz recommends.

We must now consider whether it is necessary to distinguish, among the experiences in which we have contact with literary works of art, between aesthetic and extra-aesthetic experiences. This opposition must in fact be recognized, but not in the sense in which Tatarkiewicz recommends. It is not only possible but in fact it often occurs that there is no phase of the experience of a literary work of art in which the original aesthetic experience takes place, that our attitude does not change at all, and that there is no emotional response to value, since no literary aesthetic object is constituted and no aesthetic value appears in it. Nevertheless, the constitution of a concretization of the literary work, or work of art, in question does come about. Such a non-aesthetic experience can take place, for example, when we read the *Iliad* as classical philologists in order to inform ourselves concerning the customs and way of life of the ancient Greeks or when, as Germanists, we study the prose of Thomas Mann and to this end read first *Buddenbrooks* and then perhaps *The Magic Mountain* and pay attention to the structure of the affirmative propositions in these two novels. But it is also common that we read a literary work of art as ordinary consumers; and although we are moved by nothing and so attain to no original aesthetic emotion, we still read the work to the end because we are interested in the vicissitudes of the people portrayed in it. But there are also literary works, novels for instance, which cannot be read in the aesthetic attitude at all because they are not capable of producing in us the original aesthetic emotion.

Tatarkiewicz, however, obviously wants to divide the experiences arising from contact with a literary work of art into aesthetic and extra-aesthetic in a completely different manner. That is, he feels that the "aesthetic" experiences are those in which the reader has to do with phonetic formations and phenomena and that the "extra-aesthetic" are those which relate to formations and phenomena of the remaining strata of the literary work of art, because the former would be perceived "by the senses," whereas the latter would be accessible to the reader only in thought or imagination. We see, however, that Tatarkiewicz does not even take into consideration the fact that verbal sounds, and perhaps the other phonetic formations and phenomena as well, are not individual sounds but, rather, typical sound structures, which are not given in any auditory perception but are brought to appearance in specific acts of apprehension. Second, it is clear that Tatarkiewicz has not even taken into consideration in his deliberations the particular phenomena which lead to the constitution of aesthetically relevant qualities and to the appearance of aesthetic values. His separation of "aesthetic" and "literary" experiences rests on a principle by the aid of which aesthetic experiences simply cannot be delimited. And the ultimately deciding factor is that specifically aesthetic phenomena can be brought to intuitive givenness not only in material based directly on the senses (that is, in a mode of experiencing whose sensory material is grounded in sensory feelings) but also in material that is merely "imaginatively" projected. We can thus experience aesthetically both the phonetic phenomena and the data appearing in the stratum of portrayed objectivities (e.g., interpersonal situations). The distinction between aesthetic literary experiences and experiences which are "literary" but not aesthetic must thus be made in a way completely different from that recommended by Tatarkiewicz.

If we distinguish between the various already provisionally differentiated modes of contact with, or cognition (in the broad sense introduced here) of, the literary work of art, the following four kinds of "literary" experience must be enumerated.

A.1. The nonaesthetic or extra-aesthetic experiences of the literary consumer
   2. The aesthetic experience of a literary consumer
B.1. The preaesthetic cognition of the literary work of art in the investigative attitude
   2. The cognition of an aesthetic concretization of the literary work of art carried out in the investigative attitude on the basis of an aesthetic experience

Which basic experiences (functions and operations) enter into the makeup of each of these complicated processes has been clarified in the preceding reflections. We must now supplement the details which appear in the variations of "literary" experience just enumerated. Only the variation listed under A.1. will be analyzed no further.

§ 26. *Some observations on literary aesthetic experiences*

THE LITERARY AESTHETIC experience is even more complicated than the nonaesthetic experience of literature. Within its domain fall, not only the experiences of all kinds which we discussed in Chapter 1, but also certain particular emotions and modes of behavior (activities) which simply play no part in a preaesthetic contact with literary works. Moreover, the whole process undergoes certain modifications (some acts are performed differently). Special emphasis is placed on those elements of the experience or cognition that differ from those of the preaesthetic contact with the literary work of art. This is not to deny, however, that the aesthetic experience also takes place in reading (or in hearing all the parts of a work in sequence), but this "reading" is then richer by various elements and takes a different course in its individual phases.

We can attain to the aesthetic attitude with regard to the literary work (work of art) in two different ways. It can come about in the natural way, in which the original aesthetic emotion takes place as the result of a particular aesthetically active element appearing in the work (where this emotion can be quite different according to which stratum of the work, or which phase of all the strata working together, evokes it). Or it can come about in an artificial way, so to speak, in that the reader puts himself in this attitude or has such an attitude from the start, when the title of the work informs him that he is dealing with a poem or drama. Incidentally, this artificial adoption of the aesthetic attitude can fail when it is not supported by the work read. It then has merely the result that we begin to read the assertions in the work as quasi-judgments. In fulfilling the intention of the sentences, we pass beyond the real world into the domain of the merely portrayed objectivities in the work; but this alone does not suffice to set the aesthetic experience in motion, although the modified realization of the sentence meanings belongs to this experience. We can also read scientific works in such a way that we do not realize the sentences in the form of genuine judgments but "put their validity in brackets"—as Husserl says—in order merely to understand what is being maintained in the work without immediately agreeing with the judgments expressed in the work. Not every purely intentional object nor every object portrayed in a literary work is an aesthetic object just because it is purely intentional. This is the case only when certain aesthetically relevant qualities appear in its content which accord with one another or lead to a qualitative harmony with other aesthetically relevant qualities appearing in the work. If these qualities are capable of producing the original aesthetic emotion in the reader, then an aesthetic perception of the work and the constitution of an aesthetic object come about. If this does not happen, we can read the whole literary work of art in question in the extra-aesthetic attitude only to arrive in the end at the conviction that the intention that this work should lead to an aesthetic concretization has miscarried. The reason for this can lie either in the work itself or in the reader or in both: the first is the case when there simply are no artistic values in the work which lead to the concretization of corresponding aesthetically relevant qualities, the second when the reader is not sensitive to the artistic values appearing in the work or, so to speak, makes himself insensitive to them because he wants, for example, to exclude the aesthetic apprehension of the work in question in order to cognize it "objectively" in its naked, neutral, and schematic substance. We shall return to this.

But once the original aesthetic emotion has been produced in the reader, the aesthetic experience unfolds under the further influence of the details of the work concretized during the reading, details which, having attained to concretion, are brought to apprehension by the reader. The constitution of the aesthetic object is thereby completed. By "aesthetic object" we here mean a concretization of the literary work in which is achieved the actualization and concretization of the aesthetically valent qualities determined by the artistic effectiveness of the work, as well as a harmony of those qualities and hence also a constitution of the aesthetic value. There are various possibilities here, however. Either the whole work is constituted into a single aesthetic object in the course of the aesthetic experience, or several different aesthetic objects attain to constitution in its domain. In the latter case they can exist, so to speak, indifferently, side by side, without influencing one another and without leading to the formation of a higher synthetic aesthetic whole. But they can also produce an aesthetic object which is, to a certain degree, hierarchically structured and which, despite a complex substructure, is still ultimately a single whole. How this is possible is a question I shall try to answer later. First, however, something else has to be noted.

In a literary work of art, a harmony of aesthetically relevant qualities can come into existence in aesthetic apprehension from qualities all of which all appear in a single stratum of the work, while the other strata are of neutral value in this respect. Or it may have as its foundation aesthetically valent qualities appearing in different strata or even in all strata of the work. In the former case, what is aesthetically valuable is concentrated exclusively in, for example, the phonetic or objective stratum, while the remaining strata are aesthetically neutral. In the opposite case the aesthetic harmony of these qualities embraces all strata. In so rich a polyphony of aesthetically relevant qualities there can be very different cases (or forms) of the final value-qualitative conclusion of the work, depending specifically on whether the aesthetically relevant qualities originating from different strata have an equal or differing importance for the polyphonic harmony constituted on the basis of them. If, for example, the aesthetically valent qualities which originate from one stratum (e.g., that of the portrayed objectivities) stand out, while those from, say, the stratum of phonetic phenomena recede into the background, then the synthetic polyphonic harmony of the aesthetically valent qualities takes a different form from the one it has when the roles of the qualities supporting it are distributed in the opposite way.

The way the qualitative harmony is formed in an individual aesthetic concretization of the work depends on both the work in question and the way in which the aesthetic experience takes place during the reading (which, of course, depends in turn on both the abilities of the reader and the further circumstances under which the aesthetic literary experience runs its course). It is important with regard to this that the reader, while employing, if possible, all the manifold functions which enter into the cognition of the literary work of art, at the same time make an attempt to exploit completely its artistic capacity and, on the basis of the work, to actualize all the aesthetically valent qualities founded in its strata. To speak of an attempt or of an effort on the part of the reader is somewhat inappropriate, inasmuch as the reader is unable to achieve the aesthetic apprehension of the work unless he comes to the original aesthetic emotion (which cannot be produced artificially and voluntarily). This talk is thus justified only insofar as it is possible to make oneself somewhat more sensitive to aesthetically valent qualities. But it is also possible to be inwardly closed to these qualities (or at least "hard of hearing" with regard to certain kinds), and that either temporarily or permanently. In the latter case the reader is "blind" to works of art of a certain kind and is simply unable to constitute them as aesthetic experiences and consequently also to apprehend them. But this does not mean that the works of art in question are artistically worthless and consequently incapable of leading to any valuable aesthetic objects ("have" no such aesthetic objects). As we see, various possibilities open up here for the apprehension value of the aesthetic "perception" of one and the same literary work of art, possibilities which must later be made the subject of our study.

There are various details of literary aesthetic experiences in which they are distinguished in characteristic ways from other aesthetic experiences. Above all, we must include here the fact emphasized by Tatarkiewicz, that, with the exception of the qualities which appear in the phonetic stratum of the literary work of art, all other qualities in the remaining strata are accessible, not on the basis of sense data, but only on the basis of intuitive mental images which are guided by the signitive acts of understanding of the meaning of the sentence units. Consequently, the fullest possible reactualization of the aspects of the portrayed objectivities held in readiness in the work plays a large part in the aesthetic apprehension of literary works of art. The aspects alone make possible the intuitive presence or quasi-presence of the portrayed objectivities and, among other things, of the aesthetically valent qualities appearing in them.

The second essential element of literary aesthetic experiences which distinguishes them to a certain extent from the aesthetic experience of works of painting, sculpture, and architecture is contained in the fact that a literary work of art can be apprehended only in an aesthetic experience occurring in several phases, in which all the successive parts of the work must be reconstructed one after the other, and that there is no phase of this experience in which the whole work can be apprehended all at once in full actuality. And in every phase—except for the last —only a part of the work is cognized and made familiar and always only in a temporal perspective characteristic of this phase. Every new phase of the aesthetic apprehension of the literary work of art is always providing new details of the work, which join with the echo of its previous, no longer present parts to form new combinations of qualities, which produce in the reader different modes of behavior, emotions, and intentional feelings and properly dispose or redispose him to the immediately following phases of the aesthetic experience of the work. The constitution of the aesthetic concretization or of the aesthetic literary object never occurs in a moment but lasts for a period of time, its length depending on the length of the work itself. Often, with longer works, it can never be realized without major interruptions. It is always being augmented during the reading by new material and thus often transformed completely, especially when aesthetically relevant qualities are involved; and it is also never actually completed. For in the moment in which it is first completed, it ceases to be present to the reader in its totality and moves irrevocably further from him into the past, so that he can have the entire literary work of art in its aesthetic concretization only in the form of a reverberation, of recollection, and in the retrospective aspect of temporal perspective.

In this respect, the aesthetic constitution of the literary work of art is related to the aesthetic constitution of the musical work. But the situation is not as complicated in the aesthetic apprehension of the musical work as in that of a literary work. Of course this depends to a degree on the form or composition of both the literary and the musical work. In general, however, the domain of previously apprehended parts of a musical work which still have an important influence on the apprehension of later parts is not so large and manifold as in a literary work of art. The active memory of the parts of a musical work just apprehended is extinguished relatively more quickly than in a literary work. This is connected with various peculiarities of the works here compared and of their apprehension. The connection between the individual parts of the literary work is in general much closer than in a musical work because it contains the stratum of semantic units, which determine various logical connections between the sentences and, as a consequence, also between the objective sentence correlates appertaining to them, connections which are in general not possible in a musical work. The syntactic functions, e.g., in the framework of a complex sentence, do not merely establish an inner unity of the sentence but also make it easier to a large extent to retain the whole of the sentence in active memory. An analogous role is played in the musical work by the tonal structures, which are built up on the basis of a multiplicity of sounds, establish the unity of the musical formations, and aid in a similar way in maintaining the formation in the actuality of the musical experience. But the relations between such tonal formations are not so close as, for instance, those between the sentences and sentence complexes are by virtue of the unity of meaning. To this extent it is much more difficult to retain, in active memory and in recollection, the parts already past in the aesthetic experience of the musical work than in the literary work of art. And the constitution of a literary aesthetic object is more difficult insofar as it is sometimes necessary to actualize aesthetically relevant qualities, not merely from different strata (which are not present in the musical work), but also from different, somewhat widely separated parts of the work. The aesthetic experience which takes place in the cognition of a literary work of art thus demands, at least in many cases, a much greater concentration and a more dynamic holding-together of the unfolding parts of the work than the aesthetic constitution of a musical work. Of course, these are only differences of degree between the two kinds of aesthetic experiences, but they must nevertheless be noted here. A much deeper difference exists, however, between the two kinds of aesthetic experiences just considered and those which take place in the apprehension of so-called spatial art—a picture, a work of sculpture, or a work of architecture.

With regard to the partial or gradual constitution of the

aesthetic object, the aesthetic apprehension of a work of architecture is closest to the aesthetic literary experience. For here, too, we can only regard the work sequentially in its various parts and aspects. In order to apprehend it in its totality, we must regard it from inside and out, but this is always in part merely a presumptive apprehension. To be sure, all parts of the work are simultaneous, but they cannot all be actually present at the same time. Hence there is always a longer or shorter phase of the architectural aesthetic object being constituted in its parts and aspects. The constitution of the aesthetic object of one and the same building can take place in very different ways. The actualization of the aesthetically relevant qualities can then come about in a very different sequence, from which there often results a different interplay of these qualities, carrying with it a different dynamic character. Although the building, which is the basis of the architectural work as its physical foundation, is intrinsically unchanging (viewed macroscopically) and, so to speak, static, yet every architectural aesthetic object is full of an inner dynamism, which is especially evident in the interplay of aesthetically valent qualities. When these differences are taken into account, it must be granted that there can be a multiplicity —which is in principle infinite—of aesthetic concretizations of one and the same architectural work, especially when many viewers form aesthetic concretizations of the same architectural work at different times (and historical epochs). The viewers can differ greatly from one another in their ability to actualize aesthetically relevant qualities and the harmonies founded on them. Compared with the full qualification of the architectural work of art, most architectural aesthetic objects are consequently inadequate. We could express this another way by saying that their constitution is, to be sure, concluded but is, at the same time, incomplete. It is essentially no different with the constitution of aesthetic objects in the domain of sculpture. In contrast, the situation with the aesthetic concretizations of pictures is somewhat different. To be sure, it is not true that the picture, as we might perhaps be inclined to maintain, can be apprehended aesthetically in a single moment. For even in the contemplation of a picture there are various possible standpoints, which lie in various directions and at various distances from the surface of the picture. It need not be viewed from all sides, however, but only "from the front," and even there we can secure an optimal apprehension of the picture only within a relatively limited space. It is also unnecessary to view the picture from all points within this space in order—as, for example, with an architectural work—to achieve a "full" aesthetic concretization of the picture. We can let our eyes wander a great deal over the surface of the picture in observing it from a particular point of view—which is not without significance for the aesthetic apprehension in the case of relatively large pictures—and we can thereby take various routes to the constitution of the aesthetic object. But still, in contrast to all works of art previously discussed, it is always possible to have the picture as a whole in a single moment in its full actuality. Despite all temporal duration of the aesthetic experience and also of the constitution of the aesthetic object, there exists here a moment of completion of this constitution in a more or less statically apprehended "picture." [48]

Another important element which distinguishes literary aesthetic experiences from other aesthetic experiences is their constituent of purely intellectual understanding of the semantic units which enter into the literary work. Consequently, we have access to the world of portrayed objectivities always through the conceptual schemata; we never apprehend them directly in their intuitively accessible properties. We must first objectify these objects and "clothe" them in an intuitive garb by the aid of aspects held in readiness. Connected with this is the fact that the literary aesthetic experience can never be so irrational and purely emotional as is possible with at least some musical works.[49] Even in works of purely emotional lyric poetry this element of intellectual understanding is not only present but may not be eliminated or reduced without a damaging effect on the other elements of the content of the lyric poem or of the corresponding aesthetic object. We should not make any effort

48. The problem of the constitution and completion of the aesthetic object in the domain of painting is here to be distinguished from the problem of the cognition of the picture itself as a work of art. In the latter case there are various complicated situations which would have to be considered separately. At the moment we are dealing only with the various modes of constitution of the aesthetic object in the domain of various arts without raising the question here whether and to what degree the aesthetic objects constituted thereby bring out a faithful expression of the work of art and make possible the cognition of the work of art revealing itself through them.

49. But even here there is an understanding, although of a completely different kind than in the case of literary works. This understanding relates, above all, to tonal formations and the structures of the musical work in question which result from them. That is a broad subject in itself, which cannot be treated here.

to eliminate this specific element of the literary experience or, correlatively, of the aesthetic object appertaining to it, since it enriches both in its own way. But is a special sensitivity to the aesthetically valent qualities appearing in this stratum possible during the aesthetic apprehension of the work, and is it advantageous to the constitution of the aesthetic object? And, on the other hand, are there any aesthetically valent qualities of a special kind in the stratum of semantic units? Both questions must be answered in the affirmative. Above all, certain qualities arising from the structure of the sentences and, still more, of the sentence complexes must undoubtedly be considered. In analyzing the language of a literary work we often speak of a "good" or "bad" "style." In doing so, we mainly have in mind certain peculiarities of the phonetic phenomena. Of much greater importance, however, are the advantages or disadvantages of the syntactic structures in the stratum of semantic units of the work. In this connection, some believe, for example, that in sentence formation it is an advantage (and therefore probably a positively valuable aesthetic quality) for sentences to be simple and short, since they are then "clear" and easily "understood." [50] It is, of course, a false prejudice to believe that a simple and "short" sentence is "clearer" or more "understandable" than a complex sentence consisting of many words, especially when the latter is hypotactically constructed. And it is just as great a prejudice to believe that it constitutes an advantage for the style of a work when the percentage of simple, short sentences in a work is especially high. All that matters for the time being is that "clarity" or "understandability" counts as a stylistic advantage with reference to the aesthetic "goodness" of the style, which in turn counts as a positive value of the literary work of art. But if we occupy ourselves somewhat more closely with complex, hypotactically structured sentences, we find that their various syntactic structures contain a quantity of aesthetically relevant qualities. There are various types of architectonics of "complex" sentences which are not merely "interesting," purely as structures, but also carry with them certain resulting phenomena which we have in mind when we speak, e.g., of the "difficulty" or the "easiness" of the sentence structure. This "difficulty" or "easiness" has nothing to do with

50. For this reason it has been fashionable for years to compute the number of short sentences in a literary work of art and to determine their percentage in the total number of sentences.

the difficulty of understanding the sentences, although it may accompany it.[51]

Other distinctions which also belong here are, for instance, those between "simplicity" and "artificiality" of style, between the "flowing" language of one work and those works with which we have to "dig in" again and again because the sentences are too complicated and their succession leads to no unified meaning of the sentence complex. In such distinctions are based contrasts of aesthetically valent qualities which have their foundation in the properties of the manifold semantic units. The dynamics and tempo of the unfolding sentence structures and their succession can serve as further examples of the aesthetically relevant qualities which belong here. They all play an important part in the constitution of the literary aesthetic objects, and their apprehension in the aesthetic experience of the work is quite indispensable to the constitution of this object. Only their disclosure and actualization in the aesthetic concretization of the work reveal what is actually "literary" in the structure of the work, along with the aesthetically relevant qualities, of course, which appear in the phonetic stratum. The aesthetically relevant qualities actualized in the other two strata of the literary aesthetic object are of the kind which can also be actualized in so-called plastic art, i.e., in a picture or a work of sculpture; they are thus nothing specifically literary.

In contrast, the heterogeneity and richness of the aesthetically relevant qualities capable of actualization in an aesthetic concretization, qualities which can be brought into harmony in the course of the aesthetic apprehension of the work, are a specific feature of the literary aesthetic experience and its intentional correlate. In no other aesthetic experience is such a far-reaching heterogeneity of these qualities possible. For the experience actually taking place even approximately to exhaust in this respect the domain of possibilities which are offered the experiencing subject by a genuine literary work of art, the reader must have a very fine eye for qualities of quite different basic types and also the skill effectively to actualize and to apprehend in their harmony those aesthetically valent qualities

---

51. We can think here, for instance, of the names Kleist and Thomas Mann, on the one hand, and, say, Immanuel Kant in the *Critique of Pure Reason* or *The Groundwork of the Metaphysics of Morals,* on the other. They all write in "long" complex sentences and are yet essentially different with regard to the "easiness" or "difficulty" of their sentence structure.

which he detects or which he feels to be predetermined by the work in question, and he must be able to do this during the experience itself. From the aesthetically relevant qualities which can appear in the verbal sounds of the language of the work in question, in the linguistic melody, in the various rhythms, to those qualities, already mentioned here, which can appear in the semantic units, to the very manifold aesthetically relevant qualities which can be revealed in the portrayed objects and their intuitive garb, in the situations in the life of the "hero," as metaphysical qualities, among other things, in the portrayed world—all in all, a great many qualities (but never more than a selection from among all the possible ones) are actualized in the aesthetic apprehension of a literary work of art. But they all constitute merely the qualitative material on which can be built various possible harmonies and synthetic value qualities, which appear in this multiplicity in no other art. All these aesthetically relevant phenomena are connected in relations of simultaneity and succession, modify one another, sometimes fortify one another, sometimes extinguish one another—all with a vitality and dynamism which can have its analogue perhaps only in music. This sets the aesthetically experiencing reader extraordinarily difficult tasks and requires of him not only a mind open in many directions but also the ability to move quickly from the active and creative attitude, in which the relevant qualities are actualized in their greatest possible fullness, to the receptive attitude, from one emotion to another, from one value response to another, without allowing this emotion to paralyze his ability to apprehend attentively new details of the unfolding work. We shall have to weigh all this when the problem of an adequate aesthetic apprehension of the literary work of art and the conditions of its possibility emerges before us.

§ 27. *The preaesthetic investigation of the literary work of art*

IN COMPARISON WITH the aesthetic experience of the literary work of art, its preaesthetic investigation seems to be much simpler, since it focuses on those properties of the literary work of art which are independent of the aesthetic experience. Thus it does not need to include anything which comes to actualization and final concretization only in this experience. But is this expectation actually to be fulfillled?

We must note above all that the possibility of such a purely investigative cognition of the literary work of art is extraordinarily important to the existence of literary study as the study of literary works of art themselves, as opposed to their concretizations. For only the results of this cognition allow us to oppose the literary work of art itself to its varied concretizations, in particular to its aesthetic concretizations. These results can in principle, at least, provide objective knowledge of the individual work, which remains identical in its schematic structure in all concretizations. The same unchanging skeleton is, in the concretizations, clothed, as it were, in the garb of various qualities which are not effectively (*actualiter*) contained in it and are determined by it only as certain potentialities—and are sometimes determined in an insufficient way (as, for instance, the possible completions of places of indeterminacy).

This investigative preaesthetic cognition of the literary work is above all a matter of discovering those properties and elements in it which make it a work of art, that is, which form the basis for the constitution of the aesthetically relevant qualities in the aesthetic concretizations. This cognition can begin only when the work in question has already been read in the ordinary attitude of a literary consumer. In carrying it out, we take into consideration the results of this first reading, aided by a renewed reading, which usually takes place only in individual fragments. But it is more than a mere reading, insofar as special deliberations, comparisons, and analytic and synthetic reflections are carried out which do not appear in ordinary reading. Fragments of the various possible aesthetic concretizations of the work must also be taken into consideration here. Thus it is generally a very complicated procedure, which does not dispense with the reading—indeed it always consults it—but necessarily goes beyond it. We shall shortly try to make clear why this is necessarily the case.

The preaesthetic investigation of a literary work of art is usually undertaken in order, as we say, to gain "objective" knowledge of it. The concept of "objectivity" of knowledge is well known to be very ambiguous. We cannot here make precise the various interpretations of this concept.[52] It will perhaps suffice to

52. See my article "Betrachtungen zum Problem der Objektivität," *Zeitschrift für philosophische Forschung*, Vol. XXI, nos. 1–2 (1967).

say here that the knowledge we are attempting to characterize is "objective" when it is successful in discovering the properties and structural characteristics appertaining to the literary work itself, which as such are independent of the modifications which the cognitive procedure undergoes under various circumstances, depending on who carries out this cognition and under which external conditions it occurs.

As soon as we make the demand of attaining such knowledge, we usually also desire that it be accomplished with the conscious and consistent exclusion of all "feelings." The extension of the concept "feeling" is usually not precisely determined, but there is a tendency to take it in a very broad sense. According to one opinion, any participation of so-called feeling in the process of cognition makes it impossible to obtain "objective" knowledge of the object in question because feeling plays a falsifying role in the process. The strict fulfillment of this demand is held to be the *conditio sine qua non* of all science. Consequently, it is also believed that there can be no science of literature as art, since it is thought that it is impossible to exclude the supposedly distracting role of "feeling" in contact with literary works of art (and with all works of art). How do matters stand, then, with the preaesthetic investigative[53] cognition of the literary work of art? Is it actually, and ought it to be, so completely "free of feeling"?

An important difficulty in answering this question results from the very indeterminate concept of "feeling," although it seems to all of us that we distinguish without difficulty in daily life between a person's unemotional behavior and his emotional engagement. And then a person certainly has emotional reactions to various influences on him from the outer world; he reacts with anger, hate, envy, desire, for instance, but also with "gentler" feelings, such as gratitude, loving inclination, etc., which distract him in cognition. These reactions do not leave us the peace which is indispensable to an attentive observation of a thing and its attributes or a human action. Some of them, such

---

[Also published in Roman Ingarden, *Erlebnis, Kunstwerk und Wert* (Tübingen: Max Niemeyer, 1969), pp. 219–55.—Trans.]

53. One would like to say "scientific" cognition, but that immediately produces strong protest from scholars oriented toward the natural sciences, that is, basically from positivistically oriented scholars. There are still other reasons, however, which keep us from using the term "scientific" here. For I believe that there can be various modes of "objective" knowledge of literary works of art and that only one of these should be reserved for literary studies.

as hate or envy, also make us blind to various attributes of the object under observation and sometimes let other attributes stand out in special prominence. In contrast, the "positive" feelings, such as love, are supposed to produce deceiving phenomena of positive value, while making us insensitive to negative determinations of the (beloved) object. On the whole, therefore, they falsify in the object precisely what is somehow significant for us. And such falsifying influences of emotional reactions should certainly be avoided in the preaesthetic investigative cognition of the literary work of art.[54] Not all feelings, however, involve such falsifying phenomena. On the contrary, it is certain that there are, if not exactly "feelings" of the kind mentioned above, then nonetheless emotionally colored modes of behavior (namely, intentional feeling) [55] which first make possible the cognition of certain objects or certain objective elements. For they first create an experiential access to them. Thus, not everything in a literary work of art would be accessible to cognition if we were to exclude absolutely all emotional or at least emotionally colored modes of behavior.[56] In many literary works of art various psychological (mental) states and modes of behavior of people and animals are portrayed. Human characters are revealed, and the conflicts and so forth developing among them are described. This occurs sometimes by way of direct naming of the various psychological states of affairs but

54. Relativitists in value theory, who regard every value simply as a phenomenon produced by a feeling, would then certainly ask: would this not lead all literary works to appear as something free of any value? But can we then still remain in the domain of works of art, as is demanded in this section? This depends, however, on whether all values must be apprehended in emotionally colored cognition.

55. See, in this connection, Max Scheler, "Der Formalismus in der Ethik und die materiale Wertethik," *Jahrbuch für Philosophie und phänomenologische Forschung*, Vols. I, no. 2, and II (1913–16). [Also published as Vol. II of Scheler's *Gesammelte Werke* (Bern: Francke, 1966). English translation by Manfred S. Frings and Roger L. Funk, *Formalism in Ethics and Non-Formal Ethics of Values: A New Attempt toward the Foundation of an Ethical Personalism* (Evanston, Ill.: Northwestern University Press, 1973).]

56. Two further points should be noted here. First of all, it is questionable whether all values are accessible to cognition in "intentional feeling" or only some of them—for example, moral and aesthetic values but not "artistic" values. Second, however, it may be asked which values are to be considered in the cognition of the literary work of art as a schematic structure. Only the artistic values? Or also the aesthetic values, which certainly, as is to be expected, go beyond the pure work of art but may not be fully disregarded? Both questions must be answered in what follows.

often only by description of the external appearance or external (bodily) mode of behavior of people. People are also portrayed who differ greatly from the readers themselves and from their acquaintances. How are we to be able to understand all this? It was once very common to speak of "empathy," and perhaps this could be applied in the cognition of the persons portrayed in literature, if there is actually such a thing as empathy. Basically, it is here more a matter of feeling along with the people portrayed for us, hence of a certain sympathy with them. In any case, it is no purely intellectual or mental act and also no mere mental image, but an experience in which the element of feeling, as well as the element of an emotional coexperiencing of psychological occurrences along with the portrayed persons, plays an essential role. When, in following the vicissitudes of the portrayed people, we put ourselves in their situation and thus do not merely view them from without, in a cool and detached way, but take an interest in their fate, we begin to understand them better, more vividly and intuitively, and that from their point of view. This is impossible, however, without a certain sympathy. From a completely cool—better: neutral— observation from without, the reader obtains at best only a purely conceptual knowledge that the portrayed person is or is supposed to be in a particular psychological state or mood. But then every fullness of psychological reality is lacking in the portrayed world. It is thus necessary, in a preaesthetic cognition of the literary work of art, to experience such a "sympathy" and not to behave in a purely intellectual way.

But we can still maintain that we ought to keep ourselves apart from every emotional reaction in this cognition. Thus we must neither hate nor love the people portrayed in the work. The sympathy which was just mentioned is not therefore an emotional reaction but a means of revealing certain psychological facts in their vividness and bringing them in this way to a reconstructive constitution. Only after we have succeeded in this can the investigative cognition of the corresponding elements of the work begin and lead, in acts of understanding, to apprehension of its peculiar nature. The acts of sympathy, of putting oneself vividly into situations in the lives of others, do not, however, lead automatically to the aesthetic apprehension of the concretization of the work. Indeed, they are used not only in concrete daily relations with other people but also in psychological analyses, for example. When, say, one is preparing a presentation in the theater and first reads the text of the play in company with the director in order to feel one's way into the interpersonal situations to be portrayed on the stage, one does nothing other than feel along with the portrayed person in his varying fortunes before thinking about the way in which the whole play is to take form artistically in order to make possible for the spectators an aesthetic apprehension of the drama in question. In the investigative cognition of a literary work of art in all its details we unquestionably go beyond the real world in intentionally constructing or reconstructing the corresponding objectivities. As already noted, this transcending of the real world forms a necessary but not sufficient condition of the attitude of the aesthetic experience. We can say: just as the "nature" of the real persons who are investigated in psychology includes their emotional state, their deeper mental and spiritual life, and their psychological makeup, which reveals itself in their individual modes of behavior and in various situations in their lives, so also the "nature" of the people portrayed in the literary work of art, precisely as they actually come to portrayal in it, includes the fact that, by literary means, they experience particular situations and states. They must first be constituted or reconstructed in all their plenitude by the reader as he makes himself acquainted with the work in order then to be cognized as given in the preaesthetic cognition of the work. Consequently, the preaesthetic cognition of the work of art just considered takes place on the basis of an appropriate reading, a reading which, in order to be "appropriate," must be regulated and checked in its results by the reader. That sympathy which provides the subject of cognition with the cognitive access to many facts of the inner life of others occurs, moreover, not on the basis of an original aesthetic emotion, nor with the aim of filling out these facts with aesthetically valent qualities, but merely with the attitude of obtaining genuine knowledge of how certain details of the world portrayed in the work are composed. And this attitude prevents the sympathy we feel from leading us into the aesthetic experience; it keeps us in the domain of the preaesthetic investigative cognition of the literary work of art.

As a result of the exclusion of the contemplating subject's emotional reactions from this cognition, the original aesthetic emotions, even when they begin to stir automatically in the subject of cognition, are consciously and intentionally suppressed. Thus the further course of the aesthetic experience is blocked, and hence no aesthetic concretization of the work comes about. The work of art in question unfolds before our eyes as if robbed of all actually present aesthetically relevant qualities, however much they are indicated as potential to some extent. In this sense, then, the literary work of art so viewed is aesthetically neutral. The intermittent emergence of original aesthetic emotions, which are then suppressed, is not, however, without importance. The subject of cognition notes their appearance and looks for an explanation for it. It is given by the discovery of that property or factor of the literary work of art in question which constituted the basis for the emergence of the original emotion. In this way we come to know that the work of art in question (or certain of its properties or elements) is the source of possible aesthetic activity. It contains peculiar forces which, in the presence of an observer, work upon him and can bring him to constitute an aesthetic object. Since its purpose lies in helping the reader come to the constitution of a valuable aesthetic object, the work fulfills its purpose better, and has a higher value, the more numerous the characteristics appearing in it which are so chosen as to be able to produce the original aesthetic emotion and to provide a basis for the actualization of aesthetically relevant qualities. But the work itself obviously has the value of a means of aesthetically affecting the reader. It thus has a relational value, in contrast to the aesthetic value of the object, which is immanently contained in the object and is grounded exclusively in aesthetically relevant qualities. The value of the object is thus in this sense an "absolute" value and belongs to the aesthetic object quite independently of whether the latter serves any purpose or performs any function. The first of these values I call the artistic, the second the aesthetic, value.[57] The disclosure and apprehension of artistic values belongs, among other things, to the task of the preaesthetic investigative cognition of the literary work of art; the apprehension of the aesthetic values appearing in the aesthetic concretization of the work of art is the task of a completely different cognition, which can be undertaken only after the constitution of the literary aesthetic object in the aesthetic experience.

The investigation of artistic values in the literary work of art takes place, as was just stated, in the preaesthetic cognition. The particular characteristic of the relativity of these values has the result, however, that we cannot limit ourselves here to this

57. See, in this connection, my article "Artistic and Aesthetic Values," *British Journal of Aesthetics*, Vol. IV, no. 3 (1964). [Also published in somewhat different form as "Künstlerische und ästhetische Werte" in Roman Ingarden, *Erlebnis, Kunstwerk und Wert*, pp. 153–79.—Trans.]

cognition but must also call to our aid the aesthetic experience of the concretization of this work. In order to orient ourselves as to whether certain peculiarities of the work possess an artistic value, we must, so to speak, apprehend their functional role in the predetermination and actualization of the aesthetically relevant qualities. We must thus gain an insight into the possible aesthetically relevant qualities in the relevant passage of the work, which is possible only on the basis of prior experience or of an actual aesthetic experience. Hence we must, so to speak, take samples from this experience.

The second characteristic element of the preaesthetic cognition of the literary work of art is that it is analytic in its first phases. In connection with this, it cannot be carried out continuously in a single reading from beginning to end of the work. It is rather directed at certain phases of the reading of the work; but it then interrupts this reading decisively and occasions deliberations which cannot be carried out in a continuous reading but only on the basis of an interrupted one. In its later, more advanced phases it proceeds more synthetically and makes itself more independent of the reading. In its analytical phase it is directed toward details of the work, which it makes into special objects of study (themes) and seeks to grasp for themselves. These "details" can be certain particular determinations as well as particular elements, e.g., individual strata or even individual parts of the work. During the analysis they are somewhat separated from the rest of the work by a process of abstraction, although we must guard against losing sight of their connection with other elements or traits of the work. All this distinguishes this mode of cognition from ordinary uninterrupted reading, which avoids interruptions not demanded by the work so as not to disturb the aesthetic effects connected with the continuity of an unfolding of the work from beginning to end. To put it another way: the analytic character of this mode of cognition is bound up with a certain destruction of the work of art. But at least for this phase of the cognition of the work, this is not too dangerous, since it is not a question here of apprehending the aspect of aesthetically valuable qualities in the work of art. Nonetheless, this destruction could do damage to the understanding of the inner anatomy of the work if we did not go beyond it and if the analysis were not followed by an attempt at a synthetic comprehension of the results gained by analysis with respect to the whole of the work.

But toward which details of the work is this preaesthetic investigation of the work of art directed? It is clear that we can give no rules here, not only because its course is conditioned subjectively by the prevailing interest of the subject of cognition, but also because its course is influenced by the importance and significance of the individual elements and parts of the work of art in question. Thus, when I treat here certain themes relating to the preaesthetic investigation of the work, I do so, not with the intention of systematizing this mode of investigation, but merely in order to discuss its individual steps more precisely.

The opposition of the literary work of art itself to its various possible concretizations and, in particular, to its aesthetic concretizations seemed untenable to some readers of the first Polish edition of this book. They believed that every reading yields a concretization of the work, i.e., that every reading already contains elements that are not contained in the work itself. Then there would actually be no literary work of art itself, but only its concretizations. In the face of the far-reaching differences among concretizations, we could not say which of them reconstructs the work itself and which of them stands closer to it than others, or which of them is further from the work and more or less falsifies it. Even the concept of a falsification or approximation of the work itself would be quite untenable, for there would then exist only the multiplicity of "concretizations," which could be compared only with one another and be more or less related to one another. If this interpretation were correct, the whole investigation of the literary work of art itself would be purely illusory.

Now the principle of differentiation of the literary work of art itself from its concretizations lies in the assertion that the work itself contains places of indeterminacy as well as various potential elements (e.g., aspects, aesthetically relevant qualities), whereas these are removed or actualized in part in a concretization. Thus the notion just adduced would be correct only if we were unable to read the work without having to remove the places of indeterminancy and actualize the potential elements. This, however, is not the case. We can very well refrain from filling out the places of indeterminancy. And it is impossible, even with the best of intentions, to remove all places of indeterminacy. In the concrete case, we are concerned to clarify which places of indeterminacy are present in the work being investigated. We cannot here illustrate the seeking-out of such places of indeterminacy by an example, since this would require a very extensive investigation, even if we were to choose only a short narrative for this purpose. For the number of places of indeterminacy in any work is very large. Thus, all that we want to point out here is why the knowledge of the places of indeterminacy is interesting for the cognition of the literary work of art.

First, we must note that not everything that is not stated expressly in the text of the work is therefore a "place of indeterminacy" in our sense. What is thus unspoken can be what is said (meant) implicitly and unambiguously, either as presupposition or consequence. We read, for example, in the first sentences of "Tristan" by Thomas Mann:

> Einfried, the sanatorium. A long, white, rectilinear building with a side wing, set in a spacious garden pleasingly equipped with grottoes, bowers, and little bark pavilions. Behind its slate roofs the mountains tower heavenwards, evergreen, massy, cleft with wooded ravines.
>
> Now as then Dr. Leander directs the establishment. He wears a two-pronged black beard as curly and wiry as horsehair stuffing. . . .*

It is not stated here or anywhere else in the whole text where this sanatorium "is located." This "where"—e.g., in Europe, in Germany—constitutes a place of indeterminacy which may be intended in some tacit way, if at all, by the reader and thus "filled out." And, to be sure, this added determination of the place or country not provided by the text can be accomplished in a more or less probable way. We have just named two fairly probable supplementations of the location of the sanatorium called Einfried. If we were to think involuntarily that it is located on the northern side of the Alps, perhaps in southern Bavaria, this would not conflict with the context. But we could give no decisive argument supporting this on the basis of the text, for it mentions merely some mountains which rise up "heavenwards" behind the roofs of the sanatorium. This "heavenwards" need not be taken too literally, either, especially from someone who comes from Lübeck. But such a completion of the text by the reader would not be forbidden by the text. The latitude of the "permissible" completions of this place of indeterminacy is fairly great. It is also not stated expressly that the sanatorium "is located" on the surface of the earth, but this does not constitute a "place of indeterminacy" in this story, for

* Thomas Mann, "Tristan," in *Stories of Three Decades,* translated by H. T. Lowe-Porter (New York: Alfred A. Knopf, 1938), p. 133.

it is an unambiguous presupposition of a series of determinations that are given in the text. It is so "self-evident" that it does not need to be stated. Whether or not we think it in reading is of no importance to our understanding of the story. In the same way, it is tacitly, unambiguously prejudged that Dr. Leander is a human being, and this is no place of indeterminacy either, although it belongs to what is unsaid. In the same way, too, it is not stated at the end of the story that Herr Klöterjahn's wife has actually died of the hemorrhage of the lung which she has suffered. But when we learn that Herr Spinell "lifted his eyes, slowly, scanning the house until he reached one of the windows, a curtained window, on which his gaze rested awhile, fixed and sombre" (p. 165), we believe that we have here been implicitly informed of the death of Herr Klöterjahn's wife. We believe this because of the earlier information concerning the course of her illness, the summoning by telegraph of her husband, because of Frau Spatz's words to Herr Klöterjahn, and finally because of the window curtained in mid-afternoon, provided one is aware of the custom of drawing the curtains of the room in which a person has died. It is thus once more something unstated, which, however, is no place of indeterminacy but rather an unambiguous inference from that which is effectively stated in the text. Moreover, it does not need to be stated, since it would be a dispensable piece of information. The fact that it is unstated exercises a special artistic function. It emphasizes that the death, though unstated, still weighs upon Herr Spinell and is all the more expressly present to the reader for being unstated. Hence it exercises here the function of lending to the concretization the form which brings an aesthetically relevant quality to expression at this moment. For just this reason, namely, that there is no effective statement of the death in the text of the story, this actuality does not belong to the schema of the work itself. In contrast, all the details of the death, how it came about, whether quickly or slowly, with agony or as a gentle slumber, etc., constitute the places of indeterminacy of the story by Thomas Mann—places of indeterminacy which are probably not filled out by any reader's completion and thus also not removed. Such a completion is not suggested by the text in any way and is not necessary to the artistic form of the novella. Quite the contrary, this technique of leaving these details in the dark makes the situation all the more expressive and suggestive. Their completion would involve a weakening of the aesthetic effect. In a proper reading we do not even become aware that there is a lacuna here, a place of indeterminacy in the text. In spite of this, it exists in a purely objective sense; and the possibility that it will be completed after all, in some reading, is not excluded.

As we can see, a consideration of the various cases of tacit information, and in particular of the various kinds of places of indeterminacy, can reveal their presence and also teach us about the artistic structure of the work in question. This takes place when, instead of confining ourselves merely to establishing that some place of indeterminacy or other is present, we at the same time subject it to a functional analysis. That is, when we ask, with regard to every place of indeterminacy we discover, why it was introduced into the work and what part it plays in the artistic structure of the work. The functional analysis also poses the question of what part in the structure of the work of art is played by the various possible completions of this place of indeterminacy within the whole of the concretization in question, that is, how they fit into this whole, enrich it, introduce a new voice in the harmony of other motives, accord with or disrupt this harmony, etc. This is a special analytic way of considering the literary work of art itself which goes completely beyond the ordinary reading, even if it does rely on the results of such a reading. At the same time, it requires that we constantly keep an eye on the possible aesthetic concretizations, in order to allow those aesthetically relevant qualities which are capable of being actualized to appear within the field of vision of our consideration of the work. This little example shows us that it is possible to contemplate a literary work of art in such a way that its places of indeterminacy stand out as such or, to put it differently, in such a way that it is possible to apprehend the work in its schematic structure and to oppose it to its various concretizations.

But as long as we are on the subject of places of indeterminacy, we might point out another interesting question which arises in the preaesthetic consideration insofar as this consideration also aims at discovering what is artistic in the work. Can a study of a selected work, e.g., Thomas Mann's "Tristan," show that the places of indeterminacy were not introduced in a completely chaotic or planless way but rather that, in contrast to what is stated expressly, they can be arranged according to certain kinds or types of determination of the portrayed objects or according to the kind of situations in which these objects take part, etc., and that they are employed in the work in question in an intelligible and artistically planned selection and arrangement in order to make possible an aesthetically valuable concretization? We can ask ourselves whether in "Tristan" certain characteristics of the portrayed people are generally or mostly suppressed in order to make other characteristics of these people stand out, or whether they are left undetermined so that the reader may be left a certain freedom in filling them out and thus be able to form different aesthetically valuable concretizations, or whether all persons who are somehow named in the story are portrayed with the same thoroughness or sketchiness, thus how the places of indeterminacy are grouped around these persons in the manner of their general qualitative determination. We are struck immediately by the fact that in "Tristan" only the three principal characters, Herr Klöterjahn, his wife, and Herr Spinell, are characterized by a considerable number of features of their external appearance and of the mental states indicated by their modes of behavior,[58] whereas the other characters are distinguished by only a few selected traits and otherwise consist, as it were, of "indeterminacy." This is certainly no accident, but rather a particular artistic intention. The realization of this intention is a characteristic feature of the "composition" of this novella's schematic structure. But it can also be a trait of the composition of Thomas Mann's novellas in general or, lastly, even the characteristic trait of the novella as a particular literary "genre." The way in which this artistic intention is carried out in the individual case constitutes the specific nature of this work and plays a part in the aesthetic effects which can be achieved in its varied aesthetic concretizations. The individual places of indeterminacy present in the story (taking into consideration the place they occupy in the work) can differ greatly in effectiveness according to the part they play as uncompleted places of indeterminacy and the completions they allow or more or less suggest. By virtue of this effectiveness they can help the reader to actualize qualities of different value in the aesthetic concretization. And the kind and measure of their effectiveness in this respect is what we call "artistic value." [59]

Implicitly contained in what we have already said is a

58. The various kinds of things left unsaid and, in particular, the places of indeterminacy constitute what now remains to be analyzed.

59. Of course, in a literary work of art there are still artistic values of a completely different kind, for instance the values which are realized through the positive determinations given the portrayed persons and situations.

further trait of the literary work of art as a schematic structure. We must now occupy ourselves briefly with this trait. The schema in question is not just something which contains certain gaps; it is, at the same time, something which is positively determined in itself by "filled" qualities and which constitutes, by virtue of being thus determined, the actuality of the work. But it is not simply something actual; rather, of itself it determines, through its positive determinations, various potentialities which, as potentialities, are characteristic of the work in question.[60] In the analytic, preaesthetic way of considering the literary work of art, it is very important to make clear which potential elements of the work of art are determined by the actual elements and also how and in what detail they are determined in the individual case. This is all the more important because, when the work is actualized in a concretization, various aesthetically relevant qualities can be contained in what constitutes the merely potential part of the work.

We know that to the potential elements of the literary work of art belong the "aspects," which, as I once expressed it, are only "held in readiness." There are very different ways of "holding aspects in readiness"; it takes place, for example, as a result of the content of the sentences or, to put it better, as a result of the objective states of affairs determined by means of the sentences. The appropriately selected material of the verbal sounds and other phonetic phenomena also plays a large part here. In ordinary reading we employ the means (or factors) present in the work for the actualization of the aspects, the determinations of the objective states of affairs, without being clearly aware what effects this actualization has and how it actually takes place. Only in the preaesthetic investigative cognition of the work is this made a subject of inquiry. In "Tristan," various persons taking part in the action are characterized more or less generously, but the traits employed for this purpose do not always lead us to apprehend these persons under sufficiently vivid aspects. But sometimes a single trait is already sufficient to cause the person in question to appear with particular vividness. For example, there are several gentlemen at Einfried who are almost always mentioned (for it is no more than a "mention") in the same way. We read: "There are several gentlemen with gaunt, fleshless faces who fling their legs about in that uncontrollable

60. I devoted a special investigation to these "potentialities" in my book *The Literary Work of Art*. I do not wish to repeat this here.

way that bodes no good" (p. 134); or "the gentlemen with the fleshless faces smiled and did their best to keep their legs in order" (p. 136). This short characterization is especially suited to evoke for the reader the visual aspect of these gentlemen's movements.[61] Sometimes this function is performed by the tone in which words are uttered or by the way in which they are formulated; this gives us the concrete aspect of a mental situation. In "Tristan" we read, for example, about the way in which Herr Klöterjahn behaves when he learns of his wife's hemorrhage:

> "Is she dead?" yelled Herr Klöterjahn. As he spoke he clutched the Rätin by the arm and pulled her to and fro on the sill. "Not quite? Not dead; she can see me, can't she? Brought up a little blood again, from the lung, eh? Yes, I give in, it may be from the lung. Gabriele!" he suddenly cried out, and his eyes filled with tears; you could see what a burst of good, warm, honest human feeling came over him. "Yes, I'm coming," he said, and dragged the Rätin after him as he went with long strides down the corridor. You could still hear his voice, from quite a distance, sounding fainter and fainter: "Not quite, eh? From the lung?" (p. 164–65)

This whole portrayal permits us to experience this scene in vivid intuition. The last sentence in particular is suited to evoke an acoustical "aspect" of the receding words of Herr Klöterjahn.

Now such diverse cases, and the means employed in them,

---

61. Of course, the reader must have at his disposal prior knowledge of the gait of those afflicted with locomotor ataxia if the corresponding aspect is to be awakened in him. The art of the author resides in appealing to such prior experiences, especially if these are vivid. But if the appeal is to too narrow a circle of those who possess the proper experience, and if, even then, it is made with insufficient means, the desired aspect fails to be evoked. Sometimes an author employs the naming of specific individual objects for this purpose, in the opinion that the concrete aspect is thereby produced. But this artifice fails if it is employed with insufficient means. Thus, for example, we read the following sentences at the beginning of Thomas Mann's novella "Death in Venice," after we have already learned that the story takes place in Munich: "He found the neighbourhood quite empty. Not a wagon in sight, either on the paved Ungererstrasse, with its gleaming tramlines stretching off towards Schwabing, nor on the Föhring highway" [*Stories of Three Decades,* translated by H. T. Lowe-Porter (New York: Alfred A. Knopf, 1938), p. 378]. Now, if the reader is not well acquainted with these two streets in Munich, this information is not sufficient to cause him to experience, during his reading, the corresponding aspect of the streets named. Probably not even the information that one of the streets was "paved" with "gleaming tramlines stretching off towards Schwabing" will help the reader much, because those details are not characteristic or striking enough to evoke the street for the reader.

must be investigated and also tested with a view to whether they are successful or more or less unproductive. It is clear that the mere reading of such passages does not suffice to make us aware of this. We must objectify the details of a part of the text itself in renewed intentional acts of apprehension and then further investigate what this text is able to effect with regard to the constitution of an aspect in a concretization: whether precisely those phenomena are concretized in it which we expect as a result of the relevant passage of the text. In this kind of study we thus go beyond the naked text (i.e., beyond the dual stratum of the language) to the concretization of a phase of the stratum of aspects in order not merely to have them (as we "have" them in an ordinary reading) but in order also to observe the aspect or multiplicity of aspects which appears there with regard to its content and also with regard to its mode of appearance. This kind of study takes place, so to speak, from an upper "storey," from which we survey the finished work in its differentiated details and compare these in their relations to one another. In particular, we study how a change in one member of a relation, e.g., in a series of sentences with specific syntactical properties, results in a parallel change in another member, e.g., in the aspect evoked and the mode of its appearance. In this way we apprehend the role of the sentence formations and their capacity for evoking aspects or holding them in readiness. This new "storey" or "level"—as I expressed it metaphorically—from which we view certain parts of the work in question permits the work, or one of its parts, to appear at a certain distance from the subject of cognition. This distance is indispensable if we are to apprehend the linguistic formations in their diverse functions, e.g., of holding the aspects in readiness or actualizing them, whereas in an ordinary reading the functions of the linguistic formations are only performed and not objectively apprehended by the reader. During the reading the reader's attention is directed at the portrayed objectivities, and he apprehends them from close up under the aspects they have in the concretization. The distanced surveying of various parts of the work permits the surveyor to assess their role in relation to certain other selected details of the work. The difficulty with this mode of procedure, however, as well as with the emotional neutrality of this kind of investigation, resides in the fact that many details of the concretized work no longer appear with the same vividness as in an ordinary reading or even disappear from the reader's field of vision. This applies especially for the aesthetically relevant qualities, since they must either be emotionally felt or apprehended in intentional feeling. In the analytic preaesthetic investigation they are at most intended in a conceptual way as something which is determined, by virtue of the appropriate capacities of certain properties of the literary work of art, as potentially belonging to it.

The aesthetically relevant qualities are, for the most part, only indirectly determined, by the details of the portrayed objectivities, or by multiplicities of aspects, or, finally, by the interplay of various strata of the work of art, so that we do not sense their immediate basis in the linguistic formations. Their determination depends, however, not merely on what is intentionally projected by the language in the objective stratum and the stratum of aspects but also on the way in which the objectivities are portrayed. The preaesthetic investigation of the literary work of art as regards its artistic effectiveness cannot leave out of consideration the methods of portrayal employed in it. In my book *The Literary Work of Art* I therefore made an effort[62] to indicate the various possible modes of portrayal of things, people, and events by means of the sentence correlates (in particular, states of affairs) immediately projected intentionally by the sentence meanings, and I do not wish to repeat myself here. It is now time to make clear how an analytical consideration of the modes of portrayal can or must take place if it is to be instructive with regard to the problems of literary art. In considering these modes of portrayal, the investigation becomes even further removed from the ordinary, continuously progressing reading of the work, although it presupposes such a reading and also makes frequent use of it in individual phases. It is first necessary to orient ourselves properly on the basis of the reading as to what—which things, people, events, situations in which events take place, etc.— is portrayed in the work in question. That means we must become well acquainted with the objective stratum of the work on the basis of the reading and also orient ourselves properly as to two orders of the events: the order of succession of these events in the portrayed time and the order of succession of the same events in the portrayal in the work in question. It is very seldom the case that these two orders coincide, although it is not impossible.[63] But their

62. See *The Literary Work of Art*, Chap. 7.
63. When we read the beginning of *Buddenbrooks*, it appears at first as if these two orders almost coincide. But already during the ceremonial dinner of the Buddenbrook family (in October, 1935) with its guests,

coincidence or divergence is closely connected with the mode of portrayal and results in manifold artistic effects, which in turn carry with them greatly divergent aesthetically valent phenomena in the concretization of the works in question. A large number of different possible interweavings of these two "orders" has been attempted in the modern novel, and a specific technique has been developed for consistently applying the appropriate kind of portrayal, although each author doubtless sought in this way to achieve his own artistic and aesthetic effects. And the development tends, it appears, in the direction not only of making the order of succession of the portrayal as independent as possible from the order of succession in the portrayed time but also of confusing or shattering the order in the portrayed time, so that it is almost impossible, in the limiting case, to have a purely phenomenal experience of the line of development of the occurrences or even to pursue it consciously with any success. These literary facts are familiar; and if I mention them here, I do so in order to indicate that the investigation of these various modes of portrayal (in both the novel and also, for instance, the drama) constitutes an important theme of the preaesthetic consideration of the literary work of art, a theme to which far too little attention has been given up to now. Both the purely technical artistic means employed in these diverse modes of portrayal and the aesthetic phenomena thereby obtained, especially with regard to their role in the constitution of the aesthetic values which result in the individual cases, have been far too little analyzed. We are dealing here, of course, with phenomena of temporal perspective, but in particular with the case in which there occurs a peculiar crossing of the two time orders—the portrayed time and the order of succession of the parts of the work. This crossing results in synthetic structures which carry with them specific artistic and aesthetic effects. But we are often concerned with something more, or with something other, than phenomena playing an aesthetic role. We are con-

---

the "prehistory" is revealed in different ways by the various speeches and conversations in the course of the reception—the history of the new house, the remembrance of the incident of the silver spoons during the Napoleonic wars, etc. The earlier intimate details of the family life of Johann Buddenbrook (his first wife, the marriage of his eldest son, etc.) are also mentioned and are mixed into the developing portrayal of the events at the first reception in the Buddenbrook house. This way of revealing the prehistory by means of conversations now taking place between the portrayed persons (rather than directly, by the "author") is only one possible mode of portrayal in the description of events successively developing "now."

cerned with a special structuring of the portrayed world, which is connected with various aspects of the reality, or, stated more generally, of the mode of being, in which the occurrences in this world appear or are supposed to appear according to the author's intention. The temporal order, or the strict observance of this order by the portrayed occurrences, seems to be connected somehow with the character of reality. At first it would appear that through all possible variations of the relation between the two orders, even in their greatest possible independence from each other, one thing must remain constant, namely, that any order and succession of the portrayal must reveal a clear and unambiguous order of portrayed occurrences in the portrayed time. But those literary works of art in which this latter order is clear, unbroken, and always unambiguously determined constitute only one limiting type of literary art, which is neither the only possible one nor the only artistically or aesthetically valuable one. It is characteristic of that mode of portrayal which we like to call "realism." It goes hand in hand with a series of other characteristic traits of the mode of portrayal, which will have to be studied in their own right. At least it must go hand in hand with them if the work is to contain no disharmonies (which, incidentally, can be artistically intended in many cases). It almost never comes to the point, by the way, where the two "orders" "coincide" in the sense that every new sentence appearing in the text determines a state of affairs existing in a new corresponding moment of time. In the majority of cases there are sometimes whole groups of sentences which relate to various details of the objects and events existing in a single specific moment of the portrayed time. This always occurs when the attributes of the persons and things taking part in an action are described.[64] The sentences belonging to the description can either form a continuous text or be scattered in various places in the text. Only in the former case, when the description refers to a state of affairs which exists in a single present moment, can we speak

---

64. Thus it happens in the beginning of *Buddenbrooks* that only a very short conversation takes place between those members of the Buddenbrook family who are present, but this conversation is woven into a long description of the individual persons and also of the reception room in which they are located. This description, which of course lasts some time, is yet removed, as it were, from the course of portrayed time; time stands still to a certain extent while we make ourselves acquainted with the traits of the persons present. In older novels, for instance those of Zola, the reader is first given a description several pages long, for example of a room in which something is going to occur, before anything begins to happen.

of an approximate coincidence of the two orders of succession; in other cases these orders diverge. Already the descriptions (usually given by the author) of situations and events happening in another temporal segment, interwoven with the portrayal of an occurrence, have the result that the two streams of succession (of the narration and of that which is narrated) part company. And the events which are reported later, even though they took place before the events developing in the present, must first be placed by the reader in the corresponding place in portrayed time. The text instructs the reader, as it were, how this is to be done; the manner of this instruction is not always exact and unambiguous, so that it is not always clear where the "earlier" events inserted into the narrative ought to be placed in the stream of portrayed time. And there are various methods for making this operation harder for the reader, so that, in the limiting case, he is left in a very unclear state of mind as to how the portrayed events are temporally connected. The factual and, in particular, the causal connection between the portrayed events also suffers in this case; the portrayed world begins to fall apart, sometimes on account of the artistic inability of the author, sometimes as the result of his intended artistic effectiveness.

In the face of these different possible circumstances, the following tasks, among others, present themselves for the preaesthetic investigation of the literary work of art. First, those sentences are to be compared which determine the continuing development of the occurrences in the portrayed world and thus also establish the frame of portrayed time. It immediately becomes clear to what extent the time is filled by the delineated occurrences and becomes past with them, as opposed to being merely projected as a schema with which many objects are correlated—objects which are only mentioned instead of being effectively portrayed. Finally, it also becomes clear what gaps are present in the events and consequently also in the time itself; on the other hand, it becomes clear whether the events and occurrences brought up in another order of portrayal can be fitted into the portrayed time and, if so, in what way. Moreover, those sentences which merely project the further determinations of the portrayed objectivities, but contribute nothing themselves to the "action" and to the events in the portrayed world, can also be compared. We can correlate with every portrayed objectivity the corresponding group of sentences determining it. And then we see what has actually been determined with regard to the object in question (concerning both its attributes and its participation in the events portrayed in the work) and what, on the contrary, has been passed over in silence and, in particular, constitutes a place of indeterminacy. On the other hand, it is revealed in which states of affairs the object in question is portrayed. Then the whole spectrum of the various possible modes in which it can be thus portrayed reveals itself to the observer; these modes can vary in a number of ways while portraying the same object with the same explicit determinations. In spite of this, it is not irrelevant just which modes of portrayal are employed, since each possesses a different effectiveness with respect to the intuitive concretization of the object and the distinctness of its determinations. The actual analysis of the artistic methods for making the object appear as significant and expressive as possible begins precisely with this question. It is not concerned with static or even statistical results but with a function analysis of the capacities for portrayal possessed by the projected states of affairs and their possible variations. Some of them are highly expressive, others say nothing at all; some are plain and simple, while others are composite and complicated. Some of them are striking and rich in intimated consequences, while others contain flat and unsuggestive elements. Of greater importance, however, is the fact that some states of affairs bring the nature of the object directly to distinct expression, while the others reveal only secondary, unimportant, inessential, or accidental features of the object. In particular, there are also states of affairs projected by sentences which bring aesthetically relevant qualities in the portrayed objects to intuitive actualization and consequently prepare the conditions for the constitution of a specific aesthetic value. All this must be shown in a dynamic, functional investigation of the actual states of affairs projected by sentences of the work of art in question and of the objects which come to constitution in them. This investigation continually operates on the border between the apprehension of the details of a literary work of art, considered as a schematic and aesthetically neutral formation, and the various aesthetic concretizations of the work in question, which only suggest themselves as possibilities. On a preliminary basis, it operates only on selected parts of the work which have been subjected to a functional, analytic investigation. This is a particularly difficult kind of study. On the one hand, we must maintain the "cool," aesthetically neutral attitude in the pre-aesthetic analysis, whereas, on the other hand, we must either rely on our memory of concretizations of the work previously carried out or else place ourselves in the actual aesthetic attitude and try to actualize at least the relevant fragment of the concretization of the work. Finally, we can only attempt to foresee the various possible ways of concretizing this fragment, which only suggest themselves to us. Only by contrasting the factors of neutral value in the objects portrayed in the states of affairs with the manifold aesthetically valuable qualities which are actualized in various ways can we learn what artistic capacities for constituting the value-bearing factors of the aesthetic concretizations are possessed by the states of affairs actually "realized" in the work. By analyzing the cases in which a successful constitution of these factors takes place or in which at least the suggestion of such a constitution is indicated, which alone can move the aesthetically experiencing reader to actualize it effectively, and by contrasting them with those cases in which it more or less fails, we can make ourselves aware *in concreto* and not merely in abstract conjectures of which means of artistic formation are successful and which, in contrast, fail. There is a certain kind of empirical knowledge which is generally present in the creative artist only as a kind of vague premonition, and which gives way immediately to creative activity, but which the investigator of literary art must attain to consciously in order to assess the artistic effectiveness of certain techniques of literary portrayal and thus to determine the artistic value of the work in question.

Of course, the intentional correlates of the sentences, and in particular the states of affairs which perform the function of portrayal with regard to the objects, are dependent in their "material" [*sachhaltig*] content (to use Husserl's term) and their syntactic structure, and also in their relations to one another, on the structure of the sentences which intentionally project them. Thus the effectiveness of artistic portrayal of the states of affairs is to be referred to the effectiveness of the sentences, specifically to the sentences both as specially structured semantic units and as organized phonetic material, including the phonetic phenomena arising from the succession of verbal sounds, e.g., rhythm, sentence melody, and the rest. The preaesthetic, analytical, functional consideration of the literary work of art thus extends to both linguistic strata of the work. It first attempts to apprehend certain over-all characteristics of the sentential semantic units. These are of different kinds, e.g., simplicity and complexity in the grammatical sense; simplicity in the sense of plainness of "style" in contrast to "complexity" of style; or "simplicity" in the sense of economy of means as contrasted with hypertrophy of motives. To take another example, we can have freedom in the flow of unfolding sentences or constraint (a certain stiffness) in the unfolding of the meaning of individual sentences, as well as in their succession; we can have clarity or unclarity, transparency or opacity, in the structure of sentence meaning, with its associated opacity of intention, of what the sentence is actually trying to "say," etc. These over-all characteristics of the sentence meanings cannot be apprehended by merely thinking or understanding the sentences, but only by specifically attending to the sentences as objectivities of a certain kind. These over-all characteristics are all particular qualitative factors of the whole of the sentence as soon as this whole has been constituted by our thinking the sentence in question. But they are founded in specific formal factors in the sentence structure, and these, in turn, must be discovered by an analytic procedure. The formal factors are of various kinds, including, e.g., the paratactical or hypotactical ordering of the relatively independent parts of so-called complex sentences, the accumulation of adjectival determinations of the subject of the sentence or of the relative clauses attached to it, the simplicity or complexity of the predicate, etc. Another important question is whether the individual words appearing in the sentences are unambiguous or ambiguous in an unclear way (where it is noticeable that they are ambiguous, although we cannot say at first which meanings are hidden behind the ambiguous word). The over-all qualitative characteristics of the sentences are certainly not all neutral as regards aesthetic value; hence we may ask whether they can be apprehended in a preaesthetic kind of investigation or are capable of being constituted only in an aesthetic experience and are accessible only by means of such an experience. In contrast, the just-named formal properties of the sentence meanings are certainly all of neutral aesthetic value and consequently are accessible to the preaesthetic kind of investigation of the literary work of art. Moreover, they can appear in both literary works of art and scientific works. Elucidating them is part of the task of a "logical" analysis, as it were, of the linguistic stratum of literary works in general. But this analysis performs its role in the analytical investigation of literary works of art only when it is carried out in connection with the disclosure of the over-all qualitative characteristics of the sentences in general and when the "formal" factors in the sentences are viewed under the aspect of their possible function in constituting those over-all qualitative characteristics and, further, in connection with the study of the role (function) of these characteristics in constituting various types of intentional sentence correlates or states of affairs. Only in such a functional analytical consideration is it possible to demonstrate the existence of the close connection between the syntactic structure of the sentences and the way in which the portrayed world and what occurs in it are revealed to the reader in the course of the reading. For this connection is anchored, on the one hand, in the structure of the sentences and, on the other, in the concreteness and distinctness (also sharpness) with which the portrayed world is revealed to the reader. But the complete concrete results of such an analysis show us still more: not merely the existence, but also the kind, or variety, of this connection which exists in the analyzed work.

The character of the appearance of the portrayed objectivities is connected, however, not merely with the formal structure of the sentences but also with the kinds of words which appear in these sentences. I should like to show this more precisely by a concrete example so as not to dwell in mere generalities here. I shall, of course, confine myself to individual selected cases, taking my example from so-called narrative literature, where these relationships are still relatively as simple as possible.

It is well known that Thomas Mann's *Buddenbrooks* is distinguished by the fact that the portrayed people and things, as well as the occurrences in which they participate, are shown in a very concrete way and have the semblance of an individual reality. From the beginning, the reader has the impression that he is associating with actual people in a real world and that he is a witness to the occurrences in which they are involved. By what means is this impression created? Part I of the novel describes the reception in the new house of the Buddenbrook family. The reception lasts about seven hours, and it appears that this entire time is filled with portrayed events and occurrences, although, of course, even here there are temporal phases in which we cannot tell, on the basis of the text, what is happening.[65]

In Chapter 1 we are mainly introduced to the characters and the rooms in which they spend their time. Only a minimal percentage of space is devoted to events and occurrences. The char-

65. The description of this evening occupies 36 pages in the Knopf edition. We must limit ourselves here to fragments of this narration, to the first chapter and selected parts from it.

acters and things are described in a static way by mentioning their visible attributes above all, so that the reader believes he is seeing them. Thus, in the first place, their clothing is described, with special emphasis on color. If we count the nouns and adjectives, our enumeration will confirm the general impression gained from the ordinary reading. In Chapter 1 the number of nouns and adjectives together considerably outweighs the number of verbs. If we add together the four categories of words— substantives + adjectives + finite verbs + adverbs—then the number of nominal expressions, (substantives + adjectives) makes up 71 per cent of this total, whereas the number of finite verbs makes up only 20 per cent. But if we consider separately the first three pages of Chapter 1, in which nothing actually happens as yet and only persons and things are described, the total number of the nominal expressions climbs to 79.22 per cent, whereas the number of finite verbs sinks to 14.66 per cent. If, on the other hand, we consider separately the last page of Chapter 1, in which something is already beginning to happen, the number of nominal expressions sinks to 58.9 per cent, and the number of finite verbs climbs to 32.7 per cent. If we take for comparison a segment of the first chapter of Part V of the novel, the ratio between the two groups of words is somewhat different. Here the persons involved in the action and the rooms in which they move are both familiar and thus need not be described, whereas action is taking place between the persons present. Thus the number of nominal expressions now comes to 60.4 per cent, the number of finite verbs, however, to 26.8 per cent of the total. The variations in the number of adjectives are also interesting. In the first three pages of Chapter 1 (Part I) they come to 32.4 per cent, whereas in the last phase of Chapter 1 they come to only 19.6 per cent of the total sum; in the whole of Chapter 1, however, they come to 25.08 per cent, whereas, in the first three pages of Chapter 1, Part V, of the novel they come to only 13.1 per cent. It is also worthwhile to compare the total number of adjectives appearing in Chapter 1 (Part I) with the number of those among them which determine visual properties of the portrayed objectivities. There are 237 adjectives, of which 112, or 47.25 per cent, determine visual factors. The reader's impression that Thomas Mann is, above all, portraying the visible world in this chapter is thus confirmed.[66]

66. The numerical data should not give the impression that the author greatly values statistical computations. In the first place, they are em-

The assertion concerning the connection between the peculiarities of the portrayed world and the verbal material of the
text is confirmed by this means. But it is obvious without special
investigation, since the portrayed world is only formed as a result of the content of the semantic units of the linguistic stratum
of the literary work. All the peculiarities of the dual stratum of
language have their reverberations in the portrayed world. If
certain variations appear in the language, there will be corresponding variations in the stratum of portrayed objectivities.
These correlations can be revealed by individual studies.

The great accumulation of nominal expressions and, in
particular, of adjectives in those portions of the text of Thomas
Mann's novel which we have considered is of course worthy of
attention and points to a specific technique in the mode of portrayal. It reveals the people and things to the reader, not only in
their visual attributes, but above all in their enduring attributes,
just as they would present themselves if we observed them
calmly and attentively and not, or at least not primarily, as they
would appear in the active course of their lives. But do pre-
ponderance and quantity of nominal determinations alone suffice to evoke in the reader an impression of the actuality and
individuality of the portrayed objectivities? Or to lend them the
character of intuitiveness and direct presence and proximity?
Does the mere multitude of details given make the reader feel
from the first moment as if he were at home in the Buddenbrook
house and bring him into direct relation with its inhabitants?
Does this not depend at least in large part on the choice of
adjectives used? Indeed, this choice is determined by the
exigencies of the portrayal of the individual characters. They
belong to three different generations and are also of different
ancestry. The determinations attached to the individual characters, e.g., the details of dress (and later of manner of speech,

---

ployed here only as a kind of confirmation of assertions which were established in a qualitative analytical investigation. Second, these statistical
computations are carried out in only a very small range, avoiding large
numbers, and only as an answer to questions posed by the qualitative
analysis—all this in conscious contrast to statistical computations which
are now being carried out in great numbers. Much propaganda is being
made for them in the thoroughly false conviction that so-called rigorous
and objective results of literary study can be obtained only in this way.
These computations are also being made in a completely chaotic way,
without any clear knowledge of what end they are to serve, in the false
belief that these computations themselves will make it possible to determine the goals of the investigation. But this is a separate subject,
which I do not wish to consider further at this time.

too), serve to indicate immediately the individuality of each of them, even in externals, and to create the impression of a vital and individual nature, formed by its life and its history. The determinations are chosen with care in order to give the briefest, most generous, and most pregnant information possible concerning the people whose fortunes are later portrayed. The great accumulation of details is explained by the author's intention of giving, in the fastest way possible, a concrete basis for the action which is to be developed and of doing so in a way which the author himself, in a different novel, refers to as "exhaustive" and praises as artistically successful.[67] But the statistical computation of the percentages does not explain this; rather, the extension of the statistical computation to the whole book would cause this accumulation to vanish. Nor do the statistics explain how the choice of the given determinations of the persons introduced is made or must be made so as to make possible the realization of the artistic goals of the composition of the work. This can be elucidated only by an analytical and functional study of the individual delineated traits of the portrayed persons in which we assess their function in characterizing the person in question and correctly understand their role in providing the basis for his subsequent behavior and for the course of the action which depends on it. Of course, the structure of the sentences in which these words appear must be noted and taken into consideration. For it is not easy to give so many details of the portrayed persons and of their spatial surroundings in short form without being dry or boring or doing it in sentences which are hard to read. Hence it is now necessary to return once again to the structure of the sentences, but this time from another point of view and with reference to a different function of the sentence structure, thus not with reference to the structure of the states of affairs projected by it and the way in which these states of affairs portray the corresponding objects, but rather with reference to certain peculiarities of the sentence structure itself, which play a part in the ease or difficulty of reading the text. The way in which the sentences affect the reader is also a matter of concern here. We must ask whether the course of the narrative bores the reader or not, whether it tires him or permits a smooth and pleasant reading—once again an analytical task

67. "We do not fear being called meticulous, inclining as we do to the view that only the exhaustive can be truly interesting" [*The Magic Mountain*, translated by H. T. Lowe-Porter (New York: Alfred A. Knopf, 1939), Foreword].

which cannot be solved automatically by any statistical computation. In order to make this clearer, I shall confine myself to the first section of *Buddenbrooks*.

The beginning of the novel consists of a fragment of a conversation which is at first incomprehensible. The purpose of this fragment is to arouse the reader's interest so that he will be induced to learn what it is actually about. But at first no continuation of the conversation is forthcoming. First the persons participating in it are introduced, all in a single paragraph.

> Frau Consul Buddenbrook shot a glance at her husband and came to the rescue of her little daughter. She sat with her mother-in-law on a straight white-enamelled sofa with yellow cushions and a gilded lion's head at the top. The Consul was in his easy-chair beside her, and the child perched on her grandfather's knee in the window.*

There are thus five persons whose family relationships are named and whose distribution in the room is precisely determined. In contrast, the sofa is described by a series of visual properties. And in the German text this description is so inserted between the subject and the predicate of the sentence that only a single relative clause is introduced for six determinations. In spite of the concentrated fullness of information thus given, the sentence is not difficult, and it must be said that the whole situation is skillfully projected in a sentence which is not too long.†

There follows a short sentence which forms the continuation of the conversation but which still does not explain what it is about. The situation is made clearer in part by the very long sentence which now follows in the German text, the construction of which does not appear to be very skillful or unified.‡ The German sentence occupies 13 lines (almost one hundred words) and gives first a description of "little Antonie," her dress and the way she acts, which is expressed in a series of words uttered by her. It so happens that she is supposed to recite from memory an article from the Catechism, at which she does, after all, succeed, with her mother's help. In the process the reader also learns the date of the new edition of the Catechism, which pro-

---

* Thomas Mann, *Buddenbrooks*, translated from the German by H. T. Lowe-Porter (New York: Alfred A. Knopf, 1938), p. 3. All quotations will be taken from this edition.

† The English paragraph given above is expressed in a single German sentence.

‡ The English translation breaks this sentence into several shorter ones.

vides, at the same time, the approximate date of the conversation and thus of the beginning of the whole story. Thus, much is achieved by this single sentence; but it is composed of so many successive and coordinated parts (there are, all together, 17 parts, apart from three inserted fragments of conversation) that the reader is able to follow it only with some effort. But, if one pays close attention, one will not get lost in the sentence. Its construction is transparent. It requires only a good active memory, with a wide span. If it were merely a matter of resolving the tension created by the fragments of the conversation, which are not properly intelligible, the sentence could be much shorter and easier to grasp. But it performs, at the same time, the function of creating an intuitive basis for the mode of behavior of little Tony by providing a series of traits of the child's appearance. Both are to be taken care of at the same time; hence the length and relative complexity of the sentence. The portrayal of little Tony's mode of behavior, this time by reference to her inner experiences, is then continued in the two following sentences. Then the grandfather, Monsieur Johann Buddenbrook, only mentioned until now, comes on stage and reacts in his way to Tony's words. This reaction is portrayed in three sentences. It is depicted only because it serves to characterize the old gentleman. And then in three further coordinated sentences in the German text his form is described by means of a series of traits which can be grasped visually. All these sentences give several details of the appearance and mode of behavior of the old gentleman. Their construction is relatively simple, and their meaning is easily grasped. They mainly perform the function of introducing Johann Buddenbrook to the reader by means of his concretely perceivable traits. In a similar way, the two Buddenbrook ladies are shown in respect of their concrete appearance in easily understandable sentences, whereupon, finally, the younger Consul Buddenbrook is portrayed in respect of his appearance and mode of behavior:

The Consul was leaning forward in his easy-chair, rather fidgety. He wore a cinnamon-coloured coat with wide lapels and leg-of-mutton sleeves close-fitting at the wrists, and white linen trousers with black stripes up the outside seams. His chin nestled in a stiff choker collar, around which was folded a silk cravat that flowed down amply over his flowered waistcoat.

He had his father's deep-set blue observant eyes, though their expression was perhaps more dreamy; but his features were clearer-cut and more serious, his nose was prominent and aquiline, and his cheeks, half-covered with a fair curling beard, were not so plump as the old man's [p. 4].

Just as before, the main features of what one sees of this person—the clothing, the face, the hands—are delineated here, where the traits of the clothing serve to characterize the fashion, and thus indirectly the time, of the younger generation of Buddenbrooks. This indicates a specific technique of portrayal which Thomas Mann often employs in his novels and short stories, especially at the beginning of the work in question.

All in all, this is all done in such a way that the reader makes the acquaintance of the main characters of the story awaiting him (whereupon the rooms of the house are also precisely described, in order to draw in intuitive strokes the environment in which these characters live); and they come to him portrayed in such a way that he becomes acquainted with them under vivid and distinct visual aspects. Only then does the portrayal of events follow, whereupon new characters come on stage and are often described in a similar way, but much more briefly.

We could analyze the whole novel thus, passage by passage, and make ourselves aware of the means of artistic portrayal, discovering their manifold functions in the formation of the various possible aesthetic concretizations. The connection between the elements and factors of the work of art would then begin to become evident to us. The analytical phase of the investigative cognition of the literary work of art begins to pass over into the synthetic stage.

But before we go into that, we must be allowed to say something about the investigative cognition of literary works of art which belong to a completely different literary genre. The question is, in what way are lyric poems accessible to an analytic functional investigation, or in what way can they be accessible? For someone could object that this investigation is indeed possible and capable of successful application with works of narrative art but fails utterly with a genuine lyric poem because— we could formulate it as follows—it shatters the internal unity of the poem, without which it could simply not be properly understood or be apprehended in its artistry.

The difficulty which faces us here resides above all in the fact that lyric poems are so diverse in form, function, and artistic means, and so extraordinarily rich in aesthetic effects, that we run the danger of having to undertake the analysis anew for each genuine lyric poem in order to avoid inadmissible generalizations. They are also so tender and fragile in their emotional mood that every analysis threatens to destroy them and to endanger their internal equilibrium. Thus we want here only to make clear by a few examples the difficulties with which an analytical investigation of lyric poems has to deal.

First, however, a few further words concerning some characteristic traits of "lyric" poetry. Of course there are various "lyric" poems which do not fit the characterization suggested here. They are then simply "lyric" in a different sense and present us with different tasks in their cognition.

In discussing the examples taken from so-called narrative literature, I have left out entirely the problem of the "narrator." This would introduce a certain complication into our deliberations and belongs mainly to the theory of a specific kind of literary work of art and not to the theory of its cognition, which occupies us here. But can we proceed in the same way with so-called lyric poems? Can we simply exclude the "lyrical" ego from our deliberations? This would mean reducing such a poem simply to the portraying function of the sentences and leaving out of the poem everything which is expressed by means of these sentences. It would then essentially cease to be "lyric."

The lyric poem or, more precisely, the sentences of which its text consists, constitute, when they are understood in respect of their dynamic development, a statement, an utterance of a speaker, hence of the so-called lyrical subject. The utterance of these sentences constitutes a mode of behavior of the lyrical ego, or, stated more precisely, the utterance of them belongs to its mode of behavior. Someone whose mental structure and state of mind are intentionally determined merely by the fact of uttering these sentences and by their content behaves in such a way that he utters precisely these sentences, or merely thinks them to himself. His total behavior includes something more than the utterance of these sentences, specifically, everything in the content of these sentences which relates to his total behavior and whatever they otherwise express concerning his life and his psyche. This expressing, which takes place in the tone of the utterance and in the choice of words and their succession, is part of the essential function of the lyric poem, which is nothing other than the manifestation of the lyrical ego. If we are to apprehend the full content of such a poem, we must not only think the total content of the sentences making up the poem, paying attention to their phonetic side in its dynamic unfolding and letting it affect us, but we must also understand the expressive function and concretize the lyrical subject in its mental state or in its momentary psychic transformation.

Some people speak of the "author" of the poem instead of the "lyrical ego." If this former word is supposed to denote only what is intentionally determined by the full content and the expressive function of the sentences of the poem, then this manner of speaking is unobjectionable. But if this word is supposed to denote the author in the sense of the real person (e.g., J. W. Goethe or R. M. Rilke), then it is better to avoid it and to make a strict distinction between the lyrical subject (ego) and the real poet. The lyrical subject is a purely intentional object which is projected by the total content of the sentences belonging to the poem in question and by their expressive function, and it constitutes in this way an object portrayed in the poem in question. It is inseparably bound up with the other objectivities portrayed in the poem, and also with the poem itself, into a totality. The "poet" in the strict sense is, in contrast, a real person who has "composed" the poem and written it down. He remains completely outside his poem and has, in addition, many determinations which do not pertain at all to the lyrical ego. On the other hand, he need not, and often does not, have such determinations as hold true of the lyrical ego in question. We learn about the mental states and character traits of the real poet from various other sources as well. It is also much to be doubted whether we are justified in using the poems written by him as a source of information concerning him. Sometimes there can be positive reasons for doing so, for example, when a poem is part of an actual letter from the poet to one of his acquaintances. But as soon as this same poem is taken out of the letter and published as a separate whole, it loses the character of an actual communication to someone. The lyrical subject must then be constructed exclusively from the total content of the poem (including what is expressed), and all secondary pieces of information must be left out of consideration. In the intention of the poet, the lyrical subject need not be himself at all. It can be a completely fictional figure, into which the poet transposes or feels himself or which serves him as a mask, behind which he conceals himself. The poems themselves are not simply psychological documents, as they are often held to be. At most, the mere fact that the poet composed the particular poem in a particular real situation can serve as a psychological document. Many poems would cause us great embarrassment if we had to establish that in them the poet is really trying to say something about himself rather than actually only being a "poet," someone, that is, who, with the help of selected groups of words, creates a poetic "reality" which is meant to stand as an artistic whole. We usually lack sure criteria for deciding this.

The distinction between the lyrical subject and the real poet is not just purely theoretical hair-splitting. Only by keeping these fundamentally different objectivities separate can we read and understand lyric poems in a way that is adequate to them. Setting the real poet in place of the lyrical ego only leads us to misinterpret the work of art and, as a result, also to falsify the psychology of the poet, instead of keeping to literary works of art and investigating the art of poetry.

The "portrayed world" in a lyric poem thus includes (a) the sentences or words, uttered by the lyrical ego, which make up the poem or, stated more precisely, are merely "quoted" in it; (b) the lyrical subject (ego); (c) that which the sentences of the poem are about; and (d) everything which these sentences express concerning the mental and spiritual life and the structure of the lyrical ego. Often the meaning of the sentences is formed in such a way that the words appearing in the sentences determine a store of portrayed objectivities which perform a symbolic function and consequently point to something completely other than themselves, something which is not directly meant by the literal sense of the sentences at all and only shines in a strange way through what is directly portrayed, although it is at the same time precisely that which is actually at issue. Sometimes the meaning of the sentences in a lyric poem is so constituted that what is portrayed by them retains its importance, so to speak, but in such a way that, at the same time, a completely new quality is brought to appearance precisely by means of what is portrayed, a quality which cannot be directly determined, much less shown by linguistic meanings: a metaphysical quality, for instance, or a necessary ontic relation among aesthetically relevant qualities which are qualified to constitute an aesthetic value in concrete intuitiveness and to set it before the reader's eyes or make it accessible to his intentional feeling. In this case, what is "portrayed" in such a lyric poem includes the second "reality," so to speak, which is revealed only symbolically, or the metaphysical quality, or necessary ontic relations among aesthetically relevant qualities, brought to appearance only indirectly. And the projection and apprehension of all these phenomena enable us to apprehend, along with the poem uttered by the lyrical ego, also the mode of behavior of the latter, into which the reader must, as it were, feel his way.

That the sentences forming the text of the lyric poem are actually supposed to be read as the words uttered by the lyrical ego is perhaps best shown by the acknowledged fact that the lyric poem is not supposed to be read completely silently or soundlessly but should either effectively be "read aloud"—with an adequate "declamation"—or at least be apprehended in silent reading as something in which the phonetic stratum, with all the phenomena appearing in it—line and sentence melody, the tone of delivery, which performs the expressive function, etc.—is represented in vivid imagination. A false intonation, an inadequate reproduction of the rhythm or line melody, a false pronunciation of the individual words, easily destroys the inner connection of all the elements of the poem, or threatens to destroy the prevailing equilibrium of aesthetically valent qualities, or, lastly, makes the expressive function of the spoken sentences ineffective, so that the lyric poem cannot then be constituted in its full emotionality. The result of all this is that no genuine, really valuable lyric poem can be translated into a foreign language, precisely because the phonetic stratum is then replaced by a completely different verbal material, which cannot ever perform all those functions which were performed effortlessly in the original.

Lyric poems, especially if they are great, genuine works of art, can be read either in one's own native language or in a foreign language which one has mastered to such a degree that one is able to employ it almost like one's native language.

The correct pronunciation of the lyric poem is, to be sure, indispensable to every genuine lyric poem, but it does not of itself suffice to make the literary work in question "lyric." For the words uttered by a portrayed person in a drama must also be adequately formed with regard to their phonetic properties if they are to perform their expressive function and, in particular, if they are to be exactly suited to the dramatic situation in which they are spoken. This alone does not make them "lyrical" utterances. The specifically lyrical character must yet be added in order for a lyric poem to be specifically differentiated from a speech in a drama. The mode of behavior of a lyrical subject is also completely different from the behavior of a person in a drama, who is a source of the action. This is simply not possible for the lyrical ego. It is distinguished by a peculiar sort of inactivity, by an inability to accomplish actual deeds in the world (in the portrayed world, of course, to which, incidentally, the persons in a drama also belong), deeds which produce something new in the world. The lyrical ego assumes, rather, the attitude of a reflective observer, a person who becomes conscious of something and is thereby transposed into a state of feeling or else subjected to a change of feeling. Nor does the lyrical ego inhabit a world in which it is even possible for it to perform genuine deeds. What takes place in the lyrical ego is either a simple emotional reaction or an outburst of feeling resulting from the awareness of something happening in it, with reference to a present or past event. The lyrical subject is far too occupied with what is happening within itself, and too devoted to what it feels, to be able to accomplish a deed which would produce a change in the world around it. And where, as in reflective lyric poetry, a thought of which it has become conscious results in a feeling, the excessive concentration on this feeling or the submission to it prevents the lyrical subject from performing a cool act of cognition directed at the objective world. Everything ends with a fleeting "impression," with whatever it was that obtruded upon the subject, in its emotionally determined attitude, to begin with; but there is never any serious attempt to apprehend anything in the world around it correctly. A simple, fleeting contact with the world suffices for the lyrical ego to discharge itself in a positive or negative feeling, in an awakening or a collapse. Only in religious lyric poetry, perhaps, do fragments of an ecstasy, of the attainment of a reality, momentarily appear. But here, too, the submission to the mood of delight or humility is the final note in the behavior of the lyrical subject. And only in connection with these specific factors of the behavior of the lyrical subject—with factors which would have to be investigated separately in each individual case—do further, very diverse traits of lyric poetry appear.[68]

Objects and states of affairs which are projected in the sentences of a lyric poem belong to the inner life of the lyrical ego or to his environment. This world is, in its basic existential

68. Recent German lyric poetry since 1945, which, incidentally, I know only fragmentarily, appears to me to belong to a completely different type. It is above all cool and intellectual and attempts to draw the external world in sharp, often crude strokes. The lyrical ego stands at a cool distance to this (portrayed) world and offers it, as it were, to the reader, so that he can react to it, while itself retaining the same inactivity as in the expressly emotional lyric poetry described here. The incomprehensibilities which often arise, and are to some extent programmatic, often make it so difficult, at least for the author of this book, to apprehend the actual meaning of the poem that he does not hesitate a moment in considering how the poem is to be treated and judged (1967).

character, an intentional correlate of the attitude and experience of the lyrical subject, although it is considered real in the intention of this subject. But the lyrical subject does not describe this world in an objective manner, as something whose being is completely independent of itself and completely free from all illumination and from all reflexes of the lyrical subject's mode of behavior and, in particular, from its feeling, as it is in the case of "epic" poetry. To be sure, in the latter, as in every literary work of art, this world is merely portrayed and not real in a strict sense. Nevertheless, the intention of the description aims at portraying this world in its ontic character and in its composition as something completely independent of the narrator and encountered by him, and at portraying it in its own traits. The lyrical subject, however, when it creates itself by means of what it speaks and thinks, employs certain turns of phrase, comparisons, metaphors, and sentences, all of which together determine a certain aspect of its environment, an aspect which is conditioned by its present mental state and its experience. To state it in a popular, but not quite correct, way: in a lyric poem we obtain only a "subjective picture" of a reality.

The mode of behavior characteristic of the lyrical subject has the result that that aspect is essentially different from the form in which the portrayed world appears in an epic or dramatic work. This is revealed above all in the fact that people and things in a lyric poem are drawn with a few very simple but striking or somehow significant strokes, whereas all details which are not necessary to establish the situation are left out. These strokes do not delineate the objects in question in respect of what is characteristic of them in themselves; rather, they lend them only an aspect, usually an emotional one, which emerges from their relation to the lyrical subject and which is thus of importance for the latter and constitutes an expression of this relation. As the subject sees and feels the objects of its environment, so does it speak about them and also delineate them. And it sees them and feels them only in respect of what is decisive for the experience developing within it. The objects of the lyrical subject's environment which are projected in this way play, within the whole of the objective stratum of the lyric poem, the role of stimulus and background, out of which the experiences, and in particular the feelings, of the lyrical subject grow, These feelings are usually not named by words at all or mentioned in any other way; rather, they are, so to speak, personally evoked for the reader by means of the expressive function of the spoken sentences; they can be felt by him.

As a result of this whole situation, the lyrical subject never judges in a responsible way concerning its environment, although it regards as a genuine reality the aspect of its environment which it projects. The utterances spoken by it always have the character of conscious passing convictions which flow out of its emotional life and in which the unnamed feeling welling up in it assumes the form of its effect and its culmination.

The lyrical ego is far too intimately intertwined with its environment, which is specifically colored by its immediately unfolding feeling, to be able to oppose itself to it, apprehend the traits of the environment from the distance of an objective (or objectifying) cognition, and make a judgment concerning them. If it utters certain sentences which have the external form of assertion, they are only the expression of an illumination or a revelation which grows out of its direct emotional relation to its environment.

From the essential features of the lyric poem here indicated result certain consequences which are no less important to its specific structure. The first which must be mentioned here is the special constitution of the phonetic stratum of the poem.[69] Above all, this stratum must not disappear, to be replaced, for example, by soundless signs, such as would suffice for the mere determination of the sentence meanings, e.g., in a mathematical notation. This applies, incidentally, to all literary works of art. But this stratum must be constituted in a special way, for it introduces, with its sound material and its manifold phonetic phenomena, a new element of specifically qualitative determination into the totality of the work of art, an element which enriches this totality in a peculiar way.[70]

But this element must not be arbitrary and completely

69. If I always speak of the "poem" here, I do not necessarily want to emphasize that it must be written in "verse." But, even if it is not written in verse, it still may not have the character of a "prosaic" text. It must be "poetic"; that is, the phonetic stratum must be specially constructed so that it is distinguished from ordinary language in its tone.

70. The Russian Formalists, especially, have pointed to this, speaking of an "autonomous" role of the verbal sounds. To what extent and in what sense we can speak of an "autonomy" here is a separate question. But it is certain that there can exist no "mute," "soundless" poetry. That was my reason for distinguishing, in a general consideration of literary works of art, a special stratum of phonetic formations and phenomena. See, in this connection, *The Literary Work of Art*, Chap. 4.

independent of the other strata of the work of art.[71] For both the words chosen, in respect of their sound, and the order of their succession are determined in such a way in the lyric poem as to make them able to assume the function of expressing, and indeed of expressing mental states of the lyrical subject. These mental states or, better, mental transformations taking place in the lyrical subject include very diverse things, of course, depending on the case in question. They include heterogeneous phenomena, both intellectual experiences, which lead to words, and emotional experiences, which are revealed in the tone of the utterance. And the words "emotion" and "emotional" in turn mean many different things. They refer not merely to genuine feelings but also to all possible "affections," such as longing, desire, wishing, melancholy, complaint, etc. And the phonetic form of the poem does not merely give vivid, involuntary expression to the emotion but at the same time contains certain corresponding emotional characteristics—"corresponding" in the sense of according with and being in qualitative harmony with the emotional atmosphere (mood) in which the lyrical subject finds itself in its experience of its environment. The emotional character of the phonetic stratum accords in one way or another with the emotional atmosphere of the lyrical subject and its environment. There are innumerable possible harmonies here, which differ greatly from one another and which can sometimes even culminate in discord. One thing, however, must not be: namely, that a completely neutral atmosphere, robbed of all emotional coloring, prevail in the phonetic stratum of the poem. For then this stratum could, first of all, scarcely perform the expressive function incumbent upon it, and, second, it would be completely dispensable in the structure of the poem as a work of art, since it would then perform only the function of a bearer of meaning, as in a mathematical work, and would no longer have any artistic role. It could then be replaced by a group of soundless symbols. But if the phonetic phenomena in a poem lead to a harmony with its other strata, then they cannot be replaced by

71. This makes talk of an "autonomy" of the phonetic formations questionable. The fact that in many lyric poems of the Romantic period "independent" phonetic formations have been shown to exist which do not determine any meaning but function more as melody or rhythm does not prove that they are also fully autonomous otherwise and constitute a completely meaningless formation. In these poems, too, their presence in a linguistic work of art is justified only because they perform a particular function, and indeed an ancillary function, in the whole of the poem.

another group of such phenomena without an essential change in the poem's artistic form. But there is yet another function of the phonetic stratum, which, though not irrelevant in any literary work of art, plays a special role in lyric poetry. This is the function of emotionally influencing the reader. This "influencing" can be of very different kinds; in general, it depends, on the one hand, on arousing in the reader either a merely emotional harmony with the emotional transformations appearing in the poem or a mood of understanding for these transformations and, on the other hand, on arousing the original aesthetic emotion, which enables the reader to apprehend the poem aesthetically. Of course, this dual function of the linguistic stratum of the poem can be set in motion only when appropriately constituted structures appear in it. These can be of manifold kinds and cannot be characterized in a general way according to these kinds. The result of all this is that every genuine, really valuable lyric poem is untranslatable. This holds above all with respect to the purely emotional harmony of the phonetic stratum with the other strata of the poem and, second, with respect to the correspondence among the aesthetically relevant qualities potentially determined in the various strata, qualities which, in their final phases, constitute the aesthetic value of the possible aesthetic concretizations of the poem. The reader cannot actually become clearly aware of what form all this takes in the individual case in an ordinary reading which takes place without interruption in an aesthetic attitude, however much the reader is moved and enriched by the poem and the fullness of its phenomena. But the question arises whether this can be attained with the help of an analytical investigation of the lyric poem and, if so, to what extent. Before I try to answer this, I would like to point out a characteristic trait of lyric poetry. I am referring to the temporal phenomena which are portrayed in the lyric poem and also come to appearance in the order of succession of the phases of the poem.[72] There are various possibilities which must be considered here, at least by way of indication.

In the first place, there are the so-called reflective lyric poems, in which no specific temporal moment is apparently constituted in the world surrounding the lyrical subject. Here are two examples from Rainer Maria Rilke's *Book of Pictures:*

72. We pointed them out in Chapter 2 of this book. We are concerned now with other, related problems.

CLOSING PIECE [73]

Death is great.
We are his
with laughing mouth.
When we think ourselves in the midst of life,
he dares to weep
in the midst of us.

INITIAL

Out of infinite yearnings rise
finite deeds like feeble fountains,
that early and trembling droop.
But those, else silent within us,
our happy strengths—reveal themselves
in these dancing tears.*

In the situation about which these sentences are speaking, no individual occurrence whatever takes place; consequently, it is also not unambiguously situated in a particular moment of time. A general thought about death and life or about human actions is being expressed in a poetic way. And indeed, in both cases, the peculiarities of these things which are being pointed out appear to belong to their essence, thus to something which is found in every case and is consequently supratemporal. But if we take these poems in their full content, and thus take into consideration the speaking lyrical subject, we notice that it becomes aware of what constitutes the essential trait of death or of human actions. Thus it cannot be said here, after all, that nothing whatever happens. For just this awareness or consciousness happens in the lyrical subject. But if we ask when it happens, on what day, at what hour, no answer can be given. Perhaps a literary scholar would tell us here that it is necessary to do research and find out on what date this poem was written. But this would amount to a falsification of the text. For certainly it is not a question of the date on which Rilke wrote this poem. It is a question of the insight itself taking place, that is, of someone—anyone—having it. It concerns the lyrical subject, which is not otherwise related to any reality and which is individuated only

73. We have already analyzed this poem once. We shall now do so again, from a different point of view.
* From M. D. Herter Norton, *Translations from the Poetry of Rainer Maria Rilke* (New York: W. W. Norton & Co., 1938), "Closing Piece," p. 147; "Initial," p. 59.

by the realization of this awareness, by the attainment of this insight, and, finally, by the tragic serenity arising from it. Nevertheless, it remains merely "someone" in whom all this takes place, someone who could be any one of us. The awareness, the emotion developing out of it, and the transformation of awareness into emotion all take place in time, and indeed in a single moment. The essential feature here is, on the one hand, that it is not, and is not supposed to be, a specific moment, fixed in the temporal stream, but is rather lifted above the concrete temporal stream of the real world and, on the other hand, that the situation projected in the poem displays an inner temporal structure, which is that of a moment. Everything which happens with and within the lyrical subject is condensed, as it were, into a single (to some extent supratemporal) present. This condensation into a single present takes place not merely in the content of the poem but also in the totality of the successive lines or sentences appearing in the poem. In order to apprehend the poem adequately, one must have the ability to collect both what is portrayed in it and its successive linguistic formations into a single concrete (present) moment. Otherwise the totality of the poem is shattered. Thus, once again, the question arises whether it is possible to apprehend such a lyric poem in an analytical investigative cognition and, if so, how. Can we expect anything more than an ordinary reading in this case or, rather, still less? Certainly, in an ordinary reading the reader experiences this concentration within a single present moment, and this original experience cannot be replaced by anything. But to apprehend thematically what is experienced in it, namely, that particular present-aspect in its peculiar nature, we need a special act of reflection which sets in only after we have succeeded not merely in experiencing this present-aspect but in understanding it synthetically as a result analytically set apart from the total substance of the poem. Here, as before in several places, as noted, the analytical preaesthetic investigation of the poem passes over into a synthetic collation of the results of analysis. It would be impossible without the original ordinary experience during a simple reading and without the rigorous analytical consideration. But if it is carried out on this basis, it provides something more than a naïve, ordinary reading by a literary consumer, in the sense that it brings what we merely had experience of into the cone of light of sharp apprehension, which alone provides us with genuine knowledge concerning what we at first only experienced. Not all lyric poems appear to be as concentrated as those cited above. Nevertheless, there are many such poems,[74] and thus the question of how the analytical investigative cognition can be applied to them is of special importance.

Such poems display an internal qualitative unity in a twofold sense: in relation to the harmony of the various strata, particularly in their aesthetically relevant qualities, and in relation to the temporal phenomena appearing in them. This unity is the form of a "condensed" present. In an ordinary uninterrupted reading carried out in the aesthetic attitude, both can be constituted and apprehended (or at least experienced) in their inner unity. The analytical consideration—when, for instance, we read the individual sentences in "Closing Piece" and attend to the sentence structure—seems, by contrast, to fracture the totality of the poem so thoroughly that it becomes doubtful whether the polyphonic harmony of the qualities still appears. For example, we do not then become clearly conscious of the details of the phonetic stratum. We do not notice, for instance, that there is no rhyme to the word *gross* ["great"], whereas the soft and singing (rocking) *seinen–meinen–weinen* ["his"–"think"–"weep"] contrast in a remarkable way with the short and sharp, broken *Munds–uns* ["mouth"–"us"]. Was it artistic intent that *gross* stands there alone without a rhyme, or was it merely the technical difficulty of finding an appropriate rhyme for it? And is the contrast between *seinen–meinen–weinen* and *Munds–uns* purely a matter of sound passing without residue into the formation of a feature of the musical line melody, or does it form at the same time a sensory analogue of the contrast, expressed in the content of the sentences, between life and the death which is somehow intimately bound up with it? Is this *uns* inserted into the text for reasons having to do purely with content, or is this short, broken sound in turn supposed to function symbolically as an analogue of the rupture of life by death? Is the repeated *mitten* ["in the midst of"] left in the text only through a mistake on the part of the poet, or does it evoke a special phonetic accent precisely where the two suggested, different meanings of this word are supposed to be emphasized? Without wanting to decide this question, we point to it in order to indicate how the purely phonetic side of the poem can play a role in the structure of the poem, not merely as pure sound material, but also by performing certain symbolic functions, attention to which in an analytical

74. One can find many examples in the lyric poetry of the young Goethe.

investigation contributes to the elucidation of the inner relationships among the elements of the work of art. But, first of all, the
logical structure of the content of the poem must be analyzed.
"Closing Piece" contains three sentences. The first two are simple
subject-predicate sentences, whereas the third is formally a compound hypothetical sentence. But how are we to understand the
"when" * in its first clause? Is it actually supposed to signify a
purely hypothetical "if," or does it rather mean as much as
"whenever"—"whenever," that is, "we think ourselves in the
midst of life"? We can also ask what the phrase "we are his" is
supposed to mean. Does it mean the same as "we are in his
power" or "he threatens us constantly," etc.? Each of these, however, is already an interpretation of a more prosaic kind. The
poetic phrase, even though it is not completely unambiguous,
tells us more plainly, yet in a more penetrating way, how we are
exposed to death. But let us return to the sentences themselves.
The first makes a simple, concise statement: "Death is great."
The following sentences form a proof of these statements by indicating that death infringes on both the happy realms of life
and our innermost selves. The title, too, is not without its importance. It is certainly not supposed to mean merely that this
poem appears at the end of the book, but also, and above all,
that what is revealed in it is a capstone to those very diverse
forms of life and to the human role in life which have been developed in *The Book of Pictures*. It is a significant pendant to
the meaning of the poem "Initial," also given here, in which human actions are, to be sure, drawn in poetic paraphrase as
"feeble fountains" and "dancing tears" yet, at the same time, as
the very thing in which "our happy strengths" are revealed to
us. But all this is said in such a way that it is not philosophy
(as so many critics unjustly wanted to stamp R. M. Rilke's
poetry). It is no Heideggerian tract about "being to death" [*Sein
zum Tode*]. No; in a simple, ordinary statement death is simply
revealed as present "in the midst of us," all as part of a developing awareness on the part of the "poet" or, more accurately, of
the lyrical ego, which comes about with tragic and yet shocking
serenity. The developing awareness here uttered is an expression of the person who has it and is able to bear it soberly and
serenely.

Of course, we do not become clearly conscious of all this in
the first, ordinary reading. As soon as we have apprehended it in

* German *wenn* means "when" and "if."

analytical reflection, we can return to the simple reading. And we then view the whole of the poem, if not with a new understanding, nevertheless with an all-penetrating one, which does not disturb our experience of the feeling which vibrates through the poem but, rather, allows it to unfold freely. And then we also experience the whole which the poem makes accessible to us, the whole which is the poem itself, conscious of the pervading harmony of all its elements and factors.

But someone may object that if, as above, we pose ourselves such questions concerning the phonetic phenomena and then concerning the syntactically structured meaning of the successive sentences, we have lost the sound of the changing flow and melody of the lines. We also interrupt the free, unified course of the thought and juxtapose looser, separate sentences, which no longer possess the liveliness of a developing thought. We must read the poem anew, without pause, in order to reconstruct its vivid melody; and yet it is only a reconstruction, which does not reproduce the music of the language with the same freshness as we felt in the first reading. The thought, too, which was just being revealed on the first reading, is now presented to us from the start as complete and familiar, and the effects which were connected with the first comprehension are now no longer present. In the analytical investigation of the two strata of language, we do not participate in the expressive function of the sentences appearing in the text, so that the mood of the lyrical subject eludes us, although it is forced on us and moves us in our first reading in the aesthetic attitude. An essential factor of the work of art no longer appears within the field of our experience, etc.

Now all this is true, of course. But this is not to deny the possibility and usefulness of applying such an analysis. Of course, as we have already noted, it must be preceded by an ordinary reading of the poem, so that we get the first impression of the living totality of the poem. And we must also reread the poem in an ordinary fashion after the analysis and thus obtain a synthetic apprehension of the whole. The analytical investigation inserted in between can, however, make us attentive to details which escaped us on the first reading. It can consequently enrich and perfect our later apprehension of the poem and help us apprehend the meaning of the poem much more unambiguously than in the beginning. It can inform us, as literary scholars and, in particular, as scholars interested in artistic technique, concerning the artistic structure and the artistic potential of the poem (that is, concerning its purely artistic values). All this would be impossible without the analytical investigation; for, in an ordinary reading, which we carry out as literary consumers, we do, to be sure, make use of these potentials—we exploit them in order to concretize the aesthetic values of the poem—but we are unable to become conscious of these potentials as particular artistic means. It is one thing to exploit certain capacities, to make use of certain means, and something else again to objectivize these means in their peculiar nature and effect and to cognize them as objectivities in their own right. And we cannot engage in this new cognition in an ordinary reading of the poem because it would make the simple employment of these means, and hence also the reading of the work, impossible.

Certainly, it might be said that the analytical investigation destroys precisely the "first impression" of the poem. It does away with various concrete phenomena, for example the phenomenon of condensation of a manifold of passing phases of the poem into a poetic present, and it robs us of precisely those effects which are most necessary for the constitution of the aesthetic object. Furthermore, it basically prevents us from constituting this object anew, since it shows the genuine structure of the work of art in false proportions. It destroys the hierarchy proper to the elements of the poem by observing, as if through a magnifying glass, unimportant, secondary factors, which are scarcely sounded at all in normal, ordinary aesthetic apprehension, and by lending them a proportion and significance which are not appropriate to them at all, while relegating others to the periphery, thus making them hardly detectable. The elements which are magnified and made the theme of investigation exhibit, moreover, when analyzed for themselves, factors (a microstructure, as it were) which are utterly invisible in the ordinary experience of the whole of the poem. Details are thereby drawn into the poem (work of art) which are not present in it at all and ought not to be present. For once the analysis has made them visible (and perhaps capable of being felt), they disturb, or perhaps even destroy, the hierarchy of elements and thus the "natural" harmony of qualities as well.

The reproach is thus the following: the analytical procedure in the investigation of poetry (or of art in general) renders certain features or elements of the poem invisible and consequently also results in their not being present, whereas it causes other elements, which are invisible or scarcely visible and which ought to remain so, to appear distinctly, just as a microphotograph does with very small components of things or a very sharp photograph with extremely brief exposure (a thousandth of a second) does with the troubled surface of the sea. The poem (work of art) then reveals genuinely new, unexpected details. Do they really belong to it? And should they have a voice in the intuitive assimilation of the poem as a whole? Benedetto Croce or Henri Bergson could make such a reproach by rejecting what they would call an "intellectual" analysis and postulating a merely intuitive beholding of the work of art.

The possible reproach of Croce is certainly serious, especially if it be conceded that the "intuitive"—let us adopt this word for the time being—apprehension of the poetic work or, in our own language, the aesthetic experience of the poem, is permeated with emotional factors, whose effect on the apprehended work is very hard to "bring under a concept." It may also be questioned whether the aesthetic concretization of the literary work of art (and of the work of art in general) can be cognized without the aesthetic values disappearing from the field of vision.

Moreover, the following must be noted: even when we read a work purely as "consumers," we make ourselves acquainted—as the statements of Chapter 1 have shown—with various strata of the literary work of art in complex experiences and to a certain extent we distinguish the strata from one another. But in the case of some strata (e.g., the stratum of phonetic formations and the stratum of semantic units) we do this more in passing, by way of transition to other strata and to the apprehension of the whole of the work. In the reflective cognition of the work, on the other hand, we take this whole, which is, to be sure, stratified but nevertheless has a tightly knit internal structure, and break it up into its strata without paying special attention to the rest of its elements, and we cognize these strata individually in respect of their structure. For each of these strata, too, is then dissected into individual elements and phenomenal factors, e.g., the phonetic stratum into the individual connected sets of verbal sounds (e.g., in poetry, into the individual lines or even into the individual words, so that they are apprehended individually in their peculiar nature). This is the "analytical" phase of the reflective cognition of the work. But even in this phase we would be proceeding incorrectly if we viewed the individual elements (for instance, the individual words) in complete isolation, without paying attention to those features or phenomena which belong to them as components of a certain whole and also as elements which appear in the proximity of certain other elements, and without taking into account the functions which the element under consideration performs within a certain whole.[75] The discovery of all these factors forms, as it were, the transition to the synthetic phase of the reflective cognition of the literary work of art. In this new phase, the decomposition of the work into individual fragments, which was carried out originally, is gradually overcome by the discovery of the connections among these fragments and, in particular, by the apprehension of totalities of increasingly higher order and of new connections among these totalities, up to the synopsis of the whole work in the peculiar features disclosed in the final synthesis. In spite of this concluding synthesis, the literary work of art is left, in the final result of the reflective analytical cognition, dissolved in a multiplicity of sentences, which, even when they are bound together in an intimately connected system, are nevertheless unable to constitute an adequate equivalent of the unified "picture" of the work which we can obtain in an original active reading of the work, especially when this is carried out in the aesthetic attitude. In its place, however, the reflective analytical cognition provides a clarification and a conceptual grasp of many details which, in simple reading, either are not apprehended for their own sake or are apprehended without being thematically objectified. That neither takes place in simple reading is not, as might be supposed, due to negligence but rather to the fact that a literary consumer is interested, above all, in the synthetic apprehension of the totality of the work, in which there must be a certain hierarchy with regard to the clarity and distinctness with which the individual sides and elements of the work appear and also with regard to their objectification. This hierarchy is determined to a large extent by the work itself, although often the interest and inclinations of the reader also interfere with its formation. The phase of analytical cognition of the work impairs this hierarchy to a certain extent. For in order to obtain an objective cognition of the individual sides (strata) and factors of the work, we try to bring all the elements under investigation to the same level of distinctness and thematic observation. It is to some extent as if we were observing through a powerful magnifying glass a fairly large thing which we usually see with the naked eye. We then notice many details which flow together in normal vision, but, in

75. I discussed this in Chapter 1, in the analysis of the understanding of individual words and sentences.

return, we cannot see the form of the thing as a whole. And we must first mentally connect with one another the data of the individual observations made through the magnifying glass in order to form an artificial, conceptual, cognitive equivalent of what is given at once in ordinary vision, with simultaneous haziness with regard to detail.

On what does the "thematic objectification" in the reflective cognition of the literary work of art depend? As soon as we orient ourselves reflectively on an object, we try to advert to it in such a way as to make it the center of our attention and the main subject of our acts of cognition. That which makes its way into our consciousness only incidentally and fleetingly, which is felt only emotionally, and consequently also gives only an indistinct indication of itself, becomes, by virtue of this orientation, the goal of the conscious and often intended directedness of our cognitive acts.[76] The transition from one mode of cognition to another does not always take place all at once, abruptly, but often requires concentrated attempts. For something which merely catches our attention from the periphery often appears in so indistinct a form that, even at the moment in which we begin to take an interest in it, we do not have any clear knowledge of what we are supposed to be looking for or where we are supposed to look for it. Moreover, it also happens sometimes that the very thing we are looking for vanishes from our field of vision or at least becomes less distinct precisely because we are looking for it. It is then advantageous to return for a time to the attitude of merely passive and involuntary experience in order to apprehend, as it were with a sidelong glance, what was at first indicated only very indistinctly. Only then may we return to the attitude of immediate directedness toward the phenomenon in question. But even when we have succeeded in assuming this attitude, the object, which is already in the center of our attention, may not be set off clearly and distinctly enough. Then still further attempts must be made to achieve a greater concentration and an increase in the cognitive activity of the mind so that it will be possible to apprehend the object or the phenomenon in full clarity and distinctness. Only then does it become the "theme" of our cognitive acts, and only then do we cognize it, in the exact, strict sense of the word, in the reflective attitude.

76. See, in this connection, Husserl's discussions of what he called the "modes of consciousness of actuality and inactuality" [*Aktualitäts- und Inaktualitätsmodus des Bewusstseins*] in his *Ideas*, § 35. Husserl also introduced the concept of the "theme" in a specific sense.

The results of the transition from peripheral experience to thematic cognition are varied. Emphasis has most frequently been given to the increased clarity with which the object appears and to the stronger differentiation of its features. But there are also much more important results of this transition. Only in such a thematic attitude is there a distinct opposition between what we cognize and ourselves as performer of the thematically oriented acts of cognition. What we cognize becomes an "object" in the etymological sense of the word: something which is opposed to us. And this "opposition" goes hand in hand with a certain distance, once again in a metaphorical sense, between the object of cognition and the subject of cognition, a distance which rests, among other things, upon a phenomenal separation of two distinct totalities: that of the object and that of the subject performing the cognitive act. We apprehend the object to a certain extent from without, at a certain "distance." "Distance" in the spatial sense is only a special case of the "distance" with which we are here dealing in general. The object appears in this context in the form of a structured whole, completed and closed. It is cognized as something which is situated in categorial, objective forms.[77] What takes place here is precisely what I called, above, "thematic objectification."

As a possible result of the thematic objectification of what we cognize in the reflective attitude, there arises the question of the so-called static apprehension of what is so cognized, in particular the unfolding events. The opinion is often expressed that every objectification stabilizes the event, turning what is, after all, a dynamically unfolding stream of transformations into a unity, into a constant, immutable whole. It is also often believed that visual cognition (perception or reconstructive representation) predisposes us to such a stabilizing "static" mode of apprehension of the object of cognition. Since Bergson's attack on so-called intellectual cognition, it is also often maintained that every static objectification amounts to a falsification of what we have to cognize and, consequently, that thematic objectification is to be avoided, at least in certain cases, especially where we are dealing with a dynamically unfolding stream of transformations.

It must be granted, of course, that there actually does exist the danger of a falsifying stabilization of the dynamically

77. It is not this structure, but rather the categorially structured object, which is given. What this objective categorial structure (Form I) looks like, so to speak, is a question I have tried to answer in detail in Volume II of my book *Der Streit um die Existenz der Welt;* see Chap. 8.

unfolding events which we have to cognize. A stabilization can accompany the thematic objectification but is not necessarily connected with it, and it does not always have to result in a falsification. It is true, however, that an event is able to be "objectified" only when it is already completed; during its course, we can only follow its development attentively while going along with it, as it were. Both modes of cognition are proper to events, and neither of them falsifies the events in their peculiar formal nature; but their objective properties are apprehended only in the thematic "objectifying" cognition. An event is stabilized and apprehended in an illegitimately static way only when it is divided into separate phases within which no transformations are distinguished.[78]

The questions just indicated here are important to us because various sides and factors of the work are thematically objectified as we move from the process of becoming acquainted with the literary work of art in ordinary reading (perhaps in the aesthetic attitude) as literary consumers to the reflective preaesthetic cognition of the work—sides and factors which in ordinary reading are apprehended incidentally, "nonobjectively," in peripheral experience. Depending on the manner of reading, this affects now one, now another element or factor of the work. In the usual orientation of the reader toward the portrayed objectivities, the other strata of the work are experienced only peripherally, whereas a philologically and linguistically oriented reader hardly notices the portrayed objectivities and the aspects in which they appear. For him, the peculiarities of the language will move into the foreground. This results in those "perspectival foreshortenings" which were discussed in Chapter 1. In the analytically reflective mode of cognition of the work, in which we temporarily forego the apprehension of the whole, these foreshortenings are removed insofar as those sides of the work of art which we experienced only peripherally are brought to thematic givenness, whereupon, of course, other sides and factors are temporarily experienced only peripherally or are even utterly displaced from the field of vision. Thus there occur, over and over again, a movement from the periphery to the center of attention

78. This can only be stated here, without further demonstration; for we would otherwise have to undertake complicated formal-ontological and epistemological reflections, and these would take us far from our theme. I content myself with referring to two of my works here: "Intuition und Intellekt bei Henri Bergson," *Jahrbuch für Philosophie und phänomenologische Forschung,* Vol. V (1921), and *Der Streit um die Existenz der Welt.*

and a thematic objectification of what was at first merely experienced. At the same time, other factors of the work withdraw from the center of attention and grow dim on the periphery of the reader's cognizing consciousness. And here the dangers of an unsuitable stabilization threaten various sides of the work, but these can be avoided by a careful, reflective cognition. The mistakes which may have been made in the apprehension of the work can also be set right. The distance which arises, in the thematic apprehension and objectification of the details of the work, between the observed work and our cognition permits the latter to make itself independent, to a certain degree, of the suggestions provided by the work for filling out the places of indeterminacy in a specific, often automatic way and to weigh the various possibilities for filling them out. It also makes it easier to apprehend the work itself in its purely schematic structure without involuntarily proceeding to one of its possible concretizations, so that the work itself is then at the disposal, so to speak, of the scientific analytical investigation. This is of fundamental significance for literary studies, at least in one phase of their endeavor. What then presents itself as cognized to the view of the observer I shall call the reconstruction of the literary work of art, as distinguished from the usual concretizations. The reconstruction must still be subjected to the synthetic procedure and set in relation to the possible aesthetic concretizations of the work of art.

If the analytical investigative consideration of the literary work of art (and, in particular, of lyric poetry) were carried out without a prior ordinary reading in the aesthetic attitude, it could lead us astray, at least in many cases. But it is here demanded from the start that, before analyzing the work in question, we first read it simply as consumers.[79] This first reading provides the reader with just that supposedly "intuitive" (in the Bergsonian sense) aesthetic concretization of the work demanded, for example, by Croce or Bergson and consequently also provides him with the guidelines for what can and should be sought in an analytical investigation of the work if this analysis is to lead to satisfactory results for the cognition of the work of art, the aesthetic object belonging to it, and the value of that aesthetic object. The analytical investigation provides an understanding of the structure of the work in respect of what constitutes the objective foundation of its possible aesthetic

79. This entails some danger, which I shall discuss shortly.

concretizations. Of course, there are various things which are not present in this foundation, including things which are essential to the aesthetic concretization. And it would be a mistake to demand more of this analytical cognition of the work itself than it can provide. This cognition is not merely descriptive; it must also be functional, in the sense of revealing the functions performed by the facts encountered in the work itself in constituting—with the help of the reader—the aesthetically valent qualities and the aesthetic value. Thus—as we have already noted—this analytical procedure must always have reference to the factors and aesthetically valent facts appearing in the aesthetic concretization of the work and in this way seek to understand both what must be present in the work itself in order for corresponding aesthetically valent facts to appear in the concretization and, conversely, which phenomena in the concretization result from what is contained in the work itself. Ordinary reading of the literary work, even when carried out in the aesthetic attitude, cannot provide us with this orientation. For it gives, so to speak, only the realization of one possible case, without any special information about what is contained in the work of art itself and of how we get from it to the concretization obtained. Only the transition from the cool analytical procedure to the aesthetic attitude, in which we consciously attain to the specific aesthetically valent qualities, can provide us with such information. We can then compare the work itself with the concretization. But we should not thereby undertake a mere correlation of the elements of two series of factors, for this alone would still be incapable of solving the functional problem. It would also have to be shown how and to what extent the aesthetically relevant qualities in the concretization of the work are founded in those factors of the work which are correlated with them and which, incidentally, also appear in the concretization. And this is often difficult to see. A somewhat experimental procedure, which is often applied by artists themselves, can be helpful here. Attempts are undertaken from time to time to discover what kinds of effects can be achieved with the help of certain phrases or words in the literary work of art and what is changed in the aesthetic concretization when we replace them with other words or other phrases or even with another arrangement of words or parts of sentences. Painters often do the same when they either cover up or replace with different spots of paint some part of a painting as it is being painted and study what change is brought about in the appearance of the whole. With the same end in view, literary scholars can compare the final text of a poem with various versions of it in which it has not yet ripened to its final form; they can then examine the corresponding concretizations in immediate apprehension in the aesthetic attitude in order to determine their aesthetic value.[80] If several versions of the same poem or the same picture [81] are not available, the literary scholar can himself, for example, to substitute other words for individual words of the text which are suspected of being responsible for the appearance of particular aesthetically relevant qualities and then check to see whether anything in the work or in the aesthetic concretization is thereby changed and, if so, what—e.g., whether the aesthetically relevant quality originally present vanishes as a result of the alteration of the text or changes in one way or another, or whether it is, on the contrary, completely unresponsive to the alteration. Problems concerning the foundation of aesthetically relevant qualities can be solved by such attempts, at least in some cases. Of course, this presupposes that in each of these cases we are able to "realize" the corresponding aesthetic concretizations of the poem and that we then also succeed not merely in concretizing the aesthetically relevant qualities in question but in apprehending them clearly and distinctly in the concretization.

This brings us to a new stage in our consideration of the cognition of the literary work of art, namely, to the following question. Given that the analytical investigative consideration of the literary work of art in its schematic form has already been carried out, at least to a certain degree, is it possible to secure knowledge about the aesthetic concretizations of a literary work which have already been constituted? We shall soon take up this

80. In Polish literary studies, K. Wyka recently showed, through the preserved versions of the beginning of the poem "Pan Tadeusz," how Mickiewicz made various attempts before he arrived at the final, consummate formulation. The same thing can be shown about the first Crimean sonnet by Mickiewicz, "The Akkerman Steppes." One could investigate Trakl's poems from this point of view, since he, too, wrote many versions of the same poem before he came to the final version. Professor W. Killy has written on them. It is remarkable that it is usually the case that the last version proves also to be the best (which is, of course, not a necessary result).

81. The Polish painter W. Taranczewski paints whole cycles of pictures on the same theme, with the individual pictures in such a series each composed in a different tone of color. In this case, too, we can study the way in which changes in the tone bring about pictures with a different aesthetic value, although the form and the order of the spots of color remain almost the same.

new fundamental problem and subject of our study. But first a few further remarks.

We must deal with the various modes of cognition of the literary work of art and its concretizations in sequence and, so to speak, separately. But it must not be supposed that the modes of cognition of the literary work of art distinguished by us here also take place, or ought to take place, altogether separately and independently of one another in scientific practice. We have already referred several times to the fact that there are, and indeed must be, various transitions from one mode of cognition to another. For example, we must begin with the ordinary, uninterrupted reading of the work. But we can also interrupt it in order to proceed to an analytical consideration of the work itself, or of selected parts of it, or in order to try tentatively to constitute an aesthetic concretization of the work and then afterwards return once again to the analytical mode of consideration, etc. The same applies also to the relationship between the constitution of an aesthetic concretization of a particular work and the cognitive apprehension of a concretization already constituted. These also need not take place altogether separately and in succession. It is possible to constitute partial concretizations and afterwards go on to the apprehension of the aesthetically relevant qualities already constituted in them in order subsequently to return, for example, to analytical consideration of the corresponding part of the work itself, etc. Great flexibility is required of the investigator and his sensitivity in order for him to proceed from one mode of cognition to another. And it is also necessary that the results obtained in such different ways be compared and judged properly with regard to the parts they play.

I have already said several times that the analytical investigation of the work must be preceded by an ordinary reading, because the latter can determine guidelines for this investigation. In doing so, I have noted that this involves some danger. For the first, ordinary reading, which is decisive for the rest of the investigation, can be not only imperfect but even quite incorrect. This is all the more possible since, as we all know, most readers of literary works of art, especially where great works of world literature are concerned, read very defectively. The investigations in the first two chapters of the present book have shown the complexity of the operations which are, or must be, performed by the reader during the first reading if he is to achieve a successful concretization of the work.

If the first, ordinary reading of the work is to provide guidelines for the later cognition of the work by means of the analytical procedure, then the course of the analytical consideration is threatened from the outset with regard to its correctness and purposiveness. It can be led in false directions. This danger undoubtedly actually exists, and the fortunes of literary studies up to now are the best evidence of how great the danger is that the investigation will fall into error because of it. This is not just a matter of simple lack of cultivation or chance inability on the part of individual readers. It is a matter of fashions in the way the reading is carried out, which result in mistaken concretizations of the works read. And this is much worse. These fashions are often connected with the intellectual atmosphere of the time (sometimes with the political situation of the country or of a particular class within the reading community) and have the result that sometimes a whole generation of readers simply is not adequate to the work of art in question. So it is, for instance, when literary works of art are read from the start as works for the "edification" of the reader or as works whose meaning is supposed to lie in the glorification of a political system or, finally, as works which are supposed to inform us about the vicissitudes of the author's life, and are thus not treated as works of art which embody, and also show the reader, specific aesthetic values. When an analytical consideration of the literary work of art is carried out on the basis of such a reading, which is often determined by the (misguided) literary scholarship prevailing at the time, it is guided along false paths from the start and can hardly reveal to us the structure proper to the work of art itself or the artistic values embodied in it. It was also for this reason that the process of becoming acquainted with the literary work of art in ordinary reading was here subjected to an exact analysis, so that we were given some idea of the complexity of this procedure. But this was only a description of the possible activities of the reader; the problems concerning the correctness of the reading, hence the guidelines for the critical study of the cognitive operations carried out in the reading, will be discussed only in what follows. For the time being we shall indicate only that the danger which threatens the analytical investigation as the result of a false reading of the work actually exists only when it is completely subject to the results of such a reading, confronts it wholly uncritically, and is unable to free itself from it. But this is by no means necessary and even contradicts the spirit of the analytical investigation, since it is itself critically oriented and begins its procedure with a new, careful, and attentive reading of the work. But even the first reading is treated as completely preliminary by a person beginning an analytical investigative consideration of the work. It can, to be sure, suggest certain directions of investigation, but it must not bind us. We can thus begin the investigative analytical consideration of the individual parts of the work in a relatively independent way and also satisfy ourselves by this means as to whether and to what degree the reading already carried out and the concretization obtained by it were carried out correctly. It is possible to learn in this way what must be changed in the reading or interpretation already completed in order to obtain a more correct concretization. And the new reading which follows can give us a more perfect concretization of the work and reveal to us certain aesthetically relevant qualities whose presence we did not previously suspect and whose foundation in the work of art itself we can investigate in a resumed analytical consideration. A manifold interweaving of the analytical investigation of the literary work of art in question with several newly undertaken concretizations of it thus develops, and also a more precise understanding of the connections which exist between the artistic means appearing in the work and the aesthetically valent qualities appearing in the concretizations, as well as the aesthetic values founded in them.

In particular, such cognitive contact with the literary work of art yields an understanding of how it is possible for one and the same work to have different aesthetically determined possible concretizations in which different aesthetic values appear—values which differ not only qualitatively but also in magnitude. It can thereby be shown that not all values are equally well founded in the work of art in question; to put it another way, not every concretization is—as we usually say—a correct interpretation of the work in question.

The analytical investigation of the literary work of art can give us an overview of the multiplicity of possible interpretations without realizing these concretizations itself. In connection with this, the problem of the places of indeterminacy in the literary work of art, which has already been discussed several times, emerges once again, but this time from a different perspective.

In the concretization of a literary work, several of the places of indeterminacy are usually removed by being filled out with concrete details, or at least the range of details which can fill them out is narrowed. Every such completion constitutes an augmentation of the positive determinations of the work, above all in the stratum of portrayed objectivities.[82] This increase can be artistically insignificant, that is, it can be without significance for the constitution of the aesthetically relevant qualities. Then it is, to be sure, harmless but, from this standpoint, unnecessary. But it can also be artistically significant, and indeed in two directions: either positively, as contributing somehow to the constitution of certain aesthetically relevant qualities which accord positively with the other qualities of this kind, or negatively, as either hindering the constitution of such qualities or resulting in the constitution of qualities which create a discord with the other aesthetically valent qualities. But there are two further ways in which it can be damaging to the form of the work of art. Either it removes a place of indeterminacy which ought to remain unfilled in the concretization of the work in question, or else, although it has no direct influence on the store of aesthetically valuable qualities and is also of neutral value itself, it does not accord with the other determinations of the portrayed objects, e.g., it is not in the style of the portrayed world.

In this connection, several tasks face the analytical investigation of the literary work of art, tasks which, to the best of my knowledge, have been completely overlooked by literary studies until now and which are closely connected with the artistic function of the literary work of art. Specifically:

1. Above all, it is necessary to establish what places of indeterminacy are present in the work in question. It must not be supposed, of course, that this task can ever be completely discharged. But this is hardly necessary, since there are many places of indeterminacy which play no part in the structure of the work of art. The analysis of the meanings of the sentences and connected groups of sentences must be carried out in such a way that it enables us to detect what is left unsaid or is suppressed and that, in addition, it indicates which of the places of indeterminacy are significant for the structure of the work and must be elucidated with regard to their specific nature. Judging which places of indeterminacy possess this significance is certainly not easy and presupposes a good understanding of

82. This augmentation is normally undertaken implicitly, that is, without an explicit increase or alteration in the dual stratum of language, although the increasing factor must somehow be incidentally intended by the reader.

what is actually explicitly stated in the linguistic stratum of the work. Then what is not said—what the reader does not yet know on the basis of the text of the work alone—also becomes noticeable.

2. The next step is an orientation as to which places of indeterminacy may be removed and which should, on the contrary, remain as indeterminacies of the work. This can be achieved through our awareness, as we analyze the text, that we lack certain pieces of information concerning the portrayed objects and their fortunes and do not actually understand everything. Then, too, the text of the work exercises certain suggestions on the reader, so that he removes many places of indeterminacy, whereas this does not occur in the case of other indeterminacies, which are then ignored in the reading. The analytical investigation is only supposed to bring this to clear consciousness.

3. It is necessary to gain an orientation as to the range of variability in possible completions of the places of indeterminacy which is fixed by the context determining them. This limit of variability must be viewed in a twofold way: (*a*) with regard to the determinations of the relevant place of indeterminacy alone, without taking into consideration the larger context and the other places of indeterminacy, and (*b*) with attention to how the limit of variability in completions of the relevant place of indeterminacy is narrowed by the completion of the other places of indeterminacy and the requirement of consistency in the text.[83] This narrowing can at first be viewed purely with regard to the avoidance of inconsistencies and contradictions in the aesthetically value-neutral skeleton of the literary work of art. Consideration of the possibilities for constituting aesthetically valent qualities results in the necessity for a further narrowing of the limits of variability of the artistically allowable completions of the individual places of indeterminacy.

Two circumstances can be of help in considering the limits of variability of the completions of the individual places of indeterminacy. First of all, the places of indeterminacy are for the most part determined by certain general nouns and nominal phrases. Once we take the context into consideration, the extension of these nominal expressions determines the limits of

---

83. It is the structure of the text of the work in question which sets up this requirement and its limits. Not all literary works have to be strictly consistent, but there is then—in works which are well constructed from a literary point of view—a certain "logic" (constancy) to the inconsistency.

variability of the possible completions in question. This limit, V, is always equal to or greater than 2; for, should $V = 1$, it would not be a place of indeterminacy, because then everything, even if unnamed, would be unambiguously determined. But not all cases which fall within this limit are of exactly the same kind. As has already been noted, the text to some degree suggests to the reader those cases, within the range of possible completions of a place of indeterminacy, which are obvious and whose actualization in reading is more probable. These cases must be taken into consideration in the analytical investigation of the work, and the consequences of their actualization for the formation of the concretization must be thought through. Of course, we must not forget the role of the reader in the formation of the concretization or his modifying influence, especially when he finds himself in the aesthetic attitude. Considering the great diversity of readers and their states, this influence is very hard to judge. But it is also necessary to notice that the reader, in his choice of concretizations in the aesthetic attitude, stands under the influence of the previously read parts of the work and thus adapts himself in great measure to the spirit of the work.

4. The most difficult task in the analytical investigation of the literary work first reveals itself when we are supposed to consider which aesthetically valuable qualities can be constituted as the result of a particular completion in the concretization of a place of indeterminacy. There are various possibilities here, which can be anticipated by the investigator. This means that he is forced to constitute various tentative aesthetic concretizations of the work he is investigating, to examine them for the aesthetically valent qualities appearing in them, and, at the same time, to orient himself as to which completions of the places of indeterminacy present in the work make possible the actualization of these aesthetically valent qualities. In other words, he must not read the work in question in a one-sided way and prefer the concretization which he has actualized. It cannot be doubted that this task is usually performed in too partial a way, for the number of different concretizations which suggest themselves is very large. Nevertheless, even a merely partial performance of this task is extraordinarily important for the cognition of the artistic excellence of a literary work of art. The cooperative labor of many investigators on the same work of art can, of course, be of great value here.

The study of this entire complex of problems is important

for two further reasons. It is important, not merely for the understanding of the artistic structure of an individual work of art, but also when we are concerned with clarifying general problems of the artistic effectiveness of the works of a specific literary genre (e.g., the novel, lyric poetry, the drama) or of various literary trends or styles (e.g., Romantic literature, positivistic naturalism, modern expressionist literature, etc.). That is to say, the problem arises whether the number of places of indeterminacy, as well as the selection of types of them to be found in a literary work, is perhaps characteristic of the literary genre or literary trend in question and whether the investigation of this problem, together with the information we gain on the basis of the fully determined part of the literary work of art, could then essentially augment our apprehension of the essence of these genres or literary styles. It is impossible to say in advance what results could be obtained by such an investigation. But it would be interesting to carry out coordinated investigations in the area of the modern novel and to compare in this respect the novels of a Zola, perhaps, with those of Proust, or Joyce's *Ulysses* with the novel cycle of Galsworthy or the works of Meredith. And how would it be if we compared in this respect the works of Thomas Mann, for example, with the writings of Faulkner? If we succeeded in showing that characteristic regularities in the treatment of places of indeterminacy in the literary work of art can be discovered in these cases, then it would also be possible to survey the typical multiplicities of possible aesthetic concretizations of works of the selected literary genre or literary trend.

The second important question which calls for attention relates to those places of indeterminacy in the individual literary works of art which should not be removed in the aesthetic concretizations. There are in every literary work of art, and, in particular, in genuine reflective lyric poetry, places where things are left unsaid, are suppressed, undetermined, left open, places which, despite their remarkable presence and their equally remarkable quality of escaping notice, nevertheless play an essential role in the artistic structure of the work of art. The analytical investigation of the works must bring these places out of their unnoticed state, their sojourn in the darkness of the periphery, and we must be made conscious of the fact that their artistic function would be destroyed if we were to remove them, filling them out in some way or other. By replacing them with positive particulars, we would gain nothing in these cases except for an unnecessary babble, and, in addition, we would be causing an essential disruption of the equilibrium of those elements of the work of art which, known and completely determined, are exposed to the bright light. The sensitive reader, possessed of sufficient artistic culture, passes silently over such places of indeterminacy, and just this allows him to constitute the aesthetic object intended by the artist, at least to a certain approximation. The less cultivated reader, the artistic dilettante of whom Moritz Geiger speaks, who is interested only in the fortunes of the portrayed persons, does not pay attention to the prohibition against removing such places of indeterminacy and turns well-formed works of art into cheap, aesthetically irritating gossip about the persons by garrulous expansion of what does not need to be expanded. But here, too, belong those literary scholars who affix to the sensitive and deep but at the same time merely suggestive lyric poetry of a Hölderlin or a Rilke or—to take a completely different example—a Trakl their own lyrical-metaphysical treatises, greatly attenuating by their own babbling what was justified in the work of art only as a prospect, an intimation, or a presentiment and which should so remain. Thus the literary scholar carrying out an analytical investigation of the literary work of art must rein himself in by paying strict attention to the location in the work of such places of indeterminacy as ought to remain just that in the concretization.

The treatment of this whole set of problems permits the investigator to foresee which aesthetically valuable concretizations can result from the work in question (assuming a receptive and aesthetically active reader) and to what degree they are aesthetically valuable. But this can always be achieved without making a decision as to which of the possible concretizations is the "correct" "interpretation" of the work of art in question and also without immediately making an attempt at "evaluating" it (i.e., at determining its value). But as soon as we arrive at the insight that a particular work allows various aesthetically valuable concretizations and suggests some of them to the reader, we find ourselves in that phase of our relations with the literary work in which the problem of evaluation emerges. But we are not yet sufficiently prepared at this point to set out this problem and attack it. For the time being, the only important thing is to become clearly conscious of the fact that this evaluation can be undertaken along two completely different paths: with regard to the literary work of art itself and with regard to the individual concretizations of it obtained in the aesthetic attitude. And, at the same time, it is also necessary to see clearly that different kinds of values are involved in each of these cases; in the case of the work itself, they are artistic values; in that of the aesthetic concretizations, aesthetic values. But since the work itself is contained in the concrete body of the concretization as its skeleton, we can say that in the concretization itself both the artistic values of the skeleton and the aesthetic values of the concretized whole can be brought to givenness.[84] It is useful to devote at least a few words to the radical difference between these values. Artistic value pertains to a work of art when it contains the necessary but not sufficient condition for the actualization of a value which differs from it in nature, namely, an aesthetic value, which appears in a concretization of the work of art in question. The artistic value is the value of a means, of a tool, so to speak, which has the ability to cause an aesthetic value to appear, if circumstances favor it. This supplementary condition on the actualization of the aesthetic value in question—this "favorable" circumstance—is the viewer of the work of art who knows how to exploit its capacities so as to actualize a corresponding concretization in which that aesthetic value attains phenomenal presence. This phenomenal presence has a dual foundation: in the work of art which is equipped with corresponding artistic values, and in the observer who brings it to phenomenal self-presence in the concretization, with the aid of the work of art and, in particular, its artistic values. The artistic value is an expressly relational value, the nature of which as a value resides in the fact that it is a necessary means to the actualization of something which is value-bearing in and of itself, and hence, in this sense, absolutely, and

84. It must be granted that the concretized literary work of art can embody, or, better, cause to appear, still other values—moral and pedagogical values, for example, or values of a social or general cultural kind—and that it then performs other functions in this regard in human and social life. All these possible values are of a secondary nature for the work of art, however, and will not be considered here. It is an extraordinary fact, however, that these extra-artistic and extra-aesthetic values are usually among the main ones taken into consideration by the reader and also by the critics. The reasons for this vary greatly and cannot be discussed here. Hardly the least important part is played by the fact that neither the readers nor the critics are sufficiently educated to a proper relationship with art and with aesthetic objects. They are not clearly aware of the specific nature of aesthetic values and the peculiar nature of art and, in the face of the difficulties to be overcome, save themselves by a flight from art into other realms, where it is apparently not so difficult to cognize and acknowledge values. But that is only an apparent solution.

which lends a value to whatever conditions it. This absolute value is precisely the aesthetic value whose material (value quality) is essentially only "to be looked at" and is thus exhausted in phenomenal self-presence.

In the case of every artistic value we have a very peculiar situation: on the one hand, it seems evident that, if it is to belong to a literary work of art, it must be founded in the effective details of the latter, so that we would not have to go into the role of the evaluating reader (in particular, of the "critic"). On the other hand, this value is incidentally conditioned by the aesthetic values of the possible concretizations of the work in question. This possibility is, to be sure, necessarily determined by the work, but not sufficiently determined by it. The realization of these concretizations depends in large measure upon the reader, who is not, in general, forced to form any concretization of the work at all (he can, for instance, decline to read it), nor, in the individual case, is he forced to form one with determinations which bring to appearance the aesthetic value suggested by the artistic value of the work. Whether the artistic value effectively belongs to the work is consequently conditioned by the behavior of the reader. But on the other hand the reader is not completely independent of the determinations of the work of art—a fact which we shall soon discuss. This has the effect of increasing the degree to which the aesthetic value is founded in the work of art. The artistic value rests on the fact that, in the work of art in question, a certain store of qualities is present which, in a particular concretization of the work of art, forms the necessary ontic basis for the constitution of a selection of aesthetically valent qualities (or formal factors). These qualities for their part form the foundation of the aesthetic value, which is qualitatively determined in itself. The factor which is still needed in order to provide a sufficient basis for the aesthetic value which is to be constituted must be supplied by the reader. He can sometimes supply this factor quite independently of the work of art, but he can also be moved to supply it by certain qualities of the work of art. Thus the artistic value of the work of art resides in those of its qualities by virtue of which it has an influence on the aesthetic observer and moves him in the concretization to constitute the still-missing portions of the ontic foundation of the aesthetic value. If the work of art lacks the store of qualities which enables it to direct this activity toward the observer, then the constitution of the aesthetic value in a particular concretization, insofar as a concretization takes place, is left to the ability of the observer alone, although the necessary purely ontic basis of the aesthetic value to be constituted is present in the work of art. But if this basis is missing and, nevertheless, the constitution of an aesthetic value takes place, this is then a pure creation of the observer, however much it may appear in the aesthetic object. It is in no way founded in the work of art and is in this sense not "objective." [85]

Of course, there can also be cases where the work contains the necessary and sufficient condition for the constitution of an aesthetic value in the sense that the properties of the work of art determine in an unambiguous way the full store of aesthetically relevant qualities which constitute an aesthetic object and also affect the reader in a way which suffices to force him in his relation with the work to concretize and thus bring to appearance the aesthetic value predetermined by the work. This value is then founded in the work of art and is in this sense "objective," despite the fact that its actualization depends on the activity of the observer.

Now, the first step in the evaluation of a work of art in respect of its artistic value consists in seeking that stock of properties in which the basis for a possible aesthetic value can be contained. This is done as part of the investigative consideration of the work and takes into consideration a series of its concretizations. And, if we have already found this stock of properties, we must still ask what character it has as foundation of the value, i.e., which of the possibilities just distinguished obtains. Certainly, situations of many kinds are laid open to the investigator, situations which are very hard to deal with, in particular because many situations must be judged in relation to the nature of the foundation of the value. Great caution and great patience are advisable if rash decisions are to be avoided. For when we throw open the question of value and its basis, a loud outcry is usually raised concerning the so-called criteria of value or of being valuable. It is demanded that we present completely general "criteria" of the "objectivity" of value. And, at the same time, it is maintained from the start that there are no such infallible criteria, that they would change from one age to another, from one cultural circle to another, indeed from one

85. See, in this connection, my article "Betrachtungen zum Problem der Objektivität," *Zeitschrift für philosophische Forschung*, Vol. XXI, nos. 1–2 (1967). [Also published in Roman Ingarden, *Erlebnis, Kunstwerk und Wert* (Tübingen: Max Niemeyer, 1969), pp. 219–55.—Trans.]

person to another, and that there are consequently no valid criteria and also no "objective" values, etc. I prefer not to spend any time on polemics against these widely held opinions. I believe that we are still much too poorly prepared materially, in the various artistic genres as well as in our knowledge of individual works of art and of the values appearing in them, to be able even to raise the question of the material "criteria." I believe we must obtain an increasingly deep and precise analytical cognition of works of art, and, in particular, of literary works of art, in order to be able to make progress in answering this difficult question.

Another problem which I would like to point up here concerns the basis for determining the degree of artistic value of a literary work of art. On what does it depend? This is not, of course, a question of an arbitrary decision as to which value we will or must consider higher or lower. It is a question of which objective state of affairs in the work itself or in the possible concretizations determined by it decides the degree of the artistic value. Various possible answers suggest themselves. Might we not suppose that the artistic value of a particular literary work of art increases with the number and value of its possible "correct" aesthetic concretizations? The work then contains in seminal form a number of high aesthetic values, and the capacity for determining all these values in advance and aiding in their phenomenal actualization seems to increase with their number. And this ability is just the artistic value itself. We also usually say that the really "great" literary works are just those which have been continually revived and which have experienced new successes in different cultural periods. The great Greek tragedians, the *Iliad,* the works of Shakespeare, the lyric poetry of Goethe, etc.—these are works which continually experience different concretizations and in which new aesthetic values appear without this new factor threatening the identity of the work. But a certain reservation about this conception of artistic value is produced by the very circumstance that, the more numerous the multiplicity of such possible concretizations, of various kinds, of a work of art becomes, the less the work seems to be unambiguously determined in itself and the more numerous the places of indeterminacy and potential elements it seems to contain. Its part in the formation of the concretizations and the aesthetic values constituted in them becomes insignificant, and the responsibility for actualizing these works is placed in large measure on the readers or observers of the work.[86] Thus the magnitude of the aesthetic values appearing in such works also seems not to be especially great. But we must take into consideration here the dual role of the artistic value, on the one hand in the ontic foundation of the aesthetically valent qualities and the aesthetic values based on them, and on the other hand in influencing the reader in such a way as to suggest a concretization to him. Thus, to the extent that it can be granted that "great" works of art have a relatively small share in the constitution of the aesthetic values which appear in their manifold concretizations, it must also be granted that they possess great artistic significance in awakening the interest and activity of the reader in constantly forming new concretizations.

The masterfulness of many literary works of art can also reside in the fact that they permit only a very few concretizations of high aesthetic value. The work of art is so closed in its inner structure that it has only relatively few places of indeterminacy and potential factors in respect of which it can be supplemented and actualized. It is also so rigorously constructed that the limits of variability of the completions of individual places of indeterminacy condition and delimit one another, so that the number of permissible valuable concretizations is greatly diminished. Only very few changes can be undertaken in the concretizations if the high aesthetic value of the whole is not to suffer as a result. In this internally closed character of the structure resides both the high artistic value of the work of art and the aesthetic value of the few concretizations it allows. And this value is then no lower than the value of those works which permit a great many different valuable concretizations.

In connection with what we have just said, the possibility of a different conception of the degree of artistic value is opened up. Instead of making it relative to the aesthetic values conditioned by the work in question, we ought to look to the artistic

---

86. In reading modern lyric poetry we have the impression that the poets are of the opinion that they have to leave their works undetermined as far as possible, so that the reader has at his disposal the widest possible range of permissible concretizations, which he can form in one way or another according to his will. In Germany this began as early as with Stefan George, when he left out all the punctuation marks in his poems so as not to limit the reader in his freedom to interpret the poem. Contemporary lyric poetry goes incomparably further in this direction by frequently dispensing with the formation of correct, complete sentences, for example, in order to leave the reader the freedom to supplement the poem as he sees fit. The schematic character of the literary work is then sometimes driven to the limit of absurdity.

excellence of the work and the perfection of artistic technique displayed in it, from which arise its capacity for founding the aesthetically valuable qualities and whatever capacity it may have for affecting the reader. This artistic excellence is to be admired as a particular feature of the structure of the work of art.

Thus we see that the degree of artistic value of a literary work of art can be understood in various ways and that it is differently determined in different works. It is only a question of knowing clearly what kind of value we are dealing with in the case in question and on what it is based. This circumstance, too, ought to keep us from setting up general "criteria" in advance and should induce us instead to observe the individual works of art with no prejudices and to learn what we can from them. Then the connection between artistic values and their ontic basis, which can differ from case to case, will also gradually be made clear.

This is the situation with which the investigator considering literary works of art analytically has to reckon. In the work under investigation he must, on the one hand, look for those elements and factors which intentionally determine the multiplicity of aesthetically valuable "correct" concretizations and, on the other hand, discover those properties of the work upon which are based the kind and the strength of the influence which it exerts on the reader to actualize concretizations of a specific sort in his mind. Just as attention to the possible concretizations leads the investigator beyond the literary work of art itself to a prospect on these concretizations, so, on the other hand, attention to the effective capacities of the work of art leads him in the direction of the possible reader and his various modes of behavior with regard to the literary work of art, however much the investigator may in both cases concentrate on specific sides and formations of the work of art itself. And this concentration is greatest where we want to reveal the work of art's "character of possessing artistic value" and to apprehend its peculiar nature. This is the complicated situation which faces the analytical preaesthetic consideration of literary works of art once we wish to discover the artistic value of the work of art. In the numerous studies concerning so-called literary evaluation which have appeared in recent years, no one, it seems to me, has seen this situation clearly. It must be analyzed both in general and in individual cases before we attempt to carry out a "literary evaluation" of an actual work. As is clear from our latest reflections, we are not yet sufficiently prepared to approach the problem of the "literary" or the "aesthetic" evaluation of literary works of art. For the time being, we must even leave open the question of whether this "literary evaluation" is a specific cognitive operation or a mode of behavior which goes beyond the sphere of cognition and leads into the domain of a specific kind of emotion. And here, it seems, yet another case may obtain. There are possibly different types and modes of "evaluation." One group falls within the domain of a particular kind of cognition, while another group consists of completely different modes of behavior on the part of the aesthetic receiver. But as soon as we come to the problem of evaluation or of the apprehension of the value of a literary work of art, we can no longer rest content with a mere preaesthetic analytical (possibly also synthetic) consideration of the work but must attack the problem of the mode of apprehending the aesthetic concretizations of the literary work of art.

§ 28. *The reflective cognition of the aesthetic concretization of the literary work of art*

IN THIS SECTION we shall consider one of the most important questions for the possibility of the scientific cognition of the literary work of art: whether and how it is possible without resulting in a deformation of the character of that which is aesthetically valuable.

At first glance, it seems that there are in principle no new problems here, that the same modes of reflective cognition are to be applied here which have already been discussed in the preceding section, with the sole distinction that they are to be applied to something different: no longer to the literary work of art as a schematic structure but to one of the concretizations which is constituted in the aesthetic attitude. To be sure, every concretization of a literary work of art is also schematic to a certain degree, even if some places of indeterminacy of the corresponding work of art have been removed. But a sufficient number of places of indeterminacy still remain uncompleted, so that we have reason for not regarding the concretization as a structure which is fully determined on all sides. And not all potential elements are in fact actualized in the individual concretizations. Consequently, many literary scholars are of the opinion that here nothing need be changed in their mode of procedure; [87] and if they come up against difficulties and are unsuccessful in their attempts, they attribute this to the so-called irrationality of the work of art, which is supposed to be inaccessible to rational cognition, and declare that the literary work of art is simply unknowable in its aesthetic concretization. It is believed that such a concretization should only be aesthetically experienced and that it can be known only insofar as there are certain acts of cognition in the aesthetic experience itself which can accomplish this, so long as these acts of cognition are interwoven with the texture of this experience. In this connection, some scholars are prepared to emphasize without further ado that both this experience and the acts of cognition interwoven with it lead to merely "subjective" results, by which they mean that they neither have nor can have any general validity and are actually nothing but an illusion of the investigator.

Is this conception entirely correct? Must we really give up any claim to the scientific nature of the apprehension of literary aesthetic objects? [88]

The aesthetic-reflective cognition of the literary aesthetic object presents us with greater difficulties than the analogous cognition of the aesthetic object in painting, the aesthetic object, that is, which is constituted in aesthetic intercourse with a picture which is not just a mechanical depiction of some extra-artistic reality but a work of art. At first it would seem that absorption in an aesthetic experience of any kind, regardless of what constitutes its departure object, at least makes it much more difficult to attain to a reflective cognitive attitude. Only in two cases, it appears, can we reflectively cognize an aesthetic object freely: either after the completion of the aesthetic experience, or by interrupting the course of this experience in certain phases and returning to the reflective attitude. [89] But there are distinctions, worth noting in the aesthetic experience, according to whether we are having aesthetic contact with a

---

87. To be sure, they are never aware of the distinction between the literary work of art and its aesthetic concretization.

88. Instead of "aesthetic concretization of the literary work of art" I shall now use the shorter expression "literary aesthetic object."

89. There is yet a third possibility, which I shall discuss later. But in this case there is no such freedom in the course of the cognitive operations as in the possibilities just mentioned.

picture or with a literary work of art. When we are dealing with a picture, we are dealing [90] in most cases (i.e., when the picture is not too large and is well lighted) with its physical ontic foundation, that is, with a painting, which does not change noticeably during observation. We can then generally see it as a whole in a single glance and, during the perception, constitute the picture itself as a whole in a relatively short time. And if we are placed in the aesthetic attitude shortly after the inception of observation, we can also attain fairly quickly to the constitution of the corresponding aesthetic object. In contrast to the process of becoming acquainted with a literary or a musical work of art, it is not generally necessary to become acquainted first with the successive parts of the work in a process of reading or hearing which takes a fairly long time, so that one apprehends it only afterward or even by interrupting the process of the aesthetic experience. Even in the case of a relatively short poem we successively gain new material (the parts of the poem), which serves as basis for the constitution of the literary aesthetic object. In the case of a painting, it is relatively easy, after the relatively fast process of seeing [91] and after the final constitution of the "pictorial" aesthetic object, to pass over into the reflective attitude and to cognize this object. Here it is of essential importance that the aesthetic object constituted on the basis of a picture can also be retained relatively unaltered in active memory for some time after the aesthetic experience has passed. It can then be apprehended at once as a whole. The situation is

90. See, in this connection, my book *Untersuchungen zur Ontologie der Kunst: Musikwerk, Bild, Architektur, Film* (Tübingen: Max Niemeyer, 1962), "Das Bild," pp. 138–253. [English translation, *Investigations into the Ontology of Art: The Musical Work, Painting, Architecture, the Film,* forthcoming from Northwestern University Press.]

91. There are, of course, various cases in which we perceptually observe the picture in question for a very long time and even investigate the painting in a number of manifolds of perception. This is the case, for example, when it is doubtful whether the painting set before us is really an original, e.g., by El Greco, or an excellent imitation. The correct understanding of the picture may also present special difficulties, and we may return even during the aesthetic experience to the ordinary perception of the painting and observe it from various points of view. In the former case, however, we are not dealing with the aesthetic apprehension of the picture at all, whereas in the latter we do it because we want to deepen our aesthetic apprehension of the aesthetic object and to constitute it as a correct interpretation of the work of art in question. In any case, these are exceptional cases. The process of constituting the aesthetic object usually takes place much more quickly in the case of painting than in the so-called temporal arts.

essentially different with literary (or musical) works of art, as is apparent from the studies we have already carried out. For not only are the parts which have already been read no longer actual, but, in addition, the phenomena of temporal perspective enter in and modify the form of the individual parts and their order of succession. After the reading is concluded, the work read ceases altogether to be actual, quite independently of whether it has been read in the ordinary attitude or in the aesthetic attitude. It can be revived only in active memory or in acts of recollection but, even then, only in condensed form or by running through its successive parts in recollection. Otherwise it can be apprehended only in a single temporal perspective, namely, in the one we have at the end of the work; this is a temporal perspective which is perhaps very important or even the most important for the cognition of the work, but it gives us the work only in a considerably foreshortened form. In order to accomplish a cognition of the literary aesthetic object in this time, the cognizing subject would have to be able to retain it for a relatively long time in its full vividness and freshness, although in this moment he has already fundamentally changed his attitude (that is to say, he has returned from the aesthetic attitude to the reflective). He would have to lean for support on the results of a vivid and maximally adequate memory, in which he would be given the full literary aesthetic object already constituted. In his scientific practice the literary scholar, too, often makes generous use of recollection. But, as a result, new dangers threaten, of deception or error in remembering, and, in addition, new secondary temporal perspectives begin to intervene as the cognizing subject becomes distant from the phase of the aesthetic experience.

In order to avoid this, we can proceed differently, and specifically in two different ways: either we can interrupt the work after reading a part of it and assume the reflective attitude for a time in order to cognize parts of the work already read and aesthetically constituted, afterwards returning once again to the aesthetic attitude; or we can try, during the aesthetic experience of the work, to carry out the aesthetic-reflective cognition of the individual phases of the work in new, so to speak overlaid, acts of cognition. Both modes of cognition have their defects, however, and lead to noteworthy difficulties, the former because it indubitably disrupts the normal course of the aesthetic experience, the latter because it renders more difficult or perhaps even impossible the complete devotion of the aesthetic experience to the aesthetic object being constituted. In the former case, moreover, the phenomena of temporal perspective in which the parts of the concretized work appear, and thus also the aesthetically valent factors stemming from these phenomena, are essentially disturbed and changed. In scientific practice both these procedures are applied with a greater or lesser degree of success or failure.[92] We shall gain a more distinct awareness of the results of these modes of procedure if we make clear a few features of the aesthetic-reflective cognition [93] of the literary aesthetic object.

Whereas the preaesthetic reflective cognition of the literary work of art (except for the cases already discussed previously) can run its course quite unemotionally, the situation is different in the case of the reflective cognition of the literary aesthetic object. As we recall, it is necessary to the constitution of an aesthetic object that the aesthetic emotion take place. The original aesthetic emotion and what develops out of it in the aesthetic experience constitute the specific mode of learning about the aesthetic object; we can also say that it creates direct access to the aesthetically valuable or to the aesthetic values. This emotion must form the basis of the aesthetic-reflective cognition of the literary aesthetic object if it is not to lose this access. In this case it constitutes no distracting or falsifying factor, the only question being how the character of the reflective apprehension agrees with it. As soon as this object is constituted in respect of its value, there takes place, as we recall, the act of the aesthetic value response, which grows out of the experience of the value and is a direct acknowledgment of this value. In intimate unity with the response to value, new acts of cognition must be performed, and indeed in such a way as not to infringe on or modify the results of the constitution and apprehension of the value. For only now is what has been constituted in the course of the aesthetic experience and in carrying-out the response to value the finished aesthetic object, as it is encountered. It is toward this object that we must direct our reflective cognition. This is facilitated to a certain degree by the

92. All these difficulties lose their harmful significance to a certain degree in the case of short works, e.g., short lyric poems.
93. The expression "aesthetic-reflective" cognition is meant to signify that this cognition relates to an aesthetic object, hence that it exploits the results of the aesthetic cognition but at the same time goes beyond the aesthetic experience and is reflective, i.e., aimed at apprehending some features of the (aesthetic) object. How such a cognition is possible and how it takes place—that is our problem.

fact that in the final phases of the aesthetic experience our concentration is directed toward the aesthetic object and the harmony of its qualities of aesthetic value; thus we do not first have to direct our attention toward something which is situated only on the periphery of our consciousness. While we are immersed in the contemplation of this object and enjoying the fullness of the qualitative harmony of qualities of value, something happens which takes place in every immediate experience: what we are enjoying becomes intuitively present to us in itself. It remains to fix what is thus self-given (so that it does not immediately vanish) and to conceive it in regard to its qualitative structure. However unified the finally resulting form of the harmony may be, it is not sufficient merely to apprehend its specific nature (which is unquestionably a condition on the value response and, in particular, on the enjoyment of the value), but it is also necessary to penetrate the qualitative basis on which it is founded and to apprehend [94] it in its qualitative heterogeneity. This must be followed by a conceptualization of this entire store of information so that a genuine reflective cognition of the whole is obtained. Moreover, it should be possible to present the results of this conceptualization in judgments which are unambiguously determined and intelligible to others. And here difficulties and doubts arise as to whether this entire cognitive process can be carried out in the same way as the analytical, preaesthetic cognition of the literary work of art. We must ask whether the cognition of the aesthetic concretization of the literary work of art does not differ in many details from the analytical reflective cognition of the literary work of art as a schematic formation, details which could call into question its objectivity and also its intersubjective intelligibility.

94. With literary (or musical) aesthetic objects, it is even questionable how and whether this is possible, because the previous phases of the corresponding aesthetic object pass away and elude the observer, whose concentration is directed toward the final value, although these previous phases also contribute to the constitution of this value. In this case no lasting picture is present but only a process which is always developing anew and passing away, namely, the literary work of art itself. And yet we cannot, in our apprehension of the literary aesthetic object, dispense with the basis on which the aesthetic value is founded, since then all we would have left of the whole aesthetic object would be its final value-bearing note. This can hardly be allowed, even in the ordinary aesthetic experience. But as soon as we are concerned with a cognition of the aesthetic object, in particular in a scientific investigation, we would like to say that the qualitative basis on which the aesthetic value is founded is just as important as this value itself. Hence our requirement.

The aesthetic contemplation of the value-determined form of the aesthetic concretization of the literary work of art as finally constituted in the aesthetic experience is unquestionably itself an emotionally accentuated kind of beholding which often transports us into various possible emotions. These emotions (which can go far beyond what is contained in the value response) are not in themselves emotions belonging to aesthetic apprehension, which are the key to aesthetic values. Rather, they are simply (possible) feelings of various kinds into which we are transported and which are merely an echo of the aesthetic experience. As feelings, they have it in them, at least in many cases, to be phenomenally productive, that is, to be capable of stamping phenomenal characteristics in conformity with themselves on the material which is given (encountered); and to this extent they are capable of changing, and, in particular, of falsifying, its qualitative form. The emotional states into which we are transported as a result of beholding the aesthetic object can thus burden the proper value-determined form of the aesthetic object (in particular, of the aesthetic concretization of the literary work of art) with new phenomenal factors which are basically foreign to it and which can falsify it, especially in respect of its aesthetic value. Hence we have first either to eliminate these consequential emotions or at least sharply distinguish the secondary emotional phenomena in the aesthetic object, arising from them, from the proper qualitative value form of the object in order to apprehend this form in its purity. It is, of course, much easier to dampen or utterly eliminate the feelings which are produced as a reaction, since the phenomenal characteristics in the aesthetic object arising from them then disappear, or at least can disappear. This way also seems to be the natural one, because the reflective attitude of the subject of cognition is automatically capable, at least in principle, of extinguishing the feelings prevailing in the subject. Indeed, the reflective attitude is distinguished by a certain lack of emotion. But if we actually succeed in extinguishing the feelings arising as a result of the aesthetic experience, then the lack of emotion in the reflective cognition threatens to go too far, with the result that we eliminate, at the same time, the specifically aesthetic emotion, which helps make possible and gives emotional emphasis to our seeing the value determination of the aesthetic object in question. Thereby, it seems, access to the intuitively given qualities of value and to their aesthetically valuable qualitative basis would be barred, and we would lose direct contact with the final value formation of the aesthetic object, so that nothing more would then remain for the reflective cognition of the aesthetic object to apprehend, and, indeed, precisely that which forms its essential core and *ratio essendi* would be missing. Then this value-bearing countenance of the aesthetic object could be reflectively cognized only on the basis of a vivid memory of what was phenomenally self-present in the last phase of the aesthetic experience, which is now past, whereupon all the dangers of deception and error on the part of our memory would appear again. This can be remedied chiefly by retaining the qualitative, value-bearing content of the aesthetic object in active memory and directing the reflective intention of cognition upon it, or by trying, after the phenomenal self-presence of the constituted aesthetic object has been extinguished, to experience the work of art in question anew in an aesthetic way and to achieve a new constitution of the relevant aesthetic object, in which we try again to cognize reflectively the value-bearing content of this object. We often perceive pictures and works of music, as well as literary works of art, several times (we observe, hear, or read them several times); and, however much certain dangers threaten,[95] nevertheless, it is certainly true that we can experience the same work of art several times in an aesthetic way and thereby attain to the constitution of the same aesthetic object. We then become ever more precisely and distinctly acquainted with the works which we have thus apprehended anew in their aesthetic concretization, so that, on the basis of the new concretization of the value-bearing content of the aesthetic object in question, we can increase, deepen, and check the cognitive results concerning this content which we have obtained in a previous concretization. It is a prejudice to maintain that we cannot read the same literary work of art several times with real interest and with the awakening of a new aesthetic experience, which leads to the same aesthetic object. In fact, we do this often (perhaps it occurs more often with music than with literature), both as ordinary consumers and as literary scholars. A deepening of the aesthetic apprehension, as well as a more correct understanding of the work and its aesthetic concretization, often results from such a procedure. And just as with works of music which we hear in various performances, we come also with literary works of art to the conclusion that we are dealing not merely with the same work of

95. I shall discuss this shortly.

art, as a schematic formation, but also with the same literary aesthetic object. The identity of this object remains constant, despite all differences (which we shall later discuss), through several apprehensions, although it is not to be denied that it sometimes breaks off for special reasons. We can therefore still say that we have certainly read the same literary work of art; but we have obtained [96] a completely different aesthetic object in the process. But where we succeed in preserving this identity, it is due not merely to the neutral basis of the work of art but also to the value-bearing content of the aesthetic object which is concretized in several cases. And this makes it possible for us to achieve a substantiated reflective cognition of this content, or at least it helps us to carry out this cognition and to ensure and check its results.

Of course, I am not forgetting what I have said here and in my book on the literary work of art about the numerous and varied distinctions which exist among individual concretizations of the same literary work of art. These distinctions hold in normal reading of the work by literary consumers and can be felt especially distinctly in the case of different readers or of readings by the same reader which are separated by large intervals of time. And they increase when the reading is not sufficiently attentive to the exact apprehension of the meaning of the sentences and is also carried out without sufficiently active objectification of the portrayed objectivities and without considerable vividness in the concretization of aspects—when, that is, the reading is left to chance. All these defects in reading are by no means necessary, however, and can be avoided if only the reading is oriented toward attaining as exact and adequate a reconstruction of the work as possible. The more regular, the more exact, the deciphering of the work, the more attentively the reader takes into consideration not merely the individual sentences but also the connections between them, defers to the suggestions of the text, and actively projects the portrayed world in intention in accordance with the meaning, at the same time concretizing the aspects under the influence of the poetic language and also removing, in conformity with the spirit of the work, exactly those places of indeterminacy which should be re-

96. I have carried out a special study concerning the bases of this identity and its limits in both the book *The Literary Work of Art* (Chap. 14) and the treatise "The Musical Work" in *The Ontology of Art*. Perhaps in those works I emphasized too sharply the differences among the individual concretizations, particularly the aesthetic concretizations.

moved, the more probable it is that the aesthetic concretization of the work will fall within the range of concretizations allowed by the work of art and, consequently, that the aesthetic concretizations of the same literary work of art will approximate one another. It is now common to speak, under the influence of Emil Staiger's works, of the "art of interpretation." But we should speak above all of the art of reading literary works of art, by which we do not necessarily mean talent—genius, as it were—which is incapable of being learned, but rather an "art" which, like a good craft, can be both learned and practiced. Precisely by reading the same literary work of art more than once, with a simultaneous analytical consideration of the two strata of language, divining the meaning of the sentences and connected sets of sentences and removing the unintelligibilities in the text which may at first obtrude, we come to an increasingly better understanding of the work read and thus to a more correct reconstruction of it and an aesthetic concretization ever more exactly suited to the work. In addition, of course, to the learned art of reading, various subjective conditions must yet be fulfilled which go beyond this "art" and shade off into the area of the reader's talent, at which point they may no longer be capable of being learned. These subjective conditions include the favorable circumstances under which the reading and the aesthetic concretization of the work take place. These conditions do not have to be fulfilled to the same degree with all readers or in all cases of reading. Thus, even given a correct reading and an effort to concretize the work aesthetically in the most adequate way possible, there can still be considerable differences among various concretizations of the same work, whether carried out by one and the same reader or by different readers. Nevertheless, it cannot be maintained that these differences must always and necessarily be present or that they are always so radical and profound that the literary aesthetic objects obtained either are not or must not be identifiable with one another. Consequently, they also need not lead to the constitution of radically different aesthetic values. But only if they did could a new reading of the same work of art fail to help us in the attempt to cognize reflectively its aesthetic value. The attempt to carry out a new reading for this purpose would then make no sense. But we should not assume from the start, and without taking actual experience into consideration, that this unfavorable limiting case necessarily obtains, thereby giving up, as a matter of principle, any hope of learning to read correctly and of attempting to carry out the most adequate concretization possible. But we often do so, "as a matter of principle," by proclaiming from the start the so-called subjectivity and relativity of aesthetic values. We also exclude from the start the possibility that both the aesthetically valuable qualities and the qualitatively determined values founded in them have their basis of being and determination in the constant features of the work, which are in themselves aesthetically neutral, since—as the subjectivist and relativist theory of value presupposes—these values and qualities can and do have their origin and their subjective acknowledgment only in the aesthetically experiencing reader, in his "taste." It is assumed, in addition, that there exist uneliminable differences in "taste" from one reader to another. In this case, of course, the individual literary aesthetic objects must diverge radically from one another in respect of their value and also vary radically with the mood of the reader. We cannot "step twice into the same river," we cannot realize two identical or similar aesthetic concretizations of the same work—so the subjectivists say. If this were true, of course, it would serve no purpose to reread the same work in order to have a second contact with the same aesthetic value.

Now all these principles have merely been laid down without being tested, and they will have to be given up as soon as we simply analyze the process of reading without prejudice and as soon as we ask ourselves how we actually fare in our attempts to become acquainted with a particular work in a correct reading. We then see that we can at least greatly limit the influence of changing moods during reading, as well as the influence of changes in our intellectual vigor; and, on the other hand, we can see that our attempts to learn to read a particular work are by no means fruitless. Through repeated readings we begin to understand the work better, although we must also try to see to it that the conditions under which the aesthetic concretization of the work takes place are as favorable as possible. In practice, we almost always do this. We prepare ourselves for reading, we try to eliminate all disturbing influences, etc. It is important, however, that the aesthetic concretization of the work be sustained, as it were, not "from without"—say, by taking into consideration information concerning other works or concerning the historical circumstances in which the work in question was written, as literary scholars often do, but rather "from within," by concentrating on the work itself and basing the concretization on details of the work. The reproach is often made on the part of literary scholars who are chiefly interested in problems of genesis that the work is then unintelligible. Now of course there can exist literary works, and even works of art, which are unintelligible if our apprehension of them is confined to details of the works themselves. Either these are badly written, or else they employ their unintelligibility as a special artistic technique for producing certain aesthetic effects. But in either case they must first be apprehended in their unintelligibility; and, if they are concretized in the aesthetic attitude, the result will be concretizations which correspond to their essence. It is precisely then that the value of these concretizations is correctly constituted and apprehended, quite independently of whether it is positive or negative. And if this value turns out to be negative or weak, it should be cognized precisely as such. And only then can the attempt perhaps be made to supplement the content of such a work by external information and to see whether it then becomes more intelligible and receives a different, perhaps higher or lower, aesthetic value in aesthetic concretization. We must also be clearly aware of what has been introduced into the content of the work or what in it has been modified by this procedure, so that we can strictly determine the basis on which its value has been constituted. But it is incorrect to maintain a priori that all works, even those of the highest literary merit, can become intelligible only by virtue of external information. In point of fact, such information often serves only to conceal or, in any case, to falsify. By means of this information we also read into the work various things which are basically quite foreign to it and which cast a false light on its aesthetically valuable qualities, as well as on its peculiar aesthetic value. That is, they transform exactly what is individual in the work. Every really genuine and great work of art is a peculiar kind of individual, and everything must be staked on constituting it in its individually proper nature, in its aesthetically value-bearing content, and, after the completion of its constitution, on cognizing it in its proper aesthetic value. Of course, there are also numerous literary works of art which do not possess this unique individuality and do not get beyond the level of cliché. The "mediocrity" or "lack of uniqueness" of such works must also come to distinct expression in the concretization directed toward them. Only afterwards, and on the basis of their aesthetic concretizations, is it possible to compare a trite work of this kind with other works in order to see which other works it resembles, which other work it had as its model, etc.

Such a comparison must be made. But these are all secondary problems, which already presuppose the aesthetic concretization of the work in question in all its "mediocrity."

The reflective cognition of the aesthetic value of the work of art constituted in the aesthetic experience and acknowledged in the response to value is basically the same as what we usually call the "valuation" or "evaluation" of the work of art, or at least it constitutes the theoretical basis of what is often called the "value judgment" or the judgment of value. The widespread opinion prevails that in order to make such an evaluation we must necessarily have so-called criteria for this evaluation, criteria which provide general principles of value (in a specific category of value) and which must be applied to the particular case in order to decide whether the conditions provided by the criterion are fulfilled in that special case.

Now these "criteria" as general principles constitute something external to the work of art which is to be evaluated and not a factor, arising from the essence of the work of art in question, which prescribes apodictically what must be fulfilled in the work of art if it is to possess a particular value. These criteria vary greatly in kind and origin. The opinion is often put forth that they arise from certain social or technical states of affairs (e.g., political tendencies, the prevailing economic situation, etc.) or from the conceptions of art prevailing in the period in question and that they are then simply imposed upon the work of art. As such, they are also completely independent of the actual content of the work of art, as well as of the aesthetic object constituted on the basis of it, and put it in a strange light. Finally, these criteria are, as history teaches, very changeable, varying according to the general external situation of the work, so that at different times different criteria of evaluation are applied to the same work and allow completely different values to be attributed to it (or to the corresponding aesthetic object). And then, of course, it will be said that value, and particularly aesthetic value, is "relative" to the criteria and to the situation out of which arose the criterion applied. The use of criteria in the evaluation of concretized literary works of art is also very much in fashion because it frees the person who carries out an evaluation in this way from the necessity of assiduously cognizing the work of art (the aesthetic object) on his own responsibility. To make an evaluative judgment, it is sufficient to find in the work of art in question the "features" named in the criterion, on which the value is supposed to be dependent. The work of art in question can remain otherwise unknown. Moreover, we soon gain practice in finding the relevant "features" effortlessly; there is no further need to carry out a precise analysis of the work, and the dangers connected with the successful accomplishment of the aesthetic experience need no longer be risked. The solution to the problem is relatively easy and leads, it is believed, to a sure result. If this result is not generally acknowledged, one can always claim that other criteria have been applied, which is, of course, allowed in this situation. The appeal to the prevailing criteria is basically a flight from art and is also destined for those who are blind to works of art and aesthetic values. Even they, when it is necessary for some reason or another, can subject works of art to an evaluation and thereby even achieve success in society, where they would have to keep silent without the criteria.

Now Max Scheler already protested against the use of "criteria" in the determination of values and of the valuableness of certain objects. They cannot replace the genuine intuitive seeing of values. Their application not only leads to a skeptical relativism concerning values but also robs us of all the happy times in our life when we have direct contact with and behold values, whether of a moral or aesthetic or some other nature. The mere knowledge that certain objectivities have a particular value in some sense or other, a knowledge which in the best case is given us by the application of the criteria, is unable to replace for us the immediate apprehension of values which transports us into deep emotions. Our life becomes empty and poorer in the process. On the other hand, the purpose of such objectivities as works of art is not realized; they lose their essential role in human life and then actually seem to be completely without value in themselves. Thus the application of criteria to the evaluation of works of art and the aesthetic objects which have their basis in them is, to be sure, easy and effortless, but it conflicts with the genuine essence of all art.

It appears, therefore, that the dangers which seem to threaten the possibility of cognition of an aesthetic concretization of the literary work of art can be overcome if we are chiefly concerned with cognizing an individual aesthetic concretization in its aesthetically valuable content, or at least an aesthetic concretization constituted on the basis of several individual concretizations and prescribed to a certain extent in respect of its type by the work of art in question. But there are still several dangers which seem to threaten the "objectivity" of this cognition and which have yet to be weighed.

It must be emphasized above all that the cognition of the constituted aesthetic concretization of a literary work of art cannot be analytical and, on the other hand, cannot be restricted to a merely synthetic apprehension of the finally resulting form of the aesthetic value of the concretization. It cannot and must not be analytical, that is, it must not distinguish and emphasize separately, on the one hand the individual, dependent factors of the aesthetically valuable foundation of the values finally constituted and, on the other, individual elements and factors of the aesthetically neutral basis of the aesthetic value-bearing content of the concretization, separating all these elements and factors from the value quality which has its basis in them. For this would amount to a fragmentation, a splitting-up of the unified appearance of the aesthetically concretized work of art. This would destroy that inner unity of the literary aesthetic object, which is itself the formal factor of its aesthetic value and enables the finally resulting Gestalt value quality to appear. The reflective cognition of the literary aesthetic object must apprehend it in its final value and bring its peculiar nature to clear self-givenness; it must therefore preserve and do justice to the character of wholeness of this object and its value. On the other hand, however, it is not part of the essential function of this cognition merely to set off the value quality of the finally resulting value from the whole and simply to pass by everything else in which this value has its foundation, as if it were not present in the full content of the aesthetic object. Hence this cognition has to accomplish something more than simple apprehension of the finally resulting value in its qualitative determination. The entire ground on which this value grows must also somehow be taken into consideration and brought to clear givenness, so that the whole of the literary aesthetic object is not merely had in the aesthetic experience but actually clearly cognized. How can this be done without falling into an analytical procedure? Here, I believe, lies the greatest difficulty, both for the concrete accomplishment of the cognition of the aesthetic object and for the theoretical proof that this cognition is actually possible. This is the point at which both Bergsonian intuitionism and its application to aesthetics by Croce failed, because it was not known how to overcome this difficulty. But can it be overcome? For the requirement which is here placed on the cognition of the aesthetic object appears to contradict its essence. And if it cannot be overcome, then the study of literature is indeed left with the possibility of treating literary works in a scientific way but is forced to set aside [97] everything in them which—as someone said —is "art."

Above all, we ought to exaggerate neither the absolute unity of aesthetic objects nor the radical unity or, better, simplicity of their cognition. To be sure, any Gestalt, as it appears in aesthetic value qualities, is a whole which cannot be divided into parts. Its specific nature also lies in the fact that, as a *quale* in comparison to the multiplicity of factors in which it has its basis, it introduces something completely new. It is precisely in respect of this new factor that it must be apprehended. But the presence of the Gestalt in the whole of the aesthetic object and even its appearance in the foreground do not mean that the whole background vanishes; the background continues to be visible and shines through the Gestalt quality. Consequently, I once called a relationship between a Gestalt and the qualitative basis out of which it grows a "harmonic unity." [98] We thus need apply no special analytical procedure in order to apprehend it, along with the Gestalt itself, and indeed in the same mode of givenness in which it appears in ordinary reading in the aesthetic attitude. We must only be sensitive enough, in thematic apprehension of the Gestalt, also to apprehend thematically its qualitative basis, which contains various qualities which coalesce with one another. In order to create favorable conditions, as it were, for this sensitivity, we can seek to apprehend the qualities contained in this basis by a prior analytical cognitive procedure and, after this has occurred, return to the aesthetic attitude and apprehend the Gestalt as a whole in harmonic unity with its basis. The act of apprehension is then certainly not absolutely simple, but nevertheless it constitutes a separate whole in which is apprehended the coalescent but still not absolutely simple whole of the aesthetic object. Incidentally, not all aesthetic objects are characterized by a radical inner unity in respect of their value-bearing elements. To be sure, there can exist in the aesthetic object several value qualities of such a kind that they enter into a harmonic unity with one another or lead to the constitution of only a single derived unity of value. In all these cases the inner

97. This is the problem which Knut Hanneborg, in his fine book *The Study of Literature* (Oslo: Universitetsforlaget, 1967), was also unable to overcome.

98. See *Der Streit um die Existenz der Welt,* II, pt. 1, 48 f.

structure of the store of value-bearing elements of the aesthetic object is extraordinarily tight. And here an apprehension of the whole is required which, although aiming at the whole, is yet sensitive to the multiplicity of tightly coalescent qualities; such an apprehension is, however, thoroughly within the realm of possibility. But, in addition, there are also aesthetic objects in which the inner structure is by no means so tight but presents instead a free and perhaps also complex structure. Then, of course, the reflective cognition of the aesthetic object is also much freer and need not be carried out with the greatest concentration on achieving an apprehension which is radically oriented toward the whole. Various degrees of relative freedom are possible in the connection between several simultaneously appearing qualities and Gestalt qualities. The cognition of this connection is also part of the task of the reflective cognition of the aesthetic object and provides a characterization of the form of this object. The particulars of this form can also be a valuable factor in the object and contribute to the constitution of the final value. As the limiting cases of the possible variations in the structure of the aesthetic object, we have, on the one hand, the case in which the unity of that structure is radically tight and, on the other hand, the many different cases in which the aesthetic object begins to a certain extent to fall apart and is then threatened by the fact that no unified positive aesthetic value is constituted in it. In contrast, formal factors of negative value sometimes emerge which can bring the observer to a negative value response to the whole of such an object.

Of course, as already indicated, the situation is much more complicated, and also causes much greater difficulties for the cognition of its store of value-bearing features, in the case of a literary object than, for instance, in the case of a picture. Only in short works, like short lyric poems, is it possible to cognize the aesthetic object being constituted in the aesthetic experience at once as a whole and, moreover, as a whole which embraces the entire poem. In longer works, for example novels or dramas, which break down into many chapters or acts and the reading of which requires a relatively long stretch of time, the aesthetic object constituted in the final phase of the work is—even when it forms a tight, internally structured whole—only the aesthetic expression of a mere part of the work, e.g., the final scene of a drama or the last chapter in a novel, where a more or less detectable echo of the previous parts of the work is only incidentally sounded in the background. In this case the work is so structured as to contain several separately composed parts (chapters, acts, scenes), which, in a reading carried out in the aesthetic attitude, lead to the constitution of a multiplicity of aesthetic objects which succeed one another in the reading and are also cognized in succession. The value qualities thereby revealed can be of very different kinds, and it is a feature of the art of the composition of such literary works that the successively appearing values lead, through their qualities, to a harmony[99] which, although it is extended in the time of the work, can still be apprehended synthetically afterwards, if only by a special activity of the apprehending consciousness. There are very different possibilities here, which also present manifold difficulties for the possible apprehension of such works and special problems for the method of cognition of their aesthetic concretization. But this can be developed no further here.

A new series of difficulties arises in the cognition of literary aesthetic objects as soon as we note that the results of direct cognition must be formulated in language and presented to other literary scholars in the form of a set of judgments. The chief difficulty lies in the fact that the language which we have at our disposal does not in general satisfy the demands of the cognition of aesthetic objects. Ordinary language is in general a relatively primitive tool and one suited to the realization of other aims. Other sciences, in particular mathematics and the natural sciences, have developed special "languages" for their purposes, but aesthetics and also literary studies still find themselves in a very awkward position in this respect. To be sure, ordinary language often has at its disposal very vivid, striking, and fitting expressions which, in actual situations in daily life, occur to the speaker as if automatically. But as soon as we are looking, in the purely cognitive attitude—for instance, in contact with aesthetic objects—for suitable words and phrases, the vivid words and phrases of ordinary language, which sometimes, in spite of everything, can be very useful, will not suggest themselves automatically. We then often seek them in vain, and the number of expressions in aesthetics which have already been developed is still relatively very small and very insufficient in the face of the great abundance of aesthetic forms and phenomena.

In connection with this, the range of unambiguously and exactly determined general concepts which could be used in the aesthetic consideration is extremely small. For aesthetics (as

99. The same thing takes place in works of music.

well as the aesthetically oriented study of literature) is still a relatively young discipline; and however much it has developed in recent decades, the number of different trends in investigation and of "schools"—however useful they may be in attacking the problems from different approaches—is more of a hindrance when it comes to the development of a common language and a common conceptual apparatus.[100] We have conceptual distinctions at our disposal only for very crass oppositions between aesthetic forms and phenomena. For almost none of the variations and subtle nuances of qualities, or for their modifications, which rest on their coexistence with other qualities within the framework of a whole, do we possess special names or even complex derived expressions (phrases). This makes much more difficult the conceptualization of the aesthetic object and the aesthetically valuable qualities appearing in it. The value qualities are only very vaguely determined, and we do not have names for all their varieties. For an even modestly satisfactory description of the qualitative states of affairs which appear in the content of the aesthetic object and are also apprehended and cognized in a fairly clear and direct way, it is necessary to create a completely new language, new names and phrases. This is no easy task. The difficulty lies above all in the fact that it is not possible in this case to provide "definitions" of the new names and expressions, as mathematicians do. The determination of the meanings of names (or, as one usually says, "concepts") by definition is based on a cognitive principle completely different from the one that must lie at the basis of the formation of a language for describing the qualitative determinations of aesthetic objects. There, in mathematics and in natural science, the principle of language formation—in particular, the principle of the determination of "concepts" (names) by definition—is based on the data of the analytical preaesthetic cognition, which is usually directed toward the quantitative. The determination of meanings pertains to names of artificially isolated elements or

---

100. When I think of that time forty years ago when I took up the task of working out the structure and the mode of being of the literary work of art and of the works of the other arts, I have to concede that an essential change has taken place in the general theory of art and also that a greater concentration on works of art themselves has come about in the scholarly investigation of art. An indubitable advance must be granted. But the tendency which often appears on the part of individual investigators to start all over again from the beginning without paying attention to the results already obtained stands in the way of the development of a common conceptual apparatus.

complexes of them. This provides simple designations at first; out of these are then formed names whose meaning consists of many simple meanings, like a mosaic. In contrast, the names which could be used to describe the determinations of aesthetic objects cannot be formed in such a "mosaic" way. For in this way everything which is most essential in the data of the aesthetic cognition would run through the sieve of the names (concepts) formed by definition: all specific properties of the qualitative harmony, in particular the Gestalten, which are not mosaic complexes of the qualities forming their substructure, as well as all reciprocal qualitative modifications of the aesthetically valent qualities appearing in a whole. That which forms the necessary condition of the determination of the meanings of names—namely, the availability of a multiplicity of isolated and mutually independent elements (which do not, therefore, modify one another by their appearing together), and of such elements only, thus the absence of qualitative harmonies in the relevant domain of Gestalt determinations—this is not fulfilled in the attempt to construct a language which would be suited for describing the data of aesthetic experience. If we wanted to use the term "rational language" to describe a language in which the meaning of the words, and in particular the names, is determined by definition, by providing a number of simple (elementary) meanings, we would have to call those languages which would be capable of being used for describing the data of aesthetic experience "irrational." But the conception that only a language constructed by definition is "rational," i.e., suited to science, is only a neopositivistic prejudice, which does not apply even to the languages constructed by mathematical logicians.[101] It is a fact that living ordinary language has arisen, in various national systems, in which the same logical-functional problems have been solved in a meaningful way, without mosaic definitions, and that this language is constantly being enriched by new, meaningful, and, in context, relatively unambiguous words. The new words and whole phrases always arise when, in the domain of the cultural life of the linguistic community in

101. This prejudice was expressed for many years in the well-known disdain for ordinary language and in the numerous attempts to construct artificial languages. Under the influence of neopositivistic agitation, it almost appeared unseemly to make use of ordinary language, until, one day, Wittgenstein discovered that it pays to occupy oneself with ordinary language and in this way brought it back into favor. Only it has turned out that he was fairly powerless against the problems which are posed by ordinary language.

question, some new, previously unfamiliar objects, phenomena, or functions emerge and are meaningfully named by someone, usually, as it were, involuntarily.[102] In spite of all the changes which every language undergoes in the course of time, those words are preserved which were created or discovered in close connection with the direct cognition of the objects in question by someone who was gifted with a genius for the creation of language. These can be completely new words, which, however, if they are formed in the spirit of the mother tongue or transformed from the available root words,[103] are understood immediately, without special explanations or "definitions." Only when we already have expressions which have been formed in connection with direct experience and which often possess a broad, not always homogeneous range of application, can we make these expressions precise, i.e., unambiguous. This can be done, at least in many cases, by a "definition." With all words, however, which unerringly denote singular qualities or conceive an object under such a quality, the "definition" accomplishes nothing but a correlation of the defined word with an ordered multiplicity of other words whose synthetic meaning delimits the same domain as the defined word but which never possesses exactly the same peculiar meaning as the defined word. Thus the essential nature of this word is certainly not made explicit by its "definition."

Genius in forming new words resides above all in capturing precisely and directly by means of a word that peculiar qualitative factor of the phenomenon which we are seeking to name by a linguistic expression. If we find no suitable expression in the language in question, it is necessary to form a new verbal sound, one which fits in harmoniously with the system of verbal sounds, which therefore conforms in its structure to certain general rules for the formation of verbal sounds in this lan-

102. It suffices to point here to the enrichments of languages which are connected with the discovery of the airplane and with the whole field of aeronautics or radio or television. The youth of every new generation proves especially creative in its ordinary language, which at first is not accepted by the older generation. And this occurs in a quite unorganized way and also in spite of the influence of the school, which transmits the received language of older generations and often fights for the purity of this language as well.

103. The only horrible thing is the apparent enrichment of the language, perpetrated for administrative reasons, by the introduction of atrocious neologisms, which arise from the transmutation of foreign words, above all Latin or Greek. Often technicians or specialists in the individual scientific disciplines are to blame for this.

guage, but which at the same time has the ability to awaken in the hearer the apprehension of the peculiar qualitative factor.[104] The appropriate intentional signifying factor is thereby lent to the verbal sound which has been formed, and the language is enriched by a new meaningful word. The newly formed word becomes intelligible even to those who were not witnesses to this word formation, and in this way it becomes not merely a tool of intersubjective agreement in the linguistic community in question but also a means for making common labor possible in the achievement of direct cognition of previously unknown objects (and, in particular, aesthetic objects) in respect of the factors which are characteristic of them. The task of forming new words whose meanings faithfully reproduce the peculiarities of aesthetic objects is much easier to perform when several persons have direct contact with the same work of art. But it is very important that they succeed in constituting the same (or perhaps similar) aesthetic objects, which thus display the same harmonies of both aesthetically valent qualities and the determinations forming their substructure, and that they know, on the basis of the constituted objects, how to cognize their aesthetic value. Then, confronted with the same data, they can make a common effort to discover the required new words and phrases which will be unambiguously intelligible without further ado to all those who have obtained the same results from the aesthetic experience and the reflective cognition based on it. Whether this attempt succeeds depends, of course, in large measure on the works of art in question, as well as on their mode of exposition.

In practice, various obstacles often stand in the way of solving this problem—not merely a lack of necessary abilities, but also various theoretical conceptions. One of these is the psychologistic theory that the meaning of a work is a certain mental experience which is cognitively accessible only to the one who has it. This theory today no longer seems to be very important. Another obstacle is created by the notion of the so-called subjectivity of "aesthetic impressions" (or "feelings"), as well as the theory of the relativity of all values, in particular aesthetic

104. There does not seem to be any doubt that there are phonetic formations in every ordinary language which possess this remarkable capacity, though there may be considerable mystery and unclarity as to their basis. In addition to such words, there are, just as unquestionably, in every ordinary language, and especially in the artificial languages (e.g., Esperanto), words which do not possess this capacity and which are in this sense lifeless and ineffective. Such words must then be artificially introduced into the language by definition.

values, which is often connected with it. According to this theory, each of us is supposed to "see" (perceive) the work of art in question in a completely different way and to obtain completely different and mutually incomparable aesthetic objects. From this arises the principle of *de gustibus non est disputandum* and also the assertion that we have no common language and are unable to come to any understanding.

It is well known that, of these two theories, the first proved untenable long ago, although it appears again and again in various discussions and treatises in positivistically oriented philosophical circles. The second, however, still awaits refutation and is regarded by many as indubitable. It is "good form," so to speak, to acknowledge it without reservation. But is it really true? What satisfactory proof do we have for it when we thus far possess neither a satisfactory theory of value nor a sufficient clarification of the aesthetic experience and of the cognition of aesthetic objects? [105]

In this way we approach those problems whose formulation is the task of the next chapter. But it must be stated now that it would be impossible to transmit to others in an intelligible way the results of the cognition of aesthetic objects only if it were logically proved that it is impossible for two persons who have immediate aesthetic contact with the same work of art to come to (at least) similar aesthetic objects constituted on the basis of this work of art and to cognize them in the same aesthetically valuable qualitative harmonies. But an indubitable proof of this is lacking.

With this problem is associated another question which throws light on the final, culminating phase of the cognition of objects which bear aesthetic value. This is the question of the universal validity of aesthetic evaluation. But first we must occupy ourselves for a while with this evaluation itself.

The conclusion of the reflective cognition of aesthetic objects consists in the conceptualization of the results of this cognition and leads to the establishment of a series of judgments concerning the (individual) aesthetic object in question. These are of three kinds:

105. See, in this connection, my book *Erlebnis, Kunstwerk und Wert: Vorträge zur Ästhetik 1937–1967* (Tübingen: Max Niemeyer, 1969) [Polish version: *Przeżycie–dzieło–wartość* (Cracow: Wydawn. Literackie, 1966)], in which I not only discuss the deficiencies in previous conceptions of value but also seek to differentiate the various meanings of "relativity" of value.

1. Reporting judgments, in which is contained the description of the aesthetic object in question

2. Judgments which simply determine that the object in question has a qualitatively determined value

3. Sentences which, to be sure, have the external form of judgments but which evaluate the object—in particular, the aesthetic object—that is, judge it with praise or blame. Basically these last are not genuine judgments but are rather the result of a completely different subjective operation, namely, that of "praising" (of positive evaluation) or of "condemning" (of disapproval), and do not at all have the function of determining objectively that the object in question possesses this value or that.[106]

Reporting judgments give the descriptive results of the reflective cognition (carried out on the basis of an aesthetic experience) of the individual aesthetic object in question. Hence, those judgments which describe the aesthetic experiences or mental behavior or reactions of the person having direct contact with a work of art or an aesthetic object do not belong here; they fall either within the realm of a descriptive phenomenological epistemology or within the realm of psychology. In the latter case they provide descriptions of individual mental facts which constitute the empirical material for general psychology. They have nothing to do with the judgments which refer to individual aesthetic objects. The conditions on the independent acquisition of reporting judgments concerning an aesthetic object are, above all, the following: (a) that the person judging have an aesthetic experience in which a particular aesthetic object is constituted [107] and (b) that he also carry out the final phases of the reflective cognition of the already constituted aesthetic object. On the other hand, reporting judgments form the theoretical basis for

---

106. See M. Wallis, *O zdniach estetycznych* (On Aesthetic Sentences) [I was unable to find this reference.—Trans.], where Wallis makes this distinction. I also occupied myself with these questions in my address to the Aesthetic Symposium (in connection with the International Congress of Philosophy in Venice, 1958) under the title "Bemerkungen zum Problem des ästhetischen Werturteils" (published in *Rivista di Estetica*, Vol. III, no. 3 [1958]).

107. It is of course possible for the person judging to have several such experiences relating to the same aesthetic object (or having their beginning in the same work of art) and for him then either to achieve a synthetic apprehension (constitution) of the aesthetic object in question or else to be confronted with a sort of interplay or struggle among the different aesthetic experiences. But these different possible cases must be subjected to a special analysis, which cannot be carried out here.

value judgments, i.e., for judgments which establish that the aesthetic object has a certain value. In what relation the evaluating sentences stand to these two types of "aesthetic" sentences (judgments) is a separate problem.

But the aesthetic object can have values of yet a very different kind. Thus it can, for example, have a cultural value within the totality of the achievements of a community, or the value of having a special significance in the history of a people, or an educating influence on the person who has direct contact with the literary work, and so forth. For the literary aesthetic object, however, these are only possible secondary values, which do not constitute it and which arise only from its specific essential value, although we should neither overlook their presence nor disregard their role in the total value of the object in question. These peculiar values, which constitute only aesthetic objects and whose essence consists in the fact that they must be beheld, we call aesthetic values in the specific sense. If they are absent, independently of whether they are positive or negative, we are, to be sure, dealing with an intentional object constituted on the basis of a (literary) work of art in the aesthetic experience but not, however, with an aesthetic object, regardless of whether it possesses values of some other kind. Moreover, there exist not just one but many different basic kinds (some say "categories") of aesthetic values. These values of different basic kinds can appear simultaneously in one and the same aesthetic object. But it can also be the case that only one value of a particular basic kind dominates the aesthetic object.[108] Only those value judgments (evaluations) which either establish the presence of an aesthetic value in an aesthetic object or evaluate (judge) this object from the standpoint of an aesthetic value stand in a close ontic and motivational connection with an aesthetic experience and with the associated cognition of the aesthetic object constituted by virtue of this value. Of course it is possible in the purely psychological sense to make an aesthetic value judgment even when we have neither constituted the relevant aesthetic object ourselves, independently, in direct ex-

108. In another place—first at the Fifth Aesthetic Congress in Amsterdam—I tried, on the one hand, to distinguish various basic types of aesthetically valuable objects and, on the other hand, to give a list of different aesthetic values, after which I posed the question whether necessary connections can be shown to obtain between a selection of aesthetically valuable qualities and the aesthetic value which is based on them. See my book *Erlebnis, Kunstwerk und Wert*.

perience, nor reflectively cognized it. It can even happen that this judgment is accidentally true. On the other hand, it may be false, if the reflective cognition built on the aesthetic experience is unsuccessful. We can, of course, make value judgments blindly, in a routine way (according to so-called criteria or by mere coincidence). In spite of this, an especially close connection obtains between the content of the value judgment (or evaluation), as well as the act of judging, and the experiences preparing them. The latter form the means for the foundation which has final responsibility for the former. When they are performed [109] correctly, they constitute the kind of aesthetic activity to which we must ultimately have reference and whose data prove the value judgments (evaluations) true or false. Since the results of the reflective cognition of the (constituted) aesthetic object are apprehended in the reporting aesthetic judgments, the latter (insofar as they are faithfully adapted to the data of this cognition) actually constitute the theoretical basis of the aesthetic value judgments.

Aesthetic value judgments ascribe a particular value to a particular aesthetic (in particular, a literary aesthetic) object. These are judgments about objects which possess a value and not about this value itself (concerning which reporting judgments are also possible). They can be of two kinds: either (*a*) they ascribe to the aesthetic object a "comparative value"—if we may so put it—which distinguishes this object in comparison with other aesthetic objects, which also have values, perhaps of the same kind or (*b*) they ascribe to it a proper value, which belongs to it without regard to its relation to other value-bearing objects.[110]

Among all these judgments two kinds must be differentiated: (*a*) judgments which are made about the value of certain objects themselves and (*b*) judgments which concern the founding or "foundation" of the value in the value-bearing object. The former can be general as well as individual. In the former case, they relate either to all values in general (or to the general idea of value as such) or only to certain kinds of values, e.g., only to aesthetic values or only to aesthetic values of a certain category

---

109. A new problem arises here, to which we shall have to devote the following chapter.

110. On the different meanings of the so-called relativity of values, see my article "Zum Problem der 'Relativität' der Werte" in the book *Erlebnis, Kunstwerk und Wert*, pp. 79–96. It was first presented at the third Congrès des Sociétés de Philosophie de langue française in Brussels in 1947.

(variety). The individual judgments relating to values concern an individual definite value of an aesthetic object, for example the aesthetic value which was constituted, in a particular aesthetic experience, as the value of the concretization of Rembrandt's self-portrait in the Frick Gallery in New York. On the other hand, judgments which concern the founding of a value in a particular object have the function of making clear on what, in the object in question, this value is based, i.e., in which aesthetically relevant qualities appearing in the aesthetic object in question and in which aesthetically value-neutral but artistically effective and thus valuable factors the value has its constitutive basis. The judgments of the latter kind form, as it were, the link between the value judgments and the purely descriptive reporting judgments concerning the content of an aesthetic object and allow us to understand better the connection between the value and its objective foundation. They also found, in part, the aesthetic evaluation of the aesthetic object.

Various values can appear in an aesthetic object which found the finally resulting, so-to-speak synthetic value. They must be distinguished from this synthetic value. In an aesthetic concretization of a literary work of art they can be of the following kinds. They can, for instance, be values which arise from the richness of manifold modes of portrayal of the fortunes of the persons appearing in the objective stratum. They can also be values which arise, say, from the stylistic features of the linguistic formations, or are based on the depth of the lives of the portrayed persons, or rest on the manifold aspects in which the portrayed objectivities appear, or, finally, are expressed in the harmony of the manifold aesthetically relevant qualities in the culminating phases of the work. If values of all the varieties just named appear in an aesthetically concretized work and are of such a kind that they all accord "harmoniously," a total synthetic value of the relevant concretization of the literary work of art is constituted in them whose value quality arises from the selection of value qualities of the values and nonvalues (defects) founding it. The quality of the total value which results from this selection can be of very different kinds. Either it is a "Gestalt," which lends the aesthetic object its finally founding unity; or it is only a synthetic quality, in which, so to speak, the determinations of the parts are still visible and lead to a somewhat complex but nevertheless harmoniously unified value structure; or else a qualitative conflict (a disharmony) is expressed in it, which has a lowering influence on the total value. But, in any case, the total value is not, in its qualitative content, an arithmetical sum of the values founding it or of their qualitative determinations. Which kind of synthetic binding the total value displays in its qualitative determination is, of course, a matter for the special investigation of the individual literary aesthetic objects and cannot be developed here. What has been said here is only supposed to give a fleeting prospect on the manifold diversity of possible variations. But it must be said that in previous literary investigation this task has never been carried out, and, basically, it has also never been seen. It would teach us about the value structure of a particular literary aesthetic object, and this could gradually lead us to a theory of the possible structures of aesthetic values. For the time being, we are still far from this stage and can barely make a few preparatory suggestions concerning the possibilities which present themselves here. Thus it seems probable that the appearance of several positive and nonconflicting values in a single aesthetic object leads, at least in general, to an increase in the total synthetic value resulting from them; if, on the contrary, nonvalues (defects?) appear among the component values alongside the positive values, this involves a decrease in the resulting value. But not all aesthetic values harmonize with one another. It appears that there can be positive values which conflict when present in a single aesthetic object; it is probable that this leads in general to a total value which is lower than it would be if this conflict were not present. But we would first have to check whether a conflict of a quite specific kind among the value qualities of the component values does not, on the contrary, create an effect which leads to an increase in the resulting value. It appears, for example, that the tragic quality which reveals itself in the fate of a hero portrayed in a drama is an aesthetically relevant and effective quality whose presence in the work leads to a high positive aesthetic value quality. But if we imagine a crass, grotesque character appearing in the same work, it can now become doubtful whether the contrast (or perhaps even the conflict) between these two aesthetically relevant qualities can be synthesized at all in respect of value and whether it leads to the constitution of a high positive total value or, on the contrary, essentially lowers the value which is being constituted or, finally, destroys that value altogether. The way in which these two aesthetically relevant qualities are made to appear can probably also have an influence. This could be decided in a concrete case only by subtle analytical cognition of the aesthetic concretization of a particular literary work of art. Of course, this requires a great sensitivity to the value-qualitative content of the aesthetic object on the part of the observer, and not everyone will succeed in obtaining a sure result. And in special cases a difference of opinion could develop among the investigators, and it would probably cost much effort and require the disclosure of possible mistakes in the apprehension of the aesthetic object in order to come to an agreement. For the time being, it is only important to emphasize that such tasks for investigation do exist and must be undertaken in the aesthetic consideration of literary works of art. The carrying-out of such investigations, at least on a few selected works of art, would have to convince us that both the purely theoretical consideration of the aesthetic value of concretized literary works of art and the concrete aesthetic evaluation of them constitute a very difficult task for literary study and cannot be eliminated by the few phrases with which it is usual to rest content but which say hardly anything. The carrying-out of such an aesthetic evaluation, as well as the reflective apprehension of the structure of the aesthetic value, not only demands in the individual case a correct and maximally exhaustive concretization of the work of art, down to the constitution of all possible aesthetically relevant qualities in it and of the qualitatively determined values founded in them, but also demands that we apprehend in the reflective cognition of the value-bearing aesthetic object the entire interplay of founding component values and in this way press on to the often hierarchical structure of the total value. If the investigator yields as much as possible to the suggestions of the literary work of art concerning the aesthetic constitution of the concretization, and if he is as independent as possible of the prevailing fashionable conception, there is hope that he will obtain correct results in the solution of the various problems concerning value which arise with regard to the concretized work of art which he is to evaluate.

Establishing reporting value judgments which relate to the work in question in its concretization is a procedure which, to be sure, derives from the data of the aesthetic experience and the cognition based on it, hence from data which contain many emotional and generally irrational factors but which are, in themselves, quite cool and dominated by intellectual factors. Moreover, it repeatedly subjects the judgments already made to a critical check, comparing them with various insights already gained and sometimes even carrying out certain experiments.

We try, for example, to alter or merely to dim certain parts of the work which we have already read and then observe whether changes take place in the aesthetic values which result, and what kind of changes. It is, in a word, a complicated and difficult investigative activity and not, as we sometimes hear, a simple reaction which arises in us under the influence of the work; and it is by no means an expression of the personal convictions and inclinations of the critic, as the so-called impressionistic criticism or, recently, the *"critique nouvelle"* maintains.

We have now given a survey of the most important phases of the aesthetic-reflective cognition of aesthetic concretizations of the literary work of art. It still remains for us to make clear the difference between the aesthetic experience of the literary work of art and the reflective cognition of that work or of its aesthetic concretizations. Let us now proceed to do this.

§ 29. *The difference between the aesthetic experience of the literary work of art and the reflective cognition of its aesthetic concretization*

THE FIRST, fundamental factor of this difference consists in the following: whereas the aesthetic experience is to a large extent creative, or at least cocreative, insofar as it leads to the constitution of the aesthetic concretization of the literary work of art, the reflective cognition has to do with an object which is already complete and given (encountered), and it is not supposed to be creative. To be sure, a series of perceiving, apprehending factors is, as we have seen, contained in the aesthetic experience in several of its phases, as well as a series of factors which must, in accordance with their essence, be counted among the cognitive modes of procedure in the broad sense of the word. Nevertheless, they constitute merely certain transitional phases of the entire process of constitution of the aesthetic object. But second, the function of these factors in the aesthetic experience is different from that of the reflective cognition. They do not serve to furnish the reader with a conceptual (rationalized) knowledge of the literary work of art but constitute a means of immersing the reader in the contemplation of the aesthetically relevant qualities and their harmonies in order to make it possible for him to delight in them in direct contact. In the reflective cognition of the work itself or of its aesthetic concretization, on the contrary, this function of the apprehension lapses, and its course is governed by the idea of gaining a genuine cognition of the aesthetic object. The cognitive effort is here aimed at doing justice as adequately as possible to the value-bearing harmony, to its structure and to its foundation in particular multiplicities of aesthetically relevant qualities and, ultimately, in the value-neutral determinations of the literary work of art itself.

In addition, the two processes are essentially different in their culminating phases. Whereas it is the emotionally determined value response and the contemplative delight in the constituted qualitative harmony (or in the aesthetic value) of the aesthetic object which form the culmination of the aesthetic experience, in the reflective cognition it is the aesthetic evaluation which is expressed in appropriately formulated value judgments and has its conclusion in the determination of the aesthetic value of the object in question. Whereas in the former case the culminating phase is submerged in the depths of an emotional experience par excellence, in the latter case the sober, careful, conscientious, and cautious intellectual consideration (investigation) occupies the foreground.

Although the reflective cognition of an aesthetic concretization has to do with an encountered object and consists of constant efforts to adapt itself as exactly as possible to the object, it is by no means, as might be supposed, a form of passive behavior on the part of the investigator. On the contrary, it is distinguished, as, incidentally, is every independent cognitive act, by great activity, which aims above all at the preservation of the constituted aesthetic object in vivid intuitiveness and unfalsified form in order to make possible a total and possibly also analytical beholding and apprehension of this object. A great exertion of cognitive activity also distinguishes the conceptualization of what we have succeeded in disclosing and understanding in the aesthetic object. This effort must be carried out all the more actively since traditional concepts are often lacking and we must often make ourselves independent of inherited conceptualizations and traditional views. The same also holds true of the final conceptualization of the aesthetic value of the concretization and its foundation in the structure of the work of art. Of course, the aesthetic experience is also characterized by a specific activity. But it is an activity aimed at the fullest possible apprehension of the aesthetically relevant content of the aesthetic object in the original harmony of all its relevant qualities, and, along with this, it is an activity aimed at the contemplative and emotional devotion to this object in order to do it complete justice. But this very immersion in contemplation, as well as the emotional devotion to the value-bearing substance of the aesthetic object, must be damped and even overcome to a certain extent in order to gain a certain distance from the object, a distance which makes the reflective cognition of it possible.

We have thus carried out the description of the various possible modes of behavior with regard to the literary work of art and its concretizations, as far as the main points are concerned. Of course, further, more detailed descriptive investigations are possible and desirable. But we must content ourselves with what has been said, since at this point in our study new problems of an essentially different kind present themselves, into which we still want to delve, at least in a preliminary fashion.

5 / Outlook on Some Problems for the Critical Consideration of Knowledge about the Literary Work of Art

§ 30. *Introductory remarks*

OUR PRECEDING CONSIDERATIONS, incomplete though they may be, have brought us far enough that we can already foresee the problems for a critique of knowledge which are raised by the various ways of cognizing a literary work of art. I shall try to sketch them in what follows, as far as the present state of scholarship allows.

As our investigations have shown, one must distinguish three different ways of cognizing the literary work of art (besides the usually rather casual way of becoming acquainted with the work through reading as a literary consumer). These are (1) the preaesthetic reflective cognition of the literary work itself; (2) the aesthetic experience, which leads to the aesthetic concretization of the work; and (3) the reflective cognition of this concretization in its value-bearing form.[1] The same basic types of experience enter as elements of the whole process into the store of all these kinds of cognition. Consequently, questions of a critique of knowledge which are raised concerning these processes, and in the results gained from them, are largely the same. But the differences among them, as well as the different tasks which they have to fulfill, have the result that, along with the problems common to them all, completely different

1. One can change the sequence of these modes of cognition and place the aesthetic experience first, because in many cases it is instructive for the preaesthetic reflective cognition of the work. But the sequence itself is not very important.

problems appear which are peculiar to a single variation of the cognition of a literary work of art.

Our investigation must be continued in two directions: (*a*) toward a determination of the basic values of the knowledge, both positive and negative, which arise in the consideration of each of the types of cognition of the literary work of art and (*b*) toward a discovery of the sources of possible errors in achieving this knowledge.

§ 31. *Problems for the critique of knowledge of the preaesthetic reflective cognition of the literary work of art*

THE EXPERIENCES which take place in an ordinary reading by a literary consumer in part provide a knowledge, however fragmentary, of the work and in part lead to an aesthetic experience in which the aesthetic concretization of the work is constituted. But the whole process is subject to various accidental modifications, often takes place in a way which is not consciously organized, and also serves varying purposes to which it is adapted in specific cases. Thus it is fitting to direct our attention primarily to the other modes of contact with the literary work of art which we have distinguished. I shall begin by considering the problems raised for a critique of knowledge by the preaesthetic reflective cognition of the literary work of art.

As stated above, the course of this cognition is more or less consciously directed by the idea that the purpose of the cognition is to gain "objective" knowledge about the work. In other words, we are trying to gain a number of interconnected, well-founded, true judgments about the work. But they are "true" only if they ascribe to the work only such qualities (features), as well as relations among qualities or parts, as the work possesses in itself, once it is "fixed" and "finished." In other words, the truth of judgments about the literary work of art (we shall call them "literary judgments") is no different from the truth of judgments about any other object.[2] And the concept of the "objectivity" of

2. In saying this, I have not, of course, forgotten all those difficulties connected with the explication of the concept of truth or of being true

the immediate knowledge of the literary work of art, before it is formulated into judgments, seems to be none other than that which is applied to the knowledge of real objects. Of course we must be cautious when we consider that literary works are not real and, in particular, are not ontologically autonomous but instead are intentionally projected by creative acts of the poet and are thus existentially heteronomous.[3] This must also be taken into account with regard to the concept of the "objectivity" of the immediate knowledge of an existentially heteronomous object; but it is sufficient, at least for our purposes here, if we add the condition that the knowledge of an existentially heteronomous object must do justice to its heteronomy and must ascribe to it its determinations as belonging to it in this mode of being. Certain questions and difficulties are raised in connection with literary knowledge which, it seems, do not arise with other kinds of knowledge. The concept of the truth of judgments and the related ideas of knowledge and its "objectivity" presuppose a certain concept of the object of knowledge. It is understood as something which (1) exists quite independently of the process of cognition and the judgments reached during cognition and (2) possesses its own determinations, which are attributed to it quite independently of whether and how it might be cognized.[4] Wherever the object of cognition is existentially autonomous,[5] wherever, that is, it has the basis of its being, which rests on the

---

and with the task of finding reliable criteria of truth without entering into a vicious circle. But these questions are too fundamental and too complex to be treated here.

3. In consideration of the differences in mode of being of various objects of cognition and in the way in which they can possess diverse determinations as attributes, I have tried elsewhere to differentiate in various ways the concept of "objectivity" as applied to both objects and cognition. See, in this respect, my article, "Betrachtungen zum Problem der Objektivität," *Zeitschrift für philosophische Forschung*, Vol. XXI, nos. 1–2 (1967). [Also published in Roman Ingarden, *Erlebnis, Kunstwerk und Wert* (Tübingen: Max Niemeyer, 1969), pp. 219–55.—Trans.]

4. Not all epistemologists agree to such a concept of the object of knowledge. It is rejected by the theory of knowledge of transcendental idealism. On the other hand, those who do accept it do not all agree that objects of knowledge thus defined can be cognized. The possibility is rejected by those interpreters of Kant's *Critique of Pure Reason* who have a realistic inclination.

5. See, in this connection, my *Der Streit um die Existenz der Welt*, 3 vols. (Tübingen: Max Niemeyer, 1964–66), Vol. I, § 12. [A Polish version of this work appeared as *Spór o istnienie świata* (The Controversy over the Existence of the World), 2 vols. (Cracow: Polska Akademia Nauk, 1947–48; 2d ed., Warsaw: Państwowe Wydawn. Naukowe, 1961–62). Volume I has been partially translated by Helen R. Michejda as *Time and Modes of Being* (Springfield, Ill.: Thomas, 1964).]

immanence of the qualities determining it, in itself, then the concept of the object of knowledge just given meets no difficulties in principle. But it must not be considered the most general concept of the object of knowledge, for it must be limited to existentially autonomous objectivities. As I tried to show in *The Literary Work of Art,* the literary work of art is not an object which is existentially autonomous but, rather, is existentially heteronomous; specifically, it is a purely intentional object which has its basis of being in the creative acts of consciousness of its author. Its determining qualities (more generally, its material and its form) are not immanent in it in a strict sense but are lent and attributed to it intentionally by appropriate conscious acts of the author. As soon as it is fixed in an existing intersubjective language in any kind of physical material (printing, writing, tape recording, etc.), it is in theory cognitively accessible, as a pregiven object, to any reader who has a command of the language; but it must be read and reconstructed during reading. What the reader encounters in the existentially autonomous objects under consideration are merely—in the case of a printed work—printed signs which move him to intend the corresponding words, that is, verbal sounds and their meanings. Thus the whole work in all its strata is basically reconstructed as if anew by the reader from his own resources. He does this on the basis of a correct deciphering of the printed signs and with the help of the language, which he knows and has mastered. The process of reconstruction begins with the apprehension of the verbal sounds, after which unfold, in different possible variations, all the conscious operations which we described in Chapter I. Once they have all run their course, we have a complete reconstruction or concretization of the work of art. If it is a question of apprehending the work of art in its peculiar schematic structure, in other words, of a pure reconstruction of the work, then one will avoid filling in the places of indeterminacy and actualizing its merely potential features or elements. The process of the preaesthetic reflective cognition of the work is based on such a reconstruction. That is, it is directed at the relevant work in the reconstruction which we have obtained.[6] The judgments in

6. It is tempting to consider this cognition as being simply "reflexive" (reflective), that is, as being a superstructure over the acts of reading. But it is one thing to reflect on the acts of reading (as we have done, in a sense, in Chapter I of this book) and another to direct our attention toward the objects constituted or revealed in these acts of reading, understanding, etc., and to apprehend these objects (particularly the different

which the knowledge about a work of art is contained are based on the results of the reflective preaesthetic cognition of the literary work of art. It takes three interrelated steps to reach these judgments: (*a*) the reconstruction of the work during reading, (*b*) the cognition of the reconstruction thus obtained, and (*c*) the collation of the results of this cognition into a number of interrelated judgments. As a result, the problem of the truth and of the foundation of these "literary judgments" becomes vastly more complex. At each step or on each level we find new problems which are related to the truth of literary judgments. These problems are the following:

a. Those related to the faithfulness of the reconstructing of the literary work of art during reading or to the faithfulness of the reconstruction itself

b. Those touching the objectivity of the knowledge about the work itself, or of a reconstruction faithful to it, or of its aesthetic concretization

c. Those relating to the way in which the content of the literary judgments and their interrelation are adapted to the results of the cognition of the literary work of art or its aesthetic concretization or to the qualitative composition of the work of art itself.

Each of these three contains a whole complex of problems. In particular, the problems cluster around three different questions: (1) the question of the meaning of faithfulness (or of objectivity or of adaptation), (2) the question of the possibility of achieving faithfulness (or objectivity or adaptation), and (3) the question of how faithfulness or objectivity or adaptation can be proved in the individual case. For only positive answers to these three questions could furnish proof for the truth of literary judgments.

We shall begin by considering the first complex of problems; we shall confine ourselves, of course, to the first steps in the treatment of these questions because we are concerned simply with laying the foundations and not with the construction of an

---

strata of the literary work of art) as it were secondarily by means of this attention. These new acts thus presuppose the intentional performance of the acts of reading and hence are totally different from the acts of reading. Very diverse relationships can obtain between the acts of reading and the acts of reflective analytical cognition of the work constituted or reconstituted in the acts of reading, according to what in the work analyzed is the target of the reflective preaesthetic cognition. But it would take us too far from our main theme to investigate these relationships here.

epistemology of the apprehension of literary works. Our concept of the literary work is broad enough to encompass the special case of the scientific work, so that one of the questions which arises has to do with the possibility of an objective or intersubjective science.

Ad a. I shall disregard the reconstruction of a literary work (especially a work of art) accomplished in the casual reading of a literary consumer and start with the reconstruction accomplished for the purpose of a preaesthetic reflective knowledge of the work, which thus requires a supervised and careful reading. What does it mean that such a reconstruction is "faithful" to the work? It means that it resembles the work itself in every respect, so that the work in all its details is revealed in the reconstruction. The reconstruction is "not faithful" when in some respect this is not the case. Of course there are a good many degrees of deviation from the work; sometimes the deviation is so great that the "reconstruction" [7] must be rejected as a reconstruction. In other cases it can still count as a reconstruction but demands some corrections in order to be considered faithful (in the full sense). In this context, questions arise as to (1) in what the nonfaithfulness of the reconstruction can consist, (2) the importance of the individual areas of nonfaithfulness with regard to the possibility of revealing the work itself, (3) how we can be certain whether and in what respect the reconstruction we have is faithful or not to the work itself, and (4) whether we can find guarantees (and, if so, what kind) that the reconstruction we have is or is not faithful to the work.

1. Since every literary work has many strata and, at the same time, consists of many successive parts, it contains an extraordinarily large number of elements and attributes resulting from the combination and succession of these elements. As a result, it is often quite difficult, especially with longer works, to do justice to the whole multitude of these elements and attributes. But not all the strata are equally important in constituting the work. The fundamental strata are (*a*) the stratum of phonetic formations and phenomena and (*b*) the stratum of semantic units. The faithfulness of each of the other strata, and of all of them taken together as a whole, depends

7. "Reconstruction" is taken in the objective sense to be a result of the activity of reconstructing. Understood in this sense, it forms the limiting case of the "concretization" of the work, in which all places of indeterminacy and all potentialities remain (as in the work itself); i.e., they are not filled out or actualized.

largely on the correct, faithful reconstruction of the strata named above. A chief cause of a possible nonfaithful reconstruction can thus be that not all elements of the phonetic stratum were considered in the reconstruction. This can result, first of all, from misreading (or leaving out) some verbal sound; but this is not very probable. More frequently, various phonetic phenomena can be overlooked, so that the constitutive functions they perform (such as that of holding aspects in readiness or actualizing them) are omitted, resulting in an omission in the reconstruction of the elements of the other strata dependent on them. Analogous omissions can occur in the stratum of semantic units (when the verbal sound in question is not noted and is hence not reconstructed) and can result in corresponding gaps in the stratum of portrayed objectivities. Such a gap in the semantic stratum is, however, evident even without our specially checking the text; for when the semantic interconnection among sentences or the unity of meaning in a given sentence is destroyed, the reader cannot grasp the meaning of a sentence or group of sentences, and this forces him back to the text to look for the missing element in the meaning.

More frequent and also more dangerous are falsifications in the reconstruction of the two linguistic strata, for example when a verbal sound is incorrectly reconstructed simply because the text is read incorrectly at a certain place, or when the verbal sound is apprehended correctly but the word is misunderstood, that is, reconstructed with a meaning other than the one it should have had at that place. If the work is read in one's native language, this happens rather infrequently; but the incidence increases when the work is written in another language, so that even the reader who has a command of the language can make mistakes in correctly apprehending the meaning. The worst misinterpretations or falsifications of meaning arise from an incorrect use of the syntactic functions, so that either the sentence structure is not correctly cognized and reconstructed or else the connection among sentences is interpreted incorrectly. Such falsifications are dangerous in the semantic stratum because they are not necessarily evident in the reconstruction of the work, and the reader can be convinced that he has reconstructed the work faithfully. For the falsifications do not necessarily lead to contradictions or disunity in the construction of the work. Usually the reader is made aware only by another reader of the same work that something is not in order and that a new interpretation of the text is necessary in order to intend the correct meaning. Falsifications in the semantic stratum lead automatically to corresponding falsifications in the portrayed world of the work, which in turn result in falsifications in the interconnection of the strata. The resulting inconsistencies in the portrayed world are, however, more easily noticed by the reader and can motivate him to look for their causes and thus to progress to a new reconstruction of the work, which will be more correct or more exact.

Completely new elements or factors, not present at all in the work itself, can appear in the reconstruction of the work. This happens especially in the semantic stratum; various things can be added by the reader in thought which are missing in the work. One often reads "between the lines," in a sense, and adds not only what is implicit in the text but also various things which are only creations of the reader. The reader is usually not aware of this addition; hence this kind of nonfaithfulness in reconstruction is not easy to detect.

Finally, it can happen that the strict content of all strata is reconstructed faithfully but that mistakes are made in the reconstruction of relations and connections among the elements of the various strata. These mistakes can be of great consequence for the constitution of the aesthetically relevant qualities as we pass to the aesthetic concretization of the work.

These types of incorrect reconstruction of the literary work should not be confused with the "perspectival foreshortenings" and modifications connected with temporal perspective. Modifications in the total aspect of the literary work of art result primarily from the peculiar structure of the literary work and can never be completely avoided, least of all the manifestations of temporal perspective. On the other hand, the "perspectival foreshortenings" resulting from the literary work's having several strata are more or less significant and can be compared to the differences which arise when, in finishing photographs, one "bathes" the pictures to achieve a different degree of development of various details in the picture: not all strata (or the details appearing in them) are "developed," or "pronounced," to the same degree in reading. In the pure reconstruction of the work itself this does not by itself lead to a nonfaithful reconstruction. But the foreshortenings and modifications of temporal perspective have a special significance for the aesthetic concretization of the work, since they can be accompanied by distortions in the constitution of the aesthetically revelant qualities. I shall return to this point.

2. Not all errors in the reconstruction of the literary work are equally significant. But it is difficult to give definite rules which hold for all works, since this significance is largely dependent on the structure and the peculiarities of the individual works. For instance, the omission of a semantic element can play a subordinate role in one work, while in another work it can be very decisive for the meaning of the entire work. For example, the meaning to be supplied can establish a connection among sentences without which the work falls apart. But the omitted meaning can form a dispensable accent in a thought unfolding in sentences. Everything depends on the role which the omitted semantic element plays in the work. Thus the significance of such an omission can be judged only in the framework of the work in which it occurs.[8] Similar to this is the case in which certain new elements are added in the reconstruction, where we do not of course have in mind the elements which fill out the places of indeterminacy in the work. The places of indeterminacy in the work are filled out in the concretization, especially the aesthetic concretization, of the work and are not a case of "nonfaithfulness" to the work. I shall return to these questions in discussing the aesthetic concretization of the literary work of art. Here we are concerned solely with the addition of an element in the reconstruction whose appearance was in no way provided for by the work itself. The results of such an addition can vary greatly according to the work; thus, as stated above, their significance can only be judged in relation to the whole structure of the work. We indicated the possible cases, which are quite various in their significance, in our brief description of this type of incorrect reconstruction of a work.

Perhaps we can make only the following general statement about the varying importance (significance) of a nonfaithful reconstruction of a literary work of art: the incorrectness of reconstruction is most significant when it is brought about by those changes (modifications of the work itself) introduced into the reconstruction which have taken place in the two linguistic strata of the work, because they entail accompanying alterations, which falsify the original, in the strata of the work dependent on the language, so that the whole work suffers a change in the reconstruction. In contrast, a change in the stratum of aspects held in readiness, such as the holding in readiness

8. Certain difficulties can arise in this connection, which I shall discuss later.

of an aspect or a group of aspects which were not provided for by the work itself, need not be of further consequence for the concretization. Only in an aesthetic concretization can this possibly have the serious result of making the concretization appear inadequate.

The discovery and removal of falsifications in the reconstruction of a literary work can sometimes occur only through a confrontation with another reader's reconstruction of the same work. The importance of collaboration among various readers in forming the reconstruction of a work becomes evident here, a theme we have not yet taken up. We shall discuss it later; but we must already note that there are special difficulties connected with this collaboration and hence with the formation of a common (intersubjective) reconstruction of one and the same work.

In considering the various ways in which a reconstruction can be unfaithful to the work, we become aware of the general importance of each error in reconstruction for the objective preaesthetic cognition of the work. Each error in reconstruction can be a source of nonobjectivity of this cognition, since the cognition is carried out and obtained on the basis of a reconstruction of the work gained in reading, and this reconstruction is also in a sense the object of cognition. If the reconstruction is not carried out under the guidance of a reflective cognition but rather, as it were, by itself, and if we try to fit our reflective cognition as precisely as possible to the reconstruction we have obtained without considering possible errors in it, then we apprehend the work itself in a way which is false in exactly those points where the reconstruction is not faithful to the work and is thus incorrect. Thus, in order to cognize the work as adequately as possible, we must first carry out as faithful a reconstruction as possible. Of course there are cases in which this is no problem. But in general it is wise to form the reconstruction in a reading which receives the constant assistance of the reflective preaesthetic cognition of the part of the work being reconstructed. If, during reading, we are as aware as possible of the meaning of the semantic units, the syntactic structure of the sentences, the possible ambiguity of words and groups of words, and syntactic-logical functions present among sentences, we can, at least to a certain extent, avoid errors in the reconstruction. Then it is also possible to compare the various parts of the reconstruction with one another and to check whether they accord with one another or, if they do not, whether the sources of discord are really in the text, etc., in order to remove in this way whatever errors we may find in the reconstruction and thus also to advance the reflective cognition of the work. This "correction" of the reconstruction thus takes place in both the analytic and synthetic phases of the reflective cognition of the work throughout the constitution of its reconstruction. By returning to the text, analyzing its individual parts (passages), comparing results already obtained with ever new parts of the reconstruction, etc., we confront the reconstruction we have already formed with the work itself; thus we create both the possibility of improving the reconstruction and the indispensable conditions for achieving objective results from the cognition of the work. Sometimes we can become convinced that our previous reconstruction was so deficient that it should be rejected totally and that we should undertake once again an attentive and critical reading of the work.

By virtue of the interplay between the reconstruction of the work which is complete or is in the process of being formed and the analytically and synthetically oriented reflective cognition of that reconstruction, and by means of a return to the work itself in a new phase of its reconstruction, it is possible to keep the identity of the already apprehended or intended meaning of the sentences or other semantic units intact in active memory for a certain time without having to perform completely new acts of understanding. That makes possible a continuity in the consideration of the work, or its reconstruction, so that we are concerned with a single process of looking for the peculiar form of the work (or its reconstruction), however complicated this process may be, and not with a discrete series of acts of understanding or intention which are performed independently of one another. A confrontation of the accomplished reconstruction (or its parts) with the corresponding parts of the work revealed (newly reconstructed) in a new reading permits us either to confirm its correctness or to revise and transform some of its parts. Both the intervention of the reflective cognition in the transformation of the already accomplished reconstruction and the recourse to the original form of the work in a new reading prove to be sensible and useful.

3. In connection with this whole procedure, we must pose the question, mentioned above, as to how we can be sure whether a given reconstruction is faithful to the work. It was established that we can check and correct the faithfulness of a reconstruction by means of the preaesthetic reflective cognition. But what does this mean? Simply that we return to the text and

try to understand it again, and better? Certainly. But what can we gain that is new and different by such a return except a reconstruction of one part of the work, which we can then compare with the "old" reconstruction (a process which is possible only because the identity of the meaning or the form of the old reconstruction is maintained in active memory)? Why should this new reconstruction be better and more faithful than the old one? Is it not possible that the old reconstruction is more faithful and generally better than the new? Or are both perhaps equally good? And, above all, why should we tend to believe that the new reconstruction renders the work faithfully, why should it be more "credible" than the old? Are not both equally suspect of being somehow unfaithful to the work? Are we not perpetually caught in the circle of reconstructions without being able to advance to the work and to reach it? And, finally: we go back to the text in order to let it teach us, as it were, what the work itself is like when we already know in some way, or at least suspect, that the reconstruction we have is unfaithful to the work in some respect. How can we know that without having compared it to the work in some way? One might claim that it is enough only to suspect that the reconstruction is unfaithful; and, to suspect it, we need only find contradictions or unexpected effects in the reconstruction. But if we find nothing of the sort and, having no cause for suspicion, put all our efforts into obtaining as adequate a cognition of the reconstruction as possible, it may then be asked what right we have to assert that the reconstruction we have is faithful to the work and that the knowledge about the work based on that reconstruction is objective. And, if we already know that our reconstruction is unfaithful to the work in one point, how can we judge the significance of this error if it is true that the significance depends more than anything on the role played in the work itself by the element which was falsified, or at least modified, in the reconstruction? If we have only the incorrect reconstruction at our disposal and do not know the original work, we cannot know the role of the falsified or modified element either.

Let us postpone for a moment the question whether we are actually dealing only with reconstructions or concretizations and not with the work itself. Even if this were true, the situation would not seem entirely hopeless. For even if, in rereading the work to remove an error in reconstruction, we produced only a new reconstruction, still it must be considered that it was formed with a more precise understanding of the sentences, so that these sentences can now be placed in connection with one another by means of the indications given in their content, and the portrayed objectivities which they determine can then be determined exactly as the content of the corresponding sentences demands. It seems that we can then expect the new reconstruction obtained in this way to be really more faithful to the work and more precise than a reconstruction formed without this precautionary measure. Often, of course, we are not aware that we are reconstructing the work incorrectly in various respects. Then we cannot gain objective knowledge about the work through a simple cognition of this reconstruction. But a failure of this sort can happen with any kind of empirical knowledge. Once we become aware of this eventuality, we must make it a principle that a critical check is necessary in those very cases of cognition where the cognition led to an easily achieved reconstruction and seems to be beyond any doubt. The attitude of reflective cognition in reading serves to make us more cautious and critical. But the analytical cognitive operations direct our attention to various details of the text and to the interrelations determined by them which escaped us, or could have done so, in ordinary reading. They help us to discover the ambiguity of words or phrases which might be present, as well as possible unclarity in sentence construction; they help give us a feeling for interconnections among sentences which we did not previously suspect; finally, they help us to read the text in a more active way, which enables us to carry out an appropriate objectification of the portrayed objects, a process which was not performed earlier. All this enables us to confront the new reconstruction of the text, obtained through the help of analytical observation, with the previous reconstruction. This confrontation does not merely inform us about the differences between the two reconstructions; it also shows the advantages of the new reconstruction and the shortcomings of the old one. This can happen in various ways. For example, the confrontation can call our attention to certain discrepancies among the elements of the earlier reconstruction or to unclarities in the reconstruction which we overlooked—discrepancies or unclarities which are no longer present in the new reconstruction. Of course we still have to consider the possibility that the shortcomings are not indications of an unsatisfactory reconstruction but rather that the work itself is not clear or unambiguous, so that the new reconstruction was carried out, as it were, too optimistically, although this is not very likely in view of the fact that it was gained in a critical, analytical consideration of the work. But if we suspect that the work itself is ambiguous, we must return to it; an attentive analysis of the appropriate passages in it can enable us to decide about this. A comparison of our reconstruction of the work with that of other readers can be helpful, as can a discussion about the questionable passages of the work or even a comparison of the work in question with other works by the same author. In the praxis of literary studies, this method of checking those reconstructions of literary works which have already been obtained and which do not coincide with one another has never even been tried, and yet a clarification of the situation has often been achieved. A good knowledge of the language in which the work is written and which was current at the time of writing can also help remove the difficulties which arise with regard to a correct apprehension of the work, that is, in the constitution of a faithful reconstruction.[9]

It is also not certain that we are really unable to judge the significance (for example) of a previously unreconstructed element of the work which has been noted and supplemented in a new, carefully executed reconstruction. It is, after all, possible to compare the two reconstructions and to determine, as it were empirically, what kind of consequences the newly considered element has for the structure of the work and to what extent it gives the work a structurally better or worse form, without considering for the moment what role it plays in an aesthetic concretization. We need not rely solely on our memory in such a case. What we need can be checked in a foolproof way against the printed text. This indubitably shows the great importance of printing for the cognition of literary works.

But it will be objected that all the means we have suggested for checking which reconstruction is more correct only involve us repeatedly in new reconstructions or in new linguistic formations, such as other people's statements about the literary work, which all have to be understood and reconstructed "correctly" in order for us to be certain that we have understood the text or the statements of other people with the meanings immanent in them. We are always dealing with mere reconstructions of literary formations, whether printed or spoken ("literary works" in the wider sense), although it is a question of pressing forward to the works themselves and not merely to their reconstructions,

9. I shall return shortly to the theoretical difficulties in the way of mutual understanding among various readers occasioned by such a procedure.

the appropriateness and correctness of which would in turn have to be checked in new reconstructions.

The source of all these difficulties and doubts is the fact that any linguistic formation, in particular any literary work of art, is an existentially heteronomous intentional object which arises from operations of consciousness and becomes intersubjectively accessible only when it is "attached" to some physical ontic foundation. This foundation is provided by a manuscript or a printed text or, finally, by the spoken word or merely the concrete phonetic material of the speaker. In §§ 66 and 67 of *The Literary Work of Art* I tried to overcome the difficulties resulting from this state of affairs, but here I should like to think through the questions again. The problem becomes acute only when we make certain presuppositions which are usually not explicitly stated. These presuppositions are: (*a*) There is no objective relationship between the verbal sound (as a typical form) and the verbal meaning. Any sound can be joined with any meaning; [10] the joining is determined by a special decision (we call it a "convention"). (*b*) The verbal meaning cannot be directly apprehended by the person understanding it; rather, it can be arrived at only indirectly by apprehending the experience of the person intending the meaning. (*c*) This experience, however, can be apprehended only by the one who has it or experiences it. (*d*) Even if we wanted to admit that the meaning intended in this experience is an intentional, ontically heteronomous formation, the being of this formation is so bound up with the existence of the meaning experience which determines it (however much it transcends that experience) that, when the experience is complete, this meaning too passes away or ceases to be. If this meaning is to be apprehended in its content, it must be created again in a new intentional act having the same "content," so that we have two different even if—at best—fully equal meanings, the second as a "reconstruction" of the first. But we can then never be certain that the new meaning is a faithful reconstruction of the first, because the first has already disappeared when the new one is formed and can no longer be confronted with it except in memory. But memory gives us no guarantee that what we remember is identical with the content of the actual past moment.

10. That is Democritus' standpoint, which in the *Cratylus* is opposed to Plato's. Modern linguists seem to have decided emphatically in favor of Democritus.

If we accept all these assertions in a consistent way, the result is that we cannot even be sure of thinking the same thing (the same meaning) twice. That spells the end, not only of the possibility of intersubjective understanding, but also of the possibility of understanding our own thoughts expressed in language and of continued thought about the same thing in the same way, since new meanings are always appearing, and we cannot guarantee their identity with other meanings. It is obvious that in the above assertions the disavowal of the self-identity of existentially heteronomous, purely intentional objectivities through the many different acts of consciousness projecting them goes too far. But this self-identity becomes questionable or at least incapable of proof once—as stated above—we limit the being of existentially heteronomous objectivities (in particular, of meanings) to the actual present of the conscious act intending them, so that each new linguistic mental act not only intends a new, individual meaning but also creates this meaning by intending it. And it has to create it, because the meaning intended in a previously completed act no longer exists. It is not clear for just what reasons we should recognize such a point of view; [11] probably by reason of the supposed impotence and sterility of acts of consciousness vis-à-vis existentially autonomous or real objects, which is then extended to all objectivities. Consciousness (human consciousness) is then treated as generally uncreative (in the sense of creation of any given objectivity), and the intentional correlate of the acts of consciousness is made an element of these acts independently of whether we might possibly want to emphasize at the same time that these correlates form merely a counterpart and a second whole vis-à-vis the act. If we overcome the prejudice that the intentional correlate is an element of the act of consciousness,[12] then we remove the second prejudice that the existentially heteronomous intentional object must itself cease to exist after completion of the act which

11. The results of such a view would be extremely detrimental to the mental or cognitive as well as the moral life of man. Among other things, one result would be that no decision (say, of a moral nature), no obligation we assume, could bind us. It would simply no longer exist as soon as the act of assuming an obligation or of making a decision to do something was completed.

12. The rejection of this prejudice accords with Husserl's assertion that the intentional object, or the noema of the act, is not a "real part" of the noesis. This is also the first (although insufficient) step toward overcoming transcendental idealism.

intentionally projects it. In positive terms: it may[13] then be conceded that the intentional object, especially the meaningful word of a language, can continue to exist after the acts which project it are completed. But only then can we speak meaningfully of the existence of the literary work of art after the creative acts of the author have run their course. And only then is it meaningful to speak of acts of apprehension in which the literary work of art is cognized or (in another case) misinterpreted and thus, in part at least, not cognized. And only then can we speak of a "faithful," "correct" reconstruction of the work in which the work itself is adequately revealed in its own form.

Only at this point does it become clear that there can be two types of situation in the reading of a literary work. The first is one in which the literary consumer is primarily oriented toward amusing himself by means of the work. He uses it simply as a means of forming his own concretization (or reconstruction) in order to take pleasure in it and is relatively unconcerned about the work itself. He cognizes it only to the extent that this is necessary for constituting his reconstruction. He makes no effort to progress to the original form of the work itself, basically does not apprehend it, and only pursues his own creative acts, in which his concretization of the work is constituted. Then there are two kinds of formations: the literary work of art itself (in the original) and its "reconstruction" or "concretization," which can stand in various relations to each other. Opposed to this is the second situation, in which the reader's (especially the scholar's)

---

13. I say "may" and not "must" be conceded, because it cannot be said that in every creative act of consciousness the intentionally projected object (for example, the individual sentence or a whole literary work of art) must continue to exist after completion of this act. Whether this is the case depends on the nature of the act itself: if it is included in its intention that the intended sentence or other objectivity should continue to exist, only then is there an (intentional) reason for its existentially heteronomous (continued) existence, in which case this object does continue to exist after completion of the act projecting it. That is the usual mode in which intentional objects (such as works of art) are created, and they are implicitly intended as objects which should continue to exist. This arises from the creative will of the artist but also from that of the scholar. But that is by no means always necessary. There can also be acts in which a certain object is rejected (for example, when we reject a scientific view which has previously been held), in the sense that it is no longer supposed to exist. This happens whenever the artist is dissatisfied with his composition and condemns it to nonbeing. Finally, there can be pure experiences of phantasy which serve the present moment and whose purpose it is simply to be present in that moment. They are supposed merely to amuse us and then to pass away.

whole effort is aimed at pressing forward to the characteristic form of the work, foregoing his own creation of a new reconstruction of it, so that, if a reconstruction is nevertheless involuntarily constituted, it is, so to speak, transparent and allows the scholar to apprehend the work in the original through it, the work itself, and no longer just its reconstruction. Only against the characteristic form of the work which has been brought into sight can we measure, if we wish, to what degree an obtained reconstruction is really faithful or correct or how much it deviates from the original and must falsify it if, instead of pressing forward through it to the original, we remain, rather, with the reconstruction and mistakenly hold it to be the work itself. Then all its inaccuracies are falsifications of the work. Only the reconstruction is then present to the reader, but he considers this reconstruction or concretization, with all the elements in it that are essentially foreign to the work, to be the work itself. There is no means of attaining to the work as it is in itself and of checking the extent to which the constituted reconstruction is faithful to it other than that of reading the work, but now in a different attitude, that of reflective cognition. We then leave the circle of reconstructions and concretizations; we will perhaps view them, in contrast to the newly deciphered work itself, merely as a source of the previous falsifications and will reject them as such.

It is thus not true that in our attempt to find inaccuracies in the reconstruction we are condemned to remain within the circle of repeated new concretizations and reconstructions and to be unable to find access to the work itself. The work does not cease to exist after the author writes it; and as soon as it receives its support in a physical foundation, or is fixed in such a foundation, it waits for the moment when we comprehend it in itself.

But there is still another condition to be filled if we are to gain access to the work, and the key to that is the identical language which lies, so to speak, between the work and the reader: the language in which the work is written and which the reader must master in order to find a "common language" with it. I have presupposed from the beginning that the reader has mastered this language (either as his native language or as a language he has learned very well). Now everything depends only on how it is possible to have an intersubjective common (*koinē*) language. I presented this question in my book *The Literary Work of Art* and tried to solve it in the sections indicated above. Usually we do not proceed correctly in determining that we are thinking the same thing as our acquaintances. Under pressure of the psychologism which still exercises a rather considerable influence in the field of linguistic theory, it is thought that we must somehow gain information about the mental experiences of the speaker (or the "author") in order to understand another person's speech, and, in particular, a literary work, and thus that it is only through these experiences that we can gain access to the other person's language. But since, as is usually also believed, another person's experiences are epistemically inaccessible to us, this way is actually closed to us. So one collects various data about the life and circumstances of the author in order to gain information, as one says, about the author's "intentions" and to conclude from them how he understood his speech or his work or how he wanted it to be understood. I do not mean to say that this approach is completely purposeless or without prospects. But it is very indirect, at any rate, and one can never know how effective it is and to what extent it leads to sure results. It is also quite improbable that this is the way in which mutual understanding among people, for instance between mother and child, normally comes about. This is a very extensive and difficult problem and one which we are not attempting to solve here. But it seems that there is a much shorter way of understanding someone else's speech. If it is a question of names of things or processes which can somehow be experienced, mutual understanding takes place either through mention of other nouns which clarify the meaning of the noun we are looking for or because we are in the same objective situation as the speaker, confronted with the same things and processes, and, in intending them, indicating them, we use certain words or phrases and thus orient each other as to the meaning of the words we use. Moreover, there are also immediate acts of apprehension of ideal entities and objects, and there is another way of comprehending the meaning of someone else's speech and even of confirming the self-identity of this meaning, by naming these objects and possibly also the relations obtaining among them. Those, for example, who have cooperated in a well-performed phenomenological analysis of concrete phenomena know how one can reach agreement in an absolutely clear way even about difficult phenomenal states of affairs and can thereby arrive at the formation of a subtle common language about the qualitative features of various objectivities which far surpasses so-called colloquial language. Of course there are also cases in which we cannot reach agreement about the analysis of certain essential states of affairs and are then not certain whether we are using words which have the same verbal sound but different meanings or whether we have different states of affairs in mind. If there is no apprehension of identity in such a case, then it cannot be established by a common understanding of words and phrases. At any rate, however, this approach, of confronting linguistic formations with a commonly obtained immediate knowledge (especially of the experience) of the same objectivities, is promising and leads to the possession of a common intersubjective language which is gradually formed and perfected further and further by means of further cognitions achieved in common. Literary works, and especially literary works of art, help for their part to enrich our experience and thus indirectly to further the formation of our common language.

Thus the difficulties which seem to stand in the way of the correct understanding of literary works can be removed, and it is possible, at least in theory, to understand the work itself (and not just one of its reconstructions) and to contrast it (chiefly in the dual stratum of language) with other reconstructions which have been obtained and possibly set down in writing, so as to demonstrate their accuracy or inaccuracy.

But correct understanding of the language of a literary work of art offers particular difficulties, which are not present, say, in scientific works. This is not only because the language of the literary work of art takes its material primarily from the stock of living ordinary language and does not employ a strict terminology, as do scientific works, but also because the words and expressions of ordinary language are used in a special way. Almost every word of living ordinary language is ambiguous, as any dictionary makes quite obvious. To be sure, this ambiguity is largely restricted by the context; by means of the context (if one is fortunate), a single meaning is selected from the several different meanings of the word, and the word appears with this one meaning in the sentence. But it is not always possible to remove all ambiguities of the words in this way, and there are always enough ambiguous words in any literary text. Ambiguities in sentence construction itself (or those resulting from a deficient sentence construction) are less frequent in good literary texts, as are ambiguities in the interconnection among the sentences, although even these ambiguities cannot always be avoided. Thus the reader must, in reading, pay attention to whether the text is ambiguous for one reason or another; he must be sufficiently careful and critical in reading, and in this a good knowledge of the language in which the work is written can be very helpful.

The work is cognized well in its language not merely when the reader is sufficiently sensitive to the mere presence of ambiguities but also when he recognizes which different interpretations of the text are admitted by these ambiguities and which are eliminated by the other parts of the text. And he must also orient himself as to which of these interpretations made admissible by the ambiguity have priority over other possible interpretations or whether all interpretations in the reading may be given equal consideration in the final interpretation of the text. It can be regarded as an accidental deficiency in the work if several ambiguities occur in the text, but there are also cases where the ambiguities that are present are visibly part of the artistic intent of the work. The work is then supposed to shimmer, as it were, in this ambiguity and thus achieve particular artistic effects. The reader, too, with the help of his reflective cognition of the work, must become aware of this property of the work and must apprehend it as a characteristic of the work. The results of such an ambiguity are aesthetically significant, and in an aesthetic concretization they lead to various aesthetically relevant phenomena which are calculated in advance. In poetic works, and especially in lyric poems, there is often a particular use of the linguistic formation. There are poems in which not one of the words occurring in the poem is to be taken in a "literal" sense; they are to be taken in a "metaphorical" sense. More precisely: in the language of a poem there is a "double meaning," and both meanings should be apprehended in reading and neither may be eliminated from the content of the poem. There are, so to speak, various levels of meaning, and, as a result, there is also a stratification of levels in the "reality" portrayed or expressed in the poem. One of these levels occupies the foreground, to be sure, and the "other" level is allowed only to shimmer through behind it. But the foreground level is only a means, only a way of letting the other level appear and of revealing it as the only important thing in the poem. In the end, only the second of the two meanings is supposed to be thought and intended; the first meaning merely forms an access to the second. To put it still a little more precisely: the first meaning of the text, taken in a "literal" sense, contains certain indications—for instance, discrepancies—of such a kind that, if the reader wanted to stop at the first meaning, he would have to conclude that the text was senseless, somehow stupid; but, at the same time, there are certain indications in the text that it cannot mean what it seems to, that the wording of the text is not to be taken literally, thus that one should look for another meaning, not expressly stated, which is, to be sure, suggested to a certain extent but which is not clear and is not indicated suggestively enough for the reader to be able to find it without some effort on his part. The search for this other meaning, which, though not explicit, is nevertheless supposed to count as the "real" meaning, can be undertaken in various ways. One can find the second meaning either by staying in the actual dual stratum of language (in a purely "logical" way, so to speak), or by taking into consideration the portrayed world projected by it, where those objects which correspond to the literal meaning of the text are first constituted or begin to be constituted. And then we begin to find indications in what is portrayed through the literal meaning (including what is expressed) that other objects are supposed to take the place of the objectivities already portrayed and that they should be considered under different aspects and placed in different relations. But these other objects should be seen as being somehow related (through similarity or analogy) to the objectivities first portrayed. We find that it is the new objects which are really at issue in the poem, but they are not supposed to appear themselves, directly, without the aspect of the objects first constituted; they are rather supposed to be brought to appearance with the help of those objects. The first objects are thus not supposed to disappear completely from our field of vision but should form an aspect of the later objects. It is a separate question why such an indirect way is chosen to show the objectivities to be portrayed, without naming them directly and "literally;" [14] the answer to this question belongs to the study of the structure and technique of portrayal in the art of poetry. [15] We are concerned here simply with pointing

14. Perhaps it is a question of bringing into play certain aesthetically relevant qualities which cannot be named directly, or of the presence of peculiarities in the portrayed world which can be made visible only in this indirect way, or else of a particular aesthetically relevant factor introduced into the whole of the poem by the interplay of the direct, literally intended objects and their aspects with the state of affairs brought only indirectly to appearance, a factor which cannot be made to appear in any other way. This question would have to be investigated separately for each individual work, and only then could the artistic effectiveness of this kind of portrayal be revealed and judged.

15. See for instance, in this connection, Rilke, in a poem from his *Stundenbuch* (Book of Hours):

> In the deep nights I dig for you, O Treasure!
> To seek you over the wide world I roam,
> For all abundance is but meager measure
> Of your bright beauty which is yet to come.

out the difficulties and dangers for a correct reconstruction of the work. Although it is clear in general that the literal meaning is not the actual meaning, and although the text gives us suggestions for looking for the "real" meaning, it is not as clear and simple to determine this new meaning and the portrayed world belonging to it. For the very point is that we are not told explicitly what it is ultimately about, and the relationship between the "literal" and "actual" meaning is purposely loose and allows a certain amount of room for indeterminacies. Sometimes the reader finds the "real" meaning with great accuracy; but it is equally possible to miss it, and other interpretations should not disappear from his field of vision. But how, and with what right, should he exclude these other interpretations? Perhaps it is merely a matter of letting the other interpretations vibrate in resonance with the one he chooses and of simply letting the portrayed world remain ambiguous. If we are too emphatic about choosing a single interpretation, then we have merely an "interpretation"—to use Emil Staiger's term—but not a correct, com-

---

Over the road to you the leaves are blowing,
Few follow it, the way is long and steep.
You dwell in solitude—Oh, does your glowing
Heart in some far-off valley lie asleep?

My bloody hands, with digging bruised, I've lifted,
Spread like a tree I stretch them in the air
To find you before day to night has drifted;
I reach out into space to seek you there . . .

Then, as though with a swift impatient gesture,
Flashing from distant stars on sweeping wing,
You come, and over earth a magic vesture
Steals gently as the rain falls in the spring.

[Rainer Maria Rilke, *Poems*, translated by Jessie Lemont (New York: Columbia University Press, 1943), p. 117.]

Or the more recent Gottfried Benn:

RADAR

A mist as at sea
and my belle-étage
drifts without rigging
from quay to quay.

Nowhere can it find
a place to moor
For new waves
carry it forth.

How far are Sound and Belt,
how hard to find a harbor
when one has no rigging
and fog rolls in.

[Gottfried Benn, *Gedichte: Gesammelte Werke in vier Bänden*, ed. Dieter Wellershoff (Wiesbaden: Limes, 1960), III, 447. Our trans.—R. A. C., K. O.]

plete understanding of the poem, because a correct understanding must not make a one-sided choice of a single interpretation
(not even the one most suggestively forced on the reader by the
text, which is thus perhaps most probably the "real" meaning)
to the exclusion of all others. But it is not easy to find the correct
relationship among the interpretations, to estimate the various
degrees of their probability and artistic significance, and to render them in the reconstruction with corresponding primary and
secondary emphasis. If we are to achieve a deeper understanding
of the work, we certainly must not limit ourselves to the apprehension and understanding of the dual stratum of language.
This is insufficient for a faithful reconstruction, and, all the
more, for an aesthetic concretization, of such poems (and also
sometimes of prose works). As our considerations in §§ 10–14
have already shown, still other provisions are necessary for this
purpose; they go far beyond a mere understanding of the language of the work, although they undoubtedly depend on this
understanding or on the sentence meanings of the work which
are constituted in it. To be sure, it is possible for these new provisions to be made in such a way that with their help a faithful
reconstruction of the whole work is achieved without particular
difficulties; but they need not be made in such a way, because
the understanding of the language of the work (in each of its
two strata) does not absolutely determine the way in which they
are carried through. At any rate, the sentence meanings determine the direction in which they should be made. But the way
they are carried out depends largely on the reader's mood, on his
contingent capacity for objectifying the portrayed objectivities
on the basis of the states of affairs projected by the sentences,
etc. Thus, in order to decide whether our reconstruction of the
work is faithful to it or not, we must perform a reflective analytical cognition of the text (the linguistic formations), as well as
of the possibilities resulting from its content for the constitution
of what is portrayed in the work, and check whether and to what
extent there are inaccuracies in our reconstruction. It can be
helpful to this undertaking that almost every (good) literary
work of art has its own style and own type of consistency, which,
once we have become aware of them, can serve as a guide to the
constitution of a faithful reconstruction of the work or as a
warning that those points of the reconstruction which deviate
from the style of the work and from its consistency in portrayal
of objects and in the use of artistic means can be inaccuracies
in the reconstruction of the work. Of course, all strata of the

work and all phases of its development must be considered, because only then do we see the stylistic peculiarities and the artistic consistency in the construction of the work, even if everything in the individual strata has not yet been faithfully reconstructed. The analytical consideration of the work, which is used as a check on the accuracy of the reconstruction, must thus take into account all the strata and all the phases of the work. Even a recourse to the results of another person's reading and a comparison of his results with ours can be helpful in checking the faithfulness of a reconstruction. In these various ways we not only can check our reconstruction but can also perfect it so that, after appropriate effort, we can come to a result which lends plausibility to the supposition that the literary work of art is really as it shows itself to us in a (perfected) reconstruction.

4. With the above deliberations we have answered the last of the questions we posed: we can have no absolute guarantee that our reconstruction is absolutely faithful to a literary work of art which we are investigating or that it continues to be unfaithful (inaccurate) in this or that point. This fact does not conflict with the scientific character of literary scholarship. The cognition of the literary work of art which leads to a certain reconstruction of the work is only a special case of empirical cognition in general, in which we can never gain an absolute guarantee for the objectivity [16] of the results obtained. We need not demand more of literary studies; it is simply a question of basing our assertions as firmly as possible on the given material (that is, on the literary work of art and its reconstruction).

*Ad b.** I distinguished above between the objectivity of knowledge about a literary work of art and the faithfulness (accuracy) of its reconstruction, although these two matters are closely related. The faithfulness of a reconstruction of a literary work is an instance and also a degree of similarity between the work and its reconstruction; in the limiting case it can lead to the identity of these two objectivities, so that the work itself can be revealed in the reconstruction. There is no question of such a relationship with regard to the knowledge of a literary work. No knowledge (no result of cognition) is similar to what is cognized

---

16. See, in this connection, my article "Betrachtungen zum Problem der Objektivität," *Zeitschrift für philosophische Forschung*, Vol. XXI, nos. 1–2 (1967). [Also published in Roman Ingarden, *Erlebnis, Kunstwerk und Wert* (Tübingen: Max Niemeyer, 1969), pp. 219–55.—Trans.]

* This *b*, and the *c* below, refer back to the list on p. 336, above.— Trans.

(to the object of cognition). The result of cognition is knowledge gained by us about an object. When it relates to the object, it ascribes to it just those attributes (more generally: characteristics) which it possesses in itself independently of how the object was cognized. The relationship between our knowledge and the object cognized in the process of cognition is that of neither similarity nor—as it is said—agreement; rather, it is very specific and is based on the fact that the cognitive meaning is realized by the intended attributes of the object in question.[17] If the cognitive meaning is really completely realized by the determinations of the object intended in it, determinations which exist in themselves and are given in their selfhood, then the result of the cognition is knowledge in the strict sense or, if one prefers, "objective" knowledge, which is the same thing. If one is inclined to add the attribute "objective" to the word "knowledge," this is because knowledge can be considered from various other points of view and because various other determinations can then be attributed to it. Thus, for example, the knowledge of an object can be exhaustive or not exhaustive; it can also be intuitive or not intuitive, direct or indirect, certain or only probable, etc. One often uses the word "knowledge" in a very broad sense, in which every kind of information gained in a process of cognition is held to be knowledge, independently of whether it is true or false. In that case, it is necessary to distinguish between "objective" and "nonobjective" knowledge.

Taken in this broad sense, a result of cognition relating to a literary work of art and obtained on the basis of a particular reconstruction of the work may nonetheless fail to be objective. This arises from the essential difference between the reconstruction of a literary work and the reflective cognition of the same work. Whereas a reconstruction aims at a faithful facsimile of a work, sentence by sentence, with their corresponding intentional correlates, our aim in reflective cognition of this work is to attain a system of judgments about the work, its characteristics, the way in which it is composed of its parts, its artistic structure, and the resulting artistic effectiveness, which, of course, leads us beyond the reconstruction in its development from beginning to end and demands of us completely new insights (an immediate apprehension) into the peculiar characteristics of the work. This

17. See, in this connection, Edmund Husserl, *Logische Untersuchungen*, 2 vols. (Halle: Max Niemeyer, 1900; 2d ed., 1913), Vol. II, Fifth and Sixth Investigations. [English translation by J. N. Findlay, *Logical Investigations*, 2 vols. (New York: Humanities Press, 1970).]

reflective cognition, although carried out with the aid of the work or of a faithful reconstruction, can go astray in various points and thus give us erroneous conceptions about the work. The knowledge gained is usually incomplete (does not embrace the whole work in all its parts and peculiarities); this can never be completely avoided. This incompleteness need not be considered erroneous as such; it merely demands a further augmentation of the results we have gained. But it can also lead to certain distorted conceptions about the relationships among the parts and the characteristics of the work (for example, an overemphasis on one characteristic of the work and an underemphasis on another, an incorrect apprehension of artistically important factors, etc.). Thus a new reflective cognition of the literary work of art contains a new source of possible errors which are independent to a certain extent of the reconstruction of the work. But we are often unaware that errors are contained in the results of cognition achieved in this way. Only if discrepancies or even contradictions appear in them, or if someone else calls our attention to the errors, can we apprehend them clearly and then try to remove them by new attempts at direct reflective cognition. If this cognition is still in the process of being completed, if we ourselves do not consider the results of our cognition "final," if everything is still in flux, then it is still quite probable that we will discover and remove the mistakes we have made. But as soon as we think that we have achieved the final result, only someone else's results, relating to the same work, can call our attention to the fact that there is something wrong with our own results.

But if the results of our own cognition are to be made known to other scholars, they must be expressed in a number of judgments formulated in language, and that is another source of possible errors.

Ad c. In these judgments the results of cognition are set down, and these results constitute, if not the only means, at least the most important means of making the judgments accessible to several subjects of cognition. Thus it is quite important that their content conform as adequately as possible to the results of a direct cognition. The content of a judgment will "conform" to the result of a direct cognition when it contains the same meaning intentions, with the same interconnections and deductive relationships, as are contained as original intentions in the cognition which is expressed and set down in the judgment.

We must, of course, distinguish between the truth of a judgment and the conformity of its content to the result of cognition. In a given case it is possible that a true judgment may not conform to the corresponding result of cognition (in this case the result of cognition is in itself not objective); the judgment which conforms in its content to the result of this cognition will then be false. Only a judgment conforming exactly in its content to the result of an objective cognition is true. As can be seen from the earlier considerations, making the content of a judgment conform adequately to the result of a direct cognition is often a very difficult task, which can be carried out only if one has a language developed for this purpose. In many cases, especially if the direct cognition yields really new results in a little-explored field, the existing language cannot furnish us with the words and phrases we need (even though it goes beyond the usual colloquial language and has a rather technical character). Sometimes this task is made more difficult by the fact that the existing syntactic functions and normal modes of expression in the language lead to formulations which are not equipped to render what is really present in the direct cognition, or lead to falsifications of what is present. In the first case we have the difficult responsibility of inventing new words (both nouns and verbs) which conform exactly in their meaning content to what is immediately present, capturing it accurately with their meaning intention. In the second case we have the far more difficult task of deactivating the existing syntactic functions and of trying to form new logical-syntactic functions which, despite their newness, can be incorporated into the system of the existing language without leading to contradictions. In the case of works of art, which are really the products of the originally creative activity of a genuine artist and which lead to completely original aesthetic concretizations, the requirement that we carry out an appropriate transformation of the existing language is particularly difficult to fulfill, and the failures we can experience in trying can do us out of the new discoveries we have made in the reflective cognition of the work of art. Having already discovered in direct cognition what is new and original in the work of art and what at the same time belongs to its essence, we would still be unable afterwards to express it adequately to anyone.

Even if the judgments about individual literary works of art conform as perfectly as possible to what is given in the direct literary objective cognition, one should not be deceived about the fact that even the most perfect system of judgments expressing the results can by itself give merely an equivalent of a particular work of art. We can come to comprehensive knowledge about this work of art in such a system, but it can never replace for us the concrete fullness of the work of art which we can reach, at least in principle, by direct investigative cognition. The reason for this is primarily that every system of judgments which we can achieve in scientific practice is always finite and thus cannot exhaust the plenitude of the whole multiplicity of characteristics and the often unique peculiarities of the literary work of art. This knowledge is thus always incomplete. But there are still other reasons which make it impossible for this system of judgments to form an equivalent of the work of art and to be able to replace it. The system of judgments only deepens and enriches the knowledge the reader can gain about the work in ordinary reading.

Every group of judgments about a literary work of art (as a schematic formation) which are set down, responsibly founded and internally coherent, itself constitutes an instance of a literary work. It is a scientific work about a particular individual object. The order of succession of its parts (ultimately of the individual judgments) is determined by this work's own principles of composition, which can vary greatly in different works about the same literary work of art. Theoretically, this order is independent of the order of the states of affairs which exist in the literary work of art under consideration. The judgments in a scientific work which concern a literary work can apprehend in their contents, among other things, the order of succession of the parts in the literary work of art under consideration, as well as the other interconnections among its determinations or among the states of affairs in the work; but the intentional states of affairs of the judgments in which this apprehension takes place need by no means be ordered in the same way as the states of affairs whose interconnection and order they determine. On the contrary, their order and interconnection and the interconnections in which they themselves stand have to be different from what they deal with. One could say that in a scientific work about a literary work of art there arises a completely new perspective from which this work of art is portrayed. The choice of this perspective is determined by the intentions, that is, goals, which the scholar has and is only indirectly conditioned by the structure of the work of art itself. This perspective is, of course, also different from the perspective from which we view the work of art in an ordinary, adequate reading; this is because it is only from this new, distanced perspective that the work can reveal itself in its characteristics, structural factors, artistic execution, etc., which escape us in ordinary reading because we are in a sense too close to the work. These new perspectives from which the work of art is portrayed need not always be "external perspectives." In the scientific treatment of a work of art we also can and must "drill" and make cross-sections [18] through the work of art, through which the work appears from, and is also portrayed in, various internal points, in internal perspectives. Only then can we understand the essential internal structure of the work of art. Then, particular sets of parts and factors are chosen from the plenitude of the work of art, are apprehended in their interconnections and dependencies, and are revealed in the role they play for the whole of the work of art and for its artistic profile. And only from these various external and internal aspects (usually noted by different scholars) does the literary work of art in question take shape, in its peculiar structure and its material nature, before the eyes of scholarly investigation; ultimately an identity must show itself among all these aspects. If we then return once again to reading the work and, intuitive experience and apprehension, see it develop before us in the sequence of its parts in the concrete time immanent in it, we cognize it, not only in its original, originary form, but we also have it before us in the whole wealth of determinations and structures which can be revealed only through the detour by way of a scholarly reflective cognition of the work. Of course, in the whole interplay of the different points of view, the external perspective, and the cross-sections, it happens that sometimes one and sometimes another side, stratum, detail, interconnection, relationship of dependency is emphasized and brought into the foreground, while others are treated only casually, from a distance, often hardly mentioned, so that the architecture of the work seems to become distorted in a peculiar way, and many phenomena appear which seem to be foreign to the work of art itself and which should be eliminated as soon as we want the work of art to take shape again before our eyes in its own unrelativized form. None of this can be avoided in examining the literary work of art, because only in this way can we achieve a better-founded literary work of art,

---

18. Ostap Ortwin, an important Polish critic in Lvov, writing from approximately the time of the "Young Polish" literature until the outbreak of World War II, published a collection of his critical essays in the thirties under the striking title "Cross-Section." He was murdered in the war. [Ostap Ortwin, *Próby przekrojów: Ze studjów nad teatrem, liryka i powieścią 1900–1935* (Lvov, 1936).]

which makes us independent of the various contingencies of ordinary reading. But, on the other hand, there are various dangers in this procedure, for example a distortion in the order of the elements in the work of art, an overemphasis on some of its determinations with a neglect of others, the appearance of certain phenomena foreign to the work, etc. There is the danger that in the multiplicity of perspectives and points of view we will not be able to find the borderline between the aspects arising from the nature of the work of art itself and those phenomena and modes of appearance which relate to the inclinations of the scholar and the arbitrary nature of the individually posited goals of his investigation. Of course it is possible, in reading a scholarly treatise about a particular literary work of art, to carry out a corresponding objectification (see, in this respect, § 10) of the states of affairs conveyed by the individual sentences of this treatise and thus to get closer again to the work of art and its proper form; but from the previous analyses we know that it is possible to carry out this objectification in different ways with the same store of judgments ordered in the same way. We must ask to what degree the above-mentioned relativities can be removed. It is also possible and quite advisable to read various treatments of the same work of art and to try to reconstruct synthetically from their results an apprehension of the peculiar form of the work which is free of the relativities of investigation. But there is no doubt that this procedure, whose appropriateness and legitimacy are by no means questioned, constantly poses the same very difficult question as to which of the aspects of the work of art resulting from the investigation are peculiar to the work and distinctly express its individual essence and which are only relative to the phase of investigation itself and to the individuality of the scholar and can be traced back to them. Can this question be decided at all? We should not answer at the outset with a curt "no," as comfortable as it is shallow and unproductive. But neither may we simply pass over this question.

One thing is clear at the beginning. No scholarly representation of an individual literary work of art, achieved with the help of a system of judgments, is adequate to the work of art itself, nor is it an equivalent of the work of art, nor can it replace the work. But that alone is no shortcoming or error in this representation. It is not supposed to be an equivalent of the work; thus we may not reproach it for not being such an equivalent. It performs quite different services from the ordinary but carefully and sensitively executed reading of the work of art. And both accesses to the work of art itself are justified and give us different sorts of knowledge about it; they complement each other and mutually aid a continually better, deeper, and comprehensive apprehension. The ordinary reading, regardless of what it contributes to attaining an aesthetic concretization of the work and hence to the apprehension of a particular aesthetic object, stimulates us to pose various questions with regard to the determinations and peculiarities of the work of art itself and with regard to its artistic execution and thus leads into the reflective cognition of the work of art. The reflective cognition of the work of art then forces us, as it develops, to return to the work of art in an attentive and cautious reading, which in turn allows us to carry out the reflective cognition more precisely and in a more adequate way and, after an analytical consideration, to progress to a synthetic apprehension of the work. This results in new insights into the qualities of the work of art and also in new unclarities about its various determinations, which stimulate us to further investigation. And so on. To say at the outset about this whole complicated procedure, which directs us back to the work of art itself several times, that it does not lead us out of the circle of relativities and "subjective" falsifications is, at the least, an overly comfortable decision, which in no way helps us overcome the problems we face. The difficulties cannot be overcome if we do not relinquish from the beginning the claim, made out of arrogance, to a special "scientific character." Proud of the exaggerated responsibility of our knowledge, we often remain caught in an unproductive skepticism.

One more problem, to conclude these considerations: we pointed out in Chapter 1 that in the literary work of art it is possible to accomplish the objectification of the portrayed objectivities in very different ways and that the number of these objectifications varies, depending on the qualities of the work. This fact leads to a general theoretical question. Is it possible, by making great efforts and overcoming all theoretical difficulties, to obtain a single system of judgments about a literary work of art? The expression "a single system" should be taken in such a way that the order of the judgments belonging to this system is not taken into consideration. Or, in other words, is it impossible to attain two or more true but at the same time, not concurring systems of judgments about a given literary work of art considered from a certain point of view?

For the moment, of course, I am disregarding the fact that there are places of indeterminacy in every literary work of art which can be filled out in various ways, since at present we are considering the reflective preaesthetic cognition of the work itself and not the cognition of its (possible) aesthetic concretization. The places of indeterminacy thus remain blank, and in the cognition of the work we shall merely consider which possibilities for filling them out are present in the work. Thus we are concerned for the moment only with those judgments which relate to the sides or qualities determined in the work. If it is possible in every work to perform different objectification of the objects (unambiguously) portrayed in it, then it appears that different ways of performing the objectification will result in differently determined portrayed objects and that the judgments relating to them will be different and will not agree with one another. But in what ways can the differently objectified portrayed objects differ from one another? It does not seem to be possible with regard to the material, qualitative determinations, for either these are determined in a direct and unambiguous way (if, that is, the text of the work is itself unambiguous—but we are not concerned here with the case in which it is not) in the dual linguistic stratum of the work by materially determining factors of the sentences appearing in this stratum, or else they are a necessary result of what is determined in the linguistic stratum. In order to avoid the danger of dual systems of judgments about one and the same work, it might perhaps be advisable to say that the objective stratum of the work is not fully determined, not only in the sense that the individual objectivities appearing in it are in many respects without unambiguous determination, but also in the sense that its categorial structure is in certain cases not fully determined. Or perhaps it should be admitted that the different ways of objectification of portrayed objects can lead to different categorial conceptions, which, however, do not conflict (but rather only complement one another). This question would have to be investigated on the basis of many concrete examples, since it seems that the nonambiguousness and completeness of the text of literary works of art may vary greatly. Often only a very precise analysis can reveal the real constitution of a text which at first seems to have many good qualities, to be very clear and complete. It can happen in connection with this that the material content of the sentences in the text of the work is such that it permits a twofold interpretation of the material determination of the portrayed objectivities and thus leads (if the objectification is carried out far enough) to two materially different objectivities. If we were to take these objectivities just as they are determined by the dual linguistic stratum in the work, they would not be fully determined even in respect of the material of the sides determined by the sentence meanings. Whatever may be the case with individual works, at least one thing is certain. If it should happen that the portrayed objectivities in a literary work of art are not unambiguously determined in a material or formal (categorial) sense prior to the carrying-out of the objectification and that the sides of these objectivities which are positively determined in the text are not fully determined, then it would have to be said that the completed objectification, or the form of the portrayed objectivities realized as a result of this objectification, belongs not to the pure reconstruction of the work but rather to one of its concretizations. Those judgments, then, which refer to the portrayed objectivities definitively objectified in one way or another should not be included in the system of judgments about the literary work of art itself. But we would have to include in this system a series of judgments stating what is determined about the portrayed objects by the meaning content of the dual stratum of language without the process of objectification, and what is, at the same time, left open as a multiplicity of different possible objectifications; in this way the various definitively objectified objectivities would belong to the work of art as a multiplicity of potentialities which would become actualities of a really executed constitution only in individual concretizations. Such judgments with regard to what is left open about the objectivities would then belong to the same group of judgments as those about the places of indeterminacy in the work and the possible ways of filling them out in concretizations. But if the opposite should prove to be true, if the objectivities are unambiguously determined by the text prior to objectification and we still arrive at different systems of judgments about the work, then that does not at all mean that the judgments are in conflict with one another but, rather, merely that they apply to different sides of the material and categorial determination of the portrayed objectivities. All these sides are contained in the objectivities, but within the whole of the object some qualities are more heavily stressed and more clearly distinguished because of the emphasis in the cognition and because of the apprehension of the cognition in corresponding judgments. This uneven emphasis is, of course, a kind of inadequacy in relation to the work itself, but it could be corrected by recourse to the direct cognition of the work itself and by embedding, in the unified totality of the portrayed objects, the elements which were emphasized and too sharply distinguished. In any case, nothing forces us to assume that, with respect to all those sides of the literary work of art itself, and especially the portrayed objects, which are unambiguously established in the work, we must obtain judgments which are at once true and inconsistent. On the contrary, wherever we have judgments which do not concur with one another, either they are not all true or, if they are true, they do not contradict one another but rather refer to different details of the work or to different concretizations of the work.

In concluding these remarks about the problems for the critique of knowledge posed by the preaesthetic reflective cognition of the literary work of art, we must emphasize that what we have said is merely an indication of the first perspectives on the problem and that we could develop a more detailed approach to the problem only by treating the investigative cognition of individual works.

§ 32. *Some problems for the critique of knowledge of the aesthetic experience*

THE AESTHETIC EXPERIENCE which develops in us as we read a literary work of art does not have the task of giving us knowledge about an aesthetic object. Its function is at first only that of constituting this object, hence only of forming the point of departure for a particular kind of cognition. It runs its course under the influence of what the reader has succeeded in bringing to givenness from the work of art. Thus to a certain extent it is regulated by the parts or qualities of the work brought to givenness but not completely determined by them, since the experiencing subject, with his abilities, his inclinations, and the relatively contingent moods in which he happens to be during reading, also has a more or less involuntary effect on the formation of the experience. This is the result of the reader's meeting with the work of art, but the role these two factors play is not always the same and not always equally significant. Many aesthetic experiences develop with the work predominating, but many also develop with the reader predominating, especially when he is not only receptive to what is given in the work of art but also takes a very active attitude. The increase of his activity can even be stimulated by the characteristics of the work. Thus the aesthetic experience can take very different courses, even with the same work and the same reader, and can lead to different admissible aesthetic objects. Of course, the circumstances under which the meeting comes about play an important role here, too. As I tried to show in § 24, above, in the constitution of the aesthetic object the aesthetic experience is interwoven with perceptive elements which are directed at the qualities of the work as it appears in the reconstruction. Moreover, especially in the later phases of the experience, in which the aesthetically relevant qualities and the aesthetic values or value factors founded in them have already been constituted, the experience is a form of direct contact with these values, from which results the emotional response to value of the experiencing subject and which can form the basis for a cognition of the aesthetic object constituted in the experience. These interwoven cognitive moments, however, unfold differently according to the final result or purpose of the experience. Either (*a*) the experiencing subject is simply concerned with having the experience, which is somehow of value to him, in contact with a work of art and by means of the constitution of an aesthetic object or (*b*) he is concerned in the experience with the perception, and hence also the cognition, of certain values which appear in the constituted aesthetic object. In the first case, the aesthetic experience is a feature of human life, sufficient to itself; in the second case it is a preparation and a means for the aesthetic cognition of a value-bearing object. These different aspects under which the aesthetic experience can be performed and considered lead to different problems in the critique of knowledge. Let us discuss first the questions which arise in the first case.

Ad (*a*). In the epistemological consideration of the pre-aesthetic mode of cognition of the literary work of art, the central question is the problem of the objectivity of this cognition or the truth of the judgments gained by means of it. The question of the objectivity of the aesthetic experience has no significance in the case of the self-sufficient aesthetic experience. Instead, three other questions occupy the foreground: (1) the problem of the effectiveness of the aesthetic experience; (2) the question of the acceptable variability and diversity of the aesthetic experiences which arise in the reader's contact with the same literary work of art,[19] which brings up the question

19. The experiences can belong either to the same or to different readers. We are concerned with both cases.

of the relation of the aesthetic experience to the work of art which constitutes the source of this experience; and (3) the question of the role of the aesthetic experience in the life of human beings and how this role changes according to the effective capacity of the experience.

1. What do we have in mind when we speak of the "effectiveness" of the aesthetic experience? Aesthetic experiences which unfold in us in contact with the same literary work of art not only differ among themselves but also lead to characteristically different aesthetic concretizations of the work. Some of the concretizations have fewer aesthetically relevant qualities than others, which may be distinguished by a wealth of such qualities. For instance, in what I have called the "philological" way of reading, the range of aesthetically relevant qualities is restricted to those qualities which can appear in the phonetic stratum and the stratum of semantic units. But in a reading in which we try to take into account all strata of the work in their aesthetically significant factors and to bring them together into a unity, the number of these qualities generally increases and brings out clearly the aesthetic value of the concretized work. At the same time, the places of indeterminacy can be filled out in many different ways and can lead to considerable differences among the concretizations. In all of this the varying "effectiveness" of the aesthetic experience is expressed. It has a greater effectiveness when, on the basis of the same literary work of art, it leads to an aesthetic concretization of the work which contains a greater number of aesthetic values and a higher total aesthetic value; but the condition must be fulfilled that the aesthetic values appearing in the concretization must belong to that domain of values which lies within the scope of the possible realizations of that work of art. This limitation prevents us from attributing any effectiveness, in our sense, to aesthetic experiences in which the experiencing subject is little concerned about the work of art and uses it only as a means to stimulate himself and to delight in the experience in whatever way he pleases. The minimal effectiveness is contained in an experience in which no aesthetic object is constituted and which is thus only apparently an aesthetic experience. This appearance usually arises because in the course of the experience strong emotions occur which are not themselves aesthetic but the experience of which is the source of an aesthetic emotion for the experiencing subject. The effectiveness of the aesthetic experience, understood as we have explained it, must not be confused

with the way and the degree in which an aesthetic experience "does justice to" the work of art on the basis of which it develops. This last concern is taken into account when an aesthetic experience functions as preparation for a cognition of the aesthetic concretization of a (literary) work of art and hence also for a cognition of the work of art itself (see below, under [b]).*

The effectiveness of the aesthetic experience depends primarily on the abilities of the reader, his interest in certain artistic themes, the type of imagination he possesses, the scope and activity of his imagination, the subtlety of his sensitivity, the level of activity of his emotional reaction, the type of aesthetic culture he possesses, and so on. In addition, the way in which places of indeterminacy are filled out plays an important role, because that can influence the actualization of the aesthetically valent qualities in various possible ways. Sometimes a failure to complete an important place of indeterminacy, or a completion which is not allowed by the work or is not in harmony with other features of the work or with other places which have been filled out, can lead to the destruction of the inner unity of the concretization or at least to the falsification of the harmony of its aesthetically relevant qualities. On the other hand, the intentional noncompletion of a place of indeterminacy can heighten the unity of the qualitative harmony of the concretization and thus lead to an increase in its total aesthetic value. Thus, in order to judge the effectiveness of an aesthetic experience, we need not only a knowledge of the existence of the aesthetic values which appear in the concretization belonging to the experience but also a good knowledge of the work itself and of the other possible concretizations it suggests. Only in the light of the artistic capacities or values of the work of art and by comparison with other possible concretizations of the same work do we see what our experience was able to effect aesthetically. A whole discipline could be devoted to the problems which relate to this question.

2. The different possible instances of the effective capacity of aesthetic experiences are revealed not solely by the structure of the concretization of the work emerging from an aesthetic experience but also by the varying course which an aesthetic experience can take, particularly in the way in which its final phases are formed. An experience which takes a different course

* The reference is to the (b) on p. 385.—Trans.

yields a differently constituted concretization. But the situation is quite complicated, and without intensive investigation it is impossible to state generally from which differences in the experience a differently constituted concretization arises. Nevertheless, we can give some indications here. The aesthetic values are founded in sets of aesthetically relevant qualities which, in combination, are strictly correlated with the appropriate value quality.[20] The appearance of a given value quality in an aesthetic object is dependent on whether the experiencing subject has succeeded in actualizing an appropriate selection of aesthetically valuable qualities in the concretization of the work. The concrete appearance of each of these qualities in a concretization is, however, conditioned on two sides: on the side of the reconstruction of the work and on that of the experiencing subject. In the first case we are concerned with the fact that every aesthetically valuable quality, if it has not been grafted onto the aesthetic object by the subject in an unjustified way,[21] must be founded in the corresponding value-neutral factors in the work of art. The presence in the (literary) work of art of these value-neutral factors which constitute the foundation of the aesthetically valuable qualities determines the artistic value of the work of art. The aesthetic experience gains in effectiveness when the experiencing subject, in completing the experience, succeeds in actualizing the artistic values present in the work (not necessarily in reconstructing them, for this is connected with the problems of the "justice" of the experience or of its so-called objectivity, which we shall soon discuss). The more of these factors which constitute the artistic value of the work of art we actualize, the more numerous will be the aesthetically

20. This general assertion, which presumes the existence of an internal, essential connection between various hierarchically ordered, aesthetically relevant or even irrelevant qualities and the qualitatively determined aesthetic values, cannot be analyzed here. It belongs to a general theory of aesthetic value. And I understand quite well that one can oppose a conception to this one which can likewise be supported by many arguments. We must leave this whole discussion for another investigation. Here we are merely concerned to point out that one arrives at the problems we have developed with regard to the aesthetic experience only if one speaks out in favor of the first assertion above. The whole analysis of the aesthetic experience given here points to the conclusion that the aesthetic object is not a loose conglomerate of qualities which are foreign to one another.

21. Here we encounter problems which are not connected with the mere effectiveness of the aesthetic experience and which are related to the question of what is usually called the "objectivity" of the results of the experience.

valuable qualities in the aesthetic object, and this increases the possibility of the appearance of aesthetic values. In other words, the effectiveness of the aesthetic experience can be that much greater. It does not have to be greater *ipso facto,* however, because the appearance of these values is also dependent on other factors. Among these value-neutral factors in the work of art which found the aesthetically valuable qualities there can still be differences (1) in the level of their activity in founding the aesthetically relevant qualities (among other things, whether they are both necessary and sufficient for the constitution of a particular quality of this type or merely necessary) and (2) in the level of their activity of effecting the experiencing observer of the work of art (whether they stimulate him actively enough to appropriate sensitivity and activity in projecting and vividly actualizing the aesthetically relevant qualities). The better these factors constituting the artistic values of the work of art can be actualized in the aesthetic experience, the greater the effectiveness of the experience. But the "subjective" side of the developing aesthetic experience also plays an important role. The experiencing subject must have enough sensitivity (1) to apprehend or to actualize the appropriate factors of the work of art; (2) to differentiate the aesthetically relevant qualities predetermined by them and to project them intentionally in an active way, so that they appear vividly in the (literary) work of art; and, finally, (3) to feel them in the aesthetic object after their constitution, to apprehend the aesthetic values founded in them, and to react to them in an appropriate emotional way—in other words, to form an appropriate value response to them. The type of the effectiveness of the aesthetic experience must be determined by the interdependent objective and subjective factors which influence the course of the experience. But these factors are, as was just indicated, of very different kinds and are partially independent of one another. Their total stock can thus vary greatly from case to case. On the one hand, the effectiveness of the experience can vary greatly, even with the same work of art and the same aesthetic observer. But, on the other hand, the corresponding aesthetic concretizations of the same (literary) work of art can also diverge greatly from one another. Thus it may be asked how broad the limits of possible variability of these concretizations of one and the same work can be.[22]

22. The formulation of this problem is not yet precise enough. We will soon try to arrive at a more exact statement of it.

In connection with this, we must occupy ourselves a little with the completion of the places of indeterminacy and the actualization of the potential factors of the literary work of art in concretization. Three kinds of factors may be contained in the completion of a place of indeterminacy: (1) artistically inert and aesthetically neutral factors; (2) active factors, which lead by themselves or in combination with other factors of the work of art to the constitution of aesthetically valent qualities; and (3) factors which are themselves aesthetically valent qualities. The set of factors which become actual in a concretization depends on the extent of the places of indeterminacy and on the course of the aesthetic experience. But the mere fact that certain aesthetically relevant qualities can be actualized in a concretization does not itself decide the aesthetic value of the whole concretization. For there are many places of indeterminacy and thus also many ways of filling them out which can lead to the constitution of aesthetically relevant qualities. But for the constitution of the aesthetic value of a concretization, in particular its total aesthetic value, not just any aesthetically valent qualities are sufficient; rather, these qualities must be selected in an appropriate way. And this selection of qualities, one of several possibilities in the concretizations of a given work, depends on the way in which the different places of indeterminacy are adapted to one another and on the effectiveness of the aesthetic experience. The aesthetically valent qualities in a concretization can be selected in such a way that they do not lead to harmony and thus cannot constitute an aesthetic value determined in a unified way. But these qualities can just as easily be actualized in a specially chosen combination which results in the constitution of a certain value in a concretization or even several aesthetic values which are compatible with one another or, in a favorable case, even require one another. Usually it is the case that not all elements of the selection are equally possible, that is, that many of them are more strongly suggested to the reader by the factors of the work of art determined in the work and relating to the place of indeterminacy in question. Thus they are more likely to be actualized (projected) by the experiencing subject than other qualities which belong to the same admissible group of qualities for "filling out" the places of indeterminacy. The rest now depends on the subject of the aesthetic experience of the work of art: on whether he is sufficiently active during his experience in actualizing what fills out the places of indeterminacy and on whether he has the necessary imagination and sensitivity to judge what facet of the place of indeterminacy should be brought to phenomenal presence in order to fill it out and what, on the other hand, must be passed by without notice or reaction. In other words, it depends on whether he has the aesthetic tact to admit only those ways of filling out places of indeterminacy which harmonize with one another (or possibly lead to desired contrasts) and which are not aesthetically dead but are active in the sense that they either contain aesthetically relevant qualities themselves or are the sufficient condition for constituting such qualities. It depends on whether the reader's mode of behavior and hence the course of the aesthetic experience are determined by an arbitrary and contingent mood or whether the reader makes an effort to influence or even to control the course of the aesthetic experience, especially the process of filling out the places of indeterminacy, with the intention of exploiting the opportunity provided him by the work of art so that the aesthetic object arising from the aesthetic experience will have the optimum of concretized aesthetic values permitted by the work of art. Every individual (literary) work of art permits different aesthetically valuable concretizations which cannot all be concretized at the same time, since they are usually mutually exclusive. Thus it is natural that the subject of the aesthetic experience will want to actualize different aesthetic concretizations of the same work in succession, in order to realize at least part of the possibilities offered by the work. He will try, at least to a certain extent, to direct his aesthetic experience so as to actualize different aesthetic values and bring them to phenomenal self-presence and thus have contact with them and respond to them in an appropriate emotional way. At first he may not be concerned with whether each of these actualized concretizations really does justice to the work of art, since his concern is only with the multiplicity of the phenomenally concretized values and his emotional contact with them.[23] But then we must ask whether there is not an admissible limit to this variability of aesthetic concretizations of a certain work.

In general, it is impossible to say whether every change or deviation in the course of the aesthetic experience has decisive significance for the final form of the concretization and its value; we would have to investigate individual cases, trying to

23. This is the case, for example, with ambitious and basically irresponsible theater directors who transform a dramatic work mercilessly only in order to achieve the desired stage success.

carry out several modifications in the course of our experience of the same work. But it is clear that, in all the various differences among individual aesthetic experiences which lead to a concretization of one and the same work, the formation of the final phases of the experience plays the most significant role: the phase in which the aesthetic value qualities, and hence the values, are phenomenally constituted and the phase in which the formation of the response to these values in the experience takes place. These two phases constitute the final note of the effectiveness of the experience. The higher the (constituted) aesthetic values or the final total value, the greater the acknowledgment it should find, as expected, in the value response in the final phase of the experience. It will be no ordinary pleasure but some kind of admiration, of delight, and an associated affirmation of the value—that is, a confirmation of its being, the assent that it is good that this value exists. In the constitution of a value which is positive but not especially high, the emotional value response will correspondingly assume the form of other kinds of acknowledgment or concurrence; it also becomes less active, less animated, and is no longer so "hot" but is, rather, lukewarm or even cool, and it will no longer engage the experiencing subject in the same way.[24] The factor of "affirmation" is still contained in it but is no longer so strong. Finally, when the aesthetic experience leads to the constitution of a negative value (a "nonvalue"), then the value response will be a rejection, a condemnation of this nonvalue itself as well as of the concretization. This rejection is the opposite of "affirmation"; thus it accompanies a postulate of nonbeing and the implicit confirmation that it is not good (it may be bad) for this nonvalue to exist. In the case of still greater negative values, one can even have an emotionally colored antipathy, an aversion, or even a revulsion. But two aesthetic experiences of the same literary work of art which take different courses can also lead to the constitution of two concretizations having a qualitatively different but equally high aesthetic value [25] because the same places of indeterminacy can be filled out in very different ways and, as a result, can constitute different aesthetically relevant

24. As is expressed in the common phrase, "It leaves me cold."
25. I am not forgetting that it is very difficult to substantiate how two qualitatively different values can be equally high. But, on the other hand, this is a question for the general theory of value and cannot be treated here.

qualities.[26] Then it is not impossible that, despite the equality of the value, the response to value differs because the different qualitative determination of the work demands a different response. Let us suppose, for example, a comparison between two different literary works of art. The one exhibits a crystal-clear composition, has a good distribution of the aesthetically relevant accents through the individual parts, and, as a result, has a harmony of aesthetically relevant accents. In its aesthetic concretization we see the calm charm of a "classic," rational structure. The other work, on the other hand, manifests no particular virtues of composition; yet, in aesthetic perception, many lyrical emotional elements unfold, and these also result in a harmony and a peculiar charm of a completely different kind. Both works can possess equally high values in aesthetic concretization, but the nature of the value response, although both responses give acknowledgment to the values, will be different in its final form. In the first work, the form of a calm admiration of the perfect harmony of structure will predominate, an admiration experienced from a certain contemplative distance. In the second work, the foreground will be occupied by an emotionally colored pleasure at the magic of the peculiar mood of the work. Something similar can occur in two different aesthetic concretizations of one and the same literary work of art; the one may emphasize the good structural qualities of the work, the other the subtle, lyrical, emotional mood.

In general, it is as possible for different aesthetic concretizations of the same work to be of equally high value but of different value quality as it is for equally high acknowledgments to have different qualitative determinations as value responses. In the area of aesthetic concretizations of literary works of art,

---

26. This can easily occur, for example, when the same literary work of art is read in different historical epochs. In different historical situations one fills out the places of indeterminacy in a different way and also inclines toward intercourse with different aesthetically relevant qualities and concretizes them with greater freedom, while ignoring others. But that does not mean that the valuableness of certain qualities has itself changed but only that certain aesthetically valuable qualities are popular in a certain epoch. Thus, in the concretization one creates the conditions for their appearance; but the other qualities are not concretized, although their valuableness is still retained. As long as two different ways of filling out the places of indeterminacy lie within the realm of possibilities permitted by the places of indeterminacy, it cannot be said that either way is an inadequate or false concretization of the work.

precisely because these are built up of many strata and have a quasi-temporal structure, neither a unilinear order of degrees of value nor a unilinear gradation of possible value responses to the values which may appear can be established.[27] There are several different systems of possible aesthetic values as well as several systems of possible value responses. These are determined by different basic types of harmony among the aesthetic qualities, or, if we prefer, by different materially determined categories of literary aesthetic objects, or by different styles of aesthetically valent qualitative harmonies. It is also possible for several value systems to cross in the concretizations of one and the same literary work of art, whereupon they may either conflict or harmonize with one another. This is not an expression of the frequently mentioned "relativity" or, to use a popular term, "subjectivity" of aesthetic values but rather a necessary consequence of the essential structure of the literary work of art, which admits of just these possibilities.

Of course, it was ascertained long ago, as early as the time of the Sophists, that one and the same literary work of art, and consequently any work of art in general, can lead to different value responses, which are sometimes diametrically opposed to one another. This fact quickly led to the theory of the so-called subjectivity and relativity of (aesthetic) values, summarized in the saying *De gustibus non est disputandum*. This saying legitimizes a complete anarchy in both the judgment of works of art and our contact with them. In our time this view takes the form, on the one hand, of a sensualistically colored skepticism with regard to values, which is preached by the neopositivists of various provenance (in proud consciousness of the highly "scientific" character of their viewpoint), and, on the other hand, of a historical relativism, which is derived from Hegel and Dilthey, among others. It would lead us too far afield to discuss these skeptical directions anew. It will, however, be useful to indicate the sources of this skeptical *De gustibus non est disputandum*.

The primary source of this view is a failure to distinguish between the literary work of art (or the work of art in general) and its various concretizations. As a result, the judgments referring to the aesthetic concretizations (or value responses, which, however, are not the same thing) are applied to the

27. This assertion could perhaps be made about all aesthetic objects, but that would require a special investigation.

work of art itself. It then seems that conflicting and mutually exclusive values have been ascribed to the same work of art; this, of course, would be a sorry state of affairs.

Because the skeptics do not know, or are unwilling to recognize, the difference between artistic and aesthetic values, they do not know that aesthetic values call for a judgment of value (value response) completely different from that called for by artistic values. They thus regard all judgments of value as aesthetic judgments, which they reject from the start as illegitimate and impossible to substantiate.

They do not recognize the difference between the value itself and the value response (or value judgment); and, since they basically deny the existence of all values, especially aesthetic values, they try to reduce them to "value judgments" (evaluations), which they then make relative to psychology and sociology or to the philosophy of history.

When the value itself is confused with the subjective mode of behavior toward values, especially with the value responses, then a change in the estimation of value (pleasure, value judgment, etc.) is at the same time confused with a change in the value itself or with a change in the object in respect of its having value. For example, when a given object, say, Shakespeare's plays, is esteemed highly in one epoch but not in another, then it is simply claimed that the object has lost its value. But since the skeptic believes at the same time that the object has not been changed at all in its attributes, he draws the logical conclusion that this object never possessed any kind of value at all and thus that there are no values, only changing estimations of value, which are then declared "subjective" to signify that they project fictions of value. The skeptic does not recognize that it is possible to cognize values as well as to suppose falsely that they are present. Erroneous presumption of value is supposed to take place under the influence of various feelings. No individual, psychological, or even sociologically conditioned changes in the estimations of value can alter anything, either in the values themselves or in the objects having value.

These confusions have already been unmasked, and the appropriate distinctions have been made; thus the basis for axiological skepticism has been destroyed. This is not to say, of course, that all values will be cognized correctly or that no doubt can ever be raised as to their cognition or their being and determination.

In his treatment of the problem of value as it relates to

works of art and their concretizations, the skeptic also disregards the fact that literary works of art are schematic configurations (as, in a different way, are all works of art)[28] which consequently predetermine sets of possible aesthetic concretizations. The concretizations can be as numerous as desired, but they cannot vary without limit in respect of their determination, provided the demand be made and fulfilled that they not be left to the pleasure of the literary consumer but rather be based on a faithful reconstruction of the work and "do justice" to the work. The aesthetic experience out of which they arise should not take a completely random course but should rather be regulated by a definite mode of cognizing the work of art and the previously realized parts of the concretization within the aesthetic experience. The set of aesthetic concretizations permitted by the work is then rigidly limited in its mode of determination, and its basic types are, at least in principle, clear to the understanding.

Finally: we must judge the correctness or incorrectness of the common saying *De gustibus non est disputandum* on the basis of an analysis of the relationship between an aesthetic concretization which is constituted in a definite way (and especially the aesthetic values constituted in it) and the value response and the value judgment based on and adapted to it. So long as this has not been done and the points of departure of the skeptical solution to the whole question have not been rectified, axiological skepticism and relativism with regard to aesthetic values is simply an easy way out, which serves to free its proponents from the trouble of a responsible investigation of the question.

Of course, it must be admitted that the two terms of the relation mentioned above have not yet been investigated and explicated thoroughly enough. We do not know what aesthetic values even exist or which of them can appear in the concretizations of literary works of art. And there exists no satisfactory analysis of the different emotional value responses. As things stand, however, we can still inform ourselves about the theoretical possibilities and delimit the various questions at hand.

Value responses are immediate reactions of a subject ex-

28. Max Wehrli recently established a connection between the schematic structure of the literary work of art and the problem of value, but even he has not sufficiently overcome relativistic tendencies in his treatment of aesthetic values. See Max Wehrli, *Wert und Unwert in der Dichtung* (Cologne: J. Hegner, 1965).

periencing a certain value in intuition, reactions which grow out of the subject's emotional feeling (we could also say: "grasping") of the value in its qualitative determination and which are adapted in a meaningful way to their built-in act of acknowledgment and affirmation of the self-present value quality—if, that is, there is a value response at all. Hildebrand counts such responses among the so-called attitudes [*Stellung-nahmen*], and he is certainly correct; but it must be added that there are various kinds of attitudes, which can also be quite intellectual, as, for example, the rejection of someone else's opinion as false. The value response, however, is at least partly determined by emotion, although it is not purely emotional, since it has an intentional relation to a self-present object which presents itself as having value. There is no value response at all when the immediate apprehension of value is somehow unsuccessful. An immediate apprehension of value is one in which the value, in respect of its material (quality), is intuitively (phenomenally) self-present. If this apprehension does not succeed, then either no value can come into view at all (in respect of its quality and degree),[29] or else it does so imperfectly. If, for example, the value quality fails to emerge in sufficiently intuitive intensity, distinctness, and relief, then the degree of value also becomes unclear. But if the immediate apprehension of value is successful, then the value response occurs without hesitation. It could be said that both, the apprehension of value and the value response, form a whole in terms of experience, although the value response is a different mode of behavior of the experiencing subject from the apprehension of value in the narrow sense of the word. This totality of apprehension and response is often what is meant when one speaks of "valuation," although this term can also refer to the value judgment based on this totality.[30] A value judgment is a purely intellectual act and constitutes a totality of its own, which can be absent from the valuation, in the narrow sense in which we are using this

29. This can occur for various reasons: (*a*) for "objective" reasons, when the work of art does not have sufficient artistic effectiveness, and (*b*) for subjective reasons, when the observer does not succeed in feeling and apprehending the aesthetically valent qualities on which the value is founded or when the subject is "blind" or "deaf" in a peculiar way to the value quality in question.

30. See, in this connection, my lecture to the Aesthetic Symposium of the International Congress of Philosophy in Venice, 1958: "Bemerkungen zum Problem des aesthetischen Werturteils," *Rivista di Estetica*, III, no. 3 (1958), 414–23. [Also printed in Ingarden, *Erlebnis, Kunstwerk und Wert* (Tübingen: Max Niemeyer, 1969), pp. 9–18.]

term; it can also be performed without the valuation being performed. In the latter case the value judgment is not substantiated by the valuation.

The meaningful adaptation of the value response to the value itself relates to two essentially interconnected factors of the value: its value quality and the resulting degree of value, which, precisely because it is grounded in this quality, characterizes the value in an absolute way. Only secondarily, by comparison with other values of the same value system, do we obtain a relative determination of degree. In the value response the emotional intensity corresponds to the value quality and is correlated with it according to its nature, whereas to the degree of value corresponds the "act of estimation" (mode of acknowledgment, appreciation, and affirmation, and, in the opposite case, rejection, etc.), which is at the same time a form of submission on the part of the subject to the degree of the value. Both factors in the value response are constitutive of the response. They must be present in it in some form, and they determine its nature. They are strictly correlated with each other, although the emotional intensity can vary within certain limits, while the act of acknowledgment remains constant. This corresponds to the fact that there can exist values of different quality which are still of the same degree.

If we consider the structures of the value (especially the aesthetic value) and the value response, we can say (or at least surmise) that ideally there is a strict correlation between values and value responses. That is: for every value which is constituted and provided with an appropriately unambiguous degree of value by a given value quality there is one, and only one, exactly adapted value response, which is in turn unambiguously determined in respect of its emotional intensity and its act of acknowledgment. To those value responses, however, which are constituted by an unambiguously determined act of acknowledgment but possess an emotional intensity which can vary within specific limits corresponds, within a system, a precisely delimited set of values which have the same degree of value but a value quality which can vary within fixed limits. But it seems impossible for values which are determined by an identical value quality to differ in degree, since the value quality (Hartmann calls it value material) determines the (absolute) degree of value. Of course, it is still possible for different value qualities to have the same degree of value.

But this ideal correlation, which would have to be proved in detail, cannot by itself protect us from axiological skepticism, especially in the area of aesthetic values. It is important only insofar as, of the correlated elements, the values and the value responses, the value is the constitutive element and the value response is the resulting element. As far as their existence and attributes are concerned, values are independent of value responses, but they do determine value responses. If the values are genuine and not merely apparent, they are founded in the object whose value they constitute; in order to exist, they need not first be apprehended, responded to, or judged.[31]

Notwithstanding the above, it still seems possible that there are cases in which, despite the presence of a certain value in the aesthetic object, there is either no value response or else there is one which is not correlated in an ideal sense with the value.

This fact is often mentioned [32] as a sufficient basis for aesthetic skepticism. But the saying *De gustibus non est disputandum* would be correct only (1) if it never happened that a value response either lacked this ideal correlation or was missing altogether or (2) if value responses were always defective. In the first case, there would be no basis whatever for a discussion of taste, since the basis for such a discussion resides in the fact that there are sometimes defective or inadequate value responses. In the second case, we would be unable actually to discuss taste, precisely because all value responses would be equally good or equally bad. In order to recognize that a value response does not fit the nature of the value, we must be able to

31. The subjectivists in value theory assert the opposite view. According to them, if values exist at all, they arise from the judgments, which are to a certain extent creative and which themselves change in time. But the creativity of human beings is not based on the production of certain illusions of values but on the creation of works of art or on the coproduction of aesthetic objects in which values are based. Neither apprehensions of value nor value responses are actually creative. Apprehensions of value are receptive, apprehending, and thus "passive" acts; value responses constitute a reaction, an attitude of the subject toward certain data with which he is confronted. The transcendental idealists (and also positivistic psychologists) are of the opinion that every act of consciousness is creative, at least intentionally; this is a prejudice which does not do justice to the differentiated nature of the individual basic kinds of acts of consciousness.

32. Usually, to be sure, in an unsatisfactory way, by referring to the value judgment (at best, the value response) of another observer of the same work of art, without having shown that the aesthetic experience of the other observer also led to the same constitutive result, i.e., that the corresponding concretization possesses the same values. But that different value responses should result from different concretizations is only natural and in no way supports aesthetic skepticism.

compare value responses which are fitting with value responses which are not. This is possible only when some value responses are fitting and others are not. This seems in fact to be the case, and so there exists the possibility of a discussion of "taste."

But what does it mean to say that in an individual case someone's value response is not fitting? Simply that for some reason he did not succeed in carrying out the concretization of the literary work in such a way that the appropriate aesthetic qualities, and hence also the appropriate value, were brought to phenomenal appearance in the concretization. He has to do with a different concretization, one which does not contain these values, either because he is blind to the relevant aesthetically valuable qualities or to the value associated with them or because he is incapable of constituting them. Then he either has no value response, because he does not have that to which he would have to respond, or he has a different response, because he is responding to something else. In either case, everything is in order; that is, neither furnishes an argument for a general aesthetic skepticism. Only if the aesthetic observer were to succeed in constituting a concretization of the work in which a specific set of aesthetically valuable qualities, and hence also the value founded in them, came to phenomenal self-presence for him, and he nevertheless had a value response which was not at all correlated, in an ideal sense, with the value, could it be claimed that the value response in this case was completely independent of the actual presence of the aesthetic value. And we would have sufficient reason for advocating aesthetic skepticism only if it could be asserted in general that all value responses are completely independent of both the apprehension of the value and its intuited essence (value quality plus degree of value). That would mean that, if there is any value response at all, both the response itself and its emotional content (its intensity) and act of acknowledgment are elicited by other factors, which lie beyond the work of art and our aesthetic contact with it. But aesthetic skepticism is untenable once it is admitted that the apprehension of value and the value response form a single total experience, the course of which is uniquely determined by the value intuitively given in the apprehension. It can be granted only that a given literary work of art can have different aesthetic concretizations, in which different ultimately resulting global aesthetic values can appear, or that, if the work is artistically poor, none whatever can appear. Where the aesthetic experience is sufficient to itself, where it simply serves the purpose of aesthetic consumption and is not a preparation for the cognition of the work or for an aesthetic concretization founded in the aesthetic experience, this multiplicity of different concretizations and different aesthetic values which are manifested in them is no shortcoming and no basis for aesthetic skepticism. We cannot say with certainty how much the different concretizations can differ from one another,[33] but this does not affect our argument.

But does not every literary work of art, of itself and independently of who is performing the concretization, determine a strictly delimited set of admissible aesthetic concretizations? These concretizations are admitted by the work itself because they contain a faithful reconstruction of the work and because those factors and elements within the concretization which correspond to the potential elements and places of indeterminacy in the work of art lie within the domain of possibilities determined by these two types of elements in the literary work. There can be no doubt that we may grant such an ideal correlation between a particular literary work of art and its set of possible concretizations, in which concretizations of negative as well as positive value can appear. But if any of these concretizations is to be actualized by the reader, then the corresponding aesthetic experience cannot follow an arbitrary or random course; rather, the reader must try to carry out this experience on the basis of, or in conjunction with, his faithful reconstruction of the work. The experience will then serve as a preparation for the cognition of the (admissible) aesthetic concretization of the work. We can now proceed to a discussion of case (*b*) of the aesthetic literary experience. But first, one further remark.

3. Among the many widely disseminated errors in aesthetics is the confusion of the problems discussed under (1) and (2) with the role played by the aesthetic experience in human life. It is well known that aesthetic experiences enrich and deepen human life. It is also maintained that they have a favorable influence on the formation of the personality—as is reflected in the program of "education through art"—although it might be questioned whether that influence is not greatly overestimated. In any case, however the aesthetic experience constitutes

---

33. This is impossible because the set of readers and of conditions which determine the course of the aesthetic concretization of the literary work is completely independent of the work and cannot be delimited in itself. And the reader shares the responsibility for the constitution of the concretization of the work.

a positive value for human life. Thus on almost every level of human culture we find the tendency to seek aesthetic experience. But the value of this experience is not itself aesthetic in nature but of a completely different kind, to the extent, of course, that we do not take an aesthetic attitude toward our own experiences and apprehend them as aesthetic objects, which happens not infrequently. But this apprehension of one's own experiences as aesthetic objectivities is secondary and a symptom of a certain decadence. It is much worse when it occurs because of a lack of aesthetic culture or a lack in effectiveness of the (basically only apparent) aesthetic experiences relating to various objectivities of our experience. Then this phenomenon is what Moritz Geiger calls "dilettantism in aesthetic experience." [34] It consists in a peculiar mystification, in a kind of *qui pro quo:* the aesthetic value, or the value for human life, of a (seemingly aesthetic) experience is taken for the aesthetic value of the object of this experience. In itself this object is a matter of indifference and consequently is not fully constituted; the experience itself takes the place which the object should occupy. What is, or should be, the real goal (or end) of the aesthetic experience begins to be misused as a means to other, generally nonaesthetic, ends: a means of enriching our life, of being in certain states which are somehow pleasant for us. In aesthetic theory this leads to erroneous views of the aesthetic experience, in particular to all the subjectivistic theories about the aesthetic object. Among other things, the productive capacity of the aesthetic experience is confused with the abundance of various factors, especially emotional factors, within it. To the aesthetically naïve person, who is primarily concerned with having certain experiences, it seems that the more he is moved by certain objects (especially by works of art), and the more multifarious and lively his emotional life is, the more valuable are the objects of his experience, or, in other words, the more effective his aesthetic experience is.[35] I distinguished (in § 24, above) between the aesthetic experience, and, in particular, the value response, and the emotional reaction which develops in the subject under the influence of his encounter and contact with a work of art or with an already constituted aesthetic object. This reaction is usually extra-aesthetic

34. Moritz Geiger, *Zugänge zur Ästhetik* (Leipzig: Der Neue Geist, 1928).
35. Of course, they have no idea of the effectiveness of the aesthetic experience, but that is what they have in mind, in spite of themselves.

in nature, although it is an aftereffect of the aesthetic experience. It is desired by many experiencing subjects and is often incorrectly thought to be the aesthetic experience itself. But it is not only completely foreign to the aesthetic experience but also disturbs the full and free development of that experience. In many cases it is precisely the abundance of the secondary feelings arising from the aesthetic experience which weakens its effectiveness. For example, there are literary works which are designed to awaken patriotic (or other political) feelings and are otherwise artistically primitive. The effect of these feelings on the aesthetic experience, which may, in spite of everything, develop, is to rob it of its effectiveness; they may make the aesthetic experience impossible by their intensity and vividness. But the works which elicit these feelings are often mistakenly evaluated as having high aesthetic rank. Great works of art, which lead to aesthetic objects of high value, require of the aesthetic observer a certain self-control, serenity, and concentration in order for an aesthetic concretization to be formed and its aesthetic value to be revealed. It is precisely the profound works on the highest artistic level which permit no tempestuous experiences on the part of the reader. Cheap, empty, and sensational works call for animated and varied extra-aesthetic feelings and thus are able to win over naïve and uncultivated consumers. Founding the theory of the aesthetic experience on the abundance of extra-aesthetic feelings which are sometimes connected with it; identifying its effectiveness with this abundance, confusing the aesthetic value of the concretization of the work of art with the dubious value of the extra-aesthetic feelings for human life: all this amounts to a huge misunderstanding, which is often quite detrimental to the development of aesthetics.

Ad (b). Let us now take up those problems for the critique of knowledge which have to do with the aesthetic experience in its role as a preparation for the cognition of aesthetic objects.

Just as the reconstruction of a literary work of art follows a different course when it serves as a point of departure for the preaesthetic cognition of the work, so the course of the aesthetic experience is less free when the experiencing subject wishes to cognize, in a reflective aesthetic apprehension, the aesthetic concretization of the literary work of art which he has obtained. A certain loss of freedom has advantages and disadvantages. On the one hand, it preserves us from falsifying the literary work of art and from constituting a concretization which does not correspond to its structure. But, on the other hand, it introduces an element of constraint, which prevents some sides of the aesthetic experience from developing fully. Keeping exactly to the characteristics of the work of art requires complete submission to the perception of the work and a stifling or removal of everything foreign to the work or to the aesthetic object which is to be constituted. The aesthetic experience loses the excessive multiplicity of its components and becomes simpler, but it gains in concentration and often in profundity.

If we experience a literary work of art aesthetically, with no thought of obtaining an aesthetic cognition, then it actually makes no difference whether the experience brings the reader to a concretization which accords with the "intentions" of the work. But the situation is different when the aesthetic experience is supposed to form a preparation for the aesthetic cognition of the concretization or of the work. Then the aesthetic experience must not only be effective but must also, as I expressed it above, "do justice" to the work and be adequate to it. The aesthetic experience will "do justice" to the work if it leads to a concretization which (1) is based on, and permeated in all its elements by, a faithful (correct) reconstruction of the work in respect of its determined and actual elements, to the extent that this is possible, (2) keeps within the bounds of the possibilities predetermined by the work itself for those elements (factors) in the concretization which go beyond simple reconstruction of the work—elements which make explicit what is unambiguously implicit in the work, fill out the places of indeterminacy, actualize the potential elements, and produce in intuition the aesthetically relevant qualities and their harmony, and (3) is as "similar," as "close," to the work as possible. The last of these considerations is introduced here because, for example, the places of indeterminacy admit of being completed in ways which generally vary greatly with regard to the way in which they are suited for complementing the other factors of the work. One way of filling out a place of indeterminacy may be very superficial in its style and hence uninteresting, whereas another may, for example, reveal depths in a character, intensify or resolve conflict within him, etc. It can be aesthetically neutral, or it can be a quality of great aesthetic value; it can harmonize or conflict with the ways of filling out other places of indeterminacy, etc. The determinate part of the text does not compel the reader to choose any particular one of the admissible ways of filling out the place of indeterminacy. All the admissible ways are therefore "possible." But the passage in the text will suggest to a certain extent which of these possible ways "fits" the work better, is better "suited" to it. The sensitive reader gives in to these suggestions and chooses, almost involuntarily, the appropriate way of filling out the place of indeterminacy.[36] His literary and artistic culture, his knowledge of the epoch in which the work originated, can be helpful to the reader in filling it out, although the suggestions that emanate from the work itself should always be decisive. In this way a concretization is obtained which is "close" to the work. The concretizations which are close to the work (since the same work usually has several) need not necessarily be those which, relatively, have the highest aesthetic value. If the work itself is relatively weak artistically, then the concretizations which are close to it and do it justice will usually exhibit no very high aesthetic value. A gifted reader (an original director, for example) can, however, fill out the places of indeterminacy in a way which is admitted by the work but was not anticipated, was not contained, in the "intentions" of the author, and he can concretize the work in such a way that higher values are actualized in his concretization than in a concretization which would be closer to the work.

In order to clarify still further the concept of a concretization which is close to (and does justice to) the literary work of art, let us consider a play performed on the stage.[37] The concrete performance of the actors and the whole outfitting of the stage (decorations, costumes, etc.) are only in part a realization of what the text of the drama says *expressis verbis*. Beyond this, however, they form a complement to the text corresponding to the places of indeterminacy and potential elements of the work. Even when the entire text of the work is left unchanged,[38] there can still be two radically different "productions" of the same drama. These may differ not only in the perfection of the execution, and hence also in the quality and degree of the aesthetic value which is concretized, but also in the whole style

36. The choice can be made quite consciously and intentionally in a concretization undertaken for the purposes of aesthetic cognition.

37. See, in this connection, *The Literary Work of Art*, § 57, as well as the Appendix, "The Function of Language in the Stage Play," in Roman Ingarden, *Das literarische Kunstwerk* (Halle: Max Niemeyer, 1931; 2d ed., Tübingen: Max Niemeyer, 1960; 3d ed., 1965). [English translation by George Grabowicz, *The Literary Work of Art* (Evanston, Ill.: Northwestern University Press, 1973).]

38. This usually does not happen, and the result is a reconstruction of the work which is not faithful, even if it is not necessarily incorrect.

of the production. Every important director, every new epoch in the theater, imposes a new style of portrayal on the works which are staged and thus creates prototypes for other productions, so that a fashion of interpreting a given drama is developed which also produces a change in its whole (concretized) structure. In the twentieth century we have experienced several such fashions of theatrical remodeling of dramas and know now, perhaps better than our predecessors did, the extent to which these productions have deviated from the "original" of the drama in question, by how much they miss being "close" to it. In contrast, there is also a kind of theater which wants to keep the original tradition of the production, e.g., of the classical French theater (as does the Comédie Française), and interprets any deviation from that tradition as a falsification of the original. That means that this sort of theater chooses from among all the valuable concretizations of, say, the works of Molière those concretizations which, on the basis of exact study of the work, are considered to be shaped in the "spirit" of the work, are as close to it as possible. Even the manner of speaking, of declamation, of movement on stage, of gesture by the actors, play an important part in the concretization. Even if they were able to play their roles in French, foreign actors would hardly be able to imitate all that, no matter how well they acted in other respects, even if they should happen to produce other artistic effects which would lead to the actualization of high aesthetic values. Their productions do not "do justice" to the original to the same degree, are not as "close" to it.[39] Something similar takes place in the case of purely literary works of art, although it is not so obvious there, since the aesthetic concretization actualized by

39. It is clear that in all these efforts to maintain the basic style of the original of the work, e.g., on the part of the Comédie Française or of Stanislavski's theater, there are going to be "minor" differences in the total value of the presentation from one production to another, for instance on different evenings. These differences must exist, since it is impossible for a living actor always to play his role in absolutely the same way. For that reason, theater connoisseurs often attend only the première, believing that each repetition produces a habit in the actor and causes the creativity of genius to disappear from his performance. Much greater differences result from, say, the replacement of a leading actor. All "great" actors usually create their own "school" of acting and are thus irreplaceable. It is difficult to say how close to the "original" the work they create on stage is. Still, it is clear from these examples that the concept of the "closeness" and "justice" to the original work of art is not an empty theoretical concept; rather, applied to the art of theater, it permits us to apprehend the various degrees of its application and hence the various degrees of closeness to the work of art.

the individual reader is not intersubjectively accessible to the same extent as a play produced on the stage.

We certainly run some risk in introducing the concept of an aesthetic concretization's "closeness" to the work. We could be accused of permitting or justifying a certain arbitrariness and inexactitude in the aesthetic concretization. Because the concretizations which are very "close" to the work, as well as those which are "far" from it, are equally admitted by the work, it appears at first glance that there is no sufficient reason in the structure of the work of art for calling one of these concretizations "closer" to the work than others. It does not seem impossible that there should be two concretizations equally close to the work. It seems that there is a sphere of "irrelevance" [40] here and that, within its limits, differences among the concretizations of the same work have no influence on their degree of "closeness" to the work. I have no wish to deny all these facts; on the contrary, I am even drawing attention to them. But they do not furnish a reason for rejecting the concept of "closeness" or "distance" of an aesthetic concretization in relation to the work of art. We would have to undertake further investigations, which we cannot do here, into which details of the literary work of art determine that many concretizations, however valuable they may be in other respects, do not "do justice" to the work and which details have the opposite effect. One important question concerns the degree to which the way of filling out a place of indeterminacy given in the concretization harmonizes with other elements and factors of the work itself and with the ways of filling out the other places of indeterminacy and how it thereby helps in constituting the unity of the work (and of the concretization). But there are other literary works which have a certain amount of disunity, not by accident or because of the author's lack of skill, but because that disunity constitutes a special artistic characteristic of the work and leads to special aesthetic effects (which the author intended). Thus, preservation of the unity of the work in the concretization does not of itself determine whether the concretization will be "closer" than

40. The expression is Waldemar Conrad's. See his "Der ästhetische Gegenstand," *Zeitschrift für Ästhetik und allgemeine Kunstwissenschaft*, III (1908), 71–118; IV (1909), 400–455. But Conrad does not have at his disposal a number of concepts which I have introduced here and in *The Literary Work of Art*. Still, his work is the important beginning of the ontological investigation of the work of art and for that reason should not be forgotten.

another which does not maintain that unity. A preaesthetic reflective cognition of the work preceding the aesthetic concretization can show the reader whether or not it is a unified work and thus help him to form an appropriate aesthetic concretization, which will take the unity (or disunity) of the work into account and maintain it by the choice of appropriate ways of filling out the places of indeterminacy. All other things being equal, one can thereby achieve a concretization which is closer to the work of art. But, even within the limits of the type of unity of the given work of art, the type can be achieved by various means. That is, there can be a varied selection of qualities or motifs which produce the same type of harmony with the determinate and actual elements of the work but which are not all equally "close" to the work. At this point it would be necessary to indicate further conditions on which the "closeness" of a concretization could depend. But to illustrate the new problems and difficulties which appear in the attempts to constitute an aesthetic concretization which is "close" to the literary work of art, concrete situations are needed. Our general discussion, which aims only at establishing the theoretical points of view from which to consider the relation of the concretization to one and the same work of art, cannot furnish us with these details.

But there are two difficulties which seem to call into question our justification for introducing the concept of a concretization's greater or lesser "closeness" to the work.

The first difficulty is that this concept could tempt us to demand that the concretization which is to serve the aesthetic cognition of the work of art be absolutely close to the work, i.e., "the closest" to it. The second difficulty arises from the question of how to decide whether one aesthetic concretization is "closer" to the work than another. With what is it to be compared? With the work itself? Or with other concretizations? Every concretization necessarily goes beyond the work of art. The work in itself is undetermined in respect of those elements in which the concretization goes beyond it; it thus seems that it can provide no model against which to measure the closeness of a concretization.

It is clear, however, that in this case there is no absolute closeness of the concretization to the work, since that would mean that only one concretization could attain this "absolute" closeness, through being fully approximated to the work itself. But it can fully approximate the work only in those of its factors which contain elements and factors of a faithful reconstruction of the work. But nothing in the concretization which goes beyond this reconstruction [41]—and to go beyond it is its essence and its function—can be approximated to anything unambiguously determined in the work. It cannot achieve "absolute" closeness, because its prototype is not present in the work. In just this impossibility resides the essence of the literary work of art as a schematic formation with various merely potential, and hence not unambiguously fixed and actualized, factors. The idea of absolute approximation to the work is simply not applicable, and so we cannot demand it. We can speak only of a relatively greater or lesser "closeness" to the work.

But we must still deal with the second difficulty. With what are we to compare the concretizations in order to determine their (possibly only relative) "closeness" to the work when the literary work of art itself contains places of indeterminacy and potentialities, not just in a single stratum but in various strata? Should several concretizations of the same work be compared with one another so that we can judge their relative closeness? But it will hardly be possible to achieve such a result in this way. The only result of such a comparison would be that one concretization would prove to be more unified than another, or richer in aesthetically valuable qualities, or would appear to express a given style more distinctly, etc. But all these things have to do only with the differences and similarities among the concretizations themselves; we learn nothing about their relationship to the work unless we determine that the work itself is unified or disunified in a definite sense, that it not only permits, but also unambiguously determines, a given abundance of aesthetically valuable qualities, that it has features of a certain style, etc. Thus it seems that we must find in the work itself the reason for one aesthetic concretization's being closer to it than another. But then we come up against the same difficulty we have already discussed. Do not all the characteristic features we are discussing go beyond the work itself, and are they not to be found only in the concretizations?

Is it really true, however, that we cannot compare a concretization with the work itself just because such a comparison would involve comparing certain determined features in the concretization with the blank spaces of the places of indeterminacy?

41. Except, of course, what is possibly an explication of something that is unambiguously implicit in the work.

The fact that a place of indeterminacy admits a sphere of possible ways of filling it out but does not unambiguously determine or absolutely demand any of them does not, as we have already noted, lead to the conclusion that all the possibilities are of equal value or are equally probable. The work does not furnish us with any decisions, but it gives suggestions so that we can choose more "probable," and hence more desirable, ways of filling out the places of indeterminacy from among those that are possible. To take a few commonplace examples: If a story talks about the fate of a very old man but does not say what color hair he has, then, theoretically, he can be given any color hair in the concretization; but it is more probable that he has gray hair. If he had very black hair despite his age, that would be something worth mentioning, something important about the old man who had aged so little; as such, it would be fixed in the text. Thus, if it is advisable for any aesthetic reasons, it is more probable and desirable to concretize the man as having gray hair rather than black hair. Such a way of concretizing this detail makes this concretization closer to the work than other concretizations which offer other hair colors. Analogously, when, say, in a drama, someone finds himself unexpectedly and innocently in a tragic situation and the text does not state what emotions were produced by his insight that he is in this situation—fear, astonishment, manly determination, courageous calm, etc.—then it is more probable to concretize him as being in one of these emotional states rather than as experiencing great joy or laughing heartily to himself. Of course, this stronger probability is prepared by, or based on, the work itself; the man has already been shown in various conflicts as a man with a certain moral or psychological character. This character lets the reader expect a certain kind of behavior in a tragic situation. Not all emotional attitudes of this man are equally probable for filling out the place of indeterminacy; thus not all are equally close to the work. Nor is the literary work of art a completely inactive formation in its actual and unambiguously determined elements and factors. It contains various possibilities of an activity through which it can affect the reader and cause him to form a concretization which is at least vaguely determined. Among other things, the work itself contains those factors which the reader must take into account and actualize in the reconstruction, so that, in the aesthetic concretization, he can actualize only a strictly limited set of aesthetically relevant qualities; these factors constitute the artistic values of the literary work of art. The presence of an appropriate selection of these artistic values also indicates that certain aesthetically relevant qualities should be actualized in the concretization. A special activity on the part of the artistic values causes the reader to choose a number of particular qualities from the set of possible aesthetically relevant qualities and to actualize them. The apprehension of the work of art in the preaesthetic reflective cognition in respect of the kind and the selection of the artistic values immanent in it, together with a comparison of these values with the aesthetically relevant qualities actualized in a given aesthetic concretization of the work, can show us whether or not they were actualized in accordance with the sense of the artistic capacities contained in the work. If they were so actualized, then we can recognize that that concretization is "closer" to the work than another concretization which does not actualize the relevant qualities.

Thus the situation is not so hopeless as it first appeared; we can decide whether and in what way a given aesthetic concretization is close to the work itself or is distant from it, although being still "admitted" by the work. The concept of a concretization which is close to the work itself is applicable in concrete situations and allows us to recognize that not all aesthetic concretizations of a work are equally valuable in this respect. It cannot be denied that a certain vagueness or lack of definition still remains, but this is no deficiency in the concept itself; rather, it is a necessary consequence of the essential structure of the literary work of art, on the one hand, and that of its aesthetic concretizations, on the other. But since the concretization's "closeness" to the work is part of the concept of the "justice" which an aesthetic concretization does the work of art, the latter concept also shows a certain lack of definition. Thus we cannot establish strict, unambiguously determined criteria for deciding the degree to which an aesthetic concretization does justice to the work. Still, we can establish approximate criteria, which enable us to determine the limits of "doing justice" to the work. In any case, it is useful to introduce this concept and to use it in judging aesthetic concretizations. It indicates the particular aspect under which the aesthetic concretization can and should be considered if it is to serve as the point of departure for the aesthetic cognition of the aesthetic object.

Finally, what does it mean to say that the aesthetic experience in which an aesthetic concretization of a literary work of art is constituted is "adequate"? The situation is as follows:

When, in the beginning stages of the concretization of a

work, we have already fixed a certain tendency or a way of filling out the places of indeterminacy and of actualizing the potential elements of the work, then, not only do certain strictly delimited possibilities for the further concretization of the work begin to reveal themselves, but a certain idea or, better, a final form of the concretization begins to be fixed. This final form or idea, which is not yet actualized, places certain demands on us as to the rules which must or should be followed, or the ways of concretizing which must or should be maintained in the further concretization, if a concretization in this form is finally to be constituted. When we have already chosen a certain way of concretizing the work, we have certain indications of what the concretization should be like if it is to approach that idea or form or embody it in itself and bring it to appearance. The idea which we at first have only vaguely before us can be apprehended clearly and distinctly once we succeed in embodying it and setting it in relief in the concretization. Thus the aesthetic experience is "adequate" when it leads to the constitution of a concretization which is the exact embodiment of the "idea" indicated in it. It is then certain that the aesthetic experience is guided, at least to a certain degree, by that idea, and this is so even though there may be some question whether the experience does justice to the work itself. That will depend in part on the reader's success in constituting this idea on the basis of a partial reconstruction of the work and in forming it in harmony with his preliminary understanding of the work. But the aesthetic experience is inadequate to a greater or lesser degree when the concretization constituted in it deviates more or less from the idea which suggests itself. On the basis of knowledge gained from repeated contact with the aesthetic experience of literary works of art, we know how often we are dissatisfied with a concretization which we succeed in constituting. We are then dissatisfied, not with the work itself nor with the more or less pleasant experiences we had from it, but solely with the concretization, with the formation we have come up with. We feel more or less distinctly that we could have achieved an aesthetically satisfactory concretization if only certain external disturbances, or our personal incapacity, had not hindered us. We feel that the concretization we have actually constituted would be more satisfactory if it were better fitted to the "idea" we have in mind but have not yet clearly apprehended, if the idea were better "fulfilled" or "realized." An already constituted deviation of the concretization from our preconceived idea of the work can sometimes be removed by a better understanding of a sentence which we at first ignored or did not correctly understand, or by a more vivid concretization of an aspect held in readiness in the text, or by a somewhat different objectification of the objects portrayed in one phase of the work. The concretization then represents a more exact adaptation to the idea and better satisfies its demands. That means that the corresponding aesthetic experience is more adequate to the idea and that the reformed concretization takes on for us the aspect of being as it "should" be. But it is still an open question whether the concretization which satisfies the reader is "better" because it does greater justice to the work of art, or only because it brings higher aesthetic values to appearance, or, lastly, because it only seems better to us because it concretizes values which are more important to us. Adequacy to the idea contributes to the aesthetic experience as a preparation for the aesthetic cognition of the concretized literary work of art only when the idea of the concretization which we have in mind in the course of the experience is founded in a reconstruction which is true to the work. And it is quite important that this idea be not merely the idea of a concretization chosen for random reasons but the idea of a concretization which does justice to the work and is close to it. Only then does the adequacy of the experience play a positive role in an investigation of the work from the standpoint of a critique of knowledge. Nonetheless, the reader's effort in apprehending the idea of the concretization as early as possible, and also as clearly and distinctly as possible, plays an important practical role in the course the aesthetic experience takes in its further phases. For this enhances the prospect that the experience will not be left to chance.

The considerations just mentioned open certain perspectives on the problems of the aesthetic cognition of the aesthetic concretization of literary works of art. We shall now discuss these problems.

§ 33 *Some epistemological problems in the cognition of the aesthetic concretization of the literary work of art*

THE QUESTIONS we now have to discuss are of a completely new sort and arise from a situation essentially different from that encountered in the cognition of aesthetic objects in, say, painting but similar in many points to the situation in the cognition of the musical aesthetic object. The similarity resides in the fact that in both cases an aesthetic concretization of the work of art is constituted in the course of a given stretch of time and, after its constitution, does not remain actual as a whole but passes away, as it were, and sinks into the past. In order to have the concretization again in its actuality, we must aesthetically constitute or reconstitute the literary or musical work of art in a new temporally extended experience; this cannot happen without certain changes. It is different in the case of pictures and the aesthetic objects partially founded in them. For after constituting the picture in an aesthetic experience based on the painting, the whole picture can be apprehended in a single present moment and can be aesthetically experienced anew in successive present moments by means of the enduring painting, which changes relatively little.

The temporal structure and the temporality [42] of the literary aesthetic object causes special problems in its cognition. To be sure, we become acquainted with the object by virtue of the perceptual factors of the aesthetic experience. If we did not have this original acquaintance with the work, we would be unable to gain any cognition at all of the literary aesthetic object. On the other hand, this form of becoming acquainted with the work is not sufficient for a cognition of the work which could be expressed in judgments and thus made intersubjectively accessible, as is necessary if we are to achieve a science of literary aesthetic objects. Is such a science possible and, if so, in what sense?

42. The words "temporal structure" mean that this object is constituted in a temporally extended process because it itself has phases and cannot be constituted all at once. The "temporality" of the object indicates that, after it is constituted, it passes away with the process of constitution and afterwards is accessible only to memory.

What effects does the temporal structure of these objects have on their cognition? When should the cognition be accomplished? During the course of the aesthetic experience, or after its completion? If it is supposed to be accomplished during the course of the experience, then we seem to be faced with a double difficulty. First, the object is not fully constituted in a single present moment but is built up in the course of the aesthetic experience by the actualization of successive new phases of the work of art. Two lines of development meet here: that of the aesthetic experience itself and that of the actualization of new phases of the work of art. In the early phases of this "dual process" the aesthetic object does not yet have all the determinations which it has in the last moment of the constitution. Its completion is conditioned by the fact that the object depends on all the phases of the literary work of art, which appear only in succession.[43] But how do matters stand here? Is it the case that those features of the aesthetic object's determination which are constituted in the individual phases of its constitution and on the basis of the individual parts of the literary work are "summed up" in the course of the aesthetic experience and endure to serve as a basis for the determinations which are constituted later, together with which, at the end of the entire process, they finally form a whole which is determined on many sides and waits, as it were, for the observer to apprehend it in its completion? Or is it rather the case that the determinations constituted in one phase of the aesthetic experience fade away with the moment of their constitution and are no longer actual in the later phases but at best emerge in recollection and are thereby brought up to the new present moment? It is certain that both retention and active memory perform their variable functions to keep actual for a while the no longer present determinations (or parts) of the aesthetic object which is being constituted. But is this sufficient in the case of longer literary works, e.g., long novels, which are read over a period of several weeks, with many

---

43. The claim might be advanced that the aesthetic concretization of a literary work of art is intentionally determined by the work all at once, since all parts of the work exist once they are recorded in writing. This view is untenable, however, because no aesthetic concretization of a literary work of art is intentionally determined by the work alone but requires a codetermination by the reader in order to be supplemented by those determinations which correspond to the places of indeterminacy and the potential elements of the work. And then the constitution of the literary aesthetic object can be accomplished only in a temporally extended process.

interruptions? Even a three-act play produced in the theater presents great difficulties in this regard. Only very short lyric poems can be contained in a single present moment. Should we say that in longer literary works we are dealing not with a single literary aesthetic object but with an ordered set of objects, with three objects corresponding to the acts, or, in the case of a novel, with as many aesthetic objects as there are chapters? Is it not the art of the author to shape these chapters in such a way that they all contribute to the constitution of a single particular aesthetic object? Indeed, even if it were the case, would our range of apprehension not have to contain, at the end of the work, e.g., after the last scene of the last act of a play, not just the aesthetic object constituted in the last moment but also the objects constituted earlier? Somehow there must be a synthesis, the formation of a single aesthetic object which embraces the whole work of art. This seems, at any rate, to be demanded. The question is whether it can be achieved and, if so, how.

Two things are clear at the outset: (1) This goal cannot be achieved for all literary works of art, and there are different modes and ways in which it is achieved or, in view of the peculiarities of the work in question, can be achieved. The structure and the various details of the work and its parts determine whether the latter will create the basis for the constitution of their own particular aesthetic totalities and the accompanying values, or whether they will determine a synthetic total value of the one aesthetic object. Individual works of art can vary greatly in this respect. (2) The final, all-synthesizing act of apprehension of the aesthetic object which is constituted by this means cannot be a pure experience in all its details but must be interspersed to a great extent with acts of memory and with pure mental acts of understanding. The more this final act is pure experience, purely intuitive apprehension, the greater seems to be the cognitive weight and the significance of the result it achieves. And the more it relies on recollections and mere mental acts which refer to the "earlier" aesthetic objects corresponding to the individual acts of a play or chapters of a novel, the greater is the danger of a falsification or misinterpretation of what is no longer actual. In connection with this, there is also a greater danger of a distorted synthetic apprehension of the aesthetic object which is finally constituted. But we ought to demand no more from the synthetic operation than we normally demand from the cognition of any objectivity which is constituted in a process. Of course, it is always possible to base the cognition of a literary aesthetic object on a new aesthetic experience in a new reading. But it should be remembered that we are then relying on another aesthetic concretization of the work, which can deviate in many respects from the previous one. And it is always questionable whether and to what extent the reader succeeds in achieving a new, fruitful aesthetic experience of a literary work of art with which he is already familiar, since certain subjective areas of resistance can pose a threat. In any case, this possibility should be left uninvestigated.

But there is still another question. How is one to perform investigative, reflective acts of apprehension during the aesthetic experience upon the aesthetic object being constituted? Is it possible? Are these to be new acts of cognition, based, so to speak, upon the developing aesthetic experience? Or should the perceptual factors of the aesthetic experience merely be more conscious, active, and apprehensive in order to grasp whatever aesthetic entity is being constituted? Will that not disturb the aesthetic experience which is developing in contact with the work of art or even make it impossible? Will not the emotional elements of the aesthetic experience, which are developing freely and must develop freely, be suppressed or even extinguished by such reflection? Will not the unfolding constitution of the aesthetic object be simply interrupted, so that the continued reading of the work is drained, incapable of eliciting the original aesthetic emotion? Would it not be better to avoid performing the special cognitive acts aimed at the aesthetic object during the aesthetic experience but rather wait until it is over and the aesthetic object is already complete? And would it not be better to dispense with the intuitive apprehension of the aesthetic object and to make use of revived memories rather than disturb or render impossible the constitution of this object? If the aesthetic object were really destroyed, there would be nothing left to cognize.

In this difficult situation we must not stand on principle. On the contrary, we must be willing to try different approaches and to exclude nothing a priori. The aesthetic experience can take various forms, chiefly because literary works of art are determined in many different ways and can make apprehension either easier or more difficult for the experiencing subject. The subjective conditions of aesthetic cognition also vary greatly according to circumstances and the abilities of the cognizing subject. It is possible for a work to move the reader so strongly that he is no longer capable of performing cognitive acts directed at the constituted aesthetic object in the aesthetic experience. But it can also happen that the activity of the effect of the work of art, together with the activity of the reader's emotion, actually increases his ability to apprehend the peculiarities of the aesthetic object. He then sees everything more clearly and with greater discrimination and also becomes immediately aware of the way in which that which moves him so greatly and compels his admiration is determined. It can also happen that the experiencing subject feels the correct original emotion and is prepared for an active value response only when he has a deep enough understanding of the aesthetic object being constituted and proceeds on the basis of this understanding to the purely cognitive apprehension which alone enables him to have an emotional contact with the aesthetic object. Then there is always present in the literary aesthetic experience a core of intellectual acts of understanding, because these acts are indispensable in performing the reading. In this case, the situation is much more favorable for the possibility of purely cognitive acts referring to the aesthetic object than, say, in the case of listening to a musical work, a work of romantic music, for example. As we have mentioned, all these diverse modifications of the aesthetic experience are co-determined by the peculiarities of the work itself. Thus the question of how acts of cognition are interwoven in the course of constituting the aesthetic object and of how they can have a positive or negative influence for the purposes of the cognition of the aesthetic object would have to be examined with reference to individual cases. But as far as we can survey the possible situations, it does not seem in theory that the performance of acts of cognition referring to the literary aesthetic object is impossible during the course of the aesthetic experience, however difficult it may be in an individual case and however incomplete the results of such acts might be. Even if we must check them, correct them, or even recognize them to be false, and even if they demand all these subsequent cognitive operations in order to ensure a broader and deeper cognition of the literary aesthetic object, still the cognitive acts performed during the aesthetic experience have one great advantage over the later acts: they are immediate acts of experience of a special kind, which bring the cognizing subject into a direct and intuitive relationship with the object. They can be crucial in furnishing the point of departure and the material for further understanding and treatment of the object.

Acts directed toward an already constituted aesthetic object which are performed after the completion of the aesthetic experience on the basis of acts of memory are in principle no different in kind from other acts of cognition. But acts of cognition which are interwoven with the course of the aesthetic experience, and especially those which refer to the value-bearing side of the aesthetic object and its inner structure, seem to be of a special kind and far to surpass in their power of apprehension the perceptual factors of any aesthetic experience. Their peculiar nature is still to be investigated. Here we can only say that they are rapid illuminations, intuitions of a special sort, which enable us to gain a certain distance on the aesthetic object being constituted. Only from this distance does the aesthetic object appear clearly as a whole in both its material value determination and its structure. These acts do not disturb the course of the aesthetic experience; on the contrary, they are elicited by the experience, since, although they are specifically cognitive acts, they nevertheless grow out of the aesthetic emotion, albeit not always and not for every experiencing subject. And the intuitive knowledge they supply makes such an impression that whatever it illuminates remains a lasting acquisition for us and can serve as our starting point for later acts of deliberation of a purely intellectual sort. We cannot produce these special acts of illumination at will. They must be prepared by the aesthetic experience, but they are essentially different from the perceptual factors of this experience. The aesthetic experience produces, or, more exactly, can produce, a change in the experiencing subject which enables him to have these intuitive acts of illumination.[44]

To be sure, we have not yet removed the doubts and difficulties connected with our investigation. The next question we must deal with is related to the temporality of the literary aesthetic object. As soon as it is fully constituted, it passes away. That it is constituted and exists is a unique historical fact. A second aesthetic concretization of a literary work of art, identical with the first, cannot be "realized"[45] in the same actuality. It is

44. Perhaps these illuminations are what Croce had in mind when he spoke about "intuitions," but his idea was confused with many other things, which cannot be held against him. It is extremely difficult to apprehend these acts in their individual nature, to oppose them to other acts of cognition, and especially to distinguish between them and the perceptual factors of the simple aesthetic experience. What we have said here constitutes only a bare and unsatisfactory beginning.

45. The quotation marks have been placed here because we cannot speak of a genuine realization in the sense that the object receives autonomous existence. But we can speak of "realization" in the sense of

exactly the same as in the case of a performance of a drama in the theater, which is a unique historical occurrence, a historical event uniting the entire audience and the actors on the stage, which, for that very reason, cannot be repeated; every subsequent performance of the same drama is a new event. The spectators owe whatever they can salvage from this unique, valuable reality to the activity of the aesthetic experience and the intuitive acts of cognition with which it is interwoven. We can obtain a supplementary cognition of this unique aesthetic object only through acts of memory and by immersion in vivid retrospective reflection on and understanding of the past aesthetic "reality."

A necessary correlate of this temporality and historicity of the literary aesthetic object is its absolute individuality, not only in its mode of being, but also in its full material determination. In a strict sense, the object cannot be repeated in this individuality, primarily because its full determination depends on a configuration of so many mutually independent conditions which cannot recur in just this configuration. These conditions, too, are steeped in the historical moment. The first consideration is thus that it is at least highly improbable that the same multiplicity of different mutually independent conditions could coincide again (what is absolutely identical in the two different temporal phases is the work of art itself in its schematic structure). For even the reader, though he may remain the identical human being for a while, often undergoes great changes in his qualitative determination in the course of time. An important role is played here by the circumstance that the temporal *quale*, the *quale* of the historical, concrete time in which the aesthetic concretization of a literary work of art is constituted, necessarily participates in the full determination of the concretization, co-determines the full content of the aesthetic object, and decides its strict qualitative individuality. Hence this individuality is strictly unique; it can be apprehended in immediate experience but cannot be grasped conceptually and communicated to others by means of language. If someone else were to experience the same work of art aesthetically under very similar external conditions, it is hardly to be supposed that he could actualize exactly the same aesthetic concretization with the same individual

---

fulfilling a possibility, altering what was only potential in a mode of being permitted by the nature of the objectivity in question—in our case, of the existentially heteronomous, purely intentional object constituted in acts of consciousness.

temporal *quale*. In the time which he experiences concretely, the temporal phases can have a different qualitative determination and consequently give a different temporal stamp to the concretization he realizes. In this respect, two literary aesthetic objects arising in the same intersubjective temporal phase cannot be approximated to each other. Thus, if we want to transmit to others the content of the aesthetic object we have constituted, we must try to grasp it without regard to the temporal *quale*. This is possible insofar as we ourselves can compare several aesthetic concretizations of the same literary work which we have constituted at different times and find what is constant in them, what remains, despite the varying temporal *quale*. Of course, what we obtain in this way is no longer so strictly individual. It is the common aspect of several concretizations, provided that we succeed in constituting them all in the same way—which is not, of course, easy. This comparison usually takes place with the essential help of acts of memory, which, of course, involve various dangers of deception and error.

Another essential difficulty in the cognition of an aesthetic concretization is related to the question of the extent to which such an aesthetic object in its full material determination constitutes a Gestalt and of the extent to which the finally resulting aesthetic value in its qualitative determination has a Gestalt which is based on a particular set of closely connected aesthetically valuable qualities and is united with them in a "harmonious unity."[46] The prevailing tendency among contemporary aestheticians is to maintain that the individual nature of every aesthetic object is marked by such an inner unity and Gestalt character. But there seem to be various possibilities in respect to this. It seems that, on the one hand, there are aesthetic objects (especially in plastic art) in which the inner coherence of all qualitative determinations, and in particular of the aesthetically valuable qualities, is so tight and strict that nothing may be altered in respect to their number and arrangement without bringing about an essential change in the resulting total value or even the destruction of the object itself. On the other hand, there seems to be a possibility of aesthetic objects which admit of a certain mutability in the aesthetically valuable qualities which establish the total value. The special possibilities present in this situation can be investigated only with reference to individual literary

---

46. See, in this connection, *Der Streit um die Existenz der Welt*, II, pt. 1, 48 ff.

works or their aesthetic concretizations. But the possibilities of a certain slackening in the inner qualitative structure of aesthetic objects is of particular importance for us when we consider the possibilities of a reflective cognition of aesthetic concretizations of literary works of art. As we have already determined, the literary aesthetic object is not fully constituted all at once. It is constituted in a continuity of phases or consists in a multiplicity of aesthetic objects which must then be combined so that a total value of the whole can be constituted. In both cases the relevant situation seems to be the same. It is basically ontological, but in our context it leads to special epistemological problems. This situation is the relationship between a set of aesthetically valuable qualities and the value they establish. In a given selection and inner combination these qualities form the basis, that is, the sufficient condition, for the appearance of an aesthetic value which is in turn determined by a value quality. This quality is unambiguously determined by the set of valuable qualities. The aesthetically valuable qualities find their harmony and their conclusion in the value quality. But, depending on the individual case, either the ordered set of aesthetically valuable qualities is at the same time the necessary condition of the value, or it is not, in which case it can be replaced by another appropriately chosen and ordered set of valuable qualities which constitutes a sufficient condition of the same value. As long as this set is not complete, however, the value cannot appear. To say the same thing in epistemological terms: until all qualities belonging to such a set of aesthetically valuable qualities have appeared in the aesthetic experience, the value is also unable to appear unless these qualities are replaced by another set of such qualities which is sufficient for the appearance of the value. But can it be the case that these aesthetically valuable qualities show themselves only individually and in succession, in the successive parts of the literary work, and that they accumulate, as it were, and thus continue to manifest themselves in the aesthetic experience in many successive phases, finally appearing in their totality and forcing the value founded in them to appear also? This would be one relatively favorable situation which we could expect in the cognition of the aesthetic concretization of the work of art. Of course, the most favorable situation would be if all aesthetically valuable qualities which establish a given value would appear simultaneously in the concretization of a literary work of art. For then the value would also appear with no further ado. But it is improbable that we should come across this favorable case

if the value is to be the total value of the aesthetically concretized work. But if the corresponding aesthetically valuable
qualities not only appeared in succession but also disappeared
immediately, then their appearance would be without result,
even if all of them, appearing simultaneously, would suffice to
constitute the value. Would the retention of these qualities in
active memory or even in mere mental intention be sufficient to
allow the value to manifest itself in a concretization, or at least
to be apprehended and understood?

Unfortunately, we cannot make a general statement at the
moment as to which of these cases obtains. This is impossible
not only because the situation can differ with different works,
and the problem thus cannot be dealt with in general terms.
What is much more important, and what makes our considerations more difficult, is the fact that we are in an area
which has been little investigated theoretically. Both the aesthetic values themselves in their multifarious qualitative determination and, especially, the foundation of these values in
aesthetically valuable qualities and ultimately in certain value-
neutral features of the (literary) work of art have in general remained completely unexamined. Up to now, more effort has
been spent on the negative, subversive activity of undermining
the existence of aesthetic values and the fact that they belong to
the concretized work of art, with constant talk about their
"relativity" and "subjectivity," than on the task of really looking
at these values and explaining their qualitative determinations
and discovering the sufficient foundation of their existence and
their appearance. The specific nature of these values has been
revealed up to now only to a very modest extent, and we know
just as little about the individual aesthetically valuable qualities
and the ontic connections among them.[47] But it can be expected
that it will be possible not only to compile and to elucidate the
most important aesthetically valuable qualities but also to show

47. In my lecture to the Fifth International Congress on Aesthetics
in Amsterdam in 1964, entitled "Über das System der ästhetisch wertvol-
len Qualitäten," I tried to take the first step in this direction. Unfortunately, the *Proceedings* of the Congress have not appeared to date.
I published the lecture in Polish a year ago in my book *Przeżycie—dzieło
—wartość* (Cracow: Wydawn. Literackie, 1966). I hope that this work
will soon appear in German. [A German version has appeared under the
title *Erlebnis, Kunstwerk und Wert: Vorträge zur Ästhetik 1937–1967*
(Tübingen: Max Niemeyer, 1969). The article "Problem des Systems der
ästhetisch valenten Qualitäten" is a version of the talk Ingarden mentions; it is printed on pp. 181–218.—Trans.]

that they can, and, in many cases, must, appear together in a single work of art in appropriately selected combinations and, finally, that their appearance in certain combinations must result in a certain aesthetic value in the aesthetic object. The study of the structure of various aesthetic objects is of interest, not only because in this way we can learn the essential effect of the works of art (when we apprehend them appropriately), but especially because it casts a brighter light on the difficult problem of the objective foundation of the aesthetic values in the aesthetically valuable qualities and, ultimately, in certain artistic values of the literary work of art.

In the cognition of the aesthetic concretization of a literary work of art we are concerned in the first place with discovering what aesthetic value is constituted and appears in it. But that is not the main concern of this cognition. It is basically only an empirical preparation for the real task which we must perform. This consists in an understanding, based on direct experience, of the nature of the ontic connection among the aesthetically valuable qualities appearing in the concretization: whether they only happen to appear together in the concretization, whether they are perhaps interconnected and blended in a peculiar way without sacrificing their specific distinctness, or whether they appear together necessarily. In the second place, we are concerned with understanding the mode of ontic connection between the set of aesthetically valuable qualities and the individual qualitatively determined aesthetic value which may appear. This understanding teaches us about the structure of the literary aesthetic object—and by "structure" we mean the kind of ontic connection among the above-mentioned value-bearing factors of the object. We cannot achieve this understanding without also having the qualitative factors which enter into the connection. Thus it is not a purely formal insight, but a formal insight which is founded in the material of the object. Nor is it a purely intuitive act, but rather a decidedly intellectual one. It exhibits the necessity of the inner structure of the aesthetic object under consideration or else the lack of such a necessity, hence its greater or lesser contingency. In particular, it can consist in the understanding that the value does appear but is not sufficiently founded in the aesthetically valuable qualities which are present. The appearance of the value must thus have a basis outside the aesthetic object, which makes its objectivity at least questionable.

With regard to the cognition of an aesthetic concretization

we must further explain to what extent the aesthetically valuable qualities manifested in the object are founded in the artistic values of the work of art itself or necessarily arise from factors which the reader projects to fill out certain places of indeterminacy in harmony with the work. In this way we gain insight into the necessary or contingent structure of the literary aesthetic object under investigation, even into its foundations in the work of art itself. The demonstration of the necessary ontic interconnections among all the elements under consideration here reveals a new specific value factor in the aesthetic object: the valuable nature of the necessary formal unity founded in the individual character of the material factors. And this is the optimum that can be achieved in the area of aesthetic objects. But note that this unity is only the formal culmination of the materially determined values which appear in the aesthetic object.[48] The aesthetic object is then a "realization" of the content of a particular idea which the artist must somehow have had in mind. But he also had to invent the means for the "realization" of this content; that is, he had to create the corresponding work of art. For note that the idea in question is not the idea of the work of art but only the idea of the peculiar ontic interconnection between the relevant value quality and the set of aesthetically valuable qualities which coexists with it in harmonious unity.

Of course, many doubts will immediately be raised here, above all the question of how we can discover the various necessary ontic interconnections within the aesthetic object and gain insight into their necessity. And it will be objected from a different quarter that there simply are no such interconnections and that we have no cognitive means of discovering them anyway. All that could be ascertained would be certain actual groups of factors which happen to appear together.

We shall have to forego at this time a theoretical discussion with the positivistically inclined empiricists.[49] But we should like

---

48. I do not mean that this optimum is what is most valued or what pleases most in any given cultural epoch. On the contrary, there are ages, such as the present one, in which necessary unity in the aesthetic object is not valued at all; rather, the values, or aesthetic values, which find favor are those which are in a state of decay, of "loss of center" [*Verlust der Mitte*], as H. Sedlmayr has called it. This situation clearly illustrates how we must distinguish the aesthetic value which is ultimately founded in the work of art from whatever pleases or is valued in a given epoch.

49. Husserl and his collaborators have already carried on such a discussion; it is unnecessary to repeat it here.

to point out just one factor. The apprehension of the existence or nonexistence of necessary ontic interconnections among many aesthetically valuable qualities and the aesthetic values can be made easier by the fact that it is possible to have different concretizations of the same literary work of art. In the changes which can be observed from one concretization to another we also observe, for example, how the composition of aesthetically valuable qualities in a concretization changes and what consequences that change has, say, for the constitution of the qualitative harmony of values or for the appearance of an aesthetic value. And we also see what remains constant through all the changes in the set of aesthetically valuable qualities. Thus we can work out the necessary ontic interconnections of dependent qualitative elements almost experimentally from the entire stock of individual concretizations. We can also learn how a change in the totality of aesthetically relevant qualities can cause a value already appearing to disappear or can lead to an essential modification of the value quality. This information helps us determine when we are dealing with a necessary ontic interconnection and when with a mere common appearance within the content of the aesthetic object. Of course, we should not ignore the danger of rationalizing the structure of the aesthetic object to an excessive degree.

The effort to apprehend the aesthetically relevant qualities as exhaustively as possible is of great importance in the cognition of the aesthetic concretization of a literary work of art. In the original aesthetic experience the aesthetic value usually occupies the foreground, while the qualities in which it is founded are experienced only peripherally and are not consciously apprehended by the experiencing subject. This must be changed in the aesthetic cognition of the concretization, insofar as the foundation of the value in aesthetically valuable qualities must also be apprehended clearly and consciously. Ignoring any of these qualities can either prevent the aesthetic value from appearing, so that it is not attributed to the aesthetic object, or allow it to appear, but with a noticeably altered qualitative determination. Thus not only the exactitude but also the objectivity of the results of the aesthetic cognition of the aesthetic concretization depend on the degree and the kind of completeness of the cognition. The cognition is, of course, especially dependent on the course of the aesthetic experience and hence on the form of the aesthetic concretization of the work; it operates on the material delivered by the experience, and the objectivity of its results depends on this material. But attempts to cognize the concretization can also influence the course of the aesthetic experience and guide it onto the right track. If, however, we want to relate the aesthetic object to the literary work of art itself, of which it is a concretization, then we have to refer to the critical problems discussed earlier. Here we must only emphasize that the evaluation of the aesthetic concretization is completely different from the evaluation of the work of art itself.

These, then, are a few of the general epistemological problems in the cognition of the aesthetic concretization of the literary work of art. More specific problems arise only when we approach the cognition of individual concretizations of various works and come across particular difficulties which the individual work of art presents for the subject of cognition. But we cannot discuss that here.

THE COGNITION of the aesthetic concretization of a literary work of art does not end with the immediate, intuitive apprehension of the concretization. It also involves fixing the results of the cognition in a set of judgments and corresponding concepts. The possibility of literary scholarship as a discipline which would also set itself the task of studying aesthetic concretizations depends on the extent to which this fixing in judgments and concepts can succeed. I should like to mention here just a few of the epistemological problems which arise in this context.

The first problem relates to the intersubjective verification of these judgments. The aesthetic concretization of a literary work of art is an individual object. We make a series of reporting judgments and verdicts (evaluations) about this object. This leads to the following consideration:

Individual objects can be cognized either with respect to their so-called common attributes, those which many or all individuals of the same type possess, or with respect to their "individual" attributes, those which only the object in question possesses. This holds also for the aesthetic concretizations of works of art. The only question is: to what in the concretization do judgments about the actual existence and qualitative determination of its aesthetic value refer? On the other hand, all individual objects can be divided into two classes: (*a*) those which according to their nature can be cognized immediately as the same by many properly qualified subjects of cognition and (*b*) those which are accessible to the immediate cognition of one, and only one, subject of cognition. As an example of (a) we may take any physical things or processes; as an example of (b), conscious experiences. The objectivities of the first group are called "intersubjective"; those of the second, "monosubjective."

Judgments which refer to intersubjective objectivities can be "verified" either directly, by recourse to an appropriate direct cognition which can be performed by several subjects, or else indirectly, by reduction through logical operations to judgments which can be tested directly. This reduction can also be performed by several subjects. It is of no importance whether the judgments ascribe common or individual attributes to the objects to which they refer. But this last consideration does play an essential role in the case of monosubjective objectivities. If a general judgment ascribes a common attribute to all monosubjective objectivities of a certain kind, then anyone to whom an object of this kind is given can test the truth of the judgment. As a result, even individual judgments which ascribe a common attribute to a monosubjective object can be checked in experience by those subjects to whom an object of this kind is given. This is a roundabout way of testing by means of another object. If this attribute is not found by some subject in his own experience, then that means only that it is not general; but it remains open whether it was really given to the subject who made the judgment or whether it is really to be ascribed to the object. But if it is ascertained in the experience of several subjects, then it is probable that it also appears in the individual case in question and is to be ascribed to the object. It is a different matter when an individual attribute is ascribed to a monosubjective object in a judgment. Such judgments cannot be tested directly by any other subject. If we have no reason to doubt the veracity of the judging subject in this case, then we can do nothing but take cognizance of his information, to the extent that it is intelligible. Contrary to the neopositivist view, the truth of a judgment is neither identical with nor dependent on its verification. Nonetheless, judgments about individual factors of monosubjective objectivities are contrary to scientific rigor. Their acknowledgment always involves a certain danger; and in any area of investigation in which this danger exists we are inclined to separate judgments which cannot be proven directly from those which can. But the former are not to be excluded from a rigorous discipline, nor are they to be despised as a matter of principle. They furnish information which is sometimes very valuable and irreplaceable but which must be used with appropriate caution. Let us apply this to the problems which interest us here.

Every literary work of art is an intersubjective object in its schematic structure. It is open to question, however, whether the same may be asserted of aesthetic concretizations. The doubts relating to the concretizations arise mainly from the fact that, besides the work itself, a series of purely subjective, individual factors influence the formation of a given literary work. The formation of a concretization of, say, Goethe's *Werther* or Shakespeare's *Hamlet* depends primarily on a number of external circumstances under which the reading is performed, as well as on the state of the reader himself. These factors are quite variable, are independent of the work of art being read and of one another, and cannot be predicted in their conjunctions. Thus the differences among individual concretizations of the same work are quite multifarious and, in general, unpredictable. It will happen only very rarely that two concretizations of the same work, formed by different readers, will be completely alike in all features which are crucial for the formation of the aesthetic value.[50] Even when a concretization is the result of group reading or, say, of a performance in the theater, differences among individual readers or spectators can hardly be avoided. Nor is it possible to cognize directly an aesthetic concretization constituted by another reader or spectator. We can form only an approximate and partial mental reconstruction of another person's concretization, and then only by having recourse to our own faithful reconstruction of the work and by means of information [51] furnished by the other reader or by means of an investigation of the conditions under which his concretization was formed. The results of this reconstruction can never be more than probable. Especially with regard to the significant elements of the individual aesthetic concretizations, which often characterize them individually and uniquely, with regard to what we earlier called the "idea" of the literary work of art, with regard to the metaphysical qualities, etc., we can never be certain whether someone else's concretization contains these ele-

---

50. I should not like to decide at this point whether this is theoretically impossible.

51. If the other reader were to read off his concretization aloud, the text brought to our cognizance in this way would still not contain the full concretization. We could receive only indirect and incomplete information about how the places of indeterminacy were filled out.

ments in exactly the form in which they appear in our own concretization.

The indirect means of our disposal for finding out anything more exact about it often fail almost completely for various reasons, although they are not completely without value. From the reader's behavior, for example, we can draw conclusions about certain details of the concretization he has constituted. The reader's emotional reactions, in particular, can be instructive in this respect.[52] But these actions can be incorrectly observed and interpreted, and the fact of their presence can inform us only within extremely vague limits about the exact form of the other person's concretization or, for example, about the value constituted in it. Linguistic communication by means of reporting judgments leads only in part to satisfactory results, for reasons which we have already indicated. A great deal depends on whether the other reader—and we ourselves are such a reader when, for example, in an investigation, we wish to inform others about our own concretization—is able to give a sufficient account of his concretization, whether he has sufficiently developed the necessary linguistic means for its communication, etc. He need not necessarily be a trained student of literature, but he should be capable of achieving a faithful reconstruction of the work and should be receptive to its artistic values and thus capable of apprehending the essential features of the concretization he has constituted. The linguistic rendering of the results presents special problems here; but, as we have mentioned, these difficulties should not be overestimated, and we should not deny a priori the possibility of communication. In animated conversation, especially, mutual understanding is much easier to achieve, and the words which will awaken another person to intuitive apprehension of the concretization are much easier to find. A special art of dialogue must be developed for this situation; and it is certain that progress can be made in this direction, although this is not to say that whatever is immediately given, including all aesthetically valuable qualities, can be intersubjectively named by language. If, despite several attempts, we are unable to quess a peculiar quality which, according to another person's report, appears in the concretization he has constituted, then all we can do is take cognizance of the fact that there is something in

52. A common viewing of a play in the theater, or the common hearing of a piece of music in a concert, produces special phenomena of a certain spiritual contagion, which does a good deal to make someone else's concretization easier to understand.

the other person's concretization of the work of art which is out of our reach. Then we can try to experience and to concretize the work of art aesthetically in a new way. Perhaps then we will cognize that quality which we did not recognize at first or a harmony which could then make communication with the other reader possible. But here we are certainly at the limit of what we can investigate in common with others. Without all these attempts at refining the cognition of literary aesthetic objects and overcoming the linguistic difficulties, however, we are not justified in declaring a priori, as is often done, that scientific mastery of this field is impossible. The fact that this discipline has certain limits, which, by the way, can be extended, does not mean that it has no validity. It must be remembered that it was not so long ago that we first attempted to subject literary works of art themselves to analytical investigation and to penetrate to the aesthetic concretizations founded in them with adequate means of cognition. In the study of literature, and especially in the so-called history of literature, many years were spent on various matters which go beyond the sphere of literary art, and thus much time was lost which could have been used to form a satisfactory method of investigating literary art.

Within the limits of the competence of literary scholarship there thus remain the individual literary works of art as schematic entities and the "common" ("general") attributes and structures of the concretizations, and especially of the aesthetic concretizations, of these works. At the limits of the sphere of investigation are the "individual" features of the individual aesthetic concretizations, and it might be asked whether these do not go beyond these limits and should not perhaps be turned over to literary criticism. But the solution of this problem would require a general discussion about the object, the task, and the methods of literary scholarship and other forms of knowledge about literature, which include philosophy of literature, criticism, and poetics. Such a discussion goes beyond the scope of this book.[53]

This result seems, however, to be threatened by a danger we must now discuss. Judgments that appear to be contradictory are often made about the same literary work of art, in daily life as well as in scholarly investigation, especially when it is a

53. The original Polish version of this book had an "Appendix" in which these problems were treated in outline. But the scope of the German edition forces me to dispense with the Appendix, which should in any case be greatly expanded.

question of so-called value judgments or evaluations. To the extent that this reflects a shortcoming of the individual investigator or arises from an accidental defect in the results achieved, it is something which occurs in all sciences, even the "exact" sciences, and which furnishes no reason for despising the science in which it occurs. In the course of further investigation, errors are discovered and removed, and their discovery often leads to new achievements and a transformation of the science in question (we need only consider the history of modern physics). In the case of literary scholarship, however, this fact is exploited as a reason to pass scornful judgment on any kind of knowledge about literature or any other art; this is especially common among mathematicians and natural scientists ("scientists" in the narrow sense of the word).[54] The belief is that these errors and "contradictions" are necessary in such a field and cannot be removed. Is this really the case? The existence of errors and contradictions must be readily acknowledged. We would also have to agree that it would jeopardize the scientific nature of such research if conflicting or even genuinely contradictory judgments were necessary in the field of literary study. But it is doubtful that they are necessary, and, it seems to me, no one has yet proved that they are. There are, however, certain apparent reasons for concluding that such a necessity exists. To date, there has not been a clear awareness of the difference between a literary work of art and its concretizations, nor has the need for such a distinction been realized. Instead of strictly separating two basic types of "literary" judgments, those about the literary work of art itself and those about its concretizations, the practice has been to treat all these judgments (and verdicts) as if they all applied to the "work of art" (with no consideration of what that term might mean). It seems to me that, after the introduction of our distinctions, the theoretical difficulties disappear. Neither conflict nor contradiction occurs when two judgments about two different concretizations of the same work say something different about corresponding factors of the two concretizations. The concretizations may very well differ on this point. The fact that such judgments do not agree does not constitute a shortcoming in literary study. Of course, this is true

54. If we take "science" [*Wissenschaft*], in the narrow sense of the word, then, of course, literary scholarship can never be "science" in that sense; nor does it aspire to be. There is no longer ground for argument here. There is simply no justification for holding the narrow sense of "science" to be the only possible or admissible one.

only when the point of difference between the judgments consists in a factor or attribute of the concretization which does not belong to the work itself but to supplementations of the work by new factors or elements of the concretization. If, however, we had two judgments which differed with reference to a factor of the schematic structure of the work of art itself, then we would have a real conflict or contradiction, which nevertheless can, in principle, be removed through further investigation. The admissible divergence among true judgments about different concretizations of the same work of art is not a defect in the study of literature. Our conception of the literary work of art accounts for its possibility. This is especially true of aesthetic value judgments about two different concretizations of the same work. We can only ask whether both of the values are equally close to the work or whether one of them is perhaps a higher value but does not do full justice to the work, whereas the other does. This does not affect the truth and validity of the judgments which establish these values. They can both be true, in which case they furnish the point of departure for further consideration of the closeness of these concretizations to the work itself or their distance from it.

It is a different situation, however, when two value judgments ascribe different artistic values to the same literary work of art. Then we must suspect that at least one of them is false and results from an inexact analysis of the work of art and the possibilities of its aesthetic concretizations. But then we do have the possibility of removing the conflict between the judgments by means of a new and more exact analysis of the work of art and its artistic excellence, so that this case presents no theoretical danger for literary scholarship, although it can sometimes be very difficult to find the basis of the error and form a correct verdict concerning the artistic value of the work. It is understandable, however, that these difficulties exist; their existence is rooted in our conception of the literary work of art and of artistic value. In order to be able to ascribe a given artistic value to a given work of art, we must not only apprehend the constant and actual elements of the work correctly (in other words, perform a faithful reconstruction of the work) but must also inform ourselves concerning the set of typical possible concretizations of the work and their various possible aesthetic values, to the extent that this sheds light on the artistic excellence of the work. And the reason evaluations of the work of art in respect of its artistic values often differ greatly and lead to long controversies may lie in the very fact that we can never take all possible concretizations into account but must restrict ourselves to some typical concretizations, which are easier to survey. If the work of art in question has an abundance of various possible concretizations, and if the concretizations admit values of a high order which differ from one another, then the controversy concerning the artistic value of the work will last a long time, and perhaps it will not be possible to resolve it in a single cultural epoch. But this does not speak against the "scientific character" of the evaluation of literary works of art; it is rather simply a consequence of the essential structure of the literary work of art itself and of its "life" in various cultural epochs, and a consequence of the relatively narrow limits of the literary scholar, who is often unable to see beyond the horizon of his own cultural epoch. But that should not tempt us into skepticism about literary scholarship; rather, it should spur us on to further investigation. If, whenever a value judgment concerning the appearance of a given artistic value in a work of art is expressed, we were able to ascertain that this value is ascribed to the work in relation to a definitely limited set of aesthetic concretizations, then the danger of error in judgment would be greatly reduced. In any case, there would be no cause for the frequent reproaches of so-called subjectivity and relativity in evaluation. On the contrary, we would be dealing with a judgment which correctly establishes the objective fact that a certain artistic value belongs to a given work of art in consideration of its artistic capacity for leading to the constitution of particular kinds of aesthetic concretizations under clearly defined circumstances.

We must mention one last problem here. The question is whether the evaluation of an aesthetic concretization or of the literary work itself made by one reader on the basis of the material to which he has access is automatically binding and valid for other readers. Are these readers automatically obliged to acknowledge it, or do they have the right to weigh it critically and then perhaps not acknowledge it? And, if the latter proves true, does every reader have this right, or are there certain conditions attached to it? We must emphasize that it is not the fact of the acknowledgment or nonacknowledgment of another reader's evaluation which is at stake but rather our right to acknowledge or not acknowledge this evaluation. If it is a mere question of fact, then we would be dealing with a psychological or sociological problem which does exist but does not enter into our considerations.

Let us examine this problem first with reference to the evaluation of a concretization with respect to its aesthetic value.

The right with which we are concerned is related not only to the truth (correctness) of the evaluation but also to its foundation. The evaluation is founded in the aesthetic experience and the aesthetic cognition of the concretization. The right to call such an evaluation into question belongs to anyone who is capable of giving it the necessary consideration. The right not to acknowledge such an evaluation exists: first, when the evaluation is not true (not correct), hence when it ascribes to a concretization a value which does not belong to it; and second, when an aesthetic experience and its accompanying cognition of the concretization which was formed do not lead to a concretization which is valuable in the way that the evaluation claims it to be, even though the aesthetic experience is adequate, effective, and does justice to the work. The evaluation is then unfounded. A reader does not have the right to refuse to acknowledge an evaluation when (*a*) the evaluation is correct, (*b*) it is founded in an appropriate aesthetic experience and accompanying direct, objective cognition of the concretization, and (*c*) the reader, who does not know whether the evaluation is correct, is, in addition, unable to have an appropriate aesthetic experience and an accompanying aesthetic cognition of the concretization. Thus all readers who are either incapable of completing an appropriately qualified aesthetic experience and accompanying objective aesthetic cognition, or at least have not been able to complete those operations up to the time when they question an evaluation, have no right simply to refuse to recognize an evaluation which has been advanced. They have this right only when they have fulfilled the two conditions presented above. On the other hand, only those who have performed the above-named operations as a basis have the right to advance an aesthetic evaluation. If they advance an evaluation without fulfilling these conditions, then their evaluation is unfounded, even should it accidentally be correct, and they are like a blind man speaking about colors.

This decision clearly limits the number of those who have the right to evaluate aesthetic concretizations of works of art or to treat them critically. But that does not mean, as the positivists might assert, that the evaluations and, correlatively, the aesthetic values are "relative" to a certain circle of readers or investigators. On the contrary, it is only by establishing this principle that we make it possible to obtain correct and well-founded aesthetic evaluations within a clearly defined domain. We merely demand expert preparation and qualification of those who are to have the right to carry out valid and responsible aesthetic evaluations. That is a demand made by every discipline, and one is not permitted to pronounce judgments when one is an illiterate in the field in question. We require only that the anarchy sanctioned by the saying *De gustibus non est disputandum* will not be sanctioned for all those not educated in dealing with art. The requisite education and the related culture of evaluation can be achieved only through the development of appropriate faculties, that is, through education to art. The sensitive, effective, and faithful aesthetic experience never seeks out some privileged circles of the community; in principle, it is accessible to everyone, in the sense that it can be awakened and even, to a certain extent, taught and exercised in contact with great works of art. The same is possible in any area of culture, provided one is not completely blind and deaf. But just as not everyone has to be a mathematician, so not everyone has to have an understanding of art, although it is regrettable when the revelation of art and of the values concretized thereby is not successful in a particular case. Education to seeing and hearing and even to feeling is necessary in order to be able to deal with the values of various aesthetic cultures, and ways and means must be found to make this education as productive as possible. But even this demand itself arises from an understanding of the fact that the aesthetic experience and cognition of works of art presuppose special abilities on the part of the subject.

The evaluation of the work of art itself in respect of its artistic value is, as can be seen from what we have said, much more complicated than the evaluation of its aesthetic concretizations. It requires special practice in the analytical cognition of the literary work of art and great experience with regard to the possible concretizations of the work, their various types and styles, etc., everything that a responsible literary scholar must learn before he can arrive at an evaluation of individual literary works of art. But this is a special feature of the education to the study of literature which need not be the concern of everyone, any more than mathematics or natural science need be everyone's concern. And there are very special problems related to such an education, which we cannot discuss here. But we must place great emphasis on the necessity for that education, because it is often forgotten. The beginning of this education is the cognition of individual literary works of art by means of a correctly performed reading and an adequate and productive aesthetic experience which leads to faithful and valuable aesthetic concretizations. All further problems of the study of literature, which, of course, are numerous and very complicated and should not be underestimated, depend on this beginning for their correct formulation and for the results of their attempted solution. That was one of the reasons why I have dealt with this cognition.

Afterword

THIS BOOK is a companion piece and a complement to my book *The Literary Work of Art*. It was written and published in Polish several years after that book. But thirty years passed before I was able to put it into a German edition and thus make it accessible outside Poland. I began to translate it in 1966, but it soon became obvious that mere translation would not be enough. Since writing the book, I have learned a good deal which could not be ignored in a new version of it. Many results in the field of aesthetics which I have presented since the last war at aesthetics congresses (1956 and 1958 in Venice, 1960 in Athens, 1964 in Amsterdam) will have to be reserved for another publication. The further development of this book had to be dictated by its own logic. Many questions (especially in Chaps. 4 and 5) which were simply noted as problems in the Polish version were in need of at least a provisional solution, which I have tried to provide in the German version. This led to a certain shift in the areas of concentration in the book. In many questions I had to try, even to dare, to leave the position of cautious reserve and to overcome the difficulties I saw. Thus I tried primarily to express more clearly the distinction between the literary work of art in its schematic structure and its concretizations. It had to be shown that it is possible to apprehend the work of art strictly in its schematic structure and in its mere potentialities without thereby achieving a concretization which has already been filled out and without removing the potentialities by actualizing them. This made it possible to explain and clarify the distinction between artistic and aesthetic values, which had only been intimated before. But this seemed to emphasize all the more the opposition between literary scholarship and criticism carried out in an aesthetic attitude, which had been mentioned in the appendix to the Polish version of the book. As I once argued, literary scholarship should be concerned with the cognition of the literary work of art itself, whereas the concretizations of the literary work of art which are constituted in the aesthetic experience should be the domain of literary criticism, which should operate with different means of apprehension and presentation to bring the concretizations into view for the reader but which cannot claim the same objectivity and intersubjective accessibility and must thus be excluded from the realm of science. But is it correct to say that an aesthetic concretization of a literary work of art is not accessible to a genuine cognition? I tried to give an answer to this question in Chapter 5 of the new edition. If my answer is correct, then the field of literary scholarship has been broadened to include the literary aesthetic objects, and a scientifically tested basis is provided for "literary evaluation" which until now has been excluded from science and left to the subjective feelings of the reader. Of course, Chapter 5 of the new version contains merely the theoretical possibilities and the tasks for research and paths of investigation which result from them. I should be glad if the positive research which I myself cannot carry out were to begin exploring these paths and to test in concrete investigations to what extent the paths I have indicated can really be taken. The interest in problems of "literary evaluation" which has been awakened in Germany in the past few years and which has led various authors to make positive attempts may make it easier to make this test and to carry my attempts further.

The problem is, of course, much more general and is not restricted to the cognition of literature. It rather concerns the cognition of all arts and of the aesthetic objects which are possible in them. But that brings up the problems of aesthetic value in general and the questions as to the possibility of founding these values in the formations and determinations of the work of art itself. These problems could not be treated in this book. I have tried to address them in other writings. These writings were collected in a small Polish book which I hope will appear soon in German.* That will carry the task of supplementing *The Literary Work of Art* a step further.

* The book did appear in German, under the title *Erlebnis, Kunstwerk und Wert* (Tübingen: Max Niemeyer, 1969).—Trans.

There remains only the pleasant task of giving warmest thanks to my faithful publisher, Mr. Robert Harsch-Niemeyer, for accepting this book. I owe thanks also to Mr. Hermann Wetzel, who took the trouble to correct the language of my German text and who has done me many other good services.

Lvov, 1935–36—Cracow, 1966–67

Index

Active memory, xxii, 99, 100, 100n, 101–6, 109, 110n, 112–13, 119n, 123, 124, 138, 140–43, 210, 228, 261, 302, 303, 342, 343, 397, 405

Aesthetic: activity, work as source of, 239; apprehension of work, 41, 46, 50, 53, 54, 56, 57, 62, 63, 72, 83, 89, 96, 103, 135, 140, 142, 142nn, 143, 151, 158, 163, 164, 176–78, 182, 184, 198–201, 214, 221, 224–27, 229–33, 237, 238, 271, 277, 302n, 306, 307, 385; aspect of work, 36; attitude, xvi, xvii, xxvi, 48, 48n, 52, 145, 155, 157, 172–74, 182, 184, 184n, 186, 188, 194, 196, 198, 200, 209, 218, 220–22, 224, 254, 271, 274, 276, 279, 282–85, 291, 293–94, 300, 302, 303, 311, 315, 317, 384, 422; consideration of works, 317, 328; consumption, 383; contact with work, xx, 194n; contemplation of concretization, 306; culture of reader, 90, 218, 369, 384, 418; effect, 36, 240, 243, 245, 250, 262, 311, 389; effectiveness, 46, 125n; experience, xxiii, xxvi–xxix, 7, 52, 53n, 73, 85, 88, 126n, 167, 173–79, 179n, 181, 182, 182n, 184, 185, 185n, 186–88, 188n, 189, 189n, 190, 190n, 191, 191nn, 192, 193, 193n, 194, 194n, 196, 196nn, 197, 197n, 198–201, 201n, 206–11, 211n, 212–19, 219n, 220, 220nn, 221–28, 230, 232–34, 238–40, 255, 278, 301, 302n, 303, 303–4, 304n, 305,

305n, 306, 307, 312–14, 316, 319, 322, 323, 323n, 324–26, 328–30, 332, 332n, 333, 366, 367, 367n, 368–70, 370nn, 371–74, 378, 381n, 382–86, 393, 394–97, 399–401, 401n, 402, 404, 408, 409, 417, 418–19, 422; form of work, 164, 185; goodness, 231; impression, 182, 321; literary object, 227, 228, 232, 239, 301, 301n, 302, 303, 304, 305n, 308–10, 314, 317, 324, 325, 327, 376, 396, 397n, 398, 401–4, 406, 407, 413, 422; object, xvi, xvii, xxi, xxv–xxx, 7, 53, 73, 83, 85, 91, 145, 162, 174, 178, 182, 185, 186, 186n, 187, 191, 196, 197n, 198, 198nn, 199, 200, 203, 206–11, 211n, 212–16, 216n, 217, 220, 221, 224, 226, 229, 230, 230n, 231, 239, 277, 283, 293, 294n, 296, 302, 302n, 304, 304n, 305, 305n, 306, 307, 308, 312–19, 321–23, 323n, 324, 324n, 325, 326, 328–31, 363, 366–68, 370, 370n, 371, 373, 376n, 381, 381n, 384, 385, 386, 393, 396–404, 406, 407, 407n, 408, 409, 422; observer, receiver, xvi, 166, 198n, 295, 296, 300, 371, 379n, 381n, 382, 397; perception, 23, 182, 184, 224, 375; phenomena, 222; reactions, 49; reality, 203; sensitivity, 218; totality, 398

Aesthetically: neutral, work as, 253; neutral features of work, 310; relevant content of aesthetic

Aesthetically (*continued*)
object, 331; relevant phenomena, 48, 250, 352, 353n; valent content, 199; valent factors, 46; valuable content, 313; valuable features, 62, 178, 225; value-bearing content, 311, 314; value-neutral features, 290, 326

Aesthetics, xi–xv, xxx, 3, 169, 189, 218, 219, 314, 317, 383, 421; critical, 72

Analytical consideration, investigation, of work of art, 262, 274, 276, 278, 283, 284, 286, 288, 289, 290, 291, 293, 299, 300, 309, 344–45, 363, 418. *See also* Preaesthetic

Architecture, 112, 215, 218; work of, 201, 209, 219, 227, 228, 229, 230

Artist, xvi, 174, 175, 182, 186, 198, 198n, 212, 284, 293, 348n, 359, 407; creative behavior of, 198; scholar as, 166

Artistic: accomplishments of work, 167; aspect of works, 82; capacity, 226, 254, 393; character, 92, 389; composition, 51; culture of reader, 293, 387; defects, 212; effectiveness, xxvii, 125n, 225, 249, 252, 254, 292, 353n, 357, 379n; effects, 250, 352, 388; essence of work, 164; excellence, 163, 211, 291, 298–99, 415; execution, 361, 363; features of work, xxv; form, 157, 166, 173, 243, 271; function, 157, 243, 289, 292; goals, 259; intention, xv, xx, 55, 166–67, 274, 352; level of works, 385; means, 68, 71n, 103, 165, 250, 254, 262, 277, 288, 355; methods, 253; potential, 276; structure, 244, 276, 292, 357; technique, 276, 299; whole, 95

Artistically: effective factors, 326; important factors, 358; inert factors, 372; valuable features, 83

Aspects under which portrayed objects appear, xvi, xx, 55, 56n, 57–59, 59n, 60–63, 68, 79, 86, 91, 98, 102, 104, 130n, 151, 152, 157, 221, 227, 230, 241, 246, 247, 247n, 248, 262, 282, 308, 326, 338, 341, 353, 353n, 395

Attitude: change of, in aesthetic experience, 192–94, 220, 221,

238; cognitive, investigative, 8, 10, 172, 173, 175, 178, 179, 182, 188, 210, 223, 281, 317; practical, natural, ordinary, 66, 173, 188, 194, 195, 196, 303; of reader toward work, xvi, xvii, xxiv, xxvi, 6, 37, 52, 53, 65, 67, 83, 87, 126, 127, 135, 142, 144, 150, 164, 169, 170, 171, 233, 366; reflective, 280, 281, 301, 303, 306, 349; toward scientific work, 159; toward value, 379. *See also* Aesthetic

Author, xv, xvii, xix, 14, 15, 27, 76, 78–80, 80n, 81, 82, 88, 93, 124n, 125n, 132, 149, 154n, 158, 165, 166, 247n, 250, 250n, 252, 259, 264, 287, 335, 345, 349, 350, 387, 389, 398

Basis: for aesthetic value, 305n, 306; of aesthetic value judgments, 325; of aesthetically valent qualities, 404; of harmonic unity, 315; for value in work, 296; of work of art (aesthetically neutral), 308, 314. *See also* Foundation

Belles-lettres, xxiii, 7, 92, 146, 147

Benn, Gottfried, "Radar," quoted, 354n

Bergson, Henri, 97, 105n, 106, 110n, 111n, 139, 205n, 278, 281, 283, 314; *Les Données immédiates de la conscience*, 205n

Brentano, Franz, 33n, 207n; *Von der Klassifikation der psychischen Phänomene*, 33n

Bühler, Karl, 21n, 29n

Building (physical foundation of architectual work), 198, 221

Categorial: determination of portrayed objects, 365; formation of object, 206, 215; forms, 281; structure of object, 202, 281n; structure of state of affairs, 42; structure of work, 364

Choromański, Michał, *Jealousy and Medicine*, quoted, 131–32, 133

Cocreative: activity, 53; attitude, 40; reader, xix, 41, 89

Cognition, xiii, xxix, 122, 173, 174, 320, 321, 398; acts of, 44, 48, 181, 280, 303, 304, 399, 400, 401, 401n, 404; aesthetic, xxviii,

portrayed objects, 227; presence of value qualities, 305; procedure of objectification, 45; properties of portrayed objects, 230; qualitative formations, 195; relationship with aesthetic object, 400; seeing of value, 313; self-presence of value, 379; understanding of portrayed persons, 358
Intuitively: appearing valuable qualities, 68; felt quality, 22; given value qualities, 306
Intuitiveness: of aesthetic object, 330; of aesthetic value, 265
Investigator of works, 286, 291, 296, 299, 301, 328. *See also* Literary scholar

Judgment: act of, 211; aesthetic, 212, 324, 325, 377; genuine, xxiii, 12, 13n, 36, 42, 64, 64n, 65, 67, 69, 71n, 146–50, 155, 159–62, 164, 215n, 224, 323; literary, 333, 336; in literary scholarship, 414, 415; about literary work of art, xxvii, xxviii, xxix, 145, 210, 305, 317, 322, 333, 335, 336, 357–60, 364, 366, 367, 376, 381n, 409, 410, 413, 416, 418; reporting, 323, 325, 328, 412; about results of perception, 179; theory of, 207n; value, xxix, 7, 210, 312, 324, 325, 326, 330, 377, 379, 380, 381n, 414–16; of value, 207n, 208, 209, 323, 326, 377

Knowledge: aesthetic, 210, 224; empirical, 254, 344; literary, 334; objective, xxvi, xxviii, 7, 28n, 234, 235, 235n, 333, 344, 357, 422; objectively valuable, 9; objectivity of, 333, 334, 336, 356; theory of, 334n

Linguistic formations, 248, 249, 273, 326, 345, 346, 351, 352, 355
Lipps, Theodor, 3, 203, 203n, 220n
Literary aesthetic experience, literary experience, xxvi, 218, 219, 222, 223, 226, 227, 229–32
Literary consumers, xvii, 6, 166, 171, 172, 222, 223, 273, 277, 278, 279, 282, 283, 307, 332, 333, 337, 348, 378, 385
Literary scholars, xiv, xvii, xxiv, xxvii, xxviii, 71, 80, 81, 137, 166,

169, 170, 170n, 235n, 254, 272, 276, 285, 293, 301, 303, 307, 310, 311, 348, 348n, 360, 361, 362, 412, 416, 418; positivistically oriented, 235n
Literary scholarship, study, investigation, xiv, xv, xvii, xxi, xxiii, xxiv, xxvi, xxviii, xxx, 3, 4, 78, 79, 163, 169, 170, 171, 234, 235n, 258n, 283, 287, 289, 315, 317, 327, 328, 409, 413, 414, 414n, 415, 416, 418, 419, 422; aesthetically oriented, 318; praxis of, 345; scientific character of, 356
Lyric poem, poetry, xxii, 71, 72, 81, 94, 125, 134, 134n, 135–38, 218, 230, 262, 263, 265, 266, 267, 268, 268n, 269, 269n, 270, 270n, 271, 273, 274n, 277, 278, 283, 292, 293, 302, 304n, 316, 352, 353, 398; basic types of, 52; emotional, 230; modern, 298n; reflective, 267, 271, 292; structure of, 269
Lyrical ego, "I," subject, 133, 134, 134n, 135, 136, 137, 138n, 139, 140, 141, 263–67, 267n, 268, 269, 270, 272, 273, 275, 276; attitude of, 134, 141, 268, 269; as opposed to real poet, 264

Mann, Thomas, 43n, 71n, 232n, 242, 243, 245–47, 247n, 249n, 250n, 251n, 256, 259, 259n, 260–62, 292; *Buddenbrooks*, quoted, 43n, 260, 261–62, discussed, 249n, 250n, 251n, 256–62; "Death in Venice," quoted, 247n; *Magic Mountain*, quoted, 259n; "Tristan," quoted, 242, 246, 247, discussed, 243–47
Meaning: cognitive, 357; context of, 23; determination of, 318; -determining form, 184; double, in poem, 352, 353, 354; entities, 28; ideal, 25; intentions, xvi, xvii, xix, 32, 35, 91, 148, 150, 159, 161, 224; of judgments, 164, 358, 359; of names, 319; organized structure of, 35n; sentence, xix, xx, 10–12, 24, 24n, 25, 26, 27n, 34–36, 38, 40, 43, 48, 49, 59n, 68–70, 91, 95, 98, 99, 149, 154n, 155, 156, 159, 160, 224, 226, 249, 255, 269, 276, 289, 309, 340, 342, 355, 365; of text, 33n, 162, 308, 355; unity of, 95, 228, 232, 338;